Early Jesuit Travellers in Central Asia

1603-1721

Statue of Bento de Goes
at
Villa Franca do Campo—Azores.

Early Jesuit Travellers in Central Asia

1603-1721

Cornelius Wessels

With Maps and Illustrations

Low Price Publications

2015

First Published 1924
Reprinted in **LPP** 1999, 2015

ISBN 10: 81-7536-163-8
ISBN 13: 978-81-7536-163-8

Published by
Low Price Publications
A-6, 2nd Floor, Nimri Commercial Centre,
Ashok Vihar Phase 4, Delhi 110052 (INDIA)
tel.: +91-11-27302453 fax.: +91-11-47061936
url: www.LPPindia.com e-mail: info@LPPindia.com

Printed at
D.K. Fine Art Press Pvt. Ltd.
Delhi

PRINTED IN INDIA

EARLY JESUIT TRAVELLERS IN CENTRAL ASIA 1603—1721

BY

C. WESSELS, S. J.

WITH MAP AND ILLUSTRATIONS

THE HAGUE
MARTINUS NIJHOFF
1924

PREFACE

> **"If, as is undoubtedly the case, there are still vast regions unknown and unsurveyed for future travellers to explore, there is quite as large an undiscovered region, in the buried archives of the past, for the historical explorer to unearth and make known to us."**
>
> **SIR CLEMENTS R. MARKHAM [1]).**

To many generations of geographers Central Asia, especially Tibet, was the land of mystery and darkness, isolated by nature and by man, in whose midst lay the sacred city of Lhasa, even more mysterious and unapproachable than Mecca or Kerbela; and it is only for some decades past that it has counted among the great fields of operation of modern geography. High as Mont Blanc are the desert-like plateaux of this "Roof of the World", and as if this elevation was not enough to render them difficult of access, they are set about by almost impassable mountain ranges; an arctic climate reigns in those bleak and forlorn regions. And if a traveller be so undaunted and hardy as to brave all the obstacles of nature, and to climb his way towards those icy wastes, he will find his road barred and himself ruthlessly turned back by the sparse inhabitants, inhospitable as their mountain sides. Hardly any explorer from Prejevalsky to Sven Hedin but testifies to the jealousy with which those desolate regions are guarded, and even as late as 1923 Dr. Montgomery McGovern experienced this inveterate distrust of the foreigner.

It has not always been thus. This aversion did not exist in the seventeenth and eighteenth centuries, before Chinese domination had influenced Tibet and grafted its own love of seclusion on its inhabitants. It was this milder feeling towards strangers from the West that allowed some Jesuit missionaries to explore the country. They entered it from the south and from the north, they traversed it along the valleys of the Indus and the Tsangpo, they

---

[1]) *Lost Geographical Documents.* — Geographical Journal (1913) vol. XLII, p. 34.

saw men and things unseen by any European before, they encountered hardships and dangers not less formidable than those for which we rightly admire explorers of a later date — and yet while the labours of other Jesuits contributed so largely to the opening up of China, the Philippines, Abyssinia and wide tracts of North and South America, Tibet practically remained an unknown country. They did, indeed, like their fellow-workers in other climates, record their experiences, but, strange to say, most of their writings remained hidden away in dusty archives, and the few things given to the world were vague and hazy and, to some minds, more suggestive of fiction than of fact, and thus cast a shadow of uncertainty even over the few facts that had actually become known, justifying Hedin's remark that "over the interior of the vast Asiatic Continent there hovered a pale reflection, faint and shadowy, of the journeys of Marco Polo and the old Jesuits" [1]).

This aspect of things has changed of late years. The merits of those "old Jesuits" have come more to the front, and more than once have met with due recognition at the hands of competent judges. At the same time criticism has not been idle: it has been caustic, it has even been unfair — the more unfair as being based on ignorance or superficial knowledge. What the late Dr. Siegmund Günther, of Munich, wrote to me some years ago, is eminently applicable to Tibet: "That the Jesuits have done much for our geographical knowledge is recognized on all hands; *what* they have done we hardly know at all." It is here we have one of Markham's undiscovered regions "for the historical explorer to unearth".

All the journeys that have been undertaken in Tibet by Jesuit missionaries will be treated of in the present work. The writer has had access to old books and other publications of which but few copies are known to exist, but the bulk of the information here presented was never published at all, and is derived from a large number of manuscripts which it has been his good fortune to "unearth" in the archives of the Society of Jesus. Each of the following chapters will have its own list of MSS. appended. The object which the writer has tried to keep constantly in view, is to determine the scientific value of those letters, journals &c., to place the merits of their writers in their proper light, and thus to assign to them their rightful place among those who have contributed to-

[1]) Sven Hedin, *Scientific Results of a Journey in Central Asia 1899—1902* (Stockholm 1907) IV, 531.

wards the development of geographical science. Hence the subject has been treated with such fulness as the limits of the book would permit, and, while drawing on every accessible source of information, the data furnished by the old documents have been tested by the light of the facts supplied by modern travellers.

A few points should not be forgotten, if we would arrive at an equitable judgment. Those men had not been, as a rule, prepared for their arduous undertakings by thorough geographical and ethnical studies; they did not set out richly equipped with physical instruments of various kinds; they were pioneers in the fullest sense of the word; without any precursors, without maps, without the experience of others to guide them. Nor, while they were out in regions untrodden by European foot, did they consider themselves in the first place discoverers who were making a name for themselves; geographers adding fresh data to the stock of human knowledge; explorers widening the horizon of the human mind; — before everything else they were, and remained, missionaries going out to cast abroad the seeds of the Gospel wherever human heart would give it soil; whose one ultimate purpose was to gain souls rather than to discover territories; who never lost sight of their *raison d'être*, and therefore carried into their enterprises the same indomitable energy and daring that had called them away from friends and home to brave the perils of the deep without any wish or hope of gain or glory. Thus they must not be looked upon as geographical specialists, but as honest, level-headed men, writing of their experiences in a land of bewildering strangeness; their writings should not be perused by the light of the exacting canons of the specialist who reports for a geographical magazine or to a learned society. They should be read, with a critical eye indeed, but not in a spirit of fault-finding, and as to the facts reported, with a bias in their favour unless they can be shown to have erred. Certainly they did make mistakes, as who does not? Their written accounts are often insignificant, abounding in generalities and hopelessly lacking in those points which a scientific training would have made them pick up as of first rate importance. But even so they have their merits as every pioneer has.

Each chapter of this book is complete in itself and can be read independently. Bento de Goes' journey has been placed at the head by way of introduction, because his journey carried him from Lahore *via* Kabul, Yarkand and Turfan to Su-cheu, and thus covers almost the whole of Central Asia. This chapter and the following on Andrade were published in Dutch some years ago [1]); as they appear here, they have been corrected and in large part re-written.

The writer does not feel called upon to premise a detailed geographical and physical description of Tibet. The books of travel and exploration that have appeared of late years are so numerous, and the character both of the country and its inhabitants have become so generally known that the map appended to the book may be deemed a sufficient guide for the general reader.

Finally there remains the pleasant task of recording the kind help and the valuable suggestions which I have received from so many quarters, and I wish to express here my deep sense of gratitude to the numerous friends and correspondents who have thus contributed towards the making of this book. Though it is impossible for me to mention them all individually I cannot forbear to name two whose claims transcend all others: Father Henry Hosten, S. J., of St. Joseph's College, Darjeeling, the learned writer on the mission-history of India, who more than once directed my researches in my hunt for documents; and my friend Father Thomas Neervens, S. J., but for whose generous assistance this work could not have appeared in its present garb.

St. Willebrord College, C. WESSELS, S. J.
Katwijk a. d. Rijn, Holland.
Lady Day, 1924.

---

[1]) C. Wessels, *Bento de Goes, S. J., Een ontdekkingsreiziger in Centraal Azië (1603—1607)* — Studiën, (1911) vol. LXXV, p. 72—96; 229—248.

C. Wessels, *Antonio de Andrade, S. J. Een ontdekkingsreiziger in de Himalaya en in Tibet (1624—1630)* — Studiën, (1912) vol. LXXVII, p. 408—440.

C. Wessels, *Antonio de Andrade, S. J., viajante no Himalaia e no Tibete (1624—1630)* — Traducido de original holandès por A. R. Gonzalves Viana. (Sociedade de Geographia de Lisboa) Lisboa, 1914.

CONTENTS

		page
Preface		V
List of Works referred to		X
CHAPTER	I. BENTO DE GOES (1602—1607)	1
„	II. ANTONIO DE ANDRADE (1624)	43
„	III. THE TSAPARANG MISSION (1625—1640)	69
„	IV. FRANCISCO DE AZEVEDO (1631—1632)	94
„	V. STEPHEN CACELLA AND JOHN CABRAL (1626—1632)	120
„	VI. JOHN GRUEBER AND ALBERT D'ORVILLE (1661—1664)	164
„	VII. HIPPOLYTE DESIDERI (1714—1722)	205
APPENDIX	I. AZEVEDO'S ACCOUNT OF HIS JOURNEY TO TIBET (Portuguese text)	282
„	II. LETTER OF STEPHEN CACELLA FROM CAMBIRASI, OCTOBER 4, 1627 (Portuguese text)	314
„	III, LETTER OF JOHN CABRAL FROM HUGLI, JUNE 17, 1628 (Portuguese text)	333
„	IV. LETTER OF JOHN GRUEBER FROM TYRNAU, JANUARY 13, 1670 (Latin text)	337
„	V. EULOGY ON JOHN GRUEBER (Latin text)	338
INDEX		339

LIST OF WORKS REPEATEDLY REFERRED TO IN THE COURSE OF THIS BOOK

ALLEN (B. C.), Kamrup, Assam District Gazetteers. Vol. IV. Allahabad, 1905.

ANDRADE (ANTONIO DE), S J., Novo Descobrimento do Gram Cathayo, ou Reinos de Tibet, pello Padre Antonio de Andrade da Companhia de Jesu, Portuguez, no anno de 1624. Lisboa, 1626.

ATTI E Memorie del Convegno di Geographi-Orientalisti tenuto in Macerata, il 25, 26, 27 Settembre 1910.... Onoranze Nationali al P. Matteo Ricci, Apostolo e Geografo della Cina (1610—1910—11). Macerata, 1911.

BARRETTO (FR.), S. J., Relatione delle Missioni e Christianita che appartengono alla Provincia di Malavar della Compagnia di Giesu. Roma, 1645.

BERNIER (FRANÇOIS), Travels in the Mogul Empire (1656—1668). A revised and improved Edition based upon Irving Brock's Translation by Archibald Constable. Westminster, 1891.

BESSE (L.) and H. HOSTEN, S. J., List of Portuguese Jesuit Missionaries in Bengal and Burma (1576—1742). — Journal and Proceedings of the Asiatic Society of Bengal. Vol. VII (1911) pp. 15—35.

BLOCHMANN (H.), Koch Bihar, Koch Hajo and A'sam in the 16th and 17th centuries, according to the Akbarnámah, the Pádisháhnámah and the Fathiyah i Ibriyah. — Journal Asiat. Soc. of Bengal 1872. Vol. XLI, part I, pp. 49—101.

BLUE-BOOK. Papers Relating to Bootan, (presented to Parliament by Her Majesty's command), [Blue-Book, 47], ordered by the House of Commons to be printed February 15, 1865. London, 1865.

BOECK (DR. KURT), Indische Gletscherfahrten. Reisen und Erlebnisse im Himalaja. Stuttgart—Leipzig, 1900.

BOECK (DR. KURT), Durch Indiën ins verschlossene Land Nepal. Leipzig, 1903.

BONIN (CH. E.), Les Royaumes des Neiges. (Etats Himalayens). Paris, 1911.

BOSE (KISHEN KANT), Some Account of the Country of Bhútán. Translated by D. Scott, Esq. — Asiatic Researches. Vol. XV. (Serampore 1825), pp 128—156.

BOSMANS (H.), S. J., Documents sur Albert Dorville de Bruxelles, missionnaire de la Compagnie de Jésus au XVIIe siècle et notamment sur les épisodes de son voyage vers Lisbonne et la Chine. Louvain, 1911. [Extrait des Analectes pour servir à l'histoire ecclésiastique de la Belgique. XXXVII, 1911].

BRUCE (C. G.), Kulu and Lahoul. London, 1914.

BRUCKER (J.), S. J., Benoît de Goes. (1603—1607). — Etudes 1879. (Vol. III), pp. 589—612; 678—695.

BURRARD (S. G.) and H. H. HAYDEN, A Sketch of the Geography and Geology of the Himalaya Mountains and Tibet. Vol. I. Text. Vol. II. Maps. Calcutta, 1907—1908.

CARREZ (LUD.), S. J., Atlas Geographicus Societatis Iesu, in quo delineantur quinque eius modernae Assistentiae, Provinciae tres et viginti singularumque in toto orbe Missiones, necnon et veteres eiusdem Societatis Provinciae quadraginta tres cum earum Domiciliis, quantum fieri licuit. Parisiis, 1900.

CATALOGUS Patrum ac Fratrum e Societate Iesu qui a morte S. Francisci Xaverii ad annum MDCCCLXXII Evangelio Christi Propagando in Sinis adlaboraverunt. Shanghai, 1873.

CHAUDHURI (HARENDRA NARAYAN), The Cooch Behar State and its Land Revenue Settlements. Cooch Behar, 1903.

CORDARA (JULIUS), S. J., Historiae Societatis Iesu. Pars sexta, complectens res gestas sub Mutio Vitellescho. Tomus I, Romae, 1750. II, 1859.

DAS (SARAT CHANDRA), Journey to Lhasa and Central Tibet, edited by the Hon. W. W. Rockhill. London, 1904.

DAVIS (J. F.), Remarks on the Religious and Social Institutions of the Bouteas, or Inhabitants of Boutan, from the unpublished Journal of the late Samuel Davis. — Transactions of the Royal Asiatic Society of Great Britain and Ireland. Vol. II (London, 1830), pp. 491—517.

DENIS (FERDINAND), Nouvelle Biographie Universelle par M.M. Firmin Didot Frères. Paris, 1857 etc. I, p. 546; XXI, pp. 19—20.

DESIDERI (IPPOLITO), S. J., Difesa della Compagnia di Giesu in ordine alla Missione del Tibet. Roma, 1728.

DONSEN (M.), R.K.Pr. Klein-Tibet. — Tijdschrift Kon. Nederl. Aardrijkskund. Genootschap. 2e Serie. Dl. XVIII. (1901), pp. 416—463.

DREW (FR.), The Jummoo and Kashmir Territories. A Geographical Account. London, 1875.

DU HALDE (J. B.), S. J., Description géographique, historique, chronologique, politique, et physique de l'Empire de la Chine et de la Tartarie Chinoise. 4 tomes. La Haye, 1736.

DUHR (BERNARD), S. J., Geschichte der Jesuiten in den Ländern deutscher Zunge. Band III. Regensburg, 1921.

DUTREUIL DE RHINS. (J. L.), L'Asie Centrale. Thibet et Régions limitrophes. Paris, 1889.

EDEN (ASHLEY), Report of.... in Papers Relating to Bootan (presented to Parliament by Her Majesty's Command) [Blue-Book] ordered by the House of Commons to be printed February 15, 1865. London, 1865, pp. 173—220.

FÉLIX, O. C., Jesuit Missions in Lahore. — Journal of the Panjab Historical Society. Special Number. Vol. V. No. 2, pp. 55—99. Calcutta, 1916.

FITCH, The Voyage of Master Ralph.... Merchant of London to Ormus and so to Goa in the East India, to Cambaia, Ganges, Bengala.... begun in the yeere of our Lord 1583 and ended 1591. — Hakluytus Posthumus or Purchas His Pilgrims by Samuel Purchas B. D Glascow, 1905, tom. X, pp. 165—205.

FORSYTH, Ost-Turkestan und das Pamir-plateau. Petermanns Mitteilungen. Ergänzungsheft 52. (1877).

FRANCKE (A. H.), Ph. D. Antiquities of Indian Tibet. Part I. Personal Narrative. — Archaeological Survey of India, New Imperial Series, vol. XXXVIII. Calcutta, 1914.

FRANCO (ANTONIO), S. J., Imagem da Virtude em o Noviciado da Companhia de Jesu na Corte de Lisboa. Coimbra, 1717.

FRANCO (ANTONIO), S. J., Synopsis Annalium S. J. in Lusitania ab anno 1540 ad annum 1725. Augusta Vindelicorum, 1726.

FUTTERER (DR. K.), Durch Asien. Erfahrungen, Forschungen und Sammlungen. Band I. Berlin, 1901.

GAZETTEER (The Imperial) of India. 26 vol. Oxford, 1907—1909.

GAZETTEER of the Kangra District. Parts II to IV: Kulu, Lahul and Spiti by A. H. Diack, revised by P. D. Agnew. Lahore, 1899.

GEORGI (AUG. ANT.), Alphabetum Tibetanum Missionum Apostolicarum commodo editum. Romae, 1762.

GRIFFITH (W.), Journal of the Mission which visited Bootan in 1837—38, under Captain R. Boileau Pemberton. — Journal of the Asiatic Soc. of Bengal. Vol. VIII (1839). Part. I, pp. 208—241; 251—291.

GRÜNWEDEL (A), Mythologie des Buddhismus in Tibet und der Mongolei. Leipzig, 1900.

GUERREIRO (FERNAN), S. J., Relaçam annal das cousas que fizeram os Padres da Companhia de Jesus nas Partes da India Oriental.... nos annos de 1606—1607. Lisboa, 1609.

—— Relaçam annal.... nos annos de 1607—1608. Lisboa, 1611.

HAENISCH (E.), Bruchstücke aus der Geschichte Chinas unter der Gegenwärtigen Dynastie. — T'Oung Pao. Vol. XII (1911), pp. 197—235; 375—424.

HARCOURT (A. F. P.), On the Himalayan Valleys: Kooloo, Lahoul and Spiti. — Journal of the Royal Geogr. Society. Vol. XLI (1871), pp. 245—257.

HAY (JOAN), S. J., De Rebus Japonicis, Indicis et Peruanis Epistulae recentiores. Antverpiae, 1605.

HEAWOOD (EDWARD), A History of Geographical Discovery in the seventeenth and eighteenth centuries. Cambridge, 1912.

HEDIN (SVEN), Die Geografisch-wissenschaftlichen Ergebnisse meiner Reise in Zentralasien. 1894—1897. Petermanns Mitteilungen. Ergänzungsheft 131. Gotha, 1900.

HEDIN (SVEN), Scientific Results of a Journey in Central-Asia. 1899—1902. 4 vol. Stockholm, 1907.

HEDIN (SVEN), Transhimalaja. Entdeckungen und Abenteuer in Tibet. Band I, II. Leipzig, 1909. Band III. Leipzig, 1912.

HEDIN (SVEN), Southern Tibet. Discoveries in former Times compared with my own Researches in 1906—1908. 4 vol. Stockholm, 1917.

HOLDICH (THOMAS), Tibet, the Mysterious. London, [1906].

HOSTEN (H.), S. J., Jesuit Missionaries in Northern India and Inscriptions on their Tombs, Agra. (1580—1803). Calcutta, 1907.

HOSTEN (H.), S. J., List of Jesuit Missionaries in "Mogor". (1580—1803).

— Journal and Proceedings of the Asiatic Soc. of Bengal. (New Series). Vol. VI (1910), pp. 527—542.

HUC (M.), Souvenirs d'un Voyage dans la Tartarie, le Thibet et la Chine pendant les années 1844, 1845, 1846. 2 vol. Paris, 1850.

HUC (M.), Le Christianisme en Chine, en Tartarie et au Thibet. 2 vol. Paris, 1857.

HUNTER (W. W.), A Statistical Account of Bengal. Vol. V. Districts of Dacca, Bakargang, Faridpur and Maimansingh.
Vol. X. Districts of Dárjíling and Jalpaigurí, and State of Kuch Beḥar. London, 1875. 1876.

JARRIC (P.), S. J., Thesaurus Rerum Indicarum. 3 vol. Colonia Agrippina, 1615.

KAWAGUCHI (EKAI), Three Years in Tibet. London and Madras, 1909.

KIRCHER (ATHANASIUS), S. J., China Monumentis, quà Sacris, quà Profanis, nec non variis Naturae et Artis Spectaculis aliarumque rerum memorabilium Argumentis illustrata. Amstelodami, 1667.

KIRCHER (ATHANASE), S. J., La Chine illustrée de plusieurs monuments... a quoy on a adjousté de nouveau les questions curieuses que le Serenissime Grand Duc de Toscane a fait depuis peu au P. Jean Grubere, touchant ce grand Empire.... traduit par F. S. Dalguié. Amsterdam, 1670.

KLAPROTH, Breve Notizia del Regno del Thibet, dal frà Francesco Orazio della Penna de Billi. 1730. — Nouveau Journal Asiatique. Tome XIV (Paris, 1834), pp. 177—204; 273—296; 406—432.

KOEPPEN (C. F.), Die Religion des Buddha. Vol. II. Die Lamaische Hierarchie und Kirche. Berlin, 1859.

KÖRÖS (A. CSOMA DE), Tibetan Studies, being a Reprint of the Articles contributed to the Journal of the Asiatic Society of Bengal. — Journal and Proc. of the Asiatic Soc. of Bengal. Vol. VII (1911). Calcutta, 1912.

LANDON (PERCEVAL), Lhasa, an Account of the Country and People of Central Tibet and of the Progress of the Mission sent there by the English Government in the Year 1903—1904. 2 vol.[2] London, 1905.

LAUNAY (A.), Histoire de la Mission du Thibet. 2 vol. Lille—Paris, [1903].

LETTERE Annue del Tibet del MDCXXVI et della Cina del MDCXXIV, scritte al M. R. P. Mutio Vitelleschi, Generale della Compagnia di Giesu. Roma, 1628.

LETTRES Edifiantes et Curieuses. 14 vol. Lyon, 1819.

LÉVI (SYLVAIN), Le Népal. Etude historique d'un Royaume hindou. 3 vol. — Annales du Musée Guimet. Tome XVII, XVIII, XIX. Paris, 1905.

MACHADO (BARBOSA), Bibliotheca Lusitana historica, critica e chronologica. 3 vol. Lisboa, 1741.

MANUCCI (NICOLAO), Storia do Mogor or Mogul India 1653—1708. Translated with Introduction and Notes by William Irvine. 4 vol. London, 1907—1908.

MARACCI (J.), S. J., Relation de ce qui s'est passé dans les Indes Orientales en ses trois Provinces de Goa, de Malabar, du Japon, de la Chine et autres païs nouvellement descouverts. Par les Pères de la Compagnie de Jésus. — Traduction de J. de Machault. Paris, 1651.

MARKHAM (CLEMENTS R.), Narrative of the Mission of George Bogle to

Tibet and of the Journey of Thomas Manning to Lhasa. London, 1879.

MARX (DR. K.), Three Documents relating to the History of Ladakh; Tibetan Text, Translation and Notes. — Journal of the Asiatic Soc. of Bengal. Vol. LX, Part. I (1891), pp. 97—135.

MARX (DR. K.), Three Documents relating to the History of Ladakh; Tibetan Text, Translation and Notes. — Journal of the Asiatic Soc. of Bengal. Vol. LXIII, Part I (1895), pp. 94—107.

MILLOUÉ (L. DE), Bod-Youl ou Tibet. — Annales du Musée Guimet. Tome XII. Paris, 1906.

MISSIO Apostolica Thibetano-Seraphica, das ist Neue durch Päbstlichen Gewalt in dem Grossen Thibetanische Reich von denen P. P. Capucineren aufgerichtete Mission. München, 1740.

MONSERRATE (A.), S. J., Mongolicae Legationis Commentarius or the First Jesuit Mission to Akbar by Fr. Anthony Monserrate S. J. — Jesuit Letters and Allied Papers on Mogor, Tibet, Bengal and Burma edited by the Rev. H. Hosten S. J. — Memoirs of the Asiatic Soc. of Bengal. Vol. III no. 9. (Calcutta, 1914), pp. 513—704.

MOORCROFT (WILLIAM), A Journey to Lake Manasarovara in Un-des, a Province of Little Tibet. — Asiatick Researches or Transactions of the Society instituted in Bengal etc. Vol. XII. (London, 1818), pp. 380—536.

MOORCROFT (W.), and G. TREBECK, Travels in the Himalayan Provinces of Hindustan and the Panjab; in Ladakh and Kashmir; in Peshawar, Kabul, Kunduz and Bokhara from 1819—1825. 2 vol. London, 1841.

PESCHEL (O.)-RUGE. Geschichte der Erdkunde. München, 1877.

PREJEVALSKY (N.), Mongolia, the Tangut Country and the Solitudes of Northern Tibet — translated by E. Delmar Morgan, with Introduction and Notes by Colonel Henry Yule. 2 vol. London, 1876.

PUINI (CARLO), Il Tibet (Geografia, Storia, Religione, Costumi) secondo la Relazione del Viaggio del P. Ippolito Desideri (1715—1721). — Memorie della Società Geografica Italiana. Vol. X. Roma, 1904.

RAPER (F. V.), Narrative of a Survey for the Purpose of Discovering the Sources of the Ganges. — Asiatic Researches or Transactions of the Society instituted in Bengal etc. Vol. XI. (London, 1812), pp. 446—563.

RAWLING (C. G.), The Great Plateau, being an Account of Exploration in Central Tibet, 1903, and of the Gartok Expedition, 1904—1905. London, 1905.

RECORDS of the Survey of India. Prepared under the Direction of Colonel Sir S. G. Burrard, K. C. S. I., R. E., F. R. S., Surveyor General of India. Vol. VIII. Dehra Dun 1915.

Part I. Exploration in Tibet and Neighbouring Regions 1865—1879.
pp. 1—79. Report on a Route Survey from Nepāl to Lhāsa by Pandit Nain Singh, drawn up by Capt. T. G. Montgomerie, R. E.
pp. 79—109. Narrative Report of the Trans-Himalayan Explorations by Pandit Nain Singh, drawn up by Capt. T. G. Montgomerie, R. E.
pp. 116—133. Memorandum on the Trans-Himalayan Explorations by Hari Ram, drawn up by Major T. G. Montgomerie, R. E.
pp. 160—197. Account of Pandit Nain Singh's Journey from Leh in Ladākh to Lhāsa and of his return to India *via* Assam.

pp. 199—207. Narrative of the Explorations of Explorer Lala.
pp. 209—215. Report on the Exploration of Nem Singh in Eastern Tibet, drawn up by Lieut. H. J. Harman, R. E.
Part II. Exploration in Tibet and Neighbouring Regions 1879—1892.
pp. 215—325. Report on Pandit Kishen Singh's Explorations in Great Tibet and Mongolia, by J. B. N. Hennessey, Esq. M. A., F. R. S.
pp. 325—329. Account of the Lower Tsang-Po by the Mongolian Lama Serap Gyatsho as related in 1883 to Lama Ugyen Gyatso, by Col. H. C. B. Tanner.
pp. 329—339. Kinthup's Narrative of a Journey from Darjeeling to Gyāla Sindong (Gyāla and Sengdam), Tsari and the Lower Tsang-Po, by Col. H. C. B. Tanner.
pp. 339—359. Narrative Account of Lama Ugyen Gyatso's third season's Explorations in Tibet by Lt.-Col. T. H. Holdich, R. E.
pp. 363—383. Narrative Account of Rinzin Nimgyl's Explorations in Sikkim, Bhutān and Tibet by Mr. G. W. E. Atkinson.
pp. 383—401. Report on Routes by Explorer Hari Ram from Dagmara Thāna *via* the Dudh Kosi River and Pangula pass to Ting-ri in Tibet, etc. etc. by Mr. C. Wood.

RIBEIRO (AUGUSTO), Bento de Goes — No Centenario de Bento de Goes 1607—1907. Homenagem de Soc. de Geogr. de Lisboa. Lisboa, 1907.

RICCI (MATTEO), S. J., Opere Storiche del P. Matteo Ricci, S. J., edite a cura del Comitato per le Onoranze Nazionali con Prolegomeni, Note e Tavole dal P. Pietro Tacchi Venturi, S. J. Macerata, 1911—1913.
Vol. I. I Commentarj dalla Cina.
Vol. II. Le Lettere dalla Cina.

RICHTHOFEN (FR. VON), China. Ergebnisse eigener Reisen und darauf gegründeter Studien. 2 vol. Berlin, 1877, 1882.

RITTER (CARL), Die Erdkunde von Asien. Berlin, 1832.

ROCKHILL (W. W.), The Land of the Lamas. Notes from a Journey through China, Mongolia and Tibet. London, 1891.

ROCKHILL (W. W.), Diary of a Journey through Mongolia and Tibet in 1891 and 1892. Washington, 1894.

RYDER (C. H. D.), Exploration and Survey with the Tibet Frontier Commission and from Gyangtse to Simla via Gartok. — Geographical Journal, tom. XXVI (1905), pp. 369—395.

SANDBERG (GRAHAM), The Exploration of Tibet. Its History and Particulars from 1623 to 1904. Calcutta—London, 1904.

SANDBERG (GRAHAM), Tibet and the Tibetans. London, 1906.

SCHLAGINTWEIT (HERMANN VON)—SAKÜNLUNSKI, Reisen in Indiën und Hochasiën. 4 vol. Jena, 1869—1880.

SHERRING (CH. A.), Western Tibet and the British Borderland, the Sacred Country of Hindus and Buddhists; with an Account of the Government, Religion and Customs of its Peoples. London, 1906.

SOMMERVOGEL (CARLOS), S. J., Bibliothèque de la Compagnie de Jésus. 9 vol. Bruxelles—Paris, 1890—1900.

STEIN (M. AUREL), Ancient Khotan. Detailed Report of Archaeological Exploration in Chinese Turkestan. 2 vol. Oxford, 1907.

STEIN (M. AUREL), Ruins of Desert Cathay. Personal Narrative of Explorations in Central Asia and Westernmost China. 2 vol. London, 1912.

STÖCKLEIN Jos.), S. J., Der Neue Welt-Bott. Mit allerhand Nachrichten dern Missionariorum Soc. Iesu. Vol. I. Augspurg und Grätz, 1726.

STRACHEY (R.), On the Physical Geography of the Provinces of Kumáon and Garhwál in the Himálaya Mountains, and of the adjoining Parts of Tibet. — Journal Royal Geographical Society XXI, (1851), pp. 57—86.

THÉVENOT (M.), Relations de divers Voyages Curieux. IV. Paris, 1672.
a) pp. 1—18. Voyage à la Chine des P.P. Grueber et D'Orville.
b) pp. 19—23. Ex Litteris Grueberi Kirchero inscriptis.
c) pp. 1—18. Viaggio del P. Giov. Grueber tornando da China in Europa.
d) pp. 18—23. Autres Pièces sur le suiet du Voyage du P. Grueber.

THOMSON (TH.), Western Himalaya and Tibet; a Narrative of a Journey through the Mountains of Northern India, during the Years 1847—48. London, 1852.

TRIGAULT [Trigautius] (NIC.), S. J., De Christiana Expeditione apud Sinas suscepta a Societate Iesu ex P. Mathaeï Ricci eiusdem Societatis Commentariis. Colonia Agrippina, 1617.

TRONNIER (R.), Die Durchquerung Tibets seitens der Jesuiten Johannes Grueber und Albert de Dorville im Jahre 1661. — Zeitschrift der Gesellschaft für Erdkunde zu Berlin (1904), pp. 328—361.

TSYBIKOFF (G.Ts.), Lhasa and Central Tibet. — Annual Report of the Smithsonian Institution for 1903. Washington, 1904, pp. 727—747.

TURNER (SAMUEL), An Account of an Embassy to the Court of the Teshoo Lama in Tibet; containing a Narrative of a Journey through Bootan, and Part of Tibet. Second Edition. London, 1806.

UJFALVY (K. E. VON), Aus dem Westlichen Himalaja. Leipzig, 1884.

VASCONCELLOS (E. DE), O Itinerario de Bento de Goes. — No Centenario de Bento de Goes, 1607—1907. Homenagem da Sociedade de Geographia de Lisboa. Lisboa, 1907, pp. 19—23.

WADDELL (L. AUSTINE), The Buddhism of Tibet or Lamaism, with its Mystic Cults, Symbolism and Mythology, and in its Relation to Indian Buddhism. London, 1895.

WADDELL (L. AUSTINE), Lhasa and its Mysteries. With a Record of the Expedition of 1903—1904. London, 1906.

WEGENER (GEORG), Tibet und die Englische Expedition. Halle a. S., 1904.

WHITE (J. C.), Sikkim and Bhutan. Twenty-one Years on the North-East Frontier. 1887—1908. London, 1909.

YOUNG (G. M.), A Journey to Toling and Tsaparang in Western Tibet. — Journal of the Panjab Historical Society Vol. VII. (Calcutta, 1919), no. 2, pp. 177—199.

YULE (HENRY), Cathay and the Way Thither, being a Collection of Medieval Notices of China. 2 vol. London, 1866.

YULE—CORDIER, Cathay and the Way Thither, being a Collection of Medieval Notices of China. New edition by Henri Cordier. 4 vol. London, 1915—1916.

CHAPTER I

BENTO DE GOES

The first in modern times to insist upon the merits of Bento de Goes was Carl Ritter. In his standard work *Asien* [1]) he expressed his appreciation of the work of "that courageous lay-brother of the Jesuit mission in Hindustan, whom had imposed on him the heavy task of exploring the then wholly unknown route from India to Khataja". After Ritter we have but passing references to this long-forgotten traveller [2]), till Henry Yule's book on ancient Cathay appeared, and first assigned to Goes the place to which he was entitled [3]). Nor has any later writer treated Goes' narrative more thoroughly or at greater length than Yule. He was followed in France by Jos. Brucker, S. J. [4]), whose able essay revived interest in the subject especially in Portugal, where the memory of so deserving a compatriot had almost perished. And when in 1907 the tercentenary of Goes' death (April 11, 1607) was celebrated, the Lisbon Geographical Society commemorated his work at a ceremonial gathering [5]). At the same time he was honoured by his

---

[1]) Ritter, I, 218 ff., 322 ff.; II, 437 ff.; V, 391, 422 ff., 503 ff. etc. Ritter's words, on p. 503 of vol. V: "We are the first to try and map out .... this remarkable journey of the Jesuit Father" are not quite correct, seeing it had been marked down, however roughly and imperfectly, by Athanasius Kircher S. J., on one of the maps in his *China Illustrata*, Part II, *De Variis Itineribus in Chinam susceptis*. — Before Ritter a summary of the journey had been given in Diogo de Couto's *Da Asia*, Decada Duodecima, Parte ultima, Livro V. Cap. VII. (Lisboa 1788). p. 492—498.

[2]) Ferdinand Denis (*Nouvelle Biographie*, vol. XXI, col. 19—20) writes of Goes briefly but with appreciation. Huc (*Christianisme* II, 209—233) enters more into details, but owing to the numerous inaccuracies of his work and its somewhat romantic setting his description does not make for a true picture of Goes' journey.

[3]) Yule, II, 529—596. He also gives a translation of the narrative of the journey. In 1915 there appeared a new edition by Henri Cordier. For Goes' journey see vol. IV, 169—259.

[4]) Brucker, *Etudes*, (1897) III, 589—612; 678—695. Brucker did not use Yule's book. — F. von Richthofen has a few pages on Goes in his *China*, I, 666—670.

[5]) *No Centenario de Bento de Goes. 1607—1907*: Homenagem de Sociedade de Geographia de Lisboa (Lisboa 1907).

native town of Villa Franca do Campo by the solemn unveiling of his statue. It represents Goes in the garb of a Persian merchant [1]).

A word as to the sources. Goes' diary, in which he noted down the various events day by day, has not come down to us in its entirety or in its original form. After his death it was destroyed by the Mohammedans at Su-cheu, and only a few fragments could be saved by his faithful Armenian travelling-companion Isaac, who took them to Pekin and placed them in the hands of the famous astronomer, Father Matthew Ricci, S.J. With the help of these precious remains and the oral account of the Armenian, Ricci pieced together the narrative of the journey as well as he might. That in this way inaccuracies should have crept in and that some parts should be incomplete will hardly cause surprise. Nor does it appear as clearly as might be wished which are Goes' personal notes and what is due to Ricci's vast and thorough knowledge of China. With all this, however, Ricci's narrative remains the chief source. He inserted it in his memoirs, which he began to compose two years before his death (1610). These memoirs were translated from the Italian and published in Latin by his fellow-missionary, Nicolas Trigault, a Belgian, under the somewhat pompous title of *De Christiana Expeditione apud Sinas suscepta ab Societate Jesu ex P. Matthei Ricci ejusdem Societatis Commentariis* [2]). For close upon three centuries every student had been referred to this, in many places incorrect, translation, when some years ago P. Tacchi Venturi, S. J. had the good fortune to discover Ricci's original manuscript. Italian scholars were about solemnly to commemorate the third centenary of Ricci's death, and at the request of the committee appointed to organize the national celebrations in honour of their great compatriot, Father Venturi prepared a critical

[1]) I have to thank the kindness of Señor Augusto Ribeiro for the photograph of this statue.

[2]) The first edition was published at Augsburg in 1615. We cite the second edition (Cologne 1616) corrected and enlarged by Trigault himself. Goes' journey is to be found in Book V, Chapters 11–13.

Nicolas Trigault was born at Douay March 3, 1577, entered the Society of Jesus November 22, 1594, and arrived in China in 1610. He was back in Europe on business in 1615, returning to China in 1618, where he was engaged in missionary labour till his death, which took place at Hang-cheu November 4, 1628. A memoir of Trigault was written by C. Dehaisnes, *Vie du Père Trigault de la Compagnie de Jésus* (Paris et Tournay 1864). For his journeys see the introduction to four articles by Jean Lavoix, *Du Royaume de Chine par le P. N. Trigault* in *Bulletin de l'Union géographique du Nord de la France*, (1908), p. 4 ff. A complete list of Trigault's writings is given by Sommervogel, VIII, 237–244.

edition of this remarkable work, which, we need hardly add, will be our primary authority [1]).

Goes' narrative is supplemented by four letters written by himself in the course of his expedition and addressed to the Jesuit missionaries in India. In Father Du Jarric's well-known work on India they are quoted from the annals of the mission, written by Father Fernam Guerreiro, in which they have been partially preserved [2]).

Goes had the obscurest of problems committed to him for solution: What was Cathay? Was it China or was it some other territory? As his whole journey is guided and directed by this question, which, moreover, repeatedly occurs in the later chapters of this book, a brief statement of the problem must be premised [3]).

Before the time of the Moguls (13th century) the name of Cathay had not been known in Europe. Originally it belonged to a people which was not Chinese, the Khitans, a Manchu tribe, who up to the tenth century occupied a tract of country in the north-east of China beyond the Chingan mountains. A conqueror arose among them, who soon extended their territory from the Sea of Korea to the Altai mountains, and before long they had pushed south as far as the left bank of the Hoang-ho. For two centuries Northern China and the adjoining territories formed the empire of

[1]) *Opere Storiche del P. Matteo Ricci S. J.*, edite al cura del Comitato per le Onoranze Nationali, con prolegomeni, note e tavole dal P. Pietro Tacchi Venturi S. J. — Matteo Ricci was born October 6, 1552, and entered the Society of Jesus at Rome August 15, 1571. On September 3, 1578, he landed at Goa, whence he reached Macao in 1582. The following year together with Father Rugieri he established the first mission station at Sciaochin. His works on geography and astronomy opened for him the road to Pekin, where, after a short stay in 1598, he established himself permanently in 1601. His claims as a contributor to the geographical knowledge of China are clearly brought out by Professor Ettore Ricci, *Per un Centenario: XXV Gennaio MDCI—MDCCCCI* (Macerata 1901—1904). Many particulars are also to be found in *Atti e Memorie del Convegno di Geographi-Orientalisti tenuto in Macerata il 25, 26 Settembre 1910* (Macerata 1911), which congress was held in honour of Ricci. For this writings cf. Sommervogel VI, 1792—1795.

[2]) Fernam Guerreiro, S. J., *Relaçam annal das cousas que fizeram os Padres da Companhia de Jesus nas partes da India Oriental .... nos annos de 1606—1607* (Lisboa 1609). In his *Relaçam .... nos annos 1607 e 1608* (Lisboa 1611) he gives the expedition in its general outline. p. 1—27.

Pierre du Jarric, S. J., *Histoire des choses les plus mémorables advenues .... ès Indes Orientales* etc. (Bordeaux 1614). I follow the Latin edition in three volumes published at Cologne in 1615. Petri Jarrici, *Thesaurus Rerum Indicarum.* The letters are to be found in vol. III, ch. 24 and 25.

[3]) For a full discussion cf. Yule, I, *Preliminary Essay*, cxv ff., or Yule-Cordier, I, 146 ff.

the Leaos or the Iron Dynasty. The rulers, then, being Khitans, but the country itself an outlying part of the great Chinese empire whose civilization the conquerors had made their own, the neighbouring tribes began to apply the name of Khitan, Khitat or Khitaï, to the latter country. And even to this day nearly all the nations which have come into touch with China by land, call the country Khitaï. When in their turn the Leao dynasty and its successor had to yield before the savage Mongolian hordes under Jengis-Khan (1206), the new conquerors considered themselves rulers of Khitaï or Cathay. It is well known how these nomads bursting all barriers came pouring through the gate of Dzungaria deluging western Asia with their unrestrained hosts. Every boundary line, natural or political, was effaced, and ever wider poured the plundering bands over the plains of Siberia and Sarmatia, so that in a few years the Mogul empire stretched from the Yellow River to the Danube. European civilization seemed doomed, for no human power could stem the tide of destruction. One way alone remained: — to win those barbarians for the Catholic Church and through her for civilization. Inspired with these high aims the first missionaries sought and found their way to the camp of the "Great Khan". Encouraged by the friendly welcome extended to them, they penetrated further into darkest Asia. From the accounts of these intrepid apostles Western Europe learned for a second time of a great civilized people living in the farthest East, and was thus enabled to revive and increase what it had learned as long ago as the time of Augustus. It was especially the Franciscan Friars who distinguished themselves in giving new life to those ancient records, and among them special mention must be made of John of Plano Carpini (1246), William Roebroek (1254) and Odorico de Pordenone (1316—1328). Their writings are only surpassed by the engrossing narrative of the famous Venetian Marco Polo. By all of them the country they described was called Cathay, as it was called by the Tartars, and its capital was Cambaluc [1]). "Further on," writes the keen observer Roebroek, "lies Great-Cathay, and I think it is the country which the ancients called the country of the Seres. For it is from that territory that the best silk is exported, and the people themselves call such silks seric". "The inhabitants

[1]) The name is spelt in various ways: Marco Polo writes Cambaluc, Pordenone Cambalech, others again Cambalu. The meaning of the Mongolian word *Khan-bâlig* is 'Khan's Town'.

of Cathay are of small stature, they speak mostly through the nose, and, as is the case with nearly all Asiatics, their eyes are very narrow". They write with pencils such as are used by painters, and each of their characters consists of several letters forming a whole word"[1]). All travellers speak of the great number of Christians in those remote regions, but they were mostly Nestorians, and there were repeated encounters between them and the Franciscans, when the latter were called to Cathay by Kublai-Khan towards the close of the thirteenth century [2]). In the course of the following years the Catholics increased in such numbers that Pope Clement V. thought it necessary to send them bishops, and in 1307 John e Monte Corvino was appointed Arcihbshop of Cambaluc in Cathay [3]).

The impulse, however, that was to have ended in the victory of Christianity, did not last. As early as the second half of the fourteenth century the immense Mogul empire began to totter, and it was finally destroyed through the incessant attacks of the southern Cathays, the Chinese. The number of missionaries steadily decreased and with them that of the traders, who had followed in their track. Occasional mention, indeed, is still made of friars or bishops sent out by the papal court at Avignon, but they vanish in the gathering darkness and then — all is silence. The new conquerors applying once more in the territories they had regained the ancient Chinese policy of isolation expelled all foreigners, while Islamism, temporarily repulsed by the Mongols, again closed its fatal grasp over Central Asia. In time a whole chain of Mahomedan nations severed almost completely the Far-East from the West. The knowledge of Cathay grew vaguer and vaguer. A few notices reached Europe through the narratives of the Spaniard Gonzales de Clavyo and of the Bavarian John Schiltberger, both of whom visited the court of Timur at Samarkand. At some greater length Nicolas Conti and Josaphat Barbaro spoke of what they had been told by others about Cathay, but there was no fresh first-hand information. Fancy was free to adorn and invent. A dense

---

[1]) D'Avezac, *Notice sur les Anciens Voyages de Tartarie en général et sur celui de Jean du Plan de Carpin en particulier — Recueil de voyages et de mémoires publié par la Société de Géographie* (Paris 1839) IV, 291 ff.; 327 ff.

[2]) Christianity was preached in the north-west of China as early as the seventh century, as is clearly borne out by the famous Chinese inscription discovered at Si-ngang-fu in the province of Shen-si in 1625.

[3]) Baronius, *Annales ecclesiastici ad annum 1307*, vol. XXIII, 403.

fog enveloped the famous cities of Cambaluc and Cansay, Zayton and Chinkalan, of which so many marvellous tales had been told by ancient travellers. But their elusiveness only increased their hold on the imagination. Columbus was not the only one to seek for a shorter way to Cathay, it was the object of every voyage "round by the north".

For a while the mysterious country was thrust into the background by the discovery of America and India, and on landing on the east-coast of Asia in 1514 the Portuguese heard no ancient names that might recall it. They heard of China, Pekin, Canton, without being aware that at one time these places were well-known in the West. It was only when missionaries, this time starting from the ports, penetrated into the interior, that it began to be conjectured that China might be Great Cathay and Pekin the rich city of Cambaluc. Though the ancient Franciscan missionaries and Marco Polo did not employ the names now in use, yet their descriptions tallied perfectly with the people, the customs, the products and the trade. It was Matthew Ricci especially who championed this view. He states it as early as October 12, 1596, in a letter from Nankin [1]). His opinion was strengthened by a visit to Pekin in September 1598. If Cathay, which by all writers was said to be a great country in the far East, was not China, then, so he argued, something should be known about it here, whether from war or from commercial relations. Such a country could not remain utterly unknown. His personal investigations and his discussions with the Persian traders he met with in the capital, finally disposed of every doubt as regards the identity of the two countries, and at the earliest opportunity he informed his friends in Europe and India of his results [2]).

As was to be expected his arguments did not command assent everywhere. Many unwilling to relinquish the country of legend and fable set themselves to assign to it another place on the map; they distinguished between Cathay and China in the same way as before them Ptolomy had done between the country of the Seres and that of the Sinae. As a glance at the ancient maps of Blaeu and Ortelius will show the cartographers shifted Cathay

---

[1]). Ricci, *Lettere* p. 227.

[2]) Ricci, *Commentari*, p. 296, 297. See also Prof. Ettore Ricci, *La Identificazione della Cina con il Cataio dovuta al P. Matteo Ricci*. Atti del VII Congresso Geographico Italiano (Palermo 1910) p. 6 ff.

and all the names connected with it bodily to the north, placing it in the Amur territory far beyond the new-found China and its great wall. As things were, it looked as if this uncertainty was to continue indefinitely, especially as the Portuguese, having their great colonial empire on their hands, would hardly have occasion to go in search of countries still more remote. But an unlooked for event, which happened at the court of the Great Mogul in India, again brought the question of the situation of Cathay to the fore. This, however, necessitates our turning our attention to Goes.

Bento de Goes was born in 1562 at Villa Franca do Campo, on the island of San Miguel, one of the Azores. Nothing is known with certainty about his family or his youth, though the rest of his career makes it probable that his education was thorough. Nor do we know for what reason he left his native country to sail for India, or why, when there, he joined the colonial army. After a life such as soldiers lead, and not over-edifying at that, he suddenly sobered down, and leaving his old ways begged for admittance into the Society of Jesus. His request was granted and he entered the noviciate of Goa in February 1584. Before completing his two years' noviceship he quitted and went to Ormuz. Regret soon followed and on applying he was again admitted, and by the end of March or the beginning of April 1588, being twenty-six years old, he was a novice once more [1]).

It was noticed before long that the new lay-brother, for it was in that capacity that he had been admitted, was a man of talent, and he was several times given the option of entering upon a course of theology with a view to the priesthood, but from a feeling of humility he firmly declined. These few facts are historically certain. Of late years, however, doubts have arisen in Portugal

---

1) These particulars are taken from a MS. *Annua Littera Provinciae Goanae anni 1609*, dated 27 December 1609 and addressed to the General of the Society. Under the heading "Obitus Benedicti Goesii" it contains a passage giving a short account of the Brother's life and of his journey. As his authority for the details concerning Goes' twofold admission into the Society the writer mentions Brother Antonius Magro. The latter is known to have entered the noviciate of Goa in October 1584 and must have lived with Goes under the same roof.

In the list of the members of the mission-province of Goa, dated December 1584, the following statement concerning Goes occurs under n. 116: "*Oppido Villa Franca Angrensis Diœcesis in Lusitania; 23 annos natus; robustus; ingressus est anno 1584, mense Februario; Officia domestica*".

In the list for the year 1588, drawn up 31 December 1588, his name reappears under n. 146. "*Benito de Goes, Portugues de la Isla de Sant' Miguel, de la Villa Franca, Obispado de Angra; de 26 años; robusto; de nueve meses de la Companhia.*"

whether the name of Goes is the explorer's real name, or whether he adopted it on his change of life. The point being still under discussion a few words about it will not be out of place.

The question was first raised by a romantic narrative entitled *Bento de Goes*, published by José de Torres at Ponta Delgada, Azores, in 1854. In it is described a young man called Luiz Gonçalves, who desperate from disappointed love takes ship for India and joins the army. After a few years he repents of his excesses, enters the Society of Jesus at Goa and changes his name into that of Bento de Goes. Whether this change of name is founded on fact Torres does not state. In any case his statement did not lack supporters, and for many the matter was settled, when it was found in 1903 that in the register of births at Villa Franca under date August 9, 1562 (the year of Goes' birth) there was entered the name of Luis Gonçalves, son of Manuel Gonçalves. In his memoir Ribeiro did not as yet accept the identity, though he admitted its possibility. He also drew attention to the entire absence of Goes' name in writings which might be expected to refer to him [1]). This was said with special reference to the well-known historian of the Azores, Antonio Cordeiro, S. J., who in his description of the island of San Miguel speaks at length of all men and women of note without any mention of Goes; nor is his name cited among the numerous family-names and pedigrees [2]). This is the more significant when we remember that he was a Jesuit himself, and would not have been likely to omit the name of one of his *confrères*. The same silence is observed in the preface written by J. Barbosa; he compares Cordeiro's book with the description of Tibet by Antonio de Andrade, but does not speak of Goes. Yet it is at least open to question whether the mere statement by Torres, the entry in the register for 1562, the silence of Cordeiro, and even the fact of his once mentioning the Gonçalves family at Villa Franca [3]) are arguments weighty enough to warrant the identification of the names of Goes and Gonçalves.

Whether Goes had any grave reason for changing his name it is impossible to say. We might be inclined to find a sufficient warrant for such a change in his not very exemplary life as a soldier;

---

[1]) Ribeiro, p. 6.

[2]) Antonio Cordeiro, S. J., *Historia Insulana das ilhas a Portugal sugeitas no Oceano Occidental* (Lisboa 1717), I, 171–311. We cite the reprint of 1866.

[3]) Cordeiro, *Historia Insulana* &c., I, 202.

but then, why should it not be mentioned or even hinted at by any of the early Jesuit historians? They certainly do not fail to mention the fact in parallel cases, and no plausible reason for their silence in the present instance can be adduced. The two most ancient documents bearing on Goes, the lists of the members of the mission-province of Goa for the years 1584 and 1588 content themselves with a few bare facts without reference to any change of name. Barbosa Machado's extensive bibliography is silent on the point [1]). Nor has an examination of the register of births at the parish church of Villa Franca do Campo resulted in establishing the identity. Rather the contrary. For one of those most deeply versed in the local history of Villa Franca, the Rev. Manuel Ernesto Ferreira, to whom I applied for information, thus sums up the results of his inquiry: "I have found nothing to prove the identity assumed by Torres to exist between Goes and Gonçalves. At one time I accepted it as it was the general opinion [2]); now I think it must be rejected". Why? Because it is a fact that at one time there was a family of the name of Goes at Villa Franca. Among other dates the name is entered in 1567, 1582, 1598. In the first of these entries the father's name is de Goes, in the other cases it is the name of the mother. As a curious coincidence it may be mentioned that in 1582 and 1598 the father is a Gonçalves. Could not the absence of the name of Goes in 1562 be accounted for by the very dilapidated state of those old registers? [3])

But how is Cordeiro's silence to be explained? Had he known of the work of his compatriot and fellow-Jesuit, he would have spoken of him no matter whether he was called Goes or Gonçalves; this is sufficiently apparent from the way in which he extols all

[1]) Machado. I, 504, s.v. Goes.

[2]) In his pamphlet *Elogio Historico de Bento de Goes* (Ponta Delgada 1907), p. 11 and 16.

[3]) The entries in the registers run as follows: "Hoje dezeseis dias do mês de novembro de mil quinhentos sessenta e sete baptizou o padre frei Melchior Homem, Vigario desta igreja do Archanjo São Miguel de Villa Franca, a Amador, filho de Amador de Goes," etc.

"Hoje quatorze dias do mês de dezembro de mil quinhentos sessenta e sete annos baptizou o padre Christavão da Mota a G.° [Gregorio?] filho de Sebastião Diniz e sua mulher Maria de Goes", etc.

"Hoje que são 3 de janeiro de 1582 baptizei eu padre Braz de Macedo a Leonor, filha de Simão Gonçalves e Catharina de Goes", etc.

"Hoje 16 de julho de 1598 baptizei a Antonio filho de Simão Gonçalves e de sua mulher Catharina de Goes. Foram padrinhos Jeronymo da Fonseca e Anna de Goes, filha de Amador de Goes", etc.

the great deeds of Azorians, and the only explanation of his silence is that he had no knowledge of the great traveller; which may be confirmed by the fact that none of his quotations or references betray any acquaintance with the works of Guerreiro, Trigault or Du Jarric. Goes, who entered the Society in India, who died in China, and whose very family-name, perhaps, had become extinct on the Azores by Cordeiro's time, simply escaped his notice.

The conclusion from what has been said can, in the opinion of the writer, only be that a change of name cannot be admitted.

Goes had lived for six years at Goa, when for the third time the renowned Great Mogul Akbar invited Jesuit missionaries to his court [1]). After some *pourparler* two priests, Jerome Xavier [2]) and Emmanuel Pinheiro [3]) together with Brother Goes were appointed to this difficult mission. After a perilous journey through the Indian desert they reached the capital city of Lahore May 5, 1595. Goes soon gained Akbar's confidence, and so great did his influence become that when the latter was meditating the conquest of the whole of Deccan, which necessarily involved an attack on the Portuguese settlements, Goes succeeded in dissuading him from

---

[1]) Hay, p. 691. — The stay of the Jesuit missionaries at Akbar's court is fully treated of by E. D. Maclagan, *Jesuit Missions to the Emperor Akbar* in *Journal of the Asiatic Society of Bengal*, LXV (Calcutta 1896) I, 38 ff.; see especially p. 64—110, where he speaks of the third visit. Cf. Felix p. 55—90, and Max Müllbauer, *Geschichte der Katholische Missionen in Ostindien von der Zeit Vasco da Gama's bis zur Mitte des Achtzehnten Jahrhunderts* (Freiburg in Breisgau 1852) p. 133—149. Special reference should be made to the *Mongolicae Legationis Commentarius* and the carefully prepared edition of it published by Father H. Hosten S. J. in the *Memoirs of the Asiatic Society of Bengal*. The *Commentarius* was written by Father Antonio Monserrate, S. J., during and after his stay at the court of the Great Mogul. It is strange that this commentary should have remained practically unknown, for besides being a history of the Jesuit stay at Akbar's court (1580—1583), it is a rich source of information for the history and geography of the India of those days.

[2]) Jerome Xavier, a relative of St. Francis Xavier, was born at Buro in the diocese of Pampeluna in 1549 and admitted into the Society of Jesus at Alcala May 7, 1568. He sailed for India in 1581, where he was occupied in many places, mostly as Superior. In 1617 he returned from the country of the Mogul to Goa, where he died on June 17 of the same year, before his nomination to the archiepiscopal see of Angamale (Cranganore) had reached him. He was well versed in the Persian language, in which he wrote several works. Cf. Sommervogel, VIII, 1337—1340, and for his Persian works see Maclagan, p. 110—113.

[3]) Emmanuel Pinheiro was born at Ponta Delgada on the island of San Miguel in 1544, entered the Society of Jesus March 6, 1573, and arrived in India in 1592. He died at Goa in 1618.

his project. And in 1601 wishing to negotiate a peace with the viceroy of India the Emperor knew of no more trusty ambassador than Brother Goes, and in token of his esteem he sent with him all the young Portuguese who had been carried off as prisoners of war. At Goa Goes met Father Nicholas Pimenta[1]), then Superior of the mission, a man of prudence and strong determination, fully acquainted with all the manners and customs of the Mohammedans, and who spoke Persian, the commercial language of Central Asia, with fluency. He soon learned to know and value Goes, and when the question of Cathay was again mooted, he conceived the plan of sending him on a journey of exploration to the land of mystery [2]).

It was an event at Akbar's court which had once more drawn the attention to that lost territory. "One day," Xavier wrote from Lahore to Goa in 1598, "a Mohammedan merchant, about 60 years of age, was admitted into the presence of Akbar and related that he came from Xathai by way of Mecca. Pretending to be an ambassador he had penetrated into the country and had lived in the capital, Xambalu, for thirteen years. It was a mighty empire, the king ruled over 1500 cities, some of which had an immense population. Many of the people were Isauitae [followers of Jesus] but not all, for there were also many Mussavitae [followers of Moses] and Mohammedans" [3]). Struck by those accounts Xavier personally applied to the merchant for further information. Again he was assured that there was a considerable Christian population, and in the course of his narrative the merchant descended to such details as to dress and customs, that in a subsequent letter Xavier thought he could vouch for the truth of his former communication [4]). The merchant's report was the more readily accepted, since all medieval travellers had spoken of Christian communities in Cathay. Yet the account was false. Unwittingly, as is most probable, the

---

[1]) Nicholas Pimenta born December 6, 1546, at Santarem, became a Jesuit in 1562. Having been sent to India as a visitor in 1596 to inquire into and report on the state of the mission, he successively governed the provinces of Goa and of Malabar. Most notices put his death on March 6, 1614.

[2]) Ricci, *Commentarj*, p. 526.

[3]) *Letter of Jerome Xavier from Lahore, July 25, 1598*. Hay, p. 796 ff., 875. — From the twelfth century the Mohammedans had not been strangers in the Chinese ports; as early as 878 two Arabs, Wahab and Abu Seid, had made a voyage to "the Middle Kingdom."

[4]) *Letter of Jerome Xavier from Agra, August 1, 1598* — Hay, p. 798. Du Jarric, II, 576 ff.

Mohammedan had fallen into an error into which many fell both before and after him, mistaking Chinese Buddhism for Christianity on account of the superficial and external resemblance of some ceremonies, and it is worth noticing that several travellers who borrowed their information about Cathay from Mohammedans were told the same fables about the existence of Christianity in those countries. When Josaphat Barbaro made inquiries about Cathay among the Tartars at Tana, he was assured that the inhabitants were Christians, because they had images in their temples as the Christians had. And Anthony Jenkinson was told at Bokhara in 1559 that the religion of the people of Cathay was the religion of the Christians or at least strongly resembled it [1]).

We have seen how Ricci stood for the identity of Cathay and China. But Pimenta hesitated. For Ricci's positive statements did not square with the equally positive information coming from Lahore, and while the Mohammedan informants spoke of the presence of large numbers of Christians, Ricci was silent on this point [2]). There must be a difference or an error, so Pimenta concluded, and a journey of discovery would not be out of place. Even though no new country should be found, no neglected Christian communities be discovered, the expedition might possibly result in the opening up of a new land-route shorter than the dangerous sea-voyage. He made proposals to this effect to Philip II., who charged the viceroy Ayres de Saldanha to forward the expedition to the best of his power; but, what was of far greater importance, Akbar's consent was easily obtained. He helped not only by letters of recommendation to the princes who were either his tributaries or his friends, but even contributed 400 gold pieces towards the cost of his friend's expedition, though the Khan's liberality was anything but proverbial [3]). Xavier thought rather lightly of the undertaking and a first plan, Kashmir-Rebat [4])-Caygar, mapped out by

---

1) Cf. Yule, II, 551 (Yule-Cordier IV, 201). See further Hay, p. 797. It was similar erroneous accounts that led to Andrade's journey to Tibet.

2) A few years later Ricci wrote that some traces of Christianity were still to be found in the provinces of Ho-nan and Shen-si. *Lettere*, p. 289 and p. 330, the letters of July 26, 1605, and of November 12, 1607; *Commentarj*, p. 469 ff.

3) Du Jarric, III, 204: "Erat enim natura tenacior."

4) Rebat is mentioned both in Jarric II, 579, and in Hay, p. 797. Yule II, 535 (Yule-Cordier IV, 177) cannot locate it, but surmises it is Tibet. That his conjecture is correct is borne out by the context in Hay and confirmed by the fact that on p. 863 he has twice Tebat for Rebat.

him, was easily relinquished for a longer but, as he was assured, easier and better known road, Lahore-Kabul-Badakshan [1]). He was led to adopt this plan, partly at least, by the *Theatrum Mundi,* according to which the distance between Lahore and the capital of Cathay could be covered in six months [2]). There can be no doubt that by the *Theatrum Mundi* the famous atlas of Ortelius is meant, which in fact contains a map of Russia, Muscovy and Tartary, designed and published in London by the above-mentioned Jenkinson. Commissioned by some English merchants the latter had in 1588 travelled through Russia and Turkestan with the definite object of finding the road to Cathay. He did not get beyond Bokhara, but from information received there he placed Cascara (Kashgar) on his map at 30 days' journey from the Cathay frontier; three months more would bring the traveller to the gates of Cambaluc [3]).

This then was the route Goes was to follow [4]). That as a European he might not at once have to meet opposition, he donned the garb of a Persian trader and let his hair and beard grow. That he was a Christian he neither might nor would conceal, as is sufficiently apparent from the name, Abdullah Isaï, which he adopted [5]). An ample supply of merchandise formed part of his equipment. Xavier had provided some trusty travelling-companions,

---

[1]) *Letter of Jerome Xavier from Agra, August 1, 1599.* — Hay, p. 798. In this letter Xavier also makes a casual reference to another route "by Bengal and the Kingdom of Garagata, at the extremity of Akbar's territories". To Yule this kingdom can only mean Cooch Behar State. We shall see in ch. V that this route was actually tried in 1626.

[2]) *Narratio Brevis Rerum a Societate Iesu in Regno Magni Mogor Gestarum, transcripta ex litteris P. Hieronymi Xavier, anni 1598, et P. Emmanuelis Pigneiro, anni 1598.* — Hay p. 875 ff., "Theatrum etiam mundi eiusdem regni mentionem facit: ad cuius Regiam urbem [a] Lahor anno medio perveniri potest."

[3]) A. Ortelius, *Theatrum Orbis Terrarum* (Anteverpiae 1570) fol. 104. On Cascara it is remarked: "Hinc triginta dierum itinere orientem versus incipiunt termini imperii Cathayae. Ab his limitibus ad Cambalu trium mensium iter interjacet."

[4]) The narrative of the journey is found in Ricci, Book V, ch. 12—14, p. 526—559. Ricci always writes 'di Gois'; from extant documents and early writings, however, it is certain that 'de Goes' is the correct spelling.

[5]) Du Jarric, (III 204) writes Brandae Abedulae, which he says means 'servant of God'. — On December 30, 1602, Goes writes to F. Emmanuel da Veiga from Lahore:

"O nome que agora tenho he Bandá Abudelã, que quer dizer servo de Deos; este nome me pos a P. Jeronymo Xavier quando de la me despedy." This letter occurs in the MS. *Annua de 1603 da Provincia de Goa e partes do Norte,* dated Goa December 24, 1603.

two Greeks, Leo Grimanus, a priest [1]), who spoke Turkish and Persian, and a merchant Demetrius, and four servants [2]).

Leaving Agra October 29, 1602, our party arrived at Lahore December 8 [3]). Goes' first work on arriving was to dismiss his escort of servants as both cumbersome and useless, and to look for another suitable travelling-companion. Fortune favoured him, for he found one in the Armenian Isaac, whose loyal attachment was to prove invaluable to him. As the caravan for Kashgar started from Lahore only once a year, Goes could not set out on his journey before 24 February [4]). The party consisted of about 500 persons with a long train of beasts of burden, camels and waggons. After a month they reached Athec (Attock), where they crossed the Indus, which at this point was only a bowshot wide. Thence to Kabul through the mountain districts of Afghanistan was a perilous and difficult march. They had to protect themselves not only against the severities of the climate, but even more against the bands of marauders attracted by their merchandise. The road went by Passaur (Peshawar). Jelalabad, where the Chitral valley begins, and Ghidelì (Jagdali?). Trouble arose even before they reached Peshawar and later on they were compelled to take an escort of 400 soldiers as a defence against the rapacity of the natives.

---

[1]) Guerreiro, (*Relaçam nos annos 1607 e 1608*, c. 23) calls Grimanus a deacon; Du Jarric omits this detail. As early as 1590 Grimanus had carried communications between Akbar and the Jesuit Fathers at Goa. Cf. Felix (p. 72) who calls him an Armenian.

[2]) From a detailed Latin report on the state of the mission addressed by Pimenta to the General and dated December 29, 1602, in which the Cathay expedition is briefly mentioned, we learn that Father Anthony Machado, then rector of the college at Bassein, and Goes were selected for the enterprise. The latter was to start by himself in order to reconnoitre, after which he was to return to fetch the Father, who meanwhile would learn the language. According to Felix (p. 81 note 2) Machado arrived at Agra in 1602 and died there on April 4, 1636. Why he did not join Goes, does not appear.

[3]) Ricci (*Commentarj* p. 529) places the date of the departure from Agra on January 6, 1603, which, however, is contradicted by the above-mentioned letter of Goes to Da Veiga, in which he distinctly mentions the date given in the text. Various erroneous dates are given: Brucker (p. 601) and Vasconcellos (p. 19) have October 2, Yule (II. p. 537) and Yule-Cordier (IV, p. 203) have October 31; Ettore Ricci (*La Identificatione della Cina con il Catayo* p. 8) and Machado (I, 504) have Ricci's date.

[4]) The MS. from which I quoted Goes' letter to Da Veiga contains a transcript of another letter from the same addressed to Jerome Xavier, dated Lahore February 24, 1603. For the sake of clearness I quote from the Latin translation appended to it: "Hodie ineuntis Quadragesimae feria sexta instrumentum omne trans flumen praemisimus.... Tempus est ut proficiscamur. Quare iis litteris finem impono." Huc (*Le Christianisme* II, 211) confuses the dates of the departure from Agra and the arrival at Lahore, and makes the 500 men composing the caravan into soldiers given as an escort to Goes by the King of Lahore.

They had to make their way at the point of the sword, and the narrative of the journey notes that many were mortally wounded, whilst the others nearly lost their lives in saving their valuables. In those mountainous districts with their ravine roads the beasts of burden were generally driven along the lower parts, whilst the escort made their way along the top of the rocks to prevent the brigands from crushing them by throwing heavy stones into the narrow gorge below. At this stage of his journey Goes learned some details about another no less savage tribe in the neighbourhood. "Being on their way to a small town", Ricci writes, "they met a wandering hermit, who told them that at a distance of 30 days' march there was a territory called Caferstam, which no Mohammedan was allowed to enter. Those who penetrated into the country were punished with death, while heathen merchants went about unmolested, though they were debarred from entering the temples. He added further that they never entered their temples unless clothed in black, that the country was fertile, and that it produced grapes in great abundance. Bento tasted of the wine the hermit offered him and found it in no may different from ours. Drinking wine being contrary to all usage among Mohammedans he surmised that the inhabitants were Christians" [1]).

The country in question is clearly Kafiristan, the hill-country north-east of the Kabul valley between the river Kunar and the Hindu Kush mountains. It is occupied by some tribes very jealous of their independence, who are called Kafirs (unbelievers) by the surrounding Mahommedans, though they are better known by the name of Siah-Posh from the black colour of their garments [2]). Goes' is probably the first mention of this remnant of a nation, for the Mohammedan historians of the middle-ages, on whom we must rely for the greater part of our information about the East, did not think it worth while to go into details about such despised unbelievers, against whom they preferred to preach a war of extermination. Later explorers have entirely confirmed the sparing but characteristic details given by Goes. Ritter collected all that was known about this people up to his own time, especially from Elphinstone's *Account of the Kingdom of Caubul* [3]). They are

---

1) Ricci, *Commentarj*, p. 530.

2) F. Ratzel, *Völkerkunde* (Leipzig 1888) III, 458. George Scott Robertson, *The Kafirs of the Hindu-Kush* (London 1900) p. 73.

3) Ritter, V, 202 ff.

described by Robertson as a people of strong physique, of middle height, little resembling the Afghans or Kashmiris, and the fact that they should have maintained their independence to this very day sufficiently proves their reputation for courage to be no idle rumour. The Afghan Syud Shah, who visited them in 1882, declares that his countrymen entertain greats fears of the Kafirs, one of whom is generally said to worth five Afghans in battle. Their dislike of Mohammedanism has not yet diminished, though those among their countrymen who have embraced it, suffer little on account of it. Their hatred is one more of race than of religion. Every Siah-Posh goes bare-headed till he has slain a Mohammedan, and before that time he cannot rise to any esteem among his countrymen. To be able to marry he must have killed at le ast two Mohammedans. Syud witnessed a funeral at which wine was freely served [1]).

At length after a journey of more than six months the great centre of trade, Kabul, was reached [2]). The perils encountered, however, deterred a number of travellers from continuing the journey,— a fact which imposed upon the others a compulsory rest of eight months, during which they had to recruit their thinned ranks. Goes also lost two of his companions. Grimanus could no longer endure the fatigues of the journey and returned, while Demetrius remained in the town hoping to do some good business [3]); so with the faithful Isaac as his only companion Goes joined the new caravan.

The formidable and steep mountain range of the Hindu Kush now barred their way. The easiest and most frequented of the many passes is the well-known Bamyan pass, a depression between the Hindu Kush and their western continuation the Koh-hi-Baba

---

1) *Kafiristan nach den Berichten des Missionars Hughes und des Afghanen Munschi Syud Schah* — Petermanns Mitteil. (1883) p. 406. Cf. Ritter, V, 210; Robertson, *The Kafirs* &c., p. 190, 558, 566. — Th. Holdich (*The Origin of the Kafir on the Hindu Kush* — Geographical Journal, VII, (1896) p. 48) also states that the Kafirs have long been celebrated for their wine-making.

2) J. B. Paquier, *Le Pamir* (Paris 1876, p. 65) would have us believe that it was only through stress of circumstances that Goes visited Kabul, because the repeated attacks of the Afghan tribes prevented him from following the valley of Chitral, a contention unauthorized by any of the sources. Paquier would seem to know Goes' journey only through the extract in Kircher's *China Illustrata*.

3) Demetrius went as far as Yarkand later on, where he overtook Goes, but he did not pass into China. Du Jarric's statement (III, 215) that both he and Grimanus left Goes only at Yarkand can only be accepted with regard to the former.

mountains. A more easterly route of greater difficulty but more direct was preferred. According to Ricci it went by "Ciaracàr [Charikar], where iron is found in abundance, to Paruàn [Parwan], a small town, the furthest frontier town of the empire of the Great Mogul, whose authority was consequently more a name than a reality, so that his letters freeing Goes of all taxes were of little or no use" [1]). Charikar is situated at the mouth of the Koh-Daman valley, at the very foot of the Hindu Kush, while more to the north, at the junction of the Bajgah and Sar-Ulang passes, lies Parwan, already mentioned by Edrisi as a not very large but thriving town. Most probably, therefore, the caravan took the Bajgah or Parwan pass. Ancient writers speak of this pass as a very difficult one. In the earliest description of Kabulestan dating from the sixteenth century Sultan Mohammed Baber notes it as very difficult, especially because between Parwan and the main pass there are seven smaller ones [2]). In 1837, when on his still famous expedition to the sources of the Amu-darja, the Oxus of the ancients, Lieutenant John Wood followed more or less Goes' route and tried to cross not exactly by the Parwan pass but by the one next to it, the Sar-Ulang; the enormous depth of snow in November frustrated his attempt [3]). Though Goes in 1603 probably crossed during a more favourable season, we may fully concur with the narrative and call the passage 'difficult', and we can understand that the party, to brace itself for the effort, took a five days' rest at Parwan [4]). Then followed a journey of twenty days across the moun-

---

[1]) Ricci, *Commentarj*, p. 532. — As regards the presence of iron near Charikar, the *Imperial Gazetteer of India* (X. 176) notes that large quantities of iron from the Ghorband mines are carried to Charikar.

[2]) J. Leyden and W. Erskine, *Memoirs of Zehireddin Muhammed Baber, Emperor of Hindostan &c.* (London 1826) p. 139—140.

[3]) John Wood, *A Journey to the River Oxus, 1836—1838* (London 1841); Ch. 12 treats of the country we are now considering.

[4]) The same cannot be said of each and all of the many rests chronicled in Ricci's account, and it must have struck the reader that we have been almost silent as to time and distance. As a matter of fact, this is one of the knotty points of the narrative, on which Ricci's manuscript throws no light. Errors are many. For instance: according to Ricci the journey from Attock to Peshawar took two months, a sheer impossibility, the distance being 70 kilometres. Yule, however, very acutely observes here (II, 538; Yule-Cordier IV, 181) that Goes' notes may have had 'II mensil' (from the Persian 'manzil', a day's march,) and that the Italian Ricci may have read 'II menses'.

That Goes did note down distances in his diary appears from one of his letters, quoted by Du Jarric (III, 205), in which he relates what befell him "after travelling a distance of 102 cossas, a cossa being equal to an Italian mile." From a comparison of Ricci and Du Jarric the following dates are ascertained: departure from Lahore about the

tains to Aingaràm, from where another fifteen days' march brought them to the district of Calcià. It is worth noticing that nearly a thousand years before the Buddhist pilgrim Hiuen-Tsang covered almost the same route in the same time. The name of Aingaràm beyond the mountains cannot be traced [1]), but for this we have some compensation in Goes' brief note on the people of Calcià. "The people of this country are, like the Flemings, of a fair complexion. They inhabit several villages" [2]): another indication — and again the first — of a remnant, which in these secluded mountain regions has retained the original type and the primitive customs. The liberty-loving Calcià tribes, for they are clearly in question, live scattered throughout the tracts north of the Hindu Kush, and must be carefully distinguished from the Tadshiks of the plains, whose character has been much affected by centuries of foreign domination. The Tadshiks, says Valikhanoff, are of a dark complexion, whilst among the Calciàs fair-haired people are found [3]). Ujfalvy, who made thorough studies of the many peoples of Central Asia, visited among others the Calciàs of the Amu territory and met with many persons having blue eyes, and whose beards were brown, reddish or fair-coloured. They lived close together in villages and observed strict endogamy. The meaning of Calcià in their language was, so they said, 'a hungry raven forced to retire into the mountains in order to live' [4]). The latest

middle of February 1603 — arrival at Yarkand November 1603 according to Ricci, but in any case before February 1604, when Goes wrote to India from that town — departure from Yarkand mid-November 1604 — arrival at the Chinese wall towards the end of 1605 — death at Su-cheu April 11, 1607. The computation of all the days of travel and of rest recorded in Ricci's account between Lahore and Kabul — some are evidently omitted — would place Goes' arrival at Yarkand in November 1604, just one year after the time he did arrive. Time-notices are consequently of no value as we shall have occasion to remark also in the sequel.

[1]) Wood's map gives near the Bamyan pass a place called Dara-i-Aingharan; this together with Ricci's chronology has led Yule to suppose that the caravan striking out westward from Parwan and skirting the Hindu Kush finally crossed by the Bamyan pass (Yule, II, 526; Yule-Cordier IV, 259). But this supposition is not supported by any evidence, least of all by Ricci's words (*Commentarj*, p. 532). Brucker (p. 604) finds on Wood's map a settlement I-angheram *in* the Parwan valley, but again this cannot be the place in question, since according to the narrative Aingaràm is situated *beyond* the mountains, and therefore north of them. In the supposition, the present Jaram just north of the Parwan pass would be a more likely spot.

[2]) Ricci, *Commentarj*, p. 532: "Barba e capelli rossi, come fiammenghi."

[3]) Ratzel, *Völkerkunde* (Leipzig 1888) III, 455.

[4]) Ch. De Ujfalvy, *Voyage au Zarafchane, au Ferghanah, et à Kouldja* — Bulletin de la Société de Géographie, XV (1887) p. 486—489.

testimony comes from the great explorer Sir Aurel Stein. Speaking of a friendly native of Sarikol, a province to be spoken of by Goes later on, he says: "With his tall figure, fair hair and blue eyes, he looked the very embodiment of that *Homo Alpinus* type which prevails in Sarikol. I thought of old Benedict Goëz, the lay Jesuit, who when passing in 1603 from the Upper Oxus to 'Sarcil' or Sarikol noted in the looks of the scanty inhabitants a resemblance to Flemings" [1]).

The way in which Goes became acquainted with those independent tribes was not the most pleasant. They had passed Gialalabath — perhaps Aliabad on the Kunduz river — where the Brahmins had the right of exacting tribute, given them by the king of Bucarate (Bokhara) [2]). They next arrived at Talhan (Talikhan or Talachan as it is called in other maps), once a town of importance, now a wretched village of a couple of hundred cabins and distracted by civil war. The Calciàs had risen in revolt against the Khan of Bokhara and were engaged in pillaging and plundering the neighbourhood, so that the caravan had to take shelter at Talikhan for a weary month. Setting out again at last, they were attacked near Chescàn [3]) (Teshkàn beyond Talikhan), a place under Abdulahan King of Samarkan, Burgagne (Farghana), Bucarate (Bokhara) and other adjoining kingdoms and only escaped complete ruin by paying a tribute on their merchandise. Shortly after this Goes was held up by four of the rebels, but his presence of mind saved him. To distract their attention for a moment he took his Armenian cap, in which a precious stone glittered, flinging it away as far as possible, and as the brigands darted after it and quarrelled about the division of the booty he set spurs to his horse and escaped [4]).

---

1) Stein, *Ruins of Cathay* I, 89.

2) Trigault (p. 698), writing Bruarate where Ricci had Bucarate, led Brucker to suppose an error in the narrative and made him place Gialalabath south of the Hindu Kush, as being identical with Jelalabad (Brucker, p. 602). Probably for the same reason De Vasconcellos in his memoir (p. 19) places it in the Kabul valley without any further comment. Yule (II, 559, note 1; Yule-Cordier IV, 211) bad already suspected that Trigault's reading was an inaccuracy or a copyist's error for Bacharata (Bokhara); Ricci's manuscript has fully confirmed the learned commentator's conjecture.

3) Trigault (p. 698) wrote Cheman, which completely confused Yule (II, 559) Yule-Cordier (IV, 211) and Brucker (p. 607).

4) Henry Rawlinson speaking of Hayward's journey to the Tarim basin (*On Trade Routes between Turkestan and India* — Proceedings of the Royal Geographical Society XIII (1886) p. 16—18.) takes the Calciàs described by Goes to be the same as the

Meanwhile travelling became more and more difficult. Skirting the higher uplands, so the narrative tells us, they reached Tenghi Badasciàn by a wretched road, and after a ten days' rest Ciarciunar. The district of Badakshan is evidently meant. In the town of the same name the escort made common cause with the populace and fell upon the traders. Goes notes here that 'Tenghi' means 'difficult road', and in fact, he says, the road was so narrow, that when travelling along the high bank of a large river they had to march in single file [1]). Marco Polo had already complained of the bad roads in Badakshan, and if we take the above-mentioned river to be the Padsh or upper Amu-darja, the principal watercourse of those regions, Goes' description agrees well with the findings of later travellers. Abdul Subhan, who took part in Forsyth's second expedition to Eastern Turkestan, describes the Padsh valley in the district of Gharan as very narrow and of difficult passage, where the deep and rapid river has cut itself a bed with almost perpendicular banks [2]). Thus over slowly rising ground the caravan gradually approached the formidable Pamirs, where the mightiest among the mountains of Central Asia, the huge ranges of the Tian Shan, Kuen Lun, Karakoram, Himalaya and Hindu Kush, meet and are crowned by the highest plateaux on the earth, the 'Roof of the World' as the natives call it. This 'roof', however, is no ordinary high plateau. Kostenko in 1875 and all more recent explorers describe it as a rather irregular succession of bare ridges and high-level valleys, which extend over immense distances

---

Atkashes, a fair-haired, blue-eyed robber nation belonging to the Kafir tribes. They hold the eastern passes of the Hindu Kush, especially the road through the Chitral valley, which he considers to be the ancient trade route between India and China, already described by Ptolemy. He accordingly maps out a different route for Goes and makes him go up the Kunar river from Jelalabad and thence to the Hindu Kush through the Chitral valley. Against this Vivien de St. Martin has already objected that this route cannot be made to square with Goes' stay at Talikhan and his crossing of the Pamirs (*L'Année géographique* 1869, p. 280). What, besides, would be the meaning of the journey from Kabul to Charikar and Parwan, whose topographical situation is ascertained beyond doubt? It is, moreover, anything but certain that the ancient trade route did pass through the Chitral valley. Capus, who went down it in 1888, pronounces the road to be "très difficile et peu fréquentée." (*Pamir et Tschitral* — Bulletin de la Société de Géographie (1890) p. 500.)

[1]) Ricci, *Commentarj*, p. 534. Ciarciunar cannot be located. If, as Yule conjectures (II, 526, note 1; Yule-Cordier IV, 216), it is the Persian word 'Char Chinar', 'the four plane-trees', we might have to think of it as an oasis. If we suppose an error in the time-notice, according to which Ciarciunar was reached after a day's journey from Badakshan-town, the little frontier town of Carchunar might be thought of.

[2]) Forsyth, p. 18.

between the long ranges and reach the height of Mont Blanc [1]). "Correctly described," writes George N. Curzon, "a Pamir in theory, and each Pamir in fact, is therefore neither a plain nor a down, nor a steppe, nor a plateau, but a mountain valley of glacial formation, differing only from the adjacent or other mountain valleys in its superior altitude and in the greater degree to which its trough has been filled up by glacial detritus and alluvium; it has thus approximated in appearance to a plain owing to the inability of the central stream to scour for itself a deeper channel" [2]). The snow-covered mountains which rise in every direction render, as Schultz one of the latest explorers remarks, the name of plateau, which is generally used, incorrect" [3]).

No European save Marco Polo had trod those forbidding regions before Goes, and the eighteenth century would close before Wood was to follow him. That Goes did cross the Pamir cannot be doubted. It is, indeed, denied by Alexander von Humboldt [4]) and by Ritter [5]), the latter even going so far as to place Goes' route two degrees south of the Pamir track, but this error is easily explained. For Ricci does not mention the Pamir expressly, and in neither of the two German writers is there any indication that they know of any source for the reconstruction of Goes' journey beyond Trigault's translation of Ricci. Guerreiro and Du Jarric, however, have preserved a letter from Yarkand, in which the daring traveller tells of his experiences. "While still at Hircanda [Yarkand] Benedictus de Goes wrote that he had had an exceedingly difficult and laborious journey through the Pamech desert. Of his horses five had perished through the intense cold and the entire lack of fuel together with the uncongenial state of the atmosphere, which made it almost impossible for the animals to breathe. Hence both men and beasts sometimes felt oppressed beyond endurance and gasped for breath. Against this evil men arm themselves by eating garlic, onions and dried apples, whilst the gums of the animals are rubbed with garlic. The journey through this desert takes forty days, if there is snow on the ground; otherwise it is shorter. The

---

[1]) Forsyth, p. 44 ff. — The Kirghiz call 'Pamir' any wild and uninhabited country.

[2]) George. N. Curzon, *The Pamirs and the Sources of the Oxus* — Geographical Journal VIII (1896) p. 31.

[3]) A. von Schultz, *Vorläufiger Bericht über meine Pamirexpedition 1909* — Peterm. Mitteil. (1910) p. 140.

[4]) A. von Humboldt, *Asie Centrale*, II, 387.

[5]) Ritter, V, 503 ff.

country, moreover, is notorious for its marauding bands, who lie in wait for the caravans to rob or murder them" [1]). Every one of these details has been confirmed by later explorers, and whoever wishes to obtain fuller knowledge of the life in these highlands should read Sven Hedin's interesting description of his travels through the Pamirs and of the life of the small garrison at Pamirski Post, the lonely fortress in the high valley of the Murghab, where the flag of Russia floats over the 'Roof of the World'. The climate is bleak and severe in the extreme. Scarcely two or three weeks of the summer are without a night-frost, and in the summer-nights Arved von Schultz often noted 7° C. of frost in the desert-like high valleys [2]). No one escapes the effects of the mountain-sickness with its oppression of the lungs, bleedings and quickened pulse. Like Goes Bonvalot took as a precaution a supply of dried apples with him [3]), and it is interesting to learn that the sultan of Peshawar advised his friend Burnes on his journey through Central Asia to eat plenty of onions, this being the most efficacious means to get inured to the climate of those regions [4]). Besides being a pasture ground for the wandering Kirghiz and their flocks, these inaccessible valleys have been, from time immemorial, a favourite resort for many whom political circumstances or crime had driven from their homes. Pressed by necessity they form robber bands, against which Bonvalot and Capus in 1887 thought it well to provide arms [5]).

If we have undoubted evidence for Goes' journey across the 'Roof of the World', we are ignorant as regards the road he took. Whether he went by the greater or the lesser Pamir cannot be made out from the following scanty details of Ricci's narrative, and Du Jarric gives nothing beyond what has been quoted above. It is here if anywhere that the loss of the journal is to be regretted. "From Badasciàn [Badakshan] they reached after one day's march [?] Ciarciunar, where torrential rains kept them in the open for five

---

[1]) Guerreiro, *Relaçam .... 1606–1607*, ç. 166A. Du Jarric, III, 217. — It need hardly be stated that all writers acquainted with these documents consider Goes' crossing of the Pamir to be beyond dispute.

[2]) A. von Schultz, *Vorläufiger Bericht über meine Pamirexpedition* — Peterm. Mitteil. (1910) p. 140.

[3]) G. Bonvalot, *Voyage dans l'Asie Centrale et au Pamir* — Bulletin de la Société de Géographie (1890) p. 480.

[4]) Brucker, p. 610.

[5]) Bonvalot, *Voyage dans l'Asie Centrale*, p. 479, 513.

days. Ten days later they arrived in Serpanil, a waste country, uninhabited and without food. Thence began the ascent of a steep mountain called Sacrithmà, which only the strongest horses could climb, the others going by an easier but very circuitous route" [1]. Serpanil may be traced back to Sir-i-Pamil, the 'Head of the Pamil', the native population, according to Fedschenko, using Pamil for Pamir[2]. But what and where is the Sacrithmà? Can the name, which has probably been sadly maimed, have any connection with the mountain station of Sarikbaee near the sources of the Amu-darja, as Yule suggests? [3] Or may it be a local name for some portion of the Nesa Tagh? It is certain that Goes had had to cross that range. "At last," Ricci continues, "after twenty days' march they arrived in the province of Sarcòl [Sarikol or Sírikol], where they found several villages built close together. Two days were allowed for rest on account of the jaded horses, and after another two days they found themselves at the foot of the Ciecialith. The pass lay under deep snow and during the six days' march several travellers died of cold, Goes himself only just escaping death". Under the leadership of Gordon a party belonging to Forsyth's expedition travelled along the same route in 1874 [4], as did also Aurel Stein in 1906 on his journey to Eastern Turkestan [5]. The latter crossed the Tagh-Dumbash Pamir and reached Sarikol by the Wakhjir pass. Sarikol is a small mountain district, in which a number of villages with a fairly thick population spread themselves along the Tashkurgan. By the Ciecialith is meant the high pass of Chichiklik (4350 metres), which was also followed by Stein but under far better conditions. "At length Tanghetàr [Tangitar] was reached, where Isaac fell from the high bank of the river into the water but was fortunately rescued". The Tangitar river comes from the Chichiklik plateau and unites with the Sarikol to pour their joint waters into the Serafchan or river of Yarkand. Gordon's men describe the road along the Tangitar as most terrible. At some points the track is the bed of the river itself dotted with huge boulders and deep pools [6]. Another fifteen days along this abom-

---

1) Ricci, *Commentarj*, p. 535.

2) *A. Fedschenko's Reise in Kokan und zum Nordende der Pamir 1871* — Peterm. Mitteil. (1872) p. 165.

3) Yule, II, 562; Yule-Cordier IV, 216.

4) Forsyth, p. 12.

5) Stein, *Ruins of Cathay* I, 98—99.

6) See also Stein, *Ruins of Cathay* I, 99—100.

inable road, which lost Goes six horses, and Jacorich was in sight. Yule is at a loss how to identify this place. Very likely it is Yakka-arik, which would furnish another proof for the unreliability of Ricci's time-notices; for he requires five days for the next stage, Yakka-arik—Yarkand, which is only twenty kilometers. Here Goes left the spent caravan and hurried on to Hiarcan [Yarkand], whence he sent fresh horses and supplies to those he had left behind. Finally the whole party entered Yarkand, then the capital of the kingdom of Kashgar. It was probably November 1603 [1]).

Of old the oasis of Yarkand, with its congested centre and roomy outskirts, had been, and it still is, one of the great stopping-places and emporiums on the long trade route between China and the distant West. Goes is very sparing in his details about this much frequented centre, only mentioning the great number of Mohammedan temples and a curious ceremony in the observance of the Friday as the Mohammedan weekly day of rest. On that day all believers assembled in the great mosque. As soon as the service was over, twelve men carrying leather thongs or scourges left the temple and went about striking all those who had not been present —a proceeding intended to obtain them pardon for their neglect [2]).

It need hardly be said that in such a place a Christian's very life was in danger, though, indeed, it was not the first time that fanatical Mohammedans attempted Goes' life. Even before he had left India, probably when still at Kashmir, one of the rajahs threatened to have the unbeliever crushed under the feet of his elephants, but the stranger's calm reply that he would gladly lay down his life for the true God disarmed his enemy. Others, sword in hand, tried to compel him to call on Mohammed but likewise failed, and at last the intrepid traveller found friends even among the enemies of his religion, who, respecting such courage, were ready to defend him when in danger. At Yarkand soon the rumour spread that a foreigner, a European, not a follower of Mohammed, had arrived in the town. Such a thing was unthinkable, for was not everybody persuaded that no man in his senses could fail to

---

[1]) Very cautiously Ricci writes: "Pare che questa arrivata fu l'istesso anno di 1603 in novembre." (*Commentarj*, p. 536). Du Jarric (III, 206) simply writes "November". In any case Goes arrived before February 2, 1604, the date of his letter from Yarkand.

[2]) Du Jarric, III, 213. — A similar custom is mentioned by Ibn Batuta in his own time at Khwarim. He even tried to introduce it into the Maldive Islands. The same practice is still in use at Bokhara. (Yule, II, 569; Yule-Cordier, IV, 225).

profess their religion? [1]) The commotion assumed such proportions that Goes thought it advisable to pay his respects to the king of Kashgar, who resided in the town. Some presents, among them a watch, one large and three smaller looking-glasses, but especially Goes' tactful behaviour so gratified the king that he had him sent for several times and even invited him to explain the Christian religion in the presence of his court, which gave rise to many a sharp dispute with the mollahs.

For about a year the explorer had his patience tried at Yarkand. The caravan of the Kabul traders had been disbanded, and the formation of a fresh party was attended with peculiar difficulties. The right of organizing and leading a caravan was sold by the king of Kashgar to the highest bidder, whom he appointed his ambassador investing him with absolute authority over his fellow-travellers. Then in consideration of large sums of money and presents the leader associated with himself four others with the title of ambassadors, after which he enrolled a suite of 72 travellers, who likewise had to buy their admission. Thus a caravan to Cathay put on the appearance of an embassy and it was only under this guise that it could penetrate into that country [2]).

Ricci speaks at length of this peculiar form of commercial intercourse. "Most merchants coming to this town [Su-cheu, the gate of China for caravans from Turkestan] arrive from the west pretending to be ambassadors. By very ancient treaties seven or eight countries have obtained from the Chinese government that every five years seventy-two persons in the quality of ambassadors shall bring tribute to the king, which must consist of the well-known transparent marble [jade or nephrite], diamonds, blue pigments and similar articles. This is carried to the court at the expense of the state, which also furnishes funds for the return journey. This tribute is more honourable than profitable, for no one obtains marble at greater cost than the king, who considers it incompatible with his dignity to accept anything from foreigners for nothing. They are entertained at the king's expense in such a manner that allowing for everything and deducting the necessary

---

[1]) Du Jarric, III, 204 ff. – John Wood relates that his Mohammedan hosts in Badakshan did not even remotely suspect that he could be anything but a Mohammedan, though they were well aware that he was a European and an Englishman.

[2]) Du Jarric, III, 214 ff. – The head of Goes' caravan had to pay 200 bags of musk for his appointment.

expenses they gain a gold piece a day. Hence it is that such an embassy is much sought after and membership is bought with presents from the leader, with whom the appointment rests. When the day of departure draws near they forge royal letters patent, in which they pay respectful homage to the Chinese sovereign. From several countries such embassies are admitted into the country, from Caucincinum [Cochin-China], Sian [Siam], Lenchien [Riu-Kiu Islands], Corianum [Korea] and from some petty Tartar princes. All this is an immense burden on the treasury, but the Chinese, who are well aware of the fraud, want by such devices to flatter their sovereign and make him believe that the whole world pays tribute to China, while it is the Chinese themselves who thus pay tribute to those countries" [1]). The two Jesuits Martin Martini and Alvaro Semedo speak in like terms of those pseudo-ambassadors. According to the latter the presents for the emperor always consisted of 1,000 arobas or 1,333 Italian pounds of nephrite, 340 horses, 300 very small diamonds, about 100 pounds of fine blue pigment, 600 knives, 600 files, of a total value of 7,000 crowns. The emperor's acknowledgment was worth 50,000 crowns. Xavier's Mohammedan informant at Lahore declared that he himself had penetrated into the country as a merchant-ambassador of the king of Kashgar [3]).

As the negotiations for the formation of the travelling-party dragged on, Goes was at leisure to visit Cotan (Khotan), situated in the oasis of the same name south-east of Yarkand. That he should direct his steps thither finds its explanation in an event that had taken place in the early part of his journey at Kabul. During his stay there the mother of the king of Khotan, who was also the sister of the king of Kashgar, returned to that town from a pilgrimage to Mecca. The narrative calls her Age-Hanem, the

---

[1]) Ricci, *Commentarj*, p. 550.

[2]) A. Semedo S. J., *Histoire universelle du grand royaume de la Chine* (Paris 1645) p. 27. — None of the Chinese could tell Semedo why the 600 files were included among the presents. It was ancient usage and must not be relinquished. That these fictitious embassies had their place and function in the most ancient commercial relations with China appears from what is said by Vidal de la Blache in his *Note sur l'origine du commerce de la soie par voie de mer.* Comptes Rendus de l'Académie des Inscriptions XXV (1897) p. 525: "Ce mot d'ambassade déguise probablement l'initiative des négociants grecs, qui pour s'assurer bon accueil auprès des autorités s'arrogèrent un titre officiel. Cette pratique n'avait rien d'insolite, elle était même imposée par les habitudes commerciales de l'Extrême Orient."

[3]) Hay, p. 697.

'princess-pilgrim' [1]). Very likely her rank had been no safe-guard against the rapacity of the hillmen, for she was soon short of money and turned to the merchants for aid promising to refund all on their arrival at Yarkand. This was too favourable an opportunity to secure protection on his further journey for Goes to let it pass unused. He sold part of his merchandise, and the proceeds, 600 gold pieces, were advanced to the princess free of charge. Of special importance was the stipulation that the whole sum was to be paid back in transparent marble, the stone mentioned above as forming part of the tribute carried by the ambassadors. This jade, the Yu-stone of the Chinese, the jaspis of the ancients, called nephrite by our mineralogists, has always been and still is highly valued throughout the East, especially among the Chinese, who ascribe to it certain properties. With this stone their philosophers connect the five virtues that form the basis of the Chinese moral code: Modesty, mercy, justice, meekness and frankness [2]). Every Chinese woman, writes Von Schmidt, wears nephrite ornaments of some sort, generally bracelets. Both men and women wear one as an amulet against sickness [3]). Nephrite has found its way even into Europe, and traces of it have been discovered even in the so-called prehistoric dwelling-places. As late as 1865 Damour wrote that such articles were kept in France as a protection against certain diseases, or were enclosed in the foundations of many houses to prevent their being struck by lightning [4]). For a long time there was complete ignorance as to the place where this stone, which does not occur in Europe, was found; the only thing known was that it came to the Chinese from the west. After Marco Polo, who passed through those regions between 1271 and 1275, Goes was the first European to visit the principal place of origin. It is the presence of nephrite that has given Khotan its fame throughout the East. Fortunately, on this point the narrative is fuller than it is wont to be, and Trigault has added some details from his own store of knowledge. "There is no article in which a more

---

[1]) Du Jarric, (III, 211) writes, "Ahehaxam, id est lingua Turcica, venustas Mecha descendens."

[2]) K. Bogdanowitsch, *Bericht über meine Teilnahme an der Pewzowschen Expedition* — Peterm. Mitteil. (1892) p. 52.

[3]) A. von Schmidt auf Altenstadt, *Reisherinneringen uit China* — De Aarde en haar Volken (1904) p. 225.

[4]) A. Arzruni, *Neue Beobachtungen am Nephrit und Jadeït* — Zeitschrift für Ethnologie XV (1883) p. 165.

valuable and more extensive trade is carried on than in a kind of transparent marble, which for want of a better name we call jaspis.... They [the Chinese] make of it various objects such as vases and ornaments for clothes and girdles, the value of which they enhance by artistic engravings of leaves and flowers. This marble, of which at present the country is full, is called *Yusce* by the Chinese. There are two kinds. The most valuable stone is obtained from the river Cotan [Khotan-darja] not far from the capital [Khotan] in nearly the same manner as divers fish for pearls. It is generally brought up in the shape of large pebbles. The other less valuable kind is got from the mountains and cut out in large slabs about two yards broad, after which it is made fit for transport. These mountains are at 20 days' journey from the capital and are called Can Sanguicascio, that is rock of stone [Kan-sang-i-Kash, the mine of Kash stone]. It costs an incredible amount of labour to loosen those pieces both on account of the remoteness of the spot and the hardness of the marble. It is said that this hardness may sometimes be slightly reduced by making a hot fire on the surface of the stone. For a high price the king sells the quarrying rights to some merchant, without whose consent no one is allowed to take away any stone as long as the contract lasts" [1]).

Both ancient descriptions and reports of later explorers confirm these details; one need only compare the exhaustive account in which Ritter has gathered up all that was known on the subject up to his time [2]). As the principal locality where nephrite occurs he gives the watershed of the Khotan-darja, the Karangu Tag. Hermann von Schlagintweit devotes a whole chapter to this remarkable stone [3]). In 1890 Bogdanowitsch knew of seven localities all on the northern slopes of the Kuen Lun; he gives a description of how the stone is made into articles and even how it is imitated [4]). Sven Hedin's brief description is characteristic enough to be quoted. "Kalta-Kumat, a very small village (7 kilometres north-east of Khotan), situated in the middle of what once was the bed of a river, is inhabited only by nephrite-diggers, mostly Chinese.... The nephrite-bearing soil has been officially apportioned and every

---

[1]) Trigault, p. 610. — Ricci, *Commentarj*, p. 538.

[2]) Ritter, *Asien* V, 380, Anmerkung: Der Ju (Yu) Stein, d. i. Ju-chi der Chinesen, Kasch der Turk, Yescheb der Perzer, oder Jaspis der Alten; sein Fundort in Khotan, sein Verbrauch und Handel.

[3]) Schlagintweit, IV, 161—186.

[4]) K. Bogdanowitsch — Peterm. Mitteil. (1892) p. 52 ff.

owner may dig only within his own claim. Trenches are dug only among the accumulations of stones washed down from the mountain, not where clay or sand occurs. Such trenches are to be seen in ever direction; they are generally only a couple of metres deep and wide, whilst their length is ten metres at the utmost, their shape being as a rule rectangular. It is only among the stones from the mountain that pieces of nephrite are found, which of course are water-worn. The spots for such trenches are selected at hazard, and sometimes it will be months before any piece of value is met with. White pieces with yellow spots, called *gusch*, that is flesh, have the greatest value. In the town of Khotan are a couple of factories for the production of small nephrite articles such as snuff-boxes, mouth-pieces for pipes, bracelets etc." [1]) The stone is, of course, also mentioned by Stein in his archaeological exploration of the Khotan territory, the kind referred to being of a sort of green colour, of inferior quality, quarried from a mountain side high up in the valley of the Kara-Kash. He adds: "The manner in which this inferior jade is obtained was correctly related by Goes, who speaks of the place as Cansanghicascio" [2]).

Meanwhile this little excursion of Goes' was causing days of anxiety to Isaac, who had stayed behind at Yarkand, and to Demetrius, who had arrived five months later than his former master. Though according to Goes' own assurance Khotan lay at only ten days' distance, he had been absent for a month. The Mohammedans adroitly turned this prolonged absence to account and spread the rumour that the unbeliever for being unwilling to call upon the name of Mohammed had been put to death by their priests, and they began to cast covetous glances at his belongings as unclaimed property. Fortunately at this junction the faithful Armenian saw his master, for whom he was already mourning, return safe and sound carrying a good supply of nephrite with him [3]).

In the meantime a certain Agi-Afis had been appointed head of the caravan and the intrepid European was invited to join the embassy. In order to avoid arousing the suspicions of the distrustful authorities Goes had refrained from breathing even a word

---

[1]) Hedin, *Ergebnisse*, p. 28.

[2]) Stein, *Ancient Khotan*, I, 132–133.

[3]) That the risk run by Goes was very real indeed is sufficiently borne out by the fact that Adolf von Schlagintweit, the only European who visited Khotan in the middle of the nineteenth century, never returned being murdered by fanatical Mohammedans near Kashgar in 1857.

about Cathay; in his conversations with the king he had only mentioned the kingdom of Cialis, east of Kashgar, and requested a safe-conduct for that country; which request had been supported by the king of Khotan in the name of his mother. For the same reason he now deferred accepting the proposal, so that the leader asked for the king's personal intervention to obtain Goes' compliance. He then accepted the honourable offer on condition that he should have safe-conducts given him for the whole of the rest of the journey. His old Kabul companions still tried to retain him, but at last November 14, 1604, he was at liberty to venture deeper into the deserts of Asia [1]). Dozens of travellers have in the course of the nineteenth century followed him into those lonely regions of the Tarim basin, Russians and Englishmen have opened up the country, but to no one more than to the famous Swedish explorer Sven Hedin are we indebted for the increase of our knowledge of those territories. His perilous journeys enable us to form a picture of what difficulties had to be encountered by his daring predecessor.

Eastern Turkestan or the Tarim basin is but a link in the immense chain of deserts reaching right across the Old World from the north-west coast of Africa to the steep slopes of the Chingan mountains. All round the arid sands of the Takla-Makan rise the fantastic summits of endless mountain ranges like the unscalable walls of a gigantic prison leaving a free horizon only towards the east, where the eye loses itself in the lifeless wastes of Lob-nor, behind which lies the great sea of sand, the Gobi or Shamo. Even in the very earliest periods of history it was through Turkestan that China and the West were in touch with each other. At the beginning of our era the famous silk-route lay partly within its borders and the excavations of Sven Hedin, Sir Aurel Stein and many others in the sand-buried towns plainly testify to the importanceof that country in former times [2]).

A caravan starting from Yarkand makes choice between two routes, both of which as far as possible skirt the Takla-Makan, a

---

[1]) Ricci, *Commentarj*, p. 542. — Du Jarric, III, 218.

[2]) Taking account only of the last few years we may refer to the labours of the Germans Grünwedel and Von Lecoq from 1902—1906 during three expeditions, especially in the neighbourhood of Kutsha and Turfan; of the Frenchmen Pelliot and Vaillant since 1906, mostly at Kutsha and Urumchi; of the Russians Von Oldenburg and Kolso at Turfan, Characoto and elsewhere, whilst the Japanese Zuicho Tachibana was at work both at Urumchi and Turfan.

southern route within the shadow of the Kuen Lun, a northern one along the foot of the Tian Shan. Both find their points of support in villages and oases which depend for their existence on the water-courses from the mountains, rendering artificial irrigation possible in a region where the rain-fall is exceedingly small. Goes took the northern road travelling by the oasis-towns of Aksu, Kutsha, Kurla, Turfan and Chami, from which latter place he cut across the desert into China. All these larger places are mentioned in the narrative together with a host of smaller ones, which, however, cannot be located with certainty even with the aid afforded by the detailed maps of Hedin, Stein and others. This should not surprise us for several reasons. The greater part of the journal being lost many names had to be written down by Ricci, an Italian, from the dictation of Isaac, a Persian-speaking Armenian, who had only his memory to rely upon; how much distortion such process must have entailed no one can tell. Others may have been of mere local use — a supposition which in a couple of cases comes very near to certainty, while it is not at all impossible that in a country so much ravaged by sand-storms and plundering bands many a halting-place may have been swept out of existence since the time of Goes. As early as the eighteenth century, when preparing their famous map of China, the Jesuits found it impossible to locate many places spoken of in the narrative. Father Régis thinks the difficulty was owing to the peculiarity of several towns having more than one name, the one employed by Goes having probably fallen into desuetude [1]).

"After leaving Yarkand," the narrative continues, "the first stopping-place was Jolci, where generally a toll was paid and the royal letters of exemption were inspected. Thence they reached Aksu in twenty-five days by way of Hancialix, Alcegher, Habagateth, Egriàr, Meselelec, Tallec, Horma, Toantac, Mingieda, Cape-

[1]) Régis remarks as follows: "Cette diversité de noms répand une obscurité, qui embarrasse un Géographe et qui l'expose à faire des faites grossières comme, par exemple, de multiplier les villes. C'est un défaut dont quelques-unes de nos anciennes cartes ne sont pas exemptes. On ne sait pas encore à présent, quelles sont les villes, nommées Cialis et Aramut dans l'Itinéraire du Frère Goës, qui fut envoyé pour découvrir le Cathai, quoiqu'on ne doute point que ce qu'il appelle Chiaicum ne soit Hia-yu-Koen, et ce qu'il nomme Sociou, ne soit la ville de Sou-tcheou, parce que ce que'il en rapporte fait connaître que c'est de ces villes-là qu'il parle. Mais on ne peut pas dire la même chose des autres villes, qu'on trouve nommées si différemment. Tout ce qu'on peut dire, c'est qu'apparemment ce sont des villes qui ont deux noms différents dans les diverses langues, etc." Du Halde, IV, 585.

talcòl, Cilàn, Sare, Guebedal, Cambasci, Aconterzec and Ciacor. Travelling was exceedingly difficult more particularly on account of the innumerable stones and the sandy waterless plains" [1]). Only one or two of these names can be traced. The uncertainty begins with Jolci, probably a custom-house on the edge of the oasis. Yule and Brucker have made various suggestions for the other fifteen names, but even to-day diligent study and a comparison with the material furnished by later travellers in the Tarim basin give in most cases no satisfactory results [2]). The main route being sufficiently defined, however, these obscurities do not seriously interfere with the course of the narrative [3]). As there is not a word about a stay or stop at the town of Kashgar, where Schlagintweit and Von Richthofen erroneously make Goes arrive instead of at Yarkand [4]), the caravan seems to have cut off the north-western

---

[1]) Ricci, *Commentarj*, p. 542. — In several places Trigault (p. 614) has deviated from the spelling of the manuscript.

[2] Forsyth, p. 71—76; — Ch. de Ujfalvy, *Voyage du capitaine Kouropatkine en Kachgarie*, Bulletin de la Société de Géographie de Paris, XIII (1877) p. 656—660. Hedin's and Stein's maps should be specially consulted.

[3]) The following are some conjectures:

Hancialix = Khan-Chalish? (Yule).

Egriàr = Egri-iar; this is a frequently occurring local name. as is stated by Dr. Sven Hedin in a letter to the writer on the subject of these names.

Meselelec = Mejnet, or according to Hedin, Merket-daylik.

Tallec = Tallik (Hedin), a name much used in those parts.

Horma; this word means 'date' in modern Persian; it may be objected that no date-trees are to be found in those parts (Hedin). According to Pelliot it is the Hu-eul-man of Chinese texts of the 18th century (Cf. Yule-Cordier, IV, 228).

Toantac = Tewan-tâgh, the 'low hill'; it is to this day the name of a hilly spur to the east of the road Maralbashi-Aksu (Yule-Cordier, IV, 228).

Capetalcòl = Chaptal-kul? (Brucker); Kaptar-köl, the lake of pigeons (Pelliot).

Cilàn = Tchilgan, on Hedin's map half-way between Maralbashi and Aksu.

Sare Guebedal; are two places meant or one? Taking the latter supposition Yule proposes to read Saregabedal; Brucker taking the former reads Sarc, a contraction of Sai-arik, whilst Guebedal remains unknown. According to Hassenstein (Hedin, *Ergebnisse*, p. 364) Sai or Saj means a dry stony river-bed or a stony plain at the foot of a mountain.

Cambasci = Kumbasch, on Hedin's map south of Aksu. Kam baschi means 'the first quarries'.

Aconterzec = Saksak? (Yule).

Ciacor = Shakyar? (Yule).

Hedin also remarks that there is a frequent altering of names along the Yarkand-darja and the Tarim on account of the shifting of the river-beds.

According to Paul Pelliot, Goes' route lay eastward of the present road.

[4]) Schlagintweit, IV, 213. — Von Richthofen, I, 667. — Ribeiro makes the same mistake (*Missions et Explorations Portugaises* (Lisbonne 1900) p. 22). At the time Yarkand was the capital of the kingdom of Kashgar.

corner of the Takla-Makan by taking the direction Laylik-Maralbashi, between the Kashgar-darja and the Tarim, which route was in part followed by Sven Hedin in March 1895. From Maralbashi the track runs along the edge of an arid steppe, in which oases are but rare. Speaking of the desert Goes notes that it is called Cara Catai, "which means black country of the Cathayans, because it is maintained that the inhabitants of Cathay occupied it for a long time". Roebroek also uses the name of Cara-Cathay, 'Black Cathay', to distinguish it, he says, from the country of the Cathayans, who inhabit the sea-board in the far East. But the 'Blacks' live among the mountains [1]). If Roebroek undoubtedly refers to the Tian Shan mountains, it is equally clear that Goes applies the name to the desert at their southern base. Now it appears from Chinese historians that for centuries the Chinese occupied the Gobi desert and the Tarim basin, but the inroads of the Tibetans in the eighth century put an end to the Cathay rule and at the same time to the prosperity of the country. The same supremacy of China appears moreover from the numerous archaeological finds spoken of above. Even in China Ch. E. Bonin discovered the remains of an ancient travelling-road going in the direction of the desert, defended at certain intervals by towers linked up by earthen walls. The road ran along the southern face of the wall probably to protect it from the desert sands swept up from the north [2]). Stein, too, discovered and followed over a distance of 225 kilometres an old Chinese wall, running from Aksu westward, with towers at every three to five kilometres. The road alongside of it was he says being used as early as the second century B. C. [3]).

The king at Aksu was a twelve-year-old boy, cousin to the king of Kashgar. Being well-disposed through some presents suitable to his age, sugar and the like, he received the traveller kindly. He had a festive dance performed in the presence of Goes, whom he then requested to dance after the fashion of his country, which

---

[1]) Yule, I, 176. — Plano Carpini translates the name of the people as 'Nigri Kitai.' The Chinese monk Ch'ang-ch'ung, who from 1221—1224 travelled through Central Asia to the Hindu Kush, also speaks of a country where the Karakitai live. With him, however, it is a country west of Kulcha, at the northern base of the Tian Shan in Russian Turkestan. (Dr. E. Bretschneider, *Chinesische Reisende des Mittelalters nach West-Asien*, Peterm. Mitteil. (1875) p. 373)

[2]) Charles Eudes Bonin, *Voyage de Péking au Turkestan russe* — La Géographie, III (1901) p. 173.

[3]) Dr. A. Stein, *Exploration géographique et archéologique en Asie Centrale 1906—1908*, La Géographie, XX (1909) p. 145.

little pleasure was readily accorded. After a few more visits to the king's mother and to his tutor, with the indispensable accompaniment of presents, and a compulsory rest of fifteen days to allow the stragglers to come up with them, Goes set out once more. By way of Oitogràc, Gaso, Casciani, Dellaì, Saregabedàl and Ugan, across a great many mountain streams and in part over the spurs of the Tian Shan the caravan arrived at the small town of Cucià (Kutsha or Kuchar) [1]). In this oasis, according to Merzbacher in many respects the most pleasant of all the towns in the Tarim basin, they took a whole month's rest, of which they stood greatly in need, for "the difficult journey, the heavy load of marble and the want of food had exhausted every one's strength". The fanatical vexations Goes had to suffer at the hands of the Mohammedan priests of this town made him, no doubt, welcome the moment of departure. Twenty-five days later he was at Cialis, "a small but well-fortified town." Opinions vary as regards the identity of this place, which, under this name at least, does not occur on the maps. That it is situated on the main caravan-route there can be no doubt. Ritter supposes it is Yuldus among the Tian Shan mountains [2]); Yule takes it to be Karashar [3]), since this town, which by all travellers is numbered among the principal towns along the route, is not mentioned by Goes at all; Brucker on the authority of Gaubil votes for Korla [4]). De Vasconcellos [5]) also mentions the latter place, but, without assigning any reason, prefers Chiglik, a settlement some forty-six kilometres south of Korla, from where Przewalsky approached the Lob-nor in 1876. This hamlet, however, is too far

---

[1]) Casciani and Saregabedàl are probably to be identified with the places called Tschaktschi and Sairam respectively on Hedin's maps. Oitogràc again is a local name. Regel, in his account of his expedition to Turfan, speaks of the 'tugrak', the desert poplar, one of the trees most congenial to the waterless steppes, so that Oitogràc would mean a place abounding in poplars. A. Regel, *Meine Expedition nach Turfan 1879* — Peterm. Mitteil. (1879 p. 382). Hedin and Stein frequently speak of the tograks.

Here again Pelliot has his own way of accounting for the impossibility to identify these places. "Goes", he writes, "did not go to Kuchar by the present road of Bai and Sairam. The plain of Bai is closed to the south by a mountain range not mentioned on the maps, the Chöl-tagh or 'barren mountains'. Up to the first half of the nineteenth century caravans going from Aksu to Kuchar took the route south of Chöl-tagh, and it was this road which was followed by Goes." (quoted from Yule-Cordier IV, 231.)

[2]) Ritter, I, 222.

[3]) Yule, II, 575; Yule-Cordier, IV, 234.

[4]) Brucker, p. 688. — P. Gaubil S. J. calls **Cialis 'Kouli'** in his work: ***Abrégé de l'histoire chinoise de la dynastie des Tang*** — **Mémoires concernant** les Chinois, tome XV, 404—405.

[5]) Vasconcellos, p. 22.

removed from the caravan-road and there is nothing to indicate that Goes left the usual track. Korla seems to be the most likely place both on account of Goes' remark that the town was strongly fortified and of its situation. "Korla", says Hedin, "is a small town, whose only point of importance is its geographical position on the river [the Kontje-darja], at the entrance of a narrow pass between the Tian Shan and the Kurruk Tag, and on the great caravan-road between Aksu and Kara-shahr"[1]). Even to-day Korla is a fortress with a Chinese garrison. At Cialis the reception by the Mohammedan sovereign, another relation to the king of Kashgar, threatened to be somewhat unfavourable, but in the end the passports and the necessary presents did not fail of their effect. Here also Goes could not avoid argument. One night when the king and several of his priests were discussing religious topics, the stranger was suddenly sent for. Goes went, though somewhat surprised at this nocturnal invitation, which to the anxious Isaac foreboded nothing but evil. The priests at once opened the attack, but after a hot controversy were reduced to silence, the sovereign winding up the debate with the remarkable declaration that the Christians, too, were true believers, followers of a religion which at one time had been professed by their forefathers [2]), — a vague reminiscence of the Nestorian Christian communities, which, like the settlements buried under the desert sands, have vanished without leaving a trace.

As the leader of the caravan wanted to enroll fresh associates, Goes' patience was tried for another three months, till at length he obtained the king's special leave to start by himself, which, however, alienated from him the rest of the caravan. When he was on the point of leaving the town, there arrived a large party from Cathay, who supplied him with the most valuable information. In 1601 these merchants had penetrated into the capital in the quality of ambassadors, they had even lived there for three months together with Ricci and his companions. Though unable to give their European names, each of the foreigners having assumed another name after the Chinese fashion, they could sufficiently describe their appearance, enumerate the presents offered by them to the emperor, and even, in support of their assertions, produce a piece of paper with Portuguese words written by the foreigners at

---

[1]) Hedin, *Ergebnisse*, p. 66.

[2]) Ricci, *Commentarj*, p. 545.

Pekin. They had picked it up from the sweepings of Ricci's room, that on their return home they might prove that the people using that language had penetrated into China [1]). All this could not but convince Goes that Cathay differed from China only in name, and that Cambaluc was indeed the capital city, was Pekin. Consequently what Ricci had written before his departure from Lahore was true, and he, Goes, had proved it to be so.

With Isaac and a small party he now travelled by Puccian (Pitshang or Pichan) to the fortified town of Turfan, whence after another month's delay he reached the fortress of Camul (Chami) by way of Aramuth (?).

At this point there is a slip in the narrative. Pitshang is not to the west but to the east of Turfan. The road to this oasis, passing by Karashar along the northern shore of the Bagratsh-kul, runs through an easy longitudinal valley. The German botanist A. Regel, in the employ of the Russian government, penetrated into this fertile country in 1878, though not without difficulty. He learned from the inhabitants that the present town only dated from about 150 years back, so that Goes must have stayed at the old town, the ruins of which lie a litle more eastward [2]). During the 275 years that had gone by since the passage of Goes no European had set foot in that territory save the Portuguese Jesuit D'Espinha. This was in 1756 when D'Espinha by order of the emperor Khien-long followed the army into Dzungaria in the character of topographer; on that occasion he determined the situation of Turfan and Korla [3]).

So kind was the welcome extended to our traveller at Chami, where he arrived October 17, 1605 [4]), that it induced him to stay

---

[1]) Ricci, *Commentarj*, p. 546. On p. 376 Ricci himself speaks of these Mohammedan merchants, whom he had met in Pekin at the so-called Palace of Embassies, and who once again had given him convincing proof that Cathay was really China. They also carried nephrite, by him called *iusce*, for the emperor.

[2]) A. Regel, *Turfan* — Peterm. Mitteil. (1880) p. 106.

[3]) J. Brucker S. J., *Positions géographiques déterminées par deux missionnaires jésuites dans le Turkestan Oriental et la Dzoungarie en 1756, d'après deux lettres inédites des P. P. Amiot et Gaubil.* (Lyon 1880).

[4]) Du Jarric, III, 219. — The journey from Yarkand, therefore, had lasted 11 months (14 Nov. 1604—17 Oct. 1605). Ricci would apportion the time thus: Departure from Yarkand Nov. 14, 1604 — after 25 days arrival at Aksu, 15 days' rest — after ? days arrival at Kutsha, 1 month's rest — after 25 days arrival at Cialis, 3 months' rest — then 20 days to reach Puccian — after ? days arrival at Turfan, 1 month's rest, departure Sept. 4, 1605 — after 15 days arrival at Aramuth — Oct. 17, 1605 arrival at Chami.

here for a month. The object of his journey had almost been achieved; there remained but a march across the desert, and 500 kilometres beyond the undulating sands of the Gobi, at whose northern edge he stood, rose the great Chinese wall. The shortest route is from Chami by Ansifan to Su-cheu, which was followed by Grum Grschimailo and Obrutschew in 1889 and 1894. Futterer, one of the latest explorers, assures that "this route puts no hindrances in the way save those arising from a wintry climate, drought, heat and possible sandstorms. There are no lofty mountains raising the track through difficult passes, only a few undulating rises of the ground about the middle part of the road" [1]). For all this the journey is not without its perils, as appears both from what Du Halde relates on this point as far back as 1736, and from what Kreitner reports of Mandl, who in 1881 found this road strewn with the carcases of animals that had died from lack of water or food [2]). Göes, so the narrative goes on to say, reached the northern Chinese wall near the town of Chiaicuon (Chia-yu-kuan or the 'Jade Gate', of the Great Wall) nine days after leaving Chami, and, after waiting for twenty-five days for the permission of the viceroy of Kan-su to proceed on his journey, he arrived in one day's march at Socceo (Su-cheu), surely a record journey if the number of days given be correct. These calculations, however, though probable enough in normal circumstances, seem hardly admissible in the present instance. For though the road may not be exceptionally difficult, it is never easy and was at the time anything but safe.

"The country between Cialis and the Chinese wall," Goes writes, "is notorious for its Tartar raids, so that traders always cross it in the greatest fear, sometimes even under cover of night and in the strictest silence. One often comes across the dead bodies of Mohammedans who have attempted the journey unaccompanied, though on the other hand the Tartars are not wont to kill the native population, considering them as their servants and herdsmen whom they occasionally rob of their flocks" [3]). To escape like

At the time of his excavations near Turfan Le Coq rode from the site of his operations to Kashgar by Turfan, Kutsha, Aksu and Maralbashi in 44 days. (A. von Le Coq, *A Short Account of the.... First Royal Prussian Expedition to Kurfan* — Journal of the Royal Asiatic Society (1909) p. 321).

[1]) Dr. K. Futterer, *Geographische Skizze der Wüste Gobi zwischen Hami und Sutscheu* — Peterm. Mitteil., Erganz.-heft 139 (Gotha 1902) p. 4.

[2]) G. Kreitner, *Die Wege von Ansifan durch die Wüste Gobi nach Hami* — Peterm. Mitteil. (1882) p. 416.

[3]) Ricci, *Commentarj*, p. 548.

dangers Goes and his small party journeyed only by night, and thus it becomes difficult, if not impossible, to get from Chami to Chia-yu-kuan in nine days, the distance being about 520 kilometres as the crow flies. Travelling very fast Handl covered 400 kilometres in ten days [1]). So here again an error must have crept in.

At Su-cheu, where Goes arrived towards Christmas 1605, he again met with Mohammedans on their home-journey from Pekin, who again assured him of the presence of European priests. The first thing now was to inform Ricci. Through letters from India the latter knew of the expedition, and firm in his conviction he had as late as November 12, 1605, once more written to the Superior of the mission of Goa to prove the identity of Cathay and China [2]). Of course every new arrival in the capital was questioned about our traveller but without any result. Nor did the first letter, despatched by Goes from Su-cheu immediately on his arrival, reach Ricci, because Goes did not know his Chinese name, and had, moreover, written the address in European characters. At last in the middle of November 1606 a Mohammedan handed Ricci a letter, which had been despatched at Easter [3]). In it Goes gave an account of his journey, spoke of it plainly as being very dangerous, and useless for commercial purposes. Nowhere had he found any trace of Christians and he pressed Ricci to take instant measures to enable him to get to the capital. It was his intention to return to India by way of Canton. Though the approaching winter was anything but favourable for the four months' journey from Pekin to Su-cheu, Ricci on December 11 despatched one of his trusted pupils, Fernandes, who spoke Portuguese. Little did Fernandes suspect, as he neared the town at the end of March 1607, that he came but to assist a dying man. What had happened to Goes?

Su-cheu was in reality two towns, one Chinese the other Mohammedan, and it was in the latter that Goes, a foreigner, had to take up his residence. Six months after his arrival his former travelling-companions, against whose will he had started from Cialis, entered the town, which may not have improved the situation. In general terms the narrative states that he had much to suffer at the hands of the Mohammedans, and that his funds were running out, but it

---

[1]) Kreitner, *Die Wege von Ansifan &c.* — Peterm. Mitteil. (1882) p. 416.

[2]) Du Jarric, III, 219. — He wrote to the same effect to the General of the Society of Jesus, Claudius Aquaviva, in a letter dated July 26, 1605. (Ricci, *Lettere*, p. 293).

[3]) Ricci, *Commentarj*, p. 551; *Lettere*, p. 348.

does not enter into detail. It is worth noticing, however, that even in his last letter he had warned Ricci against the untrustworthiness of the Mohammedans. At the momen the had been ill for a month, but in the night previous to Fernandes' arrival he saw in a dream that an answer had come from Pekin, and he told his faithful Armenian to go into the market-place and inquire. For a moment the old energy revived when Fernandes ushered in by Isaac entered and addressed him in Portuguese. His eyes full of tears he opened the letter from Pekin and read and re-read that last confirmation of all his toilsome travels. Cathay was China!.... He knew, but after the pronouncement of the great Ricci he could lay down his head with greater contentment. For in the complete absence of medical assistance all the cares of untiring charity could not restore his rapidly failing strength. He sank gradually and on April 11, 1607, he died far away from his brethren in the arms of his two friends [1]).

Goes had fulfilled his mission. Ascending from the sun-lit plains of Hindostan to climb the stupendous heights of Central Asia, covering a distance of more than 4,000 kilometres across elevated plateaux and sandy deserts, he was the first European of modern times to set foot on Chinese soil from the west and thus to assign to the country of legend and fable its true place on the map of the world. When looking back on his own stay at Su-cheu Sir Aurel Stein recalls in a few words of warm sympathy the memory of the great traveller who preceded him by some 300 years. "I had thought of him and his plucky perseverance at all the points — Lahore, Peshawar, the Pamirs, Sarikol, Yarkand and Khotan — where I had touched the line of his wanderings.... there is nothing to suggest even approximately the spot where his wearied limbs were laid to rest by the young Chinese convert, whom the Jesuit Fathers had despatched from Peking to his relief, and who arrived just a few days before all earthly trouble was ended" [2]).

Goes' lingering sickness and death has naturally aroused a suspicion of foul play on the part of the Mohammedans. The hypothesis of poison, already advanced by Ricci, receives some confirma-

---

[1]) Ricci, *Commentarj*, p. 553. Goes died "eleven days after Fernandes' arrival", which arrival took place "on the last day of March 1607", as is stated on the same page by Ricci. These words, therefore, dispose of all other dates such as March 16,1606, April 11, 1606 &c. Ricci himself seems to make a slip when in his letter of August 22, 1608, to Aquaviva he puts the date of Goes' death on April 10. Ricci, *Lettere*, p. 355.

[2]) Stein, *Ruins of Cathay*, II, 292.

tion from their action after his death. Though not a scholar Goes was a man of talent and a keen observer. He kept an elaborate journal, in which he accurately noted down distances, roads and their condition, places and countries. But the same journal had recorded in its pages the sums of money advanced by Goes to several of his fellow-travellers. This must have been known to them, for no sooner had he died than they possessed themselves of all his belongings, and as if by preconcerted action first threw themselves on the diary. It was mutilated and torn up, only some fragments could be saved by Isaac and Fernandes, together with a few things left by the plunderers as being of no value to them: a crucifix, the letters of the Archbishop of Goa and Jerome Xavier for the missionaries at Pekin and the three passports of the kings of Kashgar, Khotan and Cialis. But the hatred of the Mohammedans was not yet satisfied and Goes' faithful servant was not to escape scot-free. Isaac was thrown into prison and his case dragged on for months. Fernandes stood by him faithfully, which at first was extremely difficult, as he did not understand Persian. But with great diligence he learned it from Isaac at night-time, and was then able to undertake his defence. Though right was on their side, they were no match for the rich merchants, who had no difficulty in corrupting the Chinese judges. Yet, after five months, their persistance prevailed, and what was left of Goes' possessions was assigned to them. This they carried with respectful care to Ricci, and by their oral communications helped him to compose the narrative of the journey [1]).

After taking a month's rest at Pekin Isaac, well rewarded, returned to his wife and family in India. His adventures, however, were not yet ended. At Macao he took ship for Malacca, but the vessel was captured by the Dutch off Singapore. Being brought before the captain he told him of his long journey with Goes, and the simple story made such an impression that the commander

[1]) Ricci, *Commentarj*, p. 557; *Lettere*, p. 346–353, letter of March 8, 1608, to Claudius Aquaviva. — In his letter of August 22, 1608, to the same, Ricci thus refers to the composition of the narrative: "Nel tempo che qui stette Isaac, con quello che ritrovai fra gli scritti del fratello Benedetto, agiutandomi di quello che Isaac aveva visto, feci una relazione di tutto il viaggio, arrivata, stata in Socceo e morte del detto fratello Benedetto e di quello che successe al fratello Giovanni [Fernandes]" etc. (*Lettere*, p. 356). In both these letters Ricci says he has written at great length about Goes' journey to the Provincial of India, Caspar Fernandes, and to Father Francis Pasio, but these accounts have to all appearance been lost, as have also Goes' own papers carried by Fernandes to Ricci.

wishing to inform Goes' fellow-religious in Holland of this enterprise ordered him to put down everything in writing. Then having recovered all his belongings Isaac was set at liberty [1]. Whether the unnamed freebooter's narrative was ever made known in Holland I have been unable to ascertain, but the probabilities are against it. For when in 1643 Maarten Gerritszoon Vries started on his expedition, besides instructions for the exploration of Northern Japan, Van Diemen also gave him directions to search for the rich trading country of Cathay; and such was the anxiety for the success of the expedition that it had a native Tartar and four soldiers speaking both Polish and Russian among its members [2].

The evidence furnished by Goes' journey, though bound to produce its effect in time, did not obtain such immediate and widespread recognition as might have been wished, which led Yule to conclude his introductory remarks on the expedition with the words that "after the publication of this narrative inexcusable ignorance alone could continue to distinguish between Cathay and China" [3]. Yet, on the other hand, it can be no matter of surprise that Cathay did continue to live in the imaginations and aspirations of many, and that not once but repeatedly this name should occur in the writings of later missionaries as that of a country which was still being sought after. An error of centuries is not rooted up in a day — the less so at a time when reports of travellers remained unnoticed by many and communication was still so poor and defective.

---

1) Du Jarric, III, 225. *Via* Cochin Isaac safely arrived at Goa, whence on August 8, 1609, he set out for Cambay in the company of F. Emmanuel Pinario.

2) M. G. Vries, *Reise naar Japan* (ed. Leupe, Amsterdam 1858) p. 19.

3) Yule, I, XCLIIII Yule-Cordier, I, 182.

CHRONOLOGICAL SUMMARY

	1562.	Bento de Goes born at Villa Franca do Campo (São Miguel-Açores).
February	1584.	first entrance into the Society of Jesus at Goa.
April	1588.	second entrance into the Society of Jesus at Goa.
May 5,	1595.	arrival at Lahore with Jerome Xavier.
October 29,	1602.	departure from Agra for Cathay.
December 8,	1602.	arrival at Lahore.
February 24,	1603.	departure from Lahore to Kabul.
November (?)	1603.	arrival at Yarkand; (trip to Khotan).
February 2,	1604.	letter of Goes from Yarkand.
November 14,	1604.	departure from Yarkand.
December 25(?),	1604.	departure from Aksu.
September 4,	1605.	departure from Turfan.
October 17,	1605.	arrival at Chami.
Christmas (?)	1605.	arrival at Su-cheu. First letter to Ricci in Pekin.
Easter,	1606.	second letter to Ricci.
December 11,	1606.	Ricci sends Fernandes to Su-cheu.
March 31,	1607.	arrival of Fernandes at Su-cheu.
April 11,	1607.	death of Bento de Goes at Su-cheu.

CHAPTER II

ANTONIO DE ANDRADE

In the preface to their excellent work on the Himalaya mountains S. G. Burrard and H. H. Hayden rightly date the scientific exploration and study of this huge mountain range from the opening years of the nineteenth century [1]. It was in 1807 that, under the leadership of the British officers Webb and Raper, was undertaken the famous expedition to discover the sources of the Ganges. But however much one may appreciate the merits of these intrepid explorers and of those who followed them, one cannot but regret the omission in their accounts of any mention of the laborious journeys of their predecessors. Yet there were men among them who, though but pioneers, not scientific explorers, may lay claim to undeniable merits in the vast field of the history of discovery. Such a one is the Portuguese Jesuit Antonio de Andrade, who nearly 300 years ago was the first European to climb those stupendous mountain walls, to discover one of the principal sources of the sacred Ganges, and, starting from Hindostan, to penetrate into the unknown regions of Tibet. This neglect is the more to be regretted, since in the case of Andrade, if writers on the subject do make passing mention of his travels, their accounts are generally incorrect. An immediate illustration of this inaccuracy is afforded by the following quotation from Clements Markham's book on Bogle and Manning. After relating how Andrade set out for the Himalaya mountains he continues: "He climbed the terrific passes to the source of the Ganges and eventually after fearful sufferings reached the shores of the sacred lake of Mansarowar, the source of the Sutlej. Thence the undaunted missionary found his way over the lofty passes to Rudok and eventually by way of Tangut to China" [2]. These words, however com-

---

[1] Burrard, Preface, p. 1.

[2] Markham, lvi.

mendatory of Andrade's labours, are not consonant with the facts, for Andrade never saw the lake of Mansarowar, nor did he ever set foot in China. I shall indicate later a possible source of this error.

Unfortunately, these erroneous statements have been copied and repeated, they have been commented on at the cost of the character of the traveller, till misstatement has gone so far that Sir Thomas Holdich has felt justified in pronouncing the following verdict on Andrade. "The story of his travels as we possess it at present is unsatisfactory in many particulars. The letters written in 1626 to his Superior, the Jesuit General Mutio Vitelleschi, give but scanty and confused details of a journey which apparently terminated at Tsaparang on the river Sutlej. It is difficult to reconcile the account of his explorations beyond the Manasarawar lake to Rudok, and thence to Cathay and back, either with the topography of the Tibetan highlands or with the exigencies of time that would be required for such a journey. In spite of his hitherto prominent position in the field of Asiatic geography, Antonio de Andrade must be regarded as but a doubtful authority" [1]). Similarly Graham Sandberg, after stating that there exist two letters of Andrade of the years 1624 and 1626 respectively, continues: "The letters in question contain the most meagre details of the writer's travels, but a considerable display of information concerning the people and religion of the country he professed to have discovered. The scanty yet confused account of his journey, together with the absurd inapplicability of his exposition of their manners and beliefs to the Tibetans as we now know them, might excuse one for pronouncing the whole story of Andrade's visit to the country to be a fraud. How far the published effusions were the actual composition of their hero and how much was the invention of the home authorities cannot at all be determined. There is, however, beneath the bungling account printed and the manifest attempt to exaggerate the importance of the achievement, a certain substratum of correctness in two or three topographical points, which makes it extremely unlikely that the whole exploit was a fiction [2])."

---

[1]) Holdich, p. 70. The letter (not letters) referred to was written in 1624, published in 1626.

[2]) Sandberg, *Exploration*, p. 24. Sandberg's whole treatment of Andrade's travels is extremely slight; hardly a line but requires correction or qualification, since in his account almost all the errors of previous writers have been bundled together.

Though verdicts such as these can only be accounted for by the *bona fide* acceptance by their authors of statements made by others, yet they also betray neglect of the primary duty of verification by referring to the original narrative. Far different was the judgment of Carl Ritter, when in 1833 he drew attention to the work of the intrepid missionary. "Special value attaches to the artless and candid narrative from the fact that the book is rare, that the enterprise was remarkable, and that this geographical source has been left unused for two hundred years; it opened up a mountain region, which recently has had to be scientifically rediscovered." [1]) Denis is equally clear in his appreciation of Andrade's work [2]).

As matters stand, an inquiry is absolutely demanded. So this chapter is not only intended to give a general outline of Andrade's expedition, thus reviving the memory of the traveller, but to show the genuineness and reliability of his work. This will necessitate frequent reference to the findings of later travellers [3]).

As regards the narrative itself, it first appeared at Lisbon in 1626 under the title of *Novo Descobrimento do gram Cathayo, ou Reinos de Tibet, pello Padre Antonio de Andrade da Companhia de Jesu, Portuguez, no anno de 1626.* It is a verbatim reproduction of Andrade's manuscript, which is still in the possession of the Society of Jesus, and has been used by the author in writing these pages. Under the date of "Agra, November 8, 1624", he gives the Superior of the mission, Father Andreas Palmeiro, an account of his expedition. How eagerly information about this unknown

---

[1]) Ritter, II, 440. "Die Seltenheit des Berichtes, die Merkwürdigkeit des ganzen Unternehmens und die Nichtbeachtung dieser vor zwei Jahrhunderten schon eröffneten geographischen Quelle in einem Hochgebirge, dessen Passagen ganz kürzlich erst wissenschaftlich wieder entdeckt werden mussten, geben der naiven und treuherzigen Erzählung einen besonderen Werth."

[2]) Denis, I, 546. "On affirma que certain miracles s'étaient opérés sur sa tombe: le vrai miracle qu'il accomplit, ce fut celui dont il donna la preuve à l'Europe en traversant des deserts jusqu'alors inconnus."

[3]) Ritter's seems to have been the last critical study of Andrade's expedition, as Huc's cannot be considered to be such. *Le Christianisme* II, 277—301. A few brief references to Andrade are found scattered here and there: Richthofen, 1, 671; Manuel Pinheiro Chagas, *Historia de Portugal* (Lisboa 1890) IV, 161; Launy, 1, 23—30, at greater length but very slight; Puini, p. XXXII—XXXVII; etc. After the appearance of this chapter in its first form as an article in the Dutch monthly *Studiën* vol. 77 (1912) pp. 408—440, Sven Hedin published his appreciation of the Portuguese explorer in the third volume of his *Transhimalaja* p. 272 ff. and in his later work *Southern Tibet* I, 162 ff., and Heawood in *A History of Geographical Discovery* p. 131 & 411.

country was sought for is sufficiently apparent from the translations which within a few years after its first appearance were published in the principal countries of Europe; yet on the other hand it makes one wonder the more that for over two centuries these discoveries led to nothing. The title *Descobrimento do gram Cathayo* should be noted, as it shows that the belief in the existence of that country, of which Tibet was supposed to form part, was still alive. May not this same title have led some to suppose that Andrade had extended his explorations as far as China? [1])

Few biographical details of Antonio de Andrade have been preserved. He was born in 1580 at Oleiros, a small country town in the Portuguese province of Beira Baixa[2]), and entered the Society of Jesus December 15, 1596. Four years later he was sent to India, where he finished his studies. After being engaged in missionary work at Salsette and governing the colleges of Rachol and of St. Paul at Goa he had the government of all the mission stations in the territory of the Great Mogul entrusted to him. He had discharged this office for three years when he began his work of exploration.

Andrade briefly relates the occasion of his journey. It is the same which led to Goes' expedition. More than twenty years before the missionaries had heard of Christians supposed to be living in Tibet [3]), and reports to a similar effect had persistently come in,

---

[1]) An extensive bibliography is given by Sommervogel, I, 329—331, Appendix p. vi; also VIII, 1639; as the first translation he cites the Spanish one published at Madrid in 1627; it was made the basis of the others, viz. of the French translaticns of Ghent 1627, of Paris 1627, of Pont-à-Mousson 1628; of the Italian of Rome 1627, of Naples 1627, of Venice 1646; of the German of Augsburg 1627 in two editions. A Dutch translation undated appeared certainly before 1635. Besides these, mentioned by Sommervogel, I have been fortunate to discover a Spanish translation from the same hand that edited the original, published at Lisbon in 1626. This then is the oldest translation.

Extracts of varying length are given by various authors, for example by Franco, *Imagem*, pp. 376—418, almost literally, and by Cordara, p. 524—526, n. 171—179.

For the convenience of the reader all references relate to the first Lisbon edition of 1626, which as stated above is an accurate reproduction of the MS.

[2]) This is stated by the best authorities: Franco, p. 375; Machado, I, 202; J. M. Pereira d'Amaral e Pimentel, *Memorias da Villa de Oleiros e do seu Concelho* (Angra do Heroismo 1881) p. 161. Sommervogel, I, 329 is certainly wrong in speaking of Oleiros in Alemtejo, as is also Denis, 1, 546. From the above it will also be clear that Denis is wrong in saying that "l'ouvrage fut reproduit par le P. Antonio Franco, puis traduit en diverses langues."

[3]) Andrade, p. 2. Hay, p. 796. Even before Andrade's time similar reports had led Father Anthony Monserrate to the conclusion that there were Christians living beyond

though in fact they were only based on a superficial and outward similarity of some Buddhist ceremonies to those of the Catholic Church. What was more natural than a desire to ascertain the truth of these reports on the spot? Quite unexpectedly a favourable opportunity presented itself. On March 30, 1624, Andrade together with Brother Manuel Marques had left Agra to follow the Emperor on his journey to Kashmir. Arriving at Delhi he learned that a large party of Hindus were about to start on a pelgrimage to a famous temple in the Himalaya mountains at a distance of about two and a half months' journey from Agra. Here was an opportunity. These pilgrims might serve for protection and guidance in the first part of the journey meditated. No time was lost in taking the measures necessary for the government of the mission and making some preparation for the expedition; then, on the morning fixed for the departure, Andrade, his companion and two servants joined the caravan. A Hindu disguise, in which even the Delhi Christians failed to recognise him, was to see him through the first difficulties.

Travelling by the shortest route, probably through the valley of the Ganges by Hardwar, 'the Gate of Vishnu', the principal shrine of those northern parts, the caravan reached in fifteen days the borders of Hindustan, where at the foot of the mountains began the territory of the rajah of Srinagar, in what is now Kumaon, one of the divisions of the N. W. Provinces. Even at this early stage the expedition threatened to come to nothing. It had soon become evident to the pilgrims that the small band that had joined them, were neither believers nor traders They were in consequence arrested as spies, but in default of evidence they were fortunately set free early enough to allow them to continue their journey with the rest of the caravan.

---

the Himalaya mountains. I quote his words the more willingly as they contain the very first mention of Mansarowar lake. "At vero, in interiori Imao quo Agarenorum arma non penetrarunt, si Joguijs fides est tribuenda, qui multas regiones obeunt, sed multa commentitia et a se conficta narrant, verisque fabulas intermiscent: reliquiae Christianorum extant. Nam a Sacerdotibus nonnulli de Imai montis situ interrogati, dixerunt: montem esse arduum, et ascensu difficilem, in fastigio vero planum et ad habitandum accommodatum, atque in ora cujusdam stagni, quod ab incolis Mansarüor dicitur: gentem quandam pervetus quoddam oppidum incolere." Monserrate, p. 649. In his very latest work, *Southern Tibet* I, 154—156, Sven Hedin still maintains that Monserrate never mentioned Mansarowar lake; circumstances must have prevented him from becoming acquainted with the edition of the *Mongolicae Legationis Commentarius*.

Before them rose the Himalaya mountains, the 'Snowy Range', which must be crossed by those who from the tropical splendour of India venture into the chill solitudes of the high plateau of Tibet. As yet no European had set foot among these huge fastnesses that reach from the gateway of the Ganges to the gateway of the Brahmaputra. The ascent of the first mountains, so the narrative continues, was extremely difficult, ridge rose behind ridge and the paths were so narrow that they could only advance by inches, clinging to the wall of rock; while deep down below the sacred Ganges seethed and foamed, hurrying rapidly through its narrow gorge-like bed. To cheer and encourage each other the Hindus never ceased calling out the name of their pagoda with the never ending and monotonous refrain of "Ye, Badrinate, ye, ye." At every favourable point along the route stood small temples, jewels of architecture, where some jogis, the well-known fanatical Hindu self-torturers, guarded the divinity worshipped there [1]). The scenery was splendid. The lower uplands were covered with primeval forests, gigantic pine-trees "two or three times the height of the church-tower of Goa," numbers of cinnamon-trees, cypresses, lemon and chestnut trees, and flowers without number, while mountain streams leapt down all around them. At last they reached the town of Srinagar, the residence of the rajah [2]).

The name of the capital of Kashmir, Srinagar, is identical with that of the capital of Garhwal, which accounts for the fact that several writers make Andrade travel through Kashmir [3]). But not

---

[1]) In passing Andrade relates an event which shows how little the Mogul sovereigns shared the superstitious reverence of the Hindus for these self-torturers. One day when the Emperor was out hunting in Kashmir near one of the sacred lakes, he saw a jogi who had a very uncouth appearance. The hair of the naked man was more than four cubits and his nails more than a palm in length. A crowd of people thronged about the saint and worshipped his feet. The jogi took no notice whatever of the Emperor. On his return from the hunt the latter summoned the jogi who refused to go, unless they carried him or fetched him in the royal coach. Incensed at this answer the Emperor had the man dragged by the hair into his presence and gave orders that in punishment his hair and nails should be cut and himself made a show of along the roads.

[2]) Andrade, p. 4.

[3]) Thus Huc, *Christianisme*, II, 279; Max Müllbauer, *Geschichte der Katholischen Missionen in Ostindien* (Freiburg in Breisgau 1852) p. 283; Aug. Petermann, *Reisen und Aufnamen zweier Punditen in Tibet* 1865—1866 (Peterm. Mitteil. 1868, p. 234); Dr. G. Wegener, *Tibet und die Englische Expedition* (Halle a. S. 1904) p. 10, where he speaks with appreciation of Andrade, though he seems to know only one of his journeys; Sandberg, *Exploration*, p. 25; Launay, I, 23, and others. Owing to the same error Carrez (Map 42) marks Srinagar in Kashmir as a mission-station instead of Srinagar in Garhwal.

to mention Andrade's explicit statement that he did not follow the Great Mogul to Kashmir, it is abundantly clear from the narrative that the road described is the one that skirts the banks of the Alaknanda, the great source of the Ganges. Srinagar itself is situated on the left bank and at the time of Andrade's arrival was as yet a new town having been founded in the early years of the seventeenth century. It was destroyed by floods in 1894 [1]). J. Muir gives a graphic description of the yawning river-bed of the Alaknanda, which squares with the Portuguese account on every point. "The river, which is of a sea-green colour, flows at a great distance below the road, the grassy mountains, which are in some parts bare of trees, in others sprinkled with pines, sloping down steeply to its edge. The dell is narrow at the bottom and the stream is in one place so closely confined by cliffs on either hand that it looks like a canal hewn out of the mountain, the rocky banks rising square and sharp above it. In other parts the steep overhanging banks, as seen from above, are finely fringed with trees. In one place the road forms for a short way a staircase leading up the mountains, with a wall of rock rising up on the one hand, while a steep slope (which is as nearly as possible a precipice) of a thousand feet deep sinks down on the other [2])."

Very briefly Andrade brings out at this point the difference between the mountain people and the Hindus of the plains. At Srinagar the welcome was not of the kindest, and again he had to undergo a severe cross-examination as to whence he came and what was his object. Having no merchandise with him he could not possibly put himself forward as a trader, so he acknowledged frankly that he was going to Tibet for the purpose of exploration. Whether this answer was deemed satisfactory or whether the rajah had already made up his mind to stop all further advance when the stranger should have arrived at the furthest frontier of his territory, anyhow, after five or six days the traveller was released with loss of several articles which the officials had simply appropriated. A fifteen days' march along ever rising paths, and the caravan reached "the first snow-covered ridges, where it was very cold".

---

1) *Gazetteer of India*, XXIII, 105.

2) J. Muir, *Notes of a Trip to Kedarnath and Other Parts of the Snowy Range of the Himalaya in the Autumn of 1853*, (Edinburgh 1855) p. 21. The reader will find fresh support for Andrade's march along the Alaknanda in Moorcroft, *Journey*, p. 382, 384 ff.

They stood at the entrance to the world's citadel and its unscalable towers rose in every direction, one behind the other, burying their snowy summits among the clouds. Here the road winds upward to Joshimath, a settlement on the upper Alaknanda, where this river is formed by the confluence of the Vishnu-Ganga and the more easterly Dhauli. The village is 2,300 metres above sea-level. Along the banks of the wild-rushing Vishnu-Ganga, a veritable penance-road, the pilgrims ascended into ever higher regions. At a stroke Andrade paints this perilous journey through the upper mountains. "Not as hitherto by difficult rope-bridges, but over bridges formed by frozen masses of snow, which fill up the whole width of the river and underneath which the river-water breaks itself a foaming passage, we had to cross and recross the Ganges [Vishnu-Ganga], to reach at length after a journey of a month and a half the pagoda of Badrid [Badrinath] on the frontier of Scrinagar [1])." It was towards the end of May or at the beginning of June 1624, as may with some probability be conjectured from Andrade's writing a letter on May 16, 1624, "at five days' journey from Scrinagar on the way to Bardinara [Badrinath] [2])."

More than 180 years were to pass before another European would visit this sacred spot. We have already had occasion to refer to the famous expedition of Webb and Raper, who followed the route taken by Andrade. On comparing the narrative of their journey, written by Captain Raper, with that of the Portuguese missionary, whose name is not so much as mentioned, the reader might easily imagine he was reading the account of the latter. There is the same description of the rich flora, of dangerous mountain-paths, of rope-bridges and snow-bridges, details which recur regularly in the reports of later travellers. "The road is winding, with steep ascents and descents; and in some parts not a little dangerous; being formed on a ledge of rock, with here and there a small projecting point, not above five or six inches wide, to rest the foot upon; requiring the utmost care and caution in the passage....

---

[1]) Andrade, p. 8.

[2]) *Lettere annue d'Etiopiam, Malabar, Brasil, e Goa, dall'anno 1620 fin' al 1624.* Al Molto Rever. in Christo P. Mutio Vitelleschi, Preposito Generale della Compagnia di Giesù (Roma 1627) p. 342: *Lettera del P. Antonio Andrade, nel viaggio di Tibete alli 16 di Maggio del 1624* "Scrivo questa [lettera] cinque giornate de Serinangar per Bardinara." A French translation, containing a few inaccuracies, is to be found in *Histoire de ce qui s'est passé en Éthiopie, Malabar, Brasil et ès Indes Orientales.* Tirée des Lettres escrites ès années 1620 jusques à 1624 etc. (Paris 1628) p. 449–452.

We passed some very steep ascents and descents, on a rocky scarp, where the path was not broader than the palm of the hand. . . . The road was, in some parts, elevated to the height of three or four thousand feet above the bed of the river [1]).

Andrade speaks at length of the temple, which he says is visited by numerous pilgrims even from Ceylon and Bisnaga (Vijayanagar). "The temple itself is situated at the foot of a rock, from which several springs issue, one of which is so hot that it is impossible for the hand to bear the heat of the water even for a moment. This spring divides into three rivulets, which run into their several basins; in these basins the pilgrims bathe to cleanse their souls, the hot water being tempered with cold. The origin of this spring is explained by the Brahmins as follows. The Fire was very sorry for all the harm it had done on earth by burning houses, woods and fields, and came to this temple to find a cure for its affliction of spirit. It was answered that if it wished to obtain pardon it must stay. So the Fire stayed at the feet of the god and heated the water of the spring. But one fifteenth part refused to submit and still walks the earth and is the cause of all the damage."

In this temple "immense treasures have been offered in the course of centuries". Yet the pilgrims' time is very limited, since "except for three months of the year the temple is covered and as it were buried under the snow, which falls in such abundance that the villages in the neighbourhood are uninhabitable, so that during that time the people retire to a distance of three or four days [2])."

Together with Joshimath, Kedarnath and Panderkeshwar, all situated in the territory of Garhwal, Badrinath is still one of the most sacred and most frequented Hindu temples of India. It is situated 3,170 metres above sea-level against the slope of the Badrinath, which is 5,080 metres high and whose glaciers feed the Vishnu-Ganga. From November till May the inhabitants live at Joshimath [3]). Raper, who also visited the sanctuary, relates that according to the belief of the Hindus it is the work of some supernatural being. But the "structure and appearance are by no means answerable to the expectations that might be formed of a place of such reputed sanctity, and for the support of which large sums are

---

[1]) Raper, p. 509, 514, 515. See also Boeck (p. 351–361), who visited Badrinath in 1890.

[2]) Andrade, p. 8–10.

[3]) *Gazetteer of India*, VI, 179.

annually received, independent of the land-revenues appropriated for its maintenance". The bathing place itself is a large cistern called Tapta-Cúnd; it is "supplied by a spring of hot water, issuing from the mountains, by a subterranean passage, and conducted to the cistern, through a small spout, representing a dragon's or a griffin's head. Close to it is a cold spring, which is conveyed by another spout; by which means the water may be reduced to any degree of temperature between the two extremes. The water of the Tapta-Cúnd is as hot as a person can well bear; and from it issues a thick smoke, or steam, strongly tainted with a sulphurous smell.... The water from this Cúnd, independent of its supplying the cistern, is conducted through the huts and private houses, to which it imparts a suffocating warmth.... The temple of Bhadrí-Nát'h has more beneficed lands attached to it than any sacred Hindu establishment in this part of India. It is said to possess seven hundred villages, situated in different parts of Gerwál and Camáön.... The number of pilgrims who have visited Bhadrí-Nát'h this year [1808] is calculated at forty-five or fifty thousand; the greater part of these, Fakírs, who came from the most remote quarters of India. All these people assemble at Haridwár [1])."

Andrade also notes a racial difference. Though forming part of the kingdom of Srinagar, so the narrative says, the people differ from the rest of the inhabitants both in language and habits. They live principally on rice, herbs and mutton, which makes them stronger than the Hindus. As one of their peculiar traits, it is stated that they eat much snow. "Once I saw a child two or three years of age with a lump of snow in its hands. Fearing it would injure its health, I had the snow taken away and gave it some raisins; but it had no sooner tasted them than it threw them away and cried for the snow." The women cultivate the soil while the men are weavers [2]). Most probably we here have the first mention of the Bhotias, the border tribes on the outskirts of India, the description of whose characteristics by later explorers of Garhwal and Kumaun is in perfect agreement with the one here given by Andrade [3]). R. Strachey derives their name from Bod, the Tibetan

---

[1]) Raper, p. 531, 532, 536, 540. The present yearly revenue is stated by the Gazetteer of India at 7,000 rupees.

[2]) Andrade, p. 9–10.

[3]) W. Crooke, *Natives of Northern India* (London 1907) p. 12 en 49; Herbert Risley, *The People of India* (Calcutta 1908) p. 41 ff.; Sherring p. 56 ff. & p. 329.

name for Tibet, changed by the Indian people into Bhot [1]). They are described by Raper as being of more than middle height, strong and well-made, their features showing a likeness to the Tartars. Like most inhabitants of cold climates they drink much thinking that it is healthy to do so. The women cultivate the soil while the men, when the snows have melted, travel into Tibet to trade [2]).

Thus the narrative of the first British explorers confirms on every point the account given by the Portuguese missionary 180 years earlier. From the fact already adverted to, that Andrade's name is not mentioned we cannot but conclude that it was unknown to them, the English writer who passes over in silence the merit and work of others being happily rare. Yet this ignorance is much to be regretted even in the face of Horace Wilson's remark in his edition of Moorcroft's journeys, where in speaking of those ancient accounts in general and of Andrade's in particular he says: "Very little useful information was obtained from these journeys, as the accounts published of them are brief and are chiefly occupied with the personal sufferings of the travellers from the ruggedness of the route, the inclemency of the weather and the inhospitality of the people [3])." If Webb and Raper had carefully perused the old account they would have clearly perceived that on his arrival at Badrinath Andrade had actually crossed the high snow-covered ridges and therefore the Great Himalayan Range, and now stood on its *northern slope;* with greater care would the British surveyors have examined the neighbourhood, and neither Raper in his account, nor Webb in his map, would ever have placed the source of the Alaknanda on the *southern side* of the Himalaya [4]), a mistake repeated by Colebrooke in his article on the sources of the Ganges [5]). Even dusty journals will sometimes repay perusal.

---

1) R. Strachey, p. 84; Sherring p. 61.

2) Raper, p. 525 ff.; Boeck and Sherring have several typical photographs of this curious people.

3) Moorcroft. *Travels,* Preface p. xxxv.

4) Raper, p. 482, 516, 523; Webb's map precedes the article. Sir S. G. Burrard, (p. 137) in pointing out the mistake pleads extenuating circumstances: "They were so hemmed in by mountains that they entirely failed to understand that they had crossed the snowy range." W. Moorcroft, who visited lake Mansarowar in 1812 likewise failed to note that the Ganges takes its rise on the northern slope of the Himalayan Range and again stated "that it [the Ganges] does not receive the smallest streamlet from their extreme northern face, nor from a source to the northward of them." Moorcroft, *Journey*, p. 467.

5) H. F. Colebrooke, *On the Sources of the Ganges in the Himàdri or Emodus* — Asiatic Researches (London 1812) XI, 443—444.

After visiting Badrinath Andrade proceeded a little to the northward to the village of Mana, which is beyond the extreme limit of Raper and Webb's journey. This, too, is a summer settlement, not a large town as stated by the latter, situated on the Saraswati, the upper Vishnu-Ganga, 3,178 metres above sea-level. In summer it is inhabited principally by Bhotia traders, as it is the last halting place this side the Mana pass, also called Chirbitya-la or Dungri-la. Though this passage through the Zaskar Range is at an elevation of 5,604 metres, which is 800 metres above the Mont Blanc, it is quite practicable [1]). Being too much taken up with the continuance of his journey Andrade says nothing of the village. "Immediately beyond this place [Mana] there rise lofty mountains, behind which lies an awful desert, which is passable only during two months of the year. The journey requires twenty days. As there is an entire absence of trees and plants here, there are no human habitations, and the snowfall is almost uninterrupted; there being no fuel travellers live on roasted barley meal, which they mix with water and drink, taking with them nothing that requires fuel to cook. According to the natives, many people die on account of the noxious vapours that arise, for it is a fact that people in good health are suddenly taken ill and die within a quarter of an hour; but I think it is rather owing to the intense cold and the want of meat, which reduce the heat of the body." [2]) Ritter seeks for an explanation in the presence of carbonic acid springs, the usual effect of earthquakes and volcanic eruptions [3]), but we prefer to see in them the ordinary symptoms of mountain sickness, remembering what Hedin felt like when crossing the passes of the Transhimalaya at an altitude of 5,000 metres. When Fraser was on his expedition to Gangotri, the people also tried to frighten him by stories of travellers suffocated by poisonous vapours [4]). Drew,

---

[1]) Burrard, p. 92; *Gazetteer of India*, XVII, 108; Adolf Schlagintweit, who crossed by this pass September 6, 1855, calls it the Chirbitta Dhura-pass and states its height at 5, 614 metres (III, 86); a line is given to Andrade's climbing of the Mana pass (III, 55), then there is another brief reference to him saying that he was the first European who crossed the Himalaya and reached the province of Ü in Eastern Tibet but not Lhasa itself (III, 11) — an incorrect statement —, and with this all the exploration-work of this pioneer is dismissed. — Hedin on his large map of Tibet gives 5,450 metres as the height of the Mana pass.

[2]) Andrade, p. 11.

[3]) Ritter, II, 444.

[4]) J. B. Frazer, *Journal of a Tour through Part of the Snowy Range of the Himala Mountains and to the Sources of the Rivers Jumma and Ganges.* (London 1820) p. 434.

who passed several years in Kashmir and Ladakh remarks on this point as follows: "The natives whose lot occasionally leads them into the highlands, very commonly attribute these results of rarified air to some plant, which, for the purpose of their argument, they invest with the power of poisoning the air. Some of the herbs at high elevations give out a smell when rubbed, and these are brought in to account for the sickness. The much-abused onion which grows wild in some parts at a good height up, often has these things laid to it. Of course an easy answer to this hypothesis is that the effect is greatest at those heights whence all these plants and even all vegetation are absent" [1]).

For several days Andrade had been waiting for a caravan or any other opportunity to cross into Tibet when he was advised that the rajah of Srinagar had given orders to stop him from continuing his journey. It would seem that even thus early people were not anxious to throw open the sacred territory of the Dalai Lama to the mistrusted men of the West. The Portuguese, however, resolved to be beforehand with his antagonists, and having obtained sufficient information he ventured on the passage on his own account, though, as he states himself, it was not the season. Leaving his travelling-companion behind he started with two Christian servants, boys as he calls them, and one of the Mana men his guide. For two days he pushed ahead as fast as he could, but on the third morning he was overtaken by three natives, who had been sent after them by the governor of those parts. They first addressed themselves to the guide, whose wife and children they said had been thrown into prison and would certainly be put to death, unless he returned without delay. Andrade was also threatened. His companion who had stayed behind would be made answerable for his disobedience, his belongings would be confiscated, and besides, what could he gain, as he was sure to perish at this unfavourable season of the year? The guide at once retraced his steps, but Andrade refused to return, and no doubt somewhat rashly, being insufficiently equipped, proceeded on his journey accompanied by the two Christians. The road became terrible indeed. The snow was several feet deep, sometimes they sank into it up to their chests, sometimes even up to their shoulders. At some points the only way of getting on was to lie down at their full

---

1) Drew, p. 292.

length on the snow and shove themselves along struggling with hands and feet. They had hardly encamped for the night when they were overtaken by a snowstorm so violent and thick that they could not see one another though they were lying close together. The intense cold numbed their hands and feet and faces, so that Andrade hurting his finger against something lost part of it. "Having no sense of pain I should not have believed it, had not a copious flow of blood shown it to be a fact. Our feet were frozen and swollen, so much so that we did not feel it when later on they touched a piece of red-hot iron.... To this must be added a great aversion to food of any kind, and a violent thirst which could hardly be quenched by eating snow. There was water, indeed, but it flowed at a great depth under the snow, as did the river Ganges itself.... Thus the journey was continued to the summit of the mountain range, where the river Ganges takes its rise from a large pond, and from the same another river takes its rise, which waters the territories of Tibet [1])."

This last statement of Andrade's is the great controverted point of his narrative. At the beginning of this chapter we remarked on Markham's contention that Andrade reached the lake of Mansarowar [2]). This error has been added to by a work of high excellence the *Cyclopaedia of India*, which ascribes to Andrade the statement that this lake is the source of the Ganges and the Indus. "His journey was made in 1624 and is described by commentators and geographers, because of his mentioning this lake [Mansarowar] as the source of the Ganges and Indus, instead of the Sutlej. There is no doubt, however, that the voyage is genuine though we have no details of it [3])." It is hardly necessary to add that Markham's statement occurs regularly in those writers who copy from him [4]).

To substantiate his assertion the latter refers to the Portuguese edition of the journal (Lisbon 1626), in which, however, not a word is said about the sacred lake, as appears from the quotation given

---

[1]) Andrade, p. 14. The text both of the MS. and the printed edition is as follows: "Nesta forma fomos caminhando ate o alto de todas as serras onde nasce o Rio Ganga de hum grande tanque e do mesmo nasce tamben outro, que rega as terras do Tibet."

[2]) Markham, p. lvi.

[3]) E. Balfour, *Cyclopaedia of India* (Oxford 1885) I, 104, s.v. Andrade.

[4]) Sandberg *Exploration*, p. 25; Holdich, p. 70; M. von Brandt, *Aus dem Lande der lebenden Buddhas* (Hamburg 1909), p. 21; Rockhill, *Diary*, p. ix. The last-named writer makes Andrade extend his travels "along the northern base of the Kun-lun to the Koko-nor country or Tangut".

above. The mere fact that no name whatever, not even in some mutilated form, is given, should make one pause. For it is extremely difficult, not to say impossible, to admit that Andrade, whilst mentioning the name of the sacred shrine of Badrinath, should have passed over in complete silence the name of such a widely famous lake as the sacred Tso Mavang of the Tibetans. But there are weightier arguments against Markham's statement. In the first place Andrade does not speak of a lake (lago), but uses the word pool or pond (tanque), which quite suits the small glacier-basin in the Mana pass from which the Saraswati issues forth [1]). It next appears from the quotation above given that this pond was situated among the mountains, *not behind them* on the plateau, as is the case with the lake of Mansarowar. Furthermore, Markham's statement is absolutely irreconcilable with the time-notices and the sequel of Andrade's journal, as will appear further on; and it is precisely on account of this glaring contradiction that Andrade's reliability is called in question by Holdich, who in this copies directly from Markham [2]).

What is the explanation of this mistaken interpretation of Andrade's words? We know how for centuries a haze of mystery has hung about the sources of the Ganges. Before it issues from the Himalaya mountains, so Hindu mythology tells us, the sacred stream has already run a long course taking its rise from the lake of Mansarowar or from another called Bindusarovara [3]), by which is probably meant the Rakas-tal, which communicates with Mansarowar. It is this situation which is reproduced on all ancient maps, for example on d'Anville's of the year 1733. This map was based on the survey of two lamas, who, after being instructed by the well-known Pekin cartographer Father Régis S. J., had been sent to Tibet by order of the Emperor Kang-hi. The map was to include the sources of the Ganges, and the two explorers were even to bring home some of its water. Their task was completed in 1717 and they made the river issue from lake Mapama (Mansarowar) on the western side of mount Kentaisse (the Kailas mountains), whilst the river Tsanpou (Tsangpo) began east of it. But, as a revolt

---

[1]) Franco in his description of Andrade's journey uses the confusing word "lago". *Imagem da Virtude*, p. 386.

[2]) Holdich, p. 70.

[3]) H. T. Colebrooke, *On the Sources of the Ganges in the Himâdri or Emodus* — Asiatic Researches, XI, 438.

in Tibet had made it impossible for them personally to fix the situation of Kentaisse, Régis himself considered their information as of little value [1]). In 1784 a new and almost equally defective map of the sources of the Ganges was published. It had been constructed by Anquetil du Perron from the notes of Father Joseph Tieffentaller S. J., the author of the *Historisch-Geographische Beschreibung von Hindustan,* who, however, was careful to state that his personal investigations did not reach beyond Hardwar, and that he had supplied the rest from reliable Hindu information [2]). Rennell did not improve things, and the numerous theories advanced by him sufficiently show how defective was their author's knowledge of the region of the upper Ganges [3]). In discussing du Perron's map Eudes Bonin remarks that the connection between Mansarowar and Rakas-Tal, in which Ryder saw water in 1904, is called Ngangga or Ganga by the natives, and very pertinently asks if this name may not have led cartographers to consider that connection to be one of the sources of the Ganges [4]). But leaving this explanation for what it is worth and taking into account the mere fact of these persistent errors in later writers, may it not be that Andrade's description, which is brief and general, has as a matter of course been interpreted so as to fall into line with the current views?

There is yet another possibility. In 1667 Athanasius Kircher S. J. speaking of Andrade's journey in his *China Illustrata* falls into the common error, to which other incorrect statements are added. "Starting from Lahore and crossing the Ganges, he first discovered Srinagar and Ciapharanga, large and populous towns, and subsequently on the top of a high mountain a large lake, the common reservoir of the Indus, Ganges and other great rivers of India [5])." A few pages earlier he had already spoken of this common origin, at the same time referring to his map, on which,

---

[1]) Du Halde, IV, 577.

[2]) Anquetil du Perron, *Carte générale du cours du Gange et du Gagra, dressée sur les cartes particulières du P. Tieffentaller S.J., missionaire apostolique dans l'Inde.* (Paris 1784). The life and geographical work of Tieffentaller are the subject of a book by S. Notti S. J.: *Joseph Tieffentaller S. J., a forgotten Geographer of India* (Bombay 1906).

[3]) James Rennell, *Description Historique et Géographique de l'Indostan, traduit de l'anglais par J. B. Boucheseiche* (Paris an VIII, 1800) III, 101 ff. & 225; among the maps see especially n. 6.

[4]) Bonin, p. 278; see also his article *Une ancienne carte des sources du Gange* — Annales de Géographie (1911) XX, 349.

[5]) Kircher, *China Illustrata*, p. 64.

however, only the Ganges is shown issuing from the lake. This information, he tells us, he obtained from a Hindu Christian, Joseph, one of Andrade's two companions, who happened to be at Rome just then. The man, he adds, was 86 years old [1]). With the full text of Andrade before him it may be left to the reader to judge how much value is to be attached to this oral communication made forty years after the event. Most likely the fabled origin of the Ganges had played tricks on the memory of the Hindu. It is possible, as Sven Hedin believes [2]), that Kircher had some vague knowledge of Mansarowar lake from the information of the Hindu and of Father Roth S. J., the companion of Father Grueber, of whom we are to speak in a later chapter, and that he combined this with such details of Andrade's journey as were known to him. As against this, however, it should be stated that there is not a line or word in Kircher to betray personal acquaintance with Andrade's narrative. He would rather seem to have known only the title, and relying on the words *Novo Descobrimento do gram Cathayo*, he adds a fresh mistake, and makes Andrade travel *via* Rudok through the countries of the Tanguts and the Tartars into China. The scarcity of Andrade's journal and the wide circulation of Kircher's works may perhaps enable us to understand the constant repetition on the latter's authority of the error in question. Here again reference to the narrative would have proved useful.

To return to the discovery. Though the Ganges derives its waters from many quarters, we may point out that the Alaknanda is one of the chief sources. A river, Sir S. G. Burrard rightly remarks, which is fed by several glaciers, cannot be attributed to any one source, and it is probable that not a twentieth part of all the water of the Ganges is obtained from one and the same glacier. If, however, it rested with him to determine the principal source he would decide for the Alaknanda, the two principal branches of which are the Dauli and the Vishnu-Ganga [3]). On the authority of J. Herbert, who visited those regions in 1817, the Bhagirathi, which is formed by the meltings of the glacier of Gangotri, had for years been considered as the source, when in 1851 Richard Strachey protested against this view [4]). His brother, John Strachey, writes on this

[1]) Kircher, *China Illustrata*, p. 49.

[2]) Hedin, *Transhimalaja*, III, 274; *Southern Tibet*, I, 166.

[3]) Burrard, p. 139.

[4]) Strachey, p. 64.

point at greater length: "Almost every work on the Geography of India still tells us that the Ganges has its origin in the glacier, or, as it is oftener and inaccurately called, the snowbed of Gangotri, where it issues from the ice-cave, the 'Cow's mouth' of the sacred books of the Hindus. The truth is that, apart from mythology and religion and common belief, and judging as we judge less holy streams, Gangotri has no claim to be called the source of the Ganges.... The main stream is the Alaknanda, which has a much longer course and a much larger body of water than the Bhagirathi; its most distant sources are on the southern side of the watershed, near the Niti and Mána passes into Tibet, and it collects the drainage of the peaks and glaciers of the Kumáon and Garhwál Himálaya from Nanda Devi to the sacred shrines of Badrináth and Kedarnáth [1])."

Andrade, therefore, was on the Mana pass at the origin of the Vishnu-Ganga or rather of the Saraswati, as its upper reaches are called. It was, so he tells us, a large pond or pool with another outlet towards Tibet [2]). There is in fact a lake called Deb Tal drawn on John Walker's map of 1827 but no stream issues in the direction of Tibet [3]). Relying on Walker Ritter reproduced it in his map of the Himalaya mountains in 1832 [4]). The lake having disappeared from modern maps, I doubted if I could consider Walker a sufficient authority. He might have been misinformed and fuller knowledge might have led to the omission. I applied to Dr. Herm. Haack of Gotha for a solution of the difficulty. With obliging kindness, for which I wish to thank him once more, he undertook to examine Perthes' rich collection of maps, which led to the following result: "Lake Deb Tal is found on official maps up to 1865. After that the lake begins to disappear and the name alone is retained, but at present this too seems to be disappearing." This did not seem to settle the question, and to guard against the possibility of any doubt I ventured to apply to Colonel Sir S. G. Bur-

---

[1]) John Strachey, *India* (London 1888) p. 22. As an illustration of the slowness with which accepted views are modified, even in works of high excellence, we may refer to the latest edition of the *Imperial Gazetteer of India* (Oxford 1908) II, 132, where the Bhagirati still figures as the source of the Ganges.

[2]) Andrade, p. 14.

[3]) John Walker, *Newly Constructed and Extended Map of India from the Latest Surveys of the Best Authorities, inscribed to Major-General John Malcolm* (London 1827).

[4]) C. Ritter, *Entwurf zu einer Karte vom ganzen Gebirgssysteme des Himalaya nach den Quellenangaben. Nebst einer Specialkarte des hohen Himalaya in Gurwhal, Kemaoon, Almora; mit den Quellen des Ganges, Indus, Sutludsch* (Berlin 1832).

rard, Surveyor General of India, to whose work on the Himalaya mountains we have more than once had occasion to refer. He courteously furnished me with the following reply, for which I here again acknowledge my indebtedness: "The Saraswati rises at the Mana pass 20 miles north-west of the great peak of Kamet. A glacier descends from the Mana pass on the southern side and forms the ultimate source of the Vishnuganga. This glacier ends near the lake or pool of Deo Tal or Deb Tal; this pool is about 400 yards long and is canted by the lateral moraine of another glacier descending from the west. The height of Deo Tal is about 17,200 feet. A little lower down the stream than Deo Tal is another small lake, Rakas Tal. The names Deo Tal and Rakas Tal appear on the Indian maps 4 miles = 1 inch altho' the lakes are too small to be shown or drawn." This is decisive, it proves the accurracy of Walker's map, and settles the question. Only one point remains obscure namely, what Andrade meant when he spoke of the other outlet of Deo Tal towards Tibet. Such an outlet is on the face of it an impossibility, the lake being situated on the southern side of the saddle of the Mana pass. But do Andrade's words of necessity require this interpretation? Above we have translated from the Portuguese as follows: "Thus the journey was continued to the summit of the mountain range, where the river Ganges takes its rise from a large pond, and from the same [pond] another river takes its rise, which waters the territories of Tibet [1]). First of all the Portuguese text might be rendered somewhat differently, though less naturally, as follows: "Thus the journey was continued to the summit of the mountain range, where the river Ganges takes its rise from a large pond, and from the same [summit] another river takes its rise, which waters the territories of Tibet." If 'the same' is taken to refer to 'summit', all difficulty vanishes, for there is in fact on the northern side of the Mana pass a mountain stream, which joins the Sutlej near Totling. But this reading does not recommend itself to the writer; though grammatically correct, it is, to say the least, less obvious and somewhat forced and can hardly be taken to be the expression of Andrade's thought. Hence the following solution seems preferable, more especially if due account is taken of the circumstances and difficulties of this toilsome journey. One can easily imagine that Andrade

---

[1]) See the Portuguese text on p. 56, note 1.

after passing the sources of the Saraswati-Vishnuganga and then meeting the Totling-streamlet on the other side of the saddle, unguardedly connected this streamlet with the lake he had just passed, and thus ascribed a double outlet to the latter. Hedin seems to take this explanation as the obvious one. The other river "which waters the territories of Tibet," he remarks, is of course a brook which rises on the pass or in its immediate neighbourhood and goes to join the Sutlej near Totling [1]). But whichever explanation we take, or even if we suppose Andrade to have made a mistake, the importance of his expedition is in no way affected by it any more than it is diminished by the removal of his supposed discovery of lake Mansarowar from the list of his achievements.

After this long but necessary digression let us continue our journey under the guidance of the narrative. Having reached the highest point among the mountains, that is the highest point of the Mana pass, the vast plains of Tibet stretched themselves before them [2]). Behind them lay the heights, though further obstacles were still to be encountered.

"It was all one dazzling whiteness to our eyes, which had been weakened by snow-blindness, and we could make out no sign of the road we were to follow." The situation became serious especially on account of the increasing weakness of his two companions. During the night, therefore, he made up his mind that to get help the two should return to Mana, which could easily be accomplished in six days, whilst he would wait for them on the spot with some provisions. But the next morning they neither would nor dared start without him, so that Andrade, if he did not wish to lead them to certain death, was forced to go back with them. Their frozen feet made progress almost impossible and even now they might have perished, had they not been met after three days by a Bhotia sent after them by the people of Mana, who feared that the sovereign of Tibet would hold them responsible for any misadventure that should befall the stranger. After another three days' march they made some caves their temporary camp; here they were joined by Manuel Marques, who carried with him the necessary provisions, and together they waited till the snows had sufficiently melted." [3])

---

1) Hedin, *Transhimalaja*, III, 275.

2) Andrade, p. 15.

3) The account of this episode as given by Launay I, 26 is derived from a translation and incorrect.

When at length the time for starting had come, the travellers were still suffering from snow-blindness, which troubled even the natives, notwithstanding the eye-guards made of gauze. Andrade had been careful to advise the king of Tibet of his coming, whereupon the latter at once sent two guides and later on three horses to facilitate the journey. Thus in the beginning of August 1624 the first European entered the 'cidade real', the Tibetan town of Chaparangue [1]).

More than two centuries were to pass before any other European, with the exception of a few missionaries, was to reach what is now the town of Tsaparang in the valley of the Langtschen-Kamba or upper Sutlej [2]). During this period various opinions have been entertained with regard to its situation and importance. Kircher raised it to the rank of the first city of Tibet [3]), from which eminence, however, it had to step down when in the eighteenth century the sacred city of Lhasa became known. In 1812 Moorcroft entered the Sutlej valley, but brought no information about the town of Andrade [4]). It was only in 1818 that another Englishman, Fraser, learnt from two natives of those parts that Tsaparang was a place of importance and the residence of a rajah. It was said to be situated in a hilly plain at one month's distance from Gartok [5]). It is strange to find the missionary Father Huc stating as late as 1857 that the town is not found on any map and that he never heard its name mentioned during his stay in Tibet [6]). Yet it occurs on d'Anville's map of 1733 and on all later ones, whilst in 1855 Adolf Schlagintweit had visited the town. "Tsaparang", he says, "is only inhabited in summer and though it is situated on a fairly frequented trade-route, it has of late years considerably declined in prosperity [7])." He estimated the number of houses

---

[1]) Only Odorico de Pordenone reached Tibet before Andrade, but he arrived from China and did not enter the Sutlej basin. He only mentions the town of Gota (Lhasa?) in the kingdom of Riboth. Cf. H. Cordier, *Les voyages en Asie au XVIe siècle du Bienheureux Frère Odoric de Pordenone — Recueil de Voyages et de Documents pour servir à l'histoire de la Géographie depuis le XIIIe siècle jusqu'à la fin du XVIe*, tome V, Paris 1891, p. 49 ff.

[2]) There is considerable variety in the spelling of the name: Chaprang, Chabrang, Chaprung, Dschaprong, Tschaprung, Tsaprang, Tsaparang.

[3]) Kircher, *China Illustrata*, p. 49.

[4]) Moorcroft, *Journey*, p. 429 & 439.

[5]) J. B. Fraser, *Journal of a Tour through Part of the Snowy Range of the Himala Mountains and to the Sources of the Rivers Jumma and Ganges* (London 1820) p. 291.

[6]) Huc, *Christianisme*, II, 293.

[7]) Schlagintweit, III, 90.

actually inhabited at fifteen or sixteen, but the unoccupied Jong-pon-house, one of the highest-situated houses of western Tibet proved that at one time it must have been considerably greater. This also accords with the meaning of 'Chaprang', which according to Günther Schulemann is 'great residence' [1]). At present it is a poor hamlet at an altitude of 4,750 metres containing some sixteen inhabitants [2]).

The arrival of the stranger caused no slight commotion. At first the king, unable to believe that a man, not a trader, could undertake such a journey, was somewhat displeased, but after the first interview, in which the missionary explained the reason of his coming, both he and the queen showed themselves quite pleased. A religious conviction prompting such deeds of daring did not fail to impress him, and when a few weeks later Andrade insisted on being allowed to leave, as otherwise the pass would be closed, he could only obtain permission on condition of his returning the following year.

Andrade gives no description of Tsaparang only noting that it is situated on a river. The site of the town was very minutely explored by Captain G. M. Young in 1912 and with the help of his notes there is no difficulty in reconstructing the town as it was at the time of Andrade's visit. "Tsaparang", he writes, "stands on and around the base of a steep promontory which juts out like a buttress from the plateau into the river bed. The foot of the cliff is perhaps a mile from the stream. The ruins of the city are extensive and guarded on the other side by a chain of small round mud forts. Terraced fields, no longer cultivated, lie round about. Near the cliff stand the Dzongpon's house, a temple with a single lama in charge, and the dwellings of the four families which constitute the population of Tsaparang. The temples are in good preservation and are kept by the Dzongpon under lock and key [3])".

The nature of the surrounding country has been well described by Captain Rawling in his book *The Great Plateau*. It must have been at one time a vast lake silted up in the course of ages. The strata so formed have in their turn been cloven deep by the Sutlej itself and by its tributary streams. Standing in the river-bed one is

---

[1]) Günther Schulemann, *Ueber einige Geographische Namen Tibets und ihre Rechtschreibung* — Peterm. Mitteil. 1911, II, 9.

[2]) Hedin, *Transhimalaja*, III, 271.

[3]) Young, p. 195.

hemmed in by precipitous walls of crumbling mud and sandstone, wrought under the influence of sun and snow into fantastic pinnacles and ridges, above and beyond which a wide plain stretches on all sides to the skirts of the great mountains.

What Andrade tells us in the chapter given to the description of the country and the people entirely squares with our present knowledge. The district of Tsaparang with the town of the same name form part of the Tibetan province of Hundes or Nari Khorsam, which from Rakas Tal to Shipki is cut in two by the Sutlej. This river flows through a plateau 4,500 metres high, in which it has furrowed a bed or rather a gorge-like valley 900 metres deep, which, according to Colonel Sir S. G. Burrard, may be compared with the famous cañon of the Colorado River [1]). Agriculture is possible only in these lower parts watered by the river. The only tree is the poplar, while the high plateau is a treeless waste with some spare grass here and there, hardly sufficient for a nomad population [2]). From the supplies, such as corn, rice, fruit, grapes, which were sent me by the king's order, so Andrade tells us, I cannot but conclude that Tibet is a fertile country, but then the capital is a great exception, for it is the most barren spot I ever saw. Its only produce is a little corn in those parts that are watered by the river. The people keep large flocks of sheep, goats and horses on the plain, where for miles around neither trees nor plants are to be seen except in a few humid spots. It is only during three months of the year that no snow falls and grass can grow to afford pasture for the flocks. The food is mainly imported, even figs, peaches and wine, and all this has to come twelve days' journey — most probably therefore from the lower and warmer valley of the Sutlej. On account of the sterility of the country, Queiximir (Kashmir) merchants say that hell lies just underneath it.

Besides the trade with these Indian merchants, who are not allowed to settle in the town, the people had commercial intercourse with distant China, whence during Andrade's stay arrived a caravan of more than 200 traders carrying principally coarse silks and a great quantity of porcelain. This he was assured took place once a year [3]).

[1]) Burrard, p. 164.

[2]) *Explorations in Western Tibet by the Trans-Himalayan Parties of the Indian Trigonometrical Survey* — Proceedings of the Royal Geographical Society (1879) I, 445. Strachey, p. 78.

[3]) Andrade, p. 27—30.

Owing to the short duration of his visit and to his ignorance of the language his accounts of religious matters cannot but be very incomplete, though we can show his accuracy on several points. Thus he gives a description of a ceremony, which was repeated every month, and the object of which was to drive the evil spirits out of the town; this quite agrees with what we learn from the Rev. Mr. Donsen about "the destruction of the enemy", by whom the chief of evil spirits is meant [1]). Similarly, as we are told by the same Dutch Catholic missionary, who lived for five years in Little-Tibet, that every family has a lama among its next of kin, so Andrade assures us that, when a father has several sons at least one of them becomes a lama [2])". According to Dr. Karl Marx it was an ancient law in Ladakh "that every family of more than one or two children had to give up one, not the eldest however, to be made a lama [3])".

Meanwhile the time to leave had come and the indefatigable traveller left the town promising a speedy return. He was given a document in writing under the king's seal, which he transcribes in his narrative. It was couched in the following terms: "WE, the King of the Kingdoms of Potente, rejoicing at the arrival in our lands of Padre Antonio Franguim [the name of the Portuguese in India] to teach us a holy law, take him for our Chief Lama and give him full authority to teach the holy law to our people. We shall not allow that any one molest him in this, and we shall issue orders that he be given a site and all the help needed to build a house of prayer. Moreover, we shall give no credence to any malicious accusations of the Moors against the Padres, because we know that, as they have no law [religion], they oppose those who follow the truth. We earnestly desire the great Padre [the Provincial of Goa] to send us at once the said Padre Antonio that he may be of assistance to our peoples.

Given at Chaparangue" etc.

The King also gave him another letter, likewise under his seal but written in Persian, for the Kashmīrīs of Agra and Lahore, who traded with his country. He requested them to do whatever the

---

[1]) Donsen, p. 435 & 442.

[2]) Andrade does not call the Buddhist priests 'Lamas', but uses the word 'Jamba' which is no doubt connected with 'Chamba', the future incarnation of Buddha.

[3]) Marx, *Three Documents* (1891) p. 125, note 107.

Fathers should ask and to forward their goods as if they were the kings' own.

The journey was all that could be wished. The villages along the way supplied Andrade and his party with provisions: goats, rice and butter, and several men were sent along with them to see them off at the frontier. Three days beyond the capital they were overtaken by three men carrying six boxes full of figs, small but excellent, more than 2,000 of them, rareties come from the king's towns twelve or fifteen leagues from Tsaparang. It was a parting token of affection from the king and queen.

At Mana Andrade was detained by a war, which might have proved disastrous to his Tibetan friends. From this village he anxiously watched the course of events. Three rajahs, tributaries of the Tibetan king, had taken up arms against him and the opportunity was made use of by the rajah of Srinagar to invade Tibet at three points at once. One of his armies numbered 12,000 men with 11,000 muskets and twenty small pieces of artillery, the second 20,000, the third was smaller [1]).

But as a heavy snowstorm broke over the mountains, and the passes forming the lines of communication were held by the Tibetans, who offered a desperate resistance at every point, the whole enterprise failed, and peace was concluded before Andrade left Mana. At the beginning of November 1624 he was back at Agra and on the 8th he wrote the account of the first journey to the land of the living Buddha.

Though Andrade's labours are not yet over, and though we are again to meet him in the next chapter, it may be asked here, if he does not deserve more equitable treatment and a more generous appreciation than he has received at the hands of Sir Thomas Holdich and the Rev. Graham Sandberg. When, fifteen years ago, at a meeting of the Royal Geographical Society in London Dr. Sven Hedin read a paper on his Transhimalayan expedition, he had to sustain a sharp attack from the same Sir Thomas Holdich, to whom the results obtained appeared to be unsatisfactory. But the explorer very rightly reminded his critic of the enormous difficulties which had beset him on every side, how literally everything had yet to be done in that newly discovered territory, and how the information which he had been able to gather might even be

1) The printed editions have higher figures; those in the text are taken from the MS.

called remarkable. Some people were hard to please and it was always easy to ask for more. But, he concluded: "The very first traveller who, under exceptionally difficult conditions enters an unknown country and brings home with him the first knowledge of it, should be the very last to be blamed for his work" [1]).

What is here brought forward by the famous Swede in his own defence is equally applicable to the case of Antonio de Andrade. Being the first to traverse the Himalaya Range, the first to descend into Tibet, the first to bring us valuable information concerning both, he is worthy of better treatment than belittling at the hands of ill-informed critics.

---

[1]) Sven v. Hedin, *Reply to Holdich's "What we have learnt from Dr. Sven Hedin"*. – Geographical Journal, XXXIII (1909) p. 440.

CHAPTER III

THE TSAPARANG MISSION

Andrade made good his promise to return, and Ritter was mistaken when he concluded his able discussion of the first journey with the assertion that "it was long before another missionary followed Andrade through this new gateway into Tibet"[1]. For not only did Andrade himself return to Tsaparang the following year, but with him and after him several missionaries laboured in the basin of the upper Sutlej[2]. This ignorance, however, on the part of Ritter and most other authors should not surprise. The details preserved in the missionary records of the time are few and the records themselves difficult of access. Moreover, many letters from India and Tibet never saw the light, but lay, and in part are still lying, hidden away in the archives of Europe. One part of these documents, that is to say such as are in the possession of the Society of Jesus, have now been drawn upon for the writing of this and the subsequent chapters. They have been used chiefly in so far as they contribute to the history of exploration or topography, the object of the present work being to throw light on the merits of Jesuit missionaries for the enlargement of geographical knowledge. A complete history, therefore, of the Tsaparang mission is outside our scope, though glimpses of the inner life of the mission will occasionally have to be given for the sake of clearness or completeness. As regards the several missionaries who actually entered Tibet or were despatched to that country, of many it is extremely difficult to obtain anything like full information. Such biographical details, however, as are known from the publications of Franco, Hosten, Sommervogel and others, or have been gathered by the writer from unpublished documents, will be briefly related in the footnotes.

---

[1]) Ritter, II, 451.

[2]) A short chronological survey was given by Desideri, *Difesa* p. 2—6.

When Andrade sent the account of his first journey to Father Andreas Palmeiro at Goa, he accompanied it with a request for men for the mission that was to be established [1]). Three men were given him, but before their arrival at Agra Andrade, probably unwilling to risk missing the season, had started June 17, 1625, accompanied by Father Gonzales de Sousa [2]) and his companion in former perils, Brother Manuel Marques.

After a ten weeks' journey, again through Garhwal, where the rajah of Srinagar once more molested them, and, in spite of a firman from Jehangir, even robbed them of the greater part of their belongings, Tsaparang was reached a second time on August 28. At a distance of four days from the city two servants of the king had waited for them with three horses, provisions and presents. Their goods were exempted from all dues, a thing never done before, and a privilege nct to be disdained, since one tenth of the value was exacted [3]).

Andrade's knowledge of the country quickly grew. From a number of merchants coming from China with porcelain, tea and other merchandise, he learned that Tsaparang lay one and a half months' journey from 'Ussang' (Utsang), Ussang itself being within some twenty days' distance from China [4]). The following year he begins to write at greater length and on August 15 sends to the General, a memorandum of 40 pages small script divided into four chapters of very unequal length [5]). "The kingdom of Potente or Tibet comprises the kingdom of Gogue [Guge] where we are, those of Ladac, Mariul [an old name of the southern district of

---

[1]) Cordara, I, 526. The short account given on p. 526—529, n. 179—189, is incomplete and partly incorrect. Thus Cordara is mistaken in stating that the first missionaries went from Goa to Tibet together with Andrade, which statement entails an error of one or more years in all the dates relating to the arrival of the first missionaries, as appears from a comparison of Cordara's statements with Andrade's own notes and the letters of the missionaries. Franco (*Imagem* p. 400—415) gives a general outline of this second journey.

[2]) Little is known of Gonzales de Sousa. He was born at Mathozinhos (Portugal) in 1589 and entered the Society of Jesus in 1605. After six years he was sent to India and had worked in the Mogul empire since 1619, when he went to Tibet. We cannot say how long he stayed there, but it must have been a very short time; the catalogue of members of the Society of Jesus for 1627 mentions the Mogor mission as his place of residence. In the catalogue of 1633 his name does not occur, so he must have died before that date.

[3]) Andrade, *MS. Letter of September 10, 1625.*

[4]) Andrade, *MS. letter of September 10, 1625.*

[5]) See list of MSS.

Ladakh], Rudoc, Utsang and two others more to the east. Together with the great empire of the Sopô [Mongolia], which borders on China on the one side and on Moscovia on the other, they form great Tartary". A remark on Cathay shows that he was not aware of, or at least not fully alive to the decisive results of Bento de Goes' expedition. "The famous Cathayo is not a separate kingdom but a large town which is called Katay, the capital of a province situated much nearer to China and which is said to be ruled by the great king of the Sopôs" [1]).

In this new territory then, where no neglected Christians were found, though many religious ceremonies of the people bore some outward resemblance to those of the Catholic Church, they started the work they had come to do. The king kept his promise and himself urged in April 1626 the building of a church and of a house for the missionaries. An excellent site was secured in the town near the king's palace. Its position protected it from the cold and it had the sun upon it from early morning. The natives living on the spot had their dwellings pulled down but were given better houses elsewhere. To secure greater privacy the road passing near the place was turned in another direction. The king rased to the ground two of his own houses that the Fathers might have a garden with flowers for the church. On Easterday, April 12, 1626, was laid the foundation-stone of the first Christian church in Tibet [2]).

Probably one or two months after this ceremony, certainly before the completion of the church on August 15 of the same year, came the new arrivals from India. Andrade himself went to meet them at some days' distance from the town [3]). They were the Fathers Joao de Oliveira [4]), Alano

[1]) Andrade, *Letter of Aug. 15, 1726; Lettere annue del Tibet* p. 5.

[2]) Andrade, *Letter of Aug. 15, 1626; Lettere annue del Tibet*, p. 52. In his book *Die Geschichte der Dalailamas* (Heidelberg 1911, p. 129) Günther Schulemann relates that the foundations of a church were laid and that the king seemed inclined to receive baptism, but adds this puzzling statement: "Then from unknown motives Andrade gave up the undertaking, although he had already obtained assistance from India."

[3]) In the copies of the letters of Oliveira and dos Anjos (cf. List of MSS.) it is expressly stated that both had been in the mission for a year and a half when they wrote their letters in November 1627, so they may have arrived in May or June 1626, which must be considered very early in the season seeing the difficulties of the Mana pass.

[4]) John de Oliveira, who was born in 1595 at Daman, south of Surate, became a Jesuit at the age of seventeen. Sent to the Mogor mission in 1626 he went almost immediately to Tsaparang where he was engaged till October 1631, when he was called upon to share the hazards of F. de Azevedo's expedition to Leh in Ladakh, which will be spoken of in the next chapter. After his return to Agra in January 1632 he remained

dos Anjos [1]) and Francis Godinho [2]). These reinforcements, however, were not deemed sufficient by the enterprising Andrade. He had established another station at "Rodoa, a town belonging to a petty ruler, whose territory borders on Tibet" [3]), so he sent for more help from the Mogor mission. Father Antonio Pereira [4]), therefore, joined them at Tsaparang in 1627, as is stated by himself in a letter of November 12 of the same year. This Rodoa is no doubt the district and town of Rudok, situated at the northern base of the Transhimalaya mountains and the southern shore of the Nyak-tso, as appears from a letter of Andrade's, presently to be discussed, in which the town of Rudok is expressly mentioned. It is described by Littledale as "very picturesquely situated, its site covering a steep hill, which stands isolated on a plain. On the top is a large palace something similar to that at Leh, and several monasteries painted red. All the houses, which were in tiers, had once been whitewashed, but the colours had toned down, and, with the remains of an old wall round the town, the whole effect was extremely good [5])." It must remain a matter of conjecture what may have induced Andrade to go so far afield and to undertake mission work at 200 kilometres' distance

---

in the Mogor mission as appears from the list of missionaries for 1636 and 1641. After this his name is no longer mentioned but the date of his death remains unknown.

[1]) Alano dos Anjos' real name was Alain de la Beauchère. Born at Pont-à-Mousson in Lorrain in 1592 he entered the Society of Jesus in 1607, and in 1622 was sent to India where he adopted a Portuguese name. When he was directed to Tibet, he had just applied for the mission of China or Japan, as appears from a letter he wrote to the General, dated Goa, February 13, 1625. He was still there in 1633 though it is not known when he quitted that country. In 1636 he moved from Agra to Srinagar in Garhwal, where he died shortly afterwards. Southwell (*Bibliotheca Scriptorum Societatis Jesu* (Romae 1676) p. 16) speaks highly of him as a mathematician.

[2]) Francis Godinho was born at Evora (Portugal) in 1596, entered the novitiate in 1615 and sailed for India in 1619. Owing to ill-health he remained only one year in Tibet and after two years spent at Agra he definitively returned to the mission-district of Goa, where he was engaged at Daman, Diu, Goa and Bassein. He died at Goa, January 30, 1662. Sommervogel (III, 1521) confuses this missionary with a certain Francis Godin of Mons (Belgium) who never was in Tibet.

[3]) Cordara, I, 527, "Rodoa, quae est urbs reguli Thibetano accolae".

[4]) Anthony Pereira was born at Lixa (Portugal) in 1596 and joined the Society in 1612. He left for India in 1624 and was appointed to the Mogor mission in 1626. Probably in 1630 he went back from Tsaparang to Goa, for in 1631 he again set out from this place to Tibet, which, however, he did not reach, breaking off his journey at Agra. In June 1636 he was at Agra on his way to Srinagar where he stayed till October 1637. After that we lose sight of him and according to Hosten (*List.* p. 532) he probably left the Society a few years later.

[5]) Littledale, *A Journey across Tibet, from North to South, and West to Ladak.* — Geographical Journal, VII (1896) p. 477.

from Tsaparang. There are no details in any available document, and it is even impossible to state positively that Andrade went to Rudok in person. All we know is that the presence of the "Lamas of the West" was known in the neighbouring countries, for we learn from Andrade that the king of Ladakh wished to see him, and that in the same year 1627 the king of Utsang sent him a firman and a letter of invitation [1]). Whether these invitations were ever accepted there is no evidence to show. The only indication that may possibly point to a stay in Ladakh is to be found in a letter of Father de Azevedo, who, staying in 1631 at Gya with the ex-king of Mariul, calls the latter a great friend of Andrade's [2]). That the missionary should have visited Lhasa, however, is quite incorrect. Father Desideri, it is true, writes fom Leh August 5, 1715, that "it is said, but I am not sure, that ten or twelve years ago the king of the said third Tibet [Utsang] sent people to Mogor in search of Fathers of the Society of Jesus, because they say that a dress, a biretta and other things of Father Andrade are there" [3]), but this is no proof that he was ever there himself. At the early sack of the mission-buildings of Tsaparang some of Andrade's or some other missionary's garments may easily have been carried off by Tibetans and finally have found their way to Lhasa; but it is even more probable, supposing Desideri's story to be correct, that these objects had once belonged to Father Cacella, who died at Shigatse in 1630 [4]), or to the Fathers Grueber and d'Orville, who passed through Lhasa in 1661 [5]).

The only excursion Andrade speaks of is the one he made, in the company of the king, to a town at about half a day's journey from Tsaparang, where there were many temples and some 500 lamas; to celebrate the occasion as many as 2,000 had assembled from the neighbourhood [6]). No doubt the monastery-town of Totling is meant, where the dilapidated buildings still speak of the former glories of the once famous shrine in the upper valley of the Sutlej.

---

1) Andrade, *MS. Letter of September 2, 1627.* The relations with the rajah of Srinagar had also improved, for Andrade received a passport conferring exemption from taxes at the famous temple of Badrinath.

2) See Chapter IV.

3) Puini, p. 370.

4) See Chapter V.

5) See Chapter VI.

6) Andrade, *Letter of August, 16, 1626*, in *Lettere annue del Tibet*, p. 11.

Of late years it has been visited and described by Rawling [1]) and Hedin [2]).

Andrade has several things to note about the lamas, from which it appears that by the side of the more ancient 'Red-caps' the younger Gelugpa-sect of the 'Yellow-caps' was settled in Guge. The lamas, he tells us, are divided into ten or twelve kinds, differing from each other by their rites and ceremonies. They do not marry; some live in communities, others each in his own house. They wear one sleeveless garment leaving their arms bare, and over it another that comes down to their feet. Their wearing-apparel is generally red, whilst their head-gear is either red or yellow. At their religious celebrations they use trumpets generally made of metal but sometimes of the bones of human arms or legs [3]). To remind themselves of death they wear necklaces made of human bones and for the same reason they use skulls as drinking-vessels. The common people do not as a rule frequent the temples, which are nearly always closed; they go there only on two days of the year to attend the religious feasts [4]).

The missionaries must have been struck, not only during the celebrations just mentioned, but all during their sojourn in Tibet by the ubiquity of a peculiar formula of Tibetan prayer. In every spot and at every hour of the day it confronts the traveller. From city wall and temple roof, from stone heap and mountain pass the mysterious words stare forth. They are sounded in the Tibetan's ear throughout his life; he hears them as he rises in the morning, he murmurs them as he lies down at night. So intimately has this formula become woven into the life and so deeply has it impressed itself upon the land of Tibet that Hedin cannot picture to his mind its blue lakes and snow-clad mountains without this mystic legend, which Andrade was the first to publish to the world: 'Om mani padme hum'. He could not, however, interpret its meaning, because none of the lamas was able to furnish a reasonable explanation to all his questionings [5]). He also dwells on his debates on

---

[1]) Rawling, p. 285 ff.

[2]) Hedin, *Transhimalaja*, III, 264 ff.

[3]) Sherring (p. 84) mentions this custom as still existing, whilst it was noted as early as 1582 by Monserrate in his *Commentarius*, p. 594.

[4]) Andrade, *Letter of August 16, 1626; Lettere annue del Tibet*, p. 6—9.

[5]) Andrade, *Letter of August 16, 1626; Lettere annue del Tibet*, p. 36. Andrade transliterates "Om mani patmeon." When speaking of Desideri we shall return to his formula, the exact meaning of which is still a subject of controversy.

religious topics with the Buddhist priests, but as, by his own confession, he had not sufficiently mastered the language, his account must be accepted with reserve. As to the future, Andrade expected great things and his companions were equally sanguine. "It will be one of the most flourishing [missions] which the Society of Jesus possesses" [1]), wrote Anjos in November 1627. Though the number of Christians was still small, the prospects were fair. The king used all his power and influence to further the work of the missionaries, not without rousing the discontent of the lamas, whose religious chief was his own brother. Soon they were in a ferment, but no one expected that the explosion would come so soon, nor that it would be so formidable. Andrade's departure no doubt left their hands more free. Though the exact date is not known, it is certain that before 1630 he was recalled from Tibet to take upon him the honourable task of governing the whole mission-province of Goa [2]). Thus the Tsaparang mission in losing its energetic and enterprising head sustained a loss that could not be compensated for by the solicitude and care of a distant Superior. His antagonists seized the opportunity and within a short time after his departure, in the same year 1630, a revolution broke out which put an end to the reign of the friendly king.

The course of events is related by Cordara [3]), but it was described with greater fulness of detail by Andrade himself, when on February 4, 1633, he despatched from Goa an account of the missions of Mogor and Tibet to the General of the Society at Rome. It is from this document that the following particulars are taken.

For a long time there there had been a violent quarrel between Guge and Ladakh. Eighteen years before the king of Guge had had a son, the heir to the throne, born to him, but at his birth the queen had lost her reason, "so that she is still ailing". When after two years all efforts to cure her proved useless, the king resolved to contract a fresh marriage, although the Tibetan religion permits no bigamy. The new bride was a sister of the king of Ladakh and Mariul. The marriage-contract was made by proxy, but when

[1]) "Sera hua das mais florentes que tem hoje a Companhia."

[2]) From 1610 the Jesuit mission in India had consisted of the provinces of Goa and of Malabar, Cochin being the chief centre of the latter. Cf. Carrez, Map. 42 & 43. According to N. Sotuellus, *Bibliotheca Scriptorum Societatis Jesu* (Romae 1676) p. 64, Andrade went to Goa to obtain assistance, but was appointed Provincial on his arrival there. As a matter of fact the exact course of events is not known.

[3]) Cordara, I p. 527.

the new queen, on her way to her husband, was at two days' distance from Tsaparang, he suddenly forbade her to proceed and ordered her to go back to Ladakh. Andrade is quite ignorant as to what may have been the king's motive, but he is certain that this event was the main cause of the king's ruin. For Ladakh had immediately begun the war, which with occasional intervals had continued for eighteen years impoverishing the country by rendering impossible the working of fields or mines [1]).

Another cause was the great discontent among the numerous lamas at the conduct of the king. The latter had proceeded somewhat hastily in introducing the new religion and some of the measures adopted against the lamas were decidedly imprudent. We may note a few of them from Andrade's letters. Thus in 1626 he had taken away from his brother, the Chief-Lama, all his revenues, because he had received into the fraternity of lamas one hundred and thirty new candidates. His excuse was that, if his brother continued thus, he would deprive him of all his soldiers and become a dangerous rival [2]). The year after Andrade wrote that the king had become positively hostile to the lamas, in particular to his brother. All these influences, Andrade writes in his letter of February 4, 1633, came to a head at a time when the king was seriously ill. Shortly after the departure of the missionary some powerful military commanders (probably lamas, who were not by their profession excluded from such posts) rose in open revolt, called in the aid of the king of Ladakh and offered him the crown. With their help the latter laid siege to Tsaparang. The town occupied an almost impregnable position. It was built along the slopes of a hill the lower part being defended by strong walls and fortifications. From the higher middle ground there rose another eminence flattening to a sort of plateau at the top, and crowned with a second line of fortifications. This stronghold was inaccessible on all sides and could only be reached by a stairway cut out in the interior of the mountain. There was another stairway, also cut out of the rock and more than 400 metres [3]) long, leading down to two springs situated under the plateau. The castle was well victualled, and there were 1,000 fire-arms with plenty of gun-powder and ball[4]).

---

[1]) O cavar nas minas. — What mines they were is not specified.

[2]) Andrade, *Letter of August, 16, 1626; Lettere annue del Tibet*, p. 24.

[3]) Ducentas braças; 1 braça = 2,02 metres.

[4]) For a description of the present state of the palace cf. Young, p. 195.

Loyal adherents urged the king to seek shelter behind these impregnable walls, but the Chief-Lama advised submission: he should surrender on condition that the king of Ladakh after taking tribute should raise the siege. When this had lasted a month the treacherous counsel was acted upon with the result that the king and his family were kidnapped and carried off to Leh. The whole country was conquered and the Christians, numbering about 400, were singled out for retribution; many were reduced to slavery and had to share the king's exile. Part of the Tsaparang garrison had, at the last moment, retreated within the castle offering such a stubborn resistance that in the end they were allowed withdraw with military honours to Utsang. Here the viceroy of Rudok had also taken refuge leaving the town to the conquerors, who destroyed the mission and conducted the two missionaries prisoners to Leh. Soon, however, they were restored to liberty and sent back to Tsaparang. Thus far Andrade's account of the course of events.

As regards the men engaged in the Tibet mission at the time of the catastrophe, from an unpublished letter of Father de Castro, written from Bengal November 20, 1631, to Father Septalio at Milan, we learn that there were five missionaries in Tibet. No names are given, but Andrade, de Souza, Pereira and Godinho having left, they could only be dos Anjos, de Oliveira, de Azevedo, da Fonseca [1]) and Marques. Their house and church at Tsaparang were sacked but there was no loss of life.

The anonymous author of the '*Mémoire sur le Thibet et sur le royaume des Eleuthes*' in the *Lettres édifiantes* speaks of a war carried on by a Christian king of Western Tibet against the Dalai Lama. "During the reign of the Dalay-Lama Hotolon-pou-Hang, Tsang-pa-han ruled over a great part of Thibet, west of Lassa, as far as the sources of the Ganges and in the country of Sirinagar on the Ganges. Father Dandrada, a Jesuit, who was in 1624 at the court of Tsang-pa-han, assures us that this prince was a great protector of the Christian religion, and the Tartar history of that time is clear enough on the point, since it tells us that Tsang-pa-han abandoned the faith of Fo or the Lamas, that he wished to destroy it, that he ill-treated his people, that for this reason the Typa and the Dalay-Lama called to their help Kouche-han, Prince of the Eleuths of Coconor; that Couche-han came to Thibet with a con-

[1]) He had arrived in 1629; a native of Mourão, where he was born in 1600, he had entered the Society at the age of twenty.

siderable army, that a bloody battle was fought, and that Tsang-pa-han was defeated and killed in the combat" [1]).

There are in this extract facts in evident agreement with those narrated above, but it is equally clear that there is a strong admixture of error and that the author is confusing different events. This Hotolon-pou-Hang, who can be no other than the famous Dalai Lama Ngavang Lobsang, did not intervene in the affairs of Western Tibet about the year 1630. This ambitious intriguer did, indeed, wage war against one of the Tibetan kings, in which he was supported by Goutchi-Khan, the chief of the Mongolian tribes about the Koko Nor, but this was not till 1640 or later, so that there is no connection with the events at Tsapårang [2]). Nor was Ladakh at war with Central Tibet in 1630. For from the ancient chronicles, made accessible by Dr. K. Marx, it only appears that Sengge-nam-gyal, king of Ladakh in 1630, carried on a war with the central provinces of Guge or Tsaparang [3]). It was only during the reign of his second successor, Lha-ch'endelegs-nam-gyal, that there was trouble between Ladakh and Lhasa occasioned by a quarrel between the latter country and Bhutan, as also appears from Marx's data [4]).

Moreover, it may be safely asserted that, however great may have been the favour shown by the king of Tsaparang to the new preachers, he certainly never went so far as to embrace Christianity. Though Young writes that "in the course of time the king and most of his family were baptized" [5]), he adduces no proof; in fact it would be impossible to bring forward any evidence at least as far as the king is concerned. This is a safe inference from the silence on this point of all the letters both of Andrade and of those who came after him; having so much to say of him how could they or would they have passed over a point of such first rate importance? Azevedo only writes that the king was inclined to become a Christian and had even promised to receive baptism, but he adds that on account of illicit cohabitation the baptism had to be put off [5]).

It is to be regretted that Andrade does not mention the king's

---

[1]) *Lettres édifiantes*, XIII, 229.

[2]) Milloué, p. 143. Das, p. 228.

[3]) Marx, *Three Documents* (*1891*) p. 130.

[4]) Marx, *Three Documents* (*1895*) p. 96. Cf. Mir I'zzet-ullah, *Voyage dans l'Asie Centrale en 1812* — Magazin Asiatique éditée par Klaproth, II (1826) p. 11.

[5]) Young, p. 185.

[6]) Azevedo, MS. fol. 32 *Appendix I*.

name; Chodapô or Chodaipô, by which he is designated by Andrade's successors would seem to be a dynastic name. "About a thousand years ago," Azevedo writes in his diary, of which we are to speak in the next chapter, "Tibet was ruled by a king who was called Chodapô, 'the giver of the book', for having brought the book of the law from China on the other side of Uçangue." Captain Young relates that on inquiring from the lamas of Totling the name of the last king of Tsaparang he was at once answered, 'Chodakpo' [1]). Their vague memory of this king did not go far beyond this and they even seemed to confuse his reign with that of Yeshe Hod and his son in the eleventh century. Little value, therefore, attaches to their reply.

According to the Rev. A. H. Francke of the Moravian mission, famed for his historical researches on Western Tibet, Chodagpo (Jo-drag-po) would mean 'strong, severe lord'. He thinks he has found the real name of the king in two old inscriptions, one of which he discovered in 1909, at the desert camping-place of Horling on the frontier of Guge and Spiti, the other at Tabo in Spiti. The former relates that there once ruled at Tsaparang a king Khri-bkra-shis-grangs-pa-lde, and by his calculations Francke is led to place his reign between 1600 and 1630 A. D. and to infer that he is probably the very king whom Andrade visited in 1624. The second votive tablet would appear to the discoverer to confirm his result, since it not only mentions the name of the king but also bears the following legend: "He who clears away all the apostasy and darkness at the great palace of Tsabarang-rtse" [2]). But wat Francke thus takes to strengthen his conclusion, does it not in fact weaken it, and do not the words of the inscription clash with the events above recorded? The point is not further discussed in Francke's *Antiquities of Indian Tibet*, but I am enabled to quote from a letter of December 11, 1913, in which an accord is attempted. To explain the second inscription it is assumed that the king of whom we are speaking either played a double game, on the one hand helping the missionaries, and on the other courting the Buddhist party; or that after favouring Christianity he was frightened by the approaching revolution into a belated zeal for Buddhism, and to save his crown took measures of repression against the mission. Neither of these hypotheses, however, seems to fit in with the

---

[1]) Young, p. 187.

[2]) Francke, p. 36.

known facts. As to the latter supposition, besides the inherent improbability of such a radical change from protector to persecutor within the short space of one or at most two years, we should have the inexplicable silence of the letters of the missionaries. Azevedo, who instituted an inquiry into the events on the spot immediately after their occurrence, writes in the journal from which we quoted above: "The king, who was our great friend, is no longer king, but has been taken prisoner by a crafty pagan". The hypothesis also of his double dealing seems inadmissible if we remember the king's measures, especially those he took against his brother, the Chief Lama. In our opinion both the king and the missionaries in their efforts to introduce Christianity had been wanting in tact and prudence, and the revolution took them by surprise.

As to the two inscriptions of Horling and Tabo, for our present purpose at least we must leave them an open question. By the name Khri-bkra-shis-grags-pa-lde cannot be meant the usurping king, a younger brother of the king of Leh, for his name was Indra Bodhirnam-rgyal [1]). It is equally impossible to determine the name of the conquered king from the Leh chronicles, as he is only referred to as Los-long, 'the really blind'. As things are the writer cannot help confessing to some misgivings on the subject of the date 1600 to 1630; and if this date is not demonstrably certain, may we not have to look back to an earlier religious war or to the reform of Tsong-kapa for an explanation of the two inscriptions?

On February 14, 1631, still unaware of the fatal turn of events Andrade despatched the above-mentioned Father Pereira with two companions, FF. Dominic Capece [2]) and Francis Morando [3]) to the distant mission. When the first tidings reached him he at once

---

[1]) Francke, p. 36.

[2]) Dominic Capece was born at Rome in 1598 and became a Jesuit in 1619. He was sent to India in 1629 and stayed behind at Agra when on his way to Tibet in 1631. Two years later he was permanently established in the Mogor mission, where he died March 26, 1634.

[3]) Francis Morando, who was born at Parma (at Bologna according to others) in 1597 and entered the Society in 1618, went to India in 1629. Staying behind at Agra he was engaged in the Indian mission for over twenty-two years, at least till 1653, as the catalogues inform us. For sixteen years he was attached to the court of the Governor of Bengal, and in 1649 he was at Agra to have the Persian works of Father Jerome Xavier copied. (Cf. Maracci, p. 23 and 65.) He died July 7, 1655 in the new College of St. Paul in Goa. The catalogue of 1647 marks his knowledge of Hindustani and Persian: "Sabe perfeitamente as linguas Industana e Parçia." Cf. also Hosten, *The Marsden MSS. in the British Museum* — Journ. As. Soc. of Bengal. New Series VI (1910) p. 459, note 2.

appointed Father Francis de Azevedo Visitor to the mission with orders to proceed thither and report on the situation [1]). Azevedo overtook the three at Agra and ordered them to stay and await instructions, whilst he himself proceeded to Tsaparang where he arrived in the company of Marques, whom he had met in Garhwal. Azevedo has left us a very detailed account of his journey and further experiences, and this journal is in many respects so remarkable as to demand for special treatment in the next chapter. We only note here that, seeing the sad state of affairs, he resolved to go to Leh, accompanied by Oliveira, to have a personal interview with the conqueror, and, if possible, to secure his goodwill. Their suit was successful, and the king granted permission to pursue mission-work at Tsaparang, Rudok and even at Leh. Returning to India the two travellers were back at Agra January 3, 1632.

On the further state of affairs in Tibet up to the year 1635 our information is of the scantiest. What little we have is mainly obtained from the letters of Father Joseph de Castro [2]). On August 8, 1632, he writes "from Mogol" to Father Joseph Baudio that he has staying with him Father Francis Morando pending his departure for Tibet. The Superior of this mission, so we learn from letters, has gone to another station begun by the Fathers of the Cochin Province in the town of Ucangue, whose king is well disposed towards the missionaries. Thus he hopes to obtain help for his own mission because all the kings of Tibet obey the great king of Ucangue [3]). On August 28, 1632, he writes once more from Bengal, and notes that there are five Fathers actually in Tibet, and two others

---

[1]) This is stated in Andrade's letter of February 4, 1633.

[2]) Joseph de Castro was born at Turin in 1577 and entered the Society 1596. In 1610 we find him at Agra, where he seems to have lived till 1620. During the next years up to 1624 he is stationed at Sambhar. In 1626 he writes a letter "di questo Regno di Cabul", in 1627 "di Regno di Caximir", in 1631 he is chaplain to Mirza Zul Qarnin, a Catholic governor in Bengal, "at a spot 250 miles from Agra and 300 miles from Hugli." After November 24, 1632, his letters are again despatched from Agra. After working for nearly thirty-seven years in the Mogor mission he died at Lahore December 15, 1646. Later his body was conveyed to Agra and interred in the Martyrs' Chapel.

[3]) *Letter of F. de Castro Aug. 8. 1632.* ".... habiamo riceputo lettere di nostri P. P. como il P. Sup.re del Tibete era passato ad un altra residencia cominciata da nostri Padri della Provincia Australe, nella citta di Ucangue dove resida il Re mag.re di tutti qtti che confina con la China et qto Re di Ucangue favorisse assay li Nostri Padri, dadogli il necessario; con la andatta di detto Pe Sup.re si spera prospero successo con il favore divino e totale rimedio p. li Padri del Tibete, perche li reguli del Tibete obedissono a qllo grande Re di Ucangue". — We shall have occasion to return to this subject in Chapter V.

at Agra who are intended for that country. On February 6, 1633, he is a little more communicative. "Three days ago we received letters from the mission in Tibet. The five Fathers who are there, tell us that they are like prisoners in their house, because the Commander does not allow them to come back here, or to leave the place where they are, or to carry anything out of the house without his seeing it." When on October 8, 1633, he writes to the Rector of the college of Turin, things are still in the same state. Tsaparang is the only mission-station left, all the others have been swept away by the war.

Andrade meanwhile had been thoroughly informed of the state of affairs and was going back to Tsaparang in person. He would have done so earlier [1]) but his duties forbade. No sooner, however, had he been relieved of the superiorship of the mission, than he made up his mind and at once set about preparing for the doubtful journey. Six others were to go with him. While in the midst of these preparations, he suddenly died March 19, 1634, with symptoms of poisoning [2]); thus he was not to see the destruction of his foundation. Thirty-four years of his life he had spent in the vast field of the India mission.

The projected journey was now delayed for a year and in the beginning of 1635 the six missionaries set out from Goa under the leadership of Father Nuño Coresma [3]).

As noted in the list of unpublished documents copies of three of Coresma's letters to the Provincial of Goa have been preserved, so we are fairly fully acquainted with what befell the missionaries. The undertaking, then, was an utter failure, a series of reverses and disasters, which might have dashed the spirits of the most ardent. The empire of the Great Mogul was just being devastated

---

[1]) *Letter of F. de Castro, Aug. 28, 1632.*

[2]) This is stated in a letter of Father Antonio Mendez. Machado (I, 202) makes the Mohammedans. responsible, while Franco (Imagem, p. 416) explicitly states that the criminal was a Portuguese. The date of Andrade's death is wrongly given as August 20, 1633, by Denis (I, 545), and as March 6 by Launay (I, 30).

[3]) Nuño Coresma was born in 1600, probably at San Roman, a village in the district of Tordesillas in Spain. At the age of sixteen he entered the Society of Jesus, and went to India in 1625, as is stated by Franco, who calls him Nonius Quaresma. After his return from Tsaparang he was at the head of the college of Tanna, or Thana, on the island of Salsette. After 1641 his name is no longer found in the catalogues. In the list for 1653, however, it is noted, that F. Nonius Coresma on his way to India, perished in October 1650 off the coast of Mozambique near the river Licungo. Very likely he had been sent back to Europe after 1641 and was returning to his mission when he met his death.

he writes in his first letter, by a terrible famine which made itself felt as far as Garhwal and Tibet, so that the journey from Surat to Tsaparang cost no less than 3,000 rupees. But this was as nothing compared to the loss of life and of health. "Of my six companions only one reached Chaparangue with me. Two died on the way, and the other three became so ill, that it would have been inhuman to have taken them further and let them die in this desolate country" [1]). The three, therefore, were left behind at Srinagar (Garhwal), whence they probably returned to Agra. They were Father de Freytas [2]), Father Caldeira [3]) and Brother Barreiros [4]). The names of the two who died on the way have remained unknown; even in 1728 Desideri found it impossible to ascertain them. With Father Correa [5]) as his only companion Coresma went on. The crossing of the Mana pass was very trying. "The snow came up to our knees, in many places up to our waist, and a cold numbing wind was blowing." Eventually, however, they reached Tsaparang. Both the country and the people fell far short of his expectations, and in his letters he does not pretend to disguise his disappointment. "The population is very small, as appears from the fact that from the whole of the territory, which, through lack of knowledge and experience, has been called Cathayo or Tibet, it is impossible to assemble 2,000 warriors, though all are obliged to serve from their eighteenth to their eightieth year. The others are lamas.... In this town, the residence of the King, the mercantile emporium for the whole country, it is impossible to count up more than 500 inhabitants, of whom a hundred are slaves of the rajah....

[1]) Coresma, *First Letter of August 30, 1635*. In his second letter, of the same date as the first, he writes: "Alone I arrived in this mission.... without any companion of all those I took with me." (Entrey nesta Missão.... so sem companheiro algum de quantos trouxe). But this must be a slip, as appears from the very circumstantial account of the first letter.

[2]) Pietro de Freytas was born at Mondim in Portugal in 1608 and entered the Society of Jesus in India in 1630. He died whilst professor of theology at Goa May 3, 1640.

[3]) Balthasar Caldeira, born at Macao in 1609, became a Jesuit at Goa in 1627. After a three years' stay in the Mogor mission, he was active in different places, among others in Tonkin, China and Japan; he returned to India, where he filled several offices, and died at Goa May 3, 1678.

[4]) Brother Barreiros was born in 1605 at Lisbon, where he became a lay-brother of the Society of Jesus at the age of twenty. We find him at Goa in 1633; the years after his return from Garhwal he spent chiefly at Bassein, where he died March 8, 1666.

[5]) Ambrosio Correa was a native of Aveiro in the north of Portugal; born in 1606 he entered the Jesuit noviciate at Lisbon in 1622. Franco places his departure for India in 1630. After his return from Tibet he governed the college of Tanna and was at Goa at least till 1650. He died at Angola May 24, 1652.

The people are very poor and uncivilized and rude.... they live on a little roasted barley, pounded into meal, take some raw meat only occasionally, and drink one or two bowls of tea a day" [1]). The governor also who had been appointed by the king of Ladakh was anything but sympathetic and it was only the hope of presents that withheld him from turning the strangers out of the country at once. They were continually annoyed and vexed by the populace, who repeatedly bombarded their house with stones at night-time, whilst the complaints lodged with the authorities were completely disregarded. The influence of Portugal could not make itself felt here and they were left to fight their own battle; but victory seemed to Coresma to be impossible. The enormous expense was another difficulty, for the country itself had practically no resources to support the mission. "The country is mostly dry and barren, very mountainous and thinly populated. Trees are entirely wanting, not only fruit-trees but even trees for firewood. There are no herbs to serve as food, only a little barley and corn, which through want of tilled fields is very stunted. When there is no rain, the brooks are few, and the number of springs is very limited. The people have only some flocks of goats and sheep, with which they move from place to place." It was practically impossible to obtain supplies from Hindustan or Srinagar, for "the carriage of a quantity of rice bought for one rupee at Srinagar is ten or twelve rupees, as everything has to be carried along the passes [2]). The description of the sterility of the soil entirely squares with Andrade's, and is, like the latter's, fully confirmed by later travellers.

As to the Christian community, it had greatly shrunk in numbers and had been scattered in different directions, so that in Coresma's view the sacrifices that had already been made and would yet have to be made, were out of all proportion to the scanty harvest that might be expected. So the conclusion which he submits to his Superior for approval and execution is, that the mission be relinquished [3]). Correa, therefore, again crossed the Himalaya into India to carry this report to Goa.

---

[1]) Coresma, *First Letter of August 30, 1635.* In his second letter he returns to the names Cathay or Tibet, which in his opinion are entirely wrong. "In all my inquiries I have never heard that name from foreign merchants or from natives." Which should not surprise us, as the country is called Bod-yul by the native population.

[2]) Coresma, *First letter of August, 30, 1635.*

[3]) Coresma's condemnation of the Utsang mission will be of a like uncompromising nature as we shall see in Ch. V.

Coresma's explicit statement, that he stayed behind at Tsaparang with Marques as his only companion, at once raises the question as to the whereabouts of the other five missionaries, who, Castro informs us, were still there in 1633. Had new difficulties arisen? Or had the king of Ladakh gone back on the permission he had granted to Azevedo? When and how had they quitted the country? These questions must be left unanswered; we have nothing beyond Coresma's statement that he and Marques alone remained behind.

Another remark concerns Coresma's haste in judging of the state of the mission and concluding to the impossibility of working it. Having left Goa at the beginning of 1635 his arrival in the Sutlej basin cannot be placed earlier than June or July, whilst his letter is dated August 30. He had thus at most two months to acquaint himself with and enter into an exceedingly difficult state of affairs. As painted by him this state was, indeed, far from promising, and must no doubt be considered as the backwash of the revolutionary agitations. The question, however, remains whether the writer, soured, it may be, by trouble and adversity, did not see only the dark side of the picture and form his judgment with undue haste and insufficient experience. Though the rapid development of events would seem to justify Coresma, yet in the man himself we look in vain for the energy and will-power of an Andrade, for the resolve and steadfastness of purpose which remains unperturbed in the midst of a trying situation. In the circumstances he would not seem to have been the right man in the right place.

From Coresma's third letter dated Agra December 14, 1635, we learn that soon after Correa's departure the situation at Tsaparang became worse than ever, so much so that he and Marques were kept prisoners in their house by a strong body of soldiers who cut off all communication with the outside world. Finally they were banished from the country, and even before an answer from the Provincial, Father Tavarez, could have been received, they left Tsaparang, which was no longer what Andrade had called it eleven years before, the 'cidade real' in the valley of the Langtchen-Kamba [1]). They arrived at Agra December 11, 1635.

On receipt of the two letters of August 30 Tavarez placed the question before his advisers, all of whom recommended the abandonment of the mission on account of the unsatisfactory results

[1]) Though Marques is not mentioned in the letter of December 14, there can be no doubt that he left together with his Superior.

and the impossibility of increasing the support supplied from Goa [1]). The advice was acted upon, but at the same time Tavarez made some provision for a possible turn of events by sending Pereira and dos Anjos to Srinagar in Garhwal in June 1636, to devote themselves to the conversion of the Tibetan inhabitants, and to return as soon as circumstances would permit, to the country which they were now debarred from entering [2]). Dos Anjos had no sooner arrived at Srinagar than he fell ill; he died shortly afterwards. Father Stanislaus Malpichi, a Neapolitan, went to fill his place in January 1637. He advised Castro of his safe arrival adding "that the Governor of Chaparangue wrote to the petty king of Srinagar, complaining that he kept his Fathers, and he wrote to the Fathers inviting them to come to Tibet, that he is keeping their house and church intact with their other possessions and animals" [3]). All this, however, raised no sanguine expectations as appears from Castro's remark a few months later: "Though we have some news from Tibet that the King wishes again to receive us, we cannot fully trust him" [4]).

Meanwhile there were several among the missionaries who were far from approving the abandonment of the mission; thus we have preserved for us a letter of Father Antonio Mendez, who writes at length on the point to Mutius Vitelleschi, the General of the Society of Jesus. Led by their arguments the General cancelled Tavarez' decision and ordered him to send a fresh expedition into Tibet. As Tavarez had died when the order reached Goa, the matter was taken in hand by his successor Emmanuel d'Almeida, who appointed to the task Fathers Thomas de Barros [5]), Ignatius a Cruce [6]) and Aloysius de Gama [7]) with Brother Manuel Marques as their

1) Cordara, I, 528.

2) *Letter of F. de Castro, September 17, 1636.*

3) *Letter of F. de Castro, April 16, 1637.*

4) *Letter of F. de Castro, October 29, 1637.*

5) Thomas de Barros born at Coimbra in 1591, became a Jesuit at Goa in 1610. Before his appointment for Tibet he had chiefly been engaged in teaching. After the failure of the Tibet mission he was at various times Superior of different houses, was charged with the government of the whole mission-province of Goa, and died at Rachol April 13, 1658.

6) Ignatius a Cruce, also a native of Coimbra, was born in 1610, joined the Society of Jesus at the age of eighteen and was at Goa as early as 1633. He died at Badra (Bombay) September 27, 1650.

7) Aloysius de Gama was born at Laure in the diocese of Evora in 1610 and entered the noviciate at Lisbon in 1625. In 1633 he was studying at Goa. After spending three years in the Mogor mission he was Superior at Goa, then for some years at the head of the Jesuit college at Mozambique returning to Goa before 1659. After 1664 his name is nog longer found in the catalogues nor does it occur in the obituary lists.

guide. Travelling by way of Agra they joined Malpichi at Srinagar in 1640 [1]). Here they waited while Malpichi and Marques took the road of Tsaparang to find out what reliance could be placed upon the king's repeated request for missionaries. They were not kept waiting long. Very soon, Cordara tells us [2]), Malpichi returned alone, bringing the bad news that Tibet was permanently closed. On crossing the Mana pass both himself and his companion had been taken prisoners; an opportunity of escaping had presented itself, which both had seized, but Marques had been captured and for his release a heavy ransom was now exacted. He had it on trustworthy authority that both king and people, excited by the lamas, were very hostile to the Christians, and that all the buildings, except the church erected by Andrade, had been razed to the ground. It is Castro again who furnishes the last item of information [3]). He mentions the journey undertaken by Malpichi and Marques "to see if they could obtain permission from the king for the other Fathers to go thither. The king wished the return of our Fathers, but only in the hope of getting from them many rich presents, which it would be impossible for ours to give him. Consequently the said Fathers, de Barros and his companions, returned to Agra, where they are at present." He is silent about the imprisonment and escape of Malpichi and Marques, but supplies some further details about the latter's stay at Tsaparang. "The brother is still all alone in Tibete, where he occupies the house which we have at Chaparangue. A few days ago I received from him letters written in the months of August and October of last year [1641], in which he told me, that, because he wanted to go away from there, he was very badly treated and injured, so much so that humanly speaking he had no hope of getting away. And this, I believe, was another reason why the said three Fathers determined to go back to Agra, because the petty king of Tibete is considered to be a man of bad character and, above all, very dishonest. I have learned this from some merchants who have frequently gone from here to Tibete." At the request of Marques himself Castro made a last effort to obtain his release. From the father of the queen of Lahore he obtained a letter of recommendation for the king of Tsaparang, in which the latter was entreated to allow

1) *Letters of F. de Castro, Sept. 1 and Oct. 3, 1640.*

2) Cordara, I, 529.

3) *Letters of F. de Castro, August 25, 1641, and January 1, 1642.*

his prisoner to depart to Agra. The answer was a refusal. The catalogue for 1641 has a note to the effect that one of the Fathers is staying at Srinagar (Garhwal) to negotiate his release, and from the catalogue of 1647, the next available after 1641, his name is altogether absent: hence his fate is still unknown [1]).

Of the mission buildings nothing is left. Captain Young examined very closely every building round about the king's palace. "I entered every house in the city that I could, but found no trace of a church or mission. Most of the houses are amazingly well preserved although the roof timbers have been taken long ago for fuel, except in the temples themselves. The lamas no doubt abolished the mission buildings just as thoroughly as they wiped out the king's name from their chronicles. Judging by Andrade's account, the church must have been somewhere near what is now the Dzongpon's house. The inhabitants profess, truthfully I daresay, to have no tradition whatever of the Jesuits or of the king's conversion. I had already sounded the Dzongpon when I met him at Shangtze; I tried him again now, but with no better success" [2]).

No trace therefore remains save perhaps one solitary object, of which Young also speaks at the end of his account. "A row of white washed 'chortens' stands near the Dzongpon's house. One of them some forty feet high towers above the rest; and on its summit there lies horizontally a weather-beaten cross of wood. It may be that that chorten was being built, while the lamas were demolishing the church close by; and that some one carelessly, or perhaps thinking to lay up treasure for himself in two heavens, planted the rejected emblem on the Buddhist tomb" [3]).

Such was the sad ending to a day that had begun so brightly. In Srinagar, among the Garhwal mountains, mission-work was continued [4]), and developed, and fresh bands of missionaries were sent

---

[1]) There are hardly any biographical details about Marques. The writer has only been able to ascertain that he was born at Massao (?) in 1596 and entered the Society of Jesus in 1618.

[2]) Young, p. 196.

[3]) Young, p. 198.

[4]) Cf. Maracci, p. 16. Father Malpichi remained in Garhwal probably till 1644. For writing from Agra to the General Mutius Vitelleschi on May 21, 1645, he says he has been at this latter place for a year and a half. After a stay at Goa he returned about 1648 to Agra for two years, and came back a third time in 1654. From 1656 (?) to 1658 he was the tutor of prince Dárá, the eldest son of Shah Jéhan; in 1662 he was placed at

for, while the banks of the Upper Sutlej lay deserted. But though on the spot the hatred of the lamas swept away every vestige of Christianity and blotted out from the short memory of the rude inhabitants every remembrance of the preachers from the West, India did not forget. There, as we shall see in the chapter on Hippolite Desideri, the hope remained alive that one day they might be able to go back to the forbidden land beyond the mountains.

---

the head of the mission-province of Goa. After this date his name no longer occurs in the catalogues of this province, so the year of his death remains unknown. He was a native of the kingdom of Napels being born at Catanzaro in 1600. According to Manucci (I, 381) Father Malpichi was a great friend of the rajah of Srinagar.

CHRONOLOGICAL SUMMARY TO CHAPTERS II AND III

	1580.	Antonio de Andrade born at Oleiros (Portugal).
	1600.	Andrade sent to Goa.
March 30,	1624.	Andrade accompanied by Marques sets out from Agra for Tibet.
May 16,	1624.	letter of Andrade at five days' journey from Srinagar.
beginning of August	1624.	arrival at Tsaparang.
beginning of November	1624.	back at Agra.
November 8,	1624.	letter on this first expedition written from Agra to Palmeiro in Goa.
June 17,	1625.	second journey of Andrade in company with de Souza and Marques to Tsaparang.
September 10,	1625.	letter of Andrade from Tsaparang.
April 12,	1626.	laying of the foundation-stone of the first Christian Church at Tsaparang.
May or June	1626.	arrival at Tsaparang of FF. de Oliveira, dos Anjos and Godinho.
August 15,	1626.	detailed report of Andrade to the General of the Soc. of Jesus from Tsaparang.
?	1626.	return of de Souza to Agra.
?	1627.	arrival of Anthony Pereira at Tsaparang.
?	1627.	return of Godinho to Agra.
September 2,	1627.	letter of Andrade to the General from Tsaparang.
November 10,	1627.	letter of dos Anjos to F. Carvalho.
November 12,	1627.	letter of Pereira to F. Carvalho.
November 16,	1627.	letter of Oliveira to F. Carvalho.
?	1629.	arrival of Anthony da Fonseca at Tsaparang.
?	1629.	return of Andrade to Goa.
	1630.	revolution at Tsaparang.
?	1630.	return of Pereira to Goa.
August 25,	1631.	arrival of Francis de Azevedo at Tsaparang.
January 3,	1632.	arrival at Agra of Azevedo and Oliveira.

February 4.	1633.	letter of Andrade to the General from Goa.
March 19,	1634.	death of Andrade at Goa.
June or July	1635.	arrival of F.F. Coresma and Correa at Tsaparang.
August 30,	1635.	two letters of Coresma to the Provincial at Goa. — Return of Correa.
?	1635.	return of dos Anjos and Fonseca.
December 11,	1635.	return of Coresma and Marques to Agra.
December 14,	1635.	letter of Coresma to the Provincial at Goa.
June	1636.	departure of dos Anjos and Pereira for Srinagar (Garhwal).
?	1636.	death of dos Anjos.
January	1637.	arrival of Malpichi at Srinagar.
	1640.	arrival of de Barros, a Cruce, de Gama and Marques at Srinagar.
Summer	1640.	Malpichi and Marques enter Tibet and are made prisoners; Malpichi escapes, Marques is recaptured.
	1641.	Marques a prisoner at Tsaparang.

LIST OF MANUSCRIPTS TO CHAPTERS II AND III [1])

Relaçam da Missam de Tibet — Goa. February 20, 1626. 3 pp (30 × 21 c.m.). It contains a letter of Andrade from Chaparangue, Sept. 10. 1625. (Franco. *Imagem* pp. 400—402.).

Annua do Tibet do anno de 1626. Letter addressed by Andrade to the General of the Society in Rome, dated Chaparangue, Aug. 14, 1626. 40 pp. (21 × 15 c.m.).

A fragment of this MS. is reprinted by Franco in *Imagem* pp. 403—405. An Italian translation is to be found in *Lettere annue del Tibet del MDCXXVI e della Cina del MDCXXIV scritte al M. R. P. Mutuo Vitelleschi, Generale della Compagnia di Giesù.* Roma 1628.

Ao Pe. Valemtim Carvalho. Do Tibet 29 Aug. 1627. A letter signed by Ant. de Andrade, João de Oliveira and Alano dos Anjos. 2 pp. (31 × 21 c.m.).

* Letter to the General.— Tibet. Sept. 2, 1627 signed, Ant. de Andrade. 8 pp. (31 × 21 c.m.).
* Letter to the General. — Goa. Febr. 4. 1633 signed Ant. de Andrade. 6 pp. (31 × 21 c.m.). The first four pages are headed: „Da Missão do Thibet", the last two: „Da Missão do Mogor".
* Letter of João de Oliveira to F. Val. Carvalho in Goa, dated: Chaparangue Nov. 16. 1627.
* Letter of F. Alano dos Anjos to the same, dated: do Thibet, Nov. 10. 1627.
* Letter of F. Antonio Pereira to the same, dated: do Thibet, Nov. 12. 1627.

These three letters have been preserved in a transcription dated Goa, December 20. 1631. and signed by Andrade and four other missionaries. It was sent to the General at Rome. 7 pp. (31 × 21 c.m.).

* Letter of F. Nuño Coresma to the Provincial of Goa, dated: Chaparang, Aug. 30. 1635; it also bears the signatures of Ambrosio Correa and Manuel Marques.

---

[1]) All MSS. are in the possession of the Society of Jesus.

* Written in Portuguese.

* Letter of the same to the same, dated: Desto Reino do Cogue, Aug. 30. 1635.
* Letter of the same to the same, dated: Agra, Decemb. 14. 1635.
  The transcription, in which these three letters have been preserved, probably dates from 1636, and was sent to the General at Rome. $7^1/_2$ pp. (31 × 21 c.m.).
* Letter of F. Antony Mendez to the General; undated, probably of 1636. $10^1/_2$ pp. (31 × 21 c.m.).

†) Letter of F. Joseph de Castro to F. Claudio Septalio, dated: Regno di Bêgala, Nov. 20. 1631.
†) Letter of the same to F. Jos. Baudio, dated: Mogol, Aug. 8. 1632.
†) Letter of the same to F. Claud. Septalio, dated: Bêgala, Aug. 28. 1632.
†) Letter of the same to the General Mutius Vitelleschi, dated: Agra, Febr. 6. 1633.
†) Letter of the same to the same, dated: Agra, Sept. 17. 1636.
†) Letter of the same to the same, dated: Agra, Apr. 16. 1637.
†) Letter of the same to the same, dated: Agra, Oct. 29. 1637.
* Letter of the same to F. Nuño Mascarenhas at Rome, dated: Agra, Aug. 20. 1638.

†) Letter of the same to the General, dated: Agra, Sept. 1. 1640.
†) Letter of the same to the same, dated: Agra, Octob. 3. 1640.
†) Letter of the same to the same, dated: Lahore, Aug. 25. 1641.
†) Letter of the same to the same, dated: Lahore, Jan. 1. 1642.

---

* Written in Portuguese.

†) Written in Italian.

CHAPTER IV

FRANCISCO DE AZEVEDO

Father de Azevedo spent nearly the whole of his life in India. Born at Lisbon in 1578 he left his native country when still a boy and joined the Society of Jesus at Goa at the age of nineteen. On completing his studies he was stationed at several places; thus he was at Diu in 1614 and at Rachol in 1620, after which he was appointed Visitor to the mission of Monomotapa in South-Africa [1]). In 1627 he went to the Mogor mission, and he was already fifty-two, when he received his commission for Tsaparang. The full account of the expedition which he wrote in Portuguese and addressed to Father Anthony Freire, the procurator of the Indian missions in Portugal covers 44 large, closely-written pages. It is divided into two parts: from Goa to Agra (p. 1—18), and from Agra to Tibet and back (p. 18—44), of which clearly only the second comes within the scope of this book. It will be found in Appendix I printed at length and with the original pagination [2]). As, however, the route from Agra to Tsaparang has been sufficiently described and discussed in the chapter on Andrade, we shall not during this stage of his journey follow Azevedo step by step, but only dwell on such points of his description as fill up gaps in Andrade's account or supplement his statements.

As far as the author is aware, there is no work on geography or missionary enterprise dealing at any length with this expedition of Azevedo's; Desideri [3]) and Launay [4]) do not go beyond a mere

[1]) There is still extant a MS. letter of Dec. 20, 1623, written from the mission-station of Mozambique, in which he reports on the condition of the various stations along the Cuama River.

[2]) The MS. with the heading *Pera o Padre Antonio Freire, Procurador das Provincias da India da Comp. de Jesus em Portugal*, is not in Azevedo's handwriting but only signed by him. It probably dates from 1632, and is written in small, neat characters; the page measures 21.5 × 15 centimetres.

[3]) Desideri, *Difesa* p. 4.

[4]) Launay, I, 30.

mention of his departure for Tibet. Hence this chapter may be considered a first attempt to place in its proper light the pioneer work of this intrepid compatriot of Andrade's.

On June 28, 1631, Azevedo left Agra and on his arrival in the town of Srinagar was an eye-witness of a scene of oriental barbarism. The rajah of Garhwal had died. This prince, it will be remembered, after trying at first to frustrate Andrade's undertakings had afterwards become so friendly with him as to offer the missionary a site next to his own palace, if he would consent to settle in his capital. His recent death gave Azevedo an opportunity of witnessing a royal Hindu funeral. On a large pile of aromatic materials, chiefly aloe and precious sandal-wood, the body was burnt on the banks of the Alaknanda. Sixty of his wives had to follow their lord into the flames, and though some did so voluntarily, most of the wretched women had to be thrown in by main force. It was not till seven days after this barbarous ceremony that the new king, a boy of seven, could be crowned. As this would detain him too long, he resolved to push on, and was on the point of setting out when Manuel Marques arrived from Mana with the object of obtaining fresh supplies of food and sending a report on the situation at Tsaparang to Agra. From him Azevedo learnt the full truth about the revolution that had taken place, "how the king, our great friend, was no longer ruler, but the prisoner of a crafty pagan," and how the prospects of the mission, which had promised so fair, had become very gloomy indeed [1]).

Having Marques as his guide Azevedo left the capital of Garhwal July 31. Taking the mountain road along the Alaknanda, the difficulties of which are described at length, the travellers reached Jussy. "This village is situated on the slope of a famous mountain, the houses are well built and the population is numerous. The place owes its fame chiefly to a large pagoda, which is found in it, flanked by four towers of hewn stone. In front of the main entrance of this pagoda there stands on a pedestal about three metres high the statue of an angel [Anjo] made of bronze, very splendid, and the whole very artistic, not only the statue itself but more especially the features. The statue looks towards the pagoda in a kneeling posture, its hands raised to heaven" [2]). They had hardly taken lodgings for the night in one of the buildings attached to the

[1]) Azevedo, MS. fol. 26 *Appendix I.*
[2]) Azevedo, MS. fol. 27 *Appendix I.*

temple when there arrived a large procession of pilgrims with bells and perfumes, who several times made the circuit of the shrine.

It cannot be doubted that Azevedo is speaking here of the village of Josimath at the confluence of the Vishnuganga and the Dauli, to which the people of Badrinath retire in winter. Raper who visited it in 1807, estimates the number of houses "neatly built of gray stone and roofed with shingles" at between a hundred and a hundred and fifty. He mentions two temples. One contains the image of Nara-singha, one of the Hindu deities, put up there by a native of Kumaon, of the Josi (Jyátshi) class of the Brahmins, to which the place is supposed to owe its name. "The building is said to be three hundred years old, but it has the appearance of being of much later date, and resembles a private habitation much more than a Hindu place of worship. It is built with gable ends and covered in with a sloping roof of plates of copper" [1]). This description can hardly be made to square with Azevedo's notes given above, which far better apply to the ancient temple buildings also described by Raper. These are situated in the higher part of the village in a large open space in which the pilgrims pass the night. The temples "are raised on a terrace about ten feet high and in the centre of the area stands the principal one, sacred to Vishnu. It is surrounded by a wall about thirty feet square: at each angle and in the centre of each face are inferior temples, containing different deities. Several of them were destroyed and thrown down by the earthquake; and most of them are in a very tottering condition. Those which suffered the least and have the images perfect, are the temples of Vishnu, Ganesa, Surya or the sun, and the Naudevi. Of these the statues representing the two former are carved in a very superior style of workmanship [2])." A bronze statue such as is described by Azevedo is not mentioned by Raper; it may possibly have been wrecked by the earthquake above referred to. Dr. K. Boeck, who visited Josimath in 1890, speaks of a large temple to which several hostelries belong, and of a smaller shrine in the neighbourhood, but he gives no description [3]).

Azevedo has also much to say of the pagoda of Badrinath, by him called Badry. "The whole consists of three badly built low

[1]) Raper, p. 516.

[2]) Raper, p. 517.

[3]) Boeck, *Gletscherfahrten*, p. 347, 349.

cottages. The best of the three contains on an altar two images of the god, one of gold and one of stone. In its immediate neighbourhood there rise three springs, two of which are cold and one is warm, the water of which is so hot that one cannot possibly hold one's hand in it even during the short space required to say two words. This water is conducted to several basins, where the pilgrims may bathe.... Besides the wealth flowing hither from all parts of India the kings of the neighbourhood have given a large number of villages for the maintenace of the temple" [1]). Raper was told that 700 villages belonged to the pagoda [2]); Traill, however, in his '*Statistical Sketch of Kumaun*' puts the number at 226, yielding an annual revenue of only 2,000 rupees. From the temple-registers of 1820 he found that the revenue for that year, together with the offerings, amounted to 15,750 rupees, besides 3,000 rupees' worth of gold and silver presents [3]). At present the annual income is 7,000 rupees [4]).

"Three times a day," continues our traveller, who seems to have had an eye for detail, "food is offered to the god, in the morning four measures of the best rice with some cocoa-nuts, a large quantity of butter and some cake, at midday four handfuls of boiled rice and many spices, and in the afternoon some refreshments. All this is placed before the god, whereupon the doors are closed; after a while the good things are taken away and divided among the Brahmin and his ministers as the god is satisfied with the odour alone.... The mountain district of the pagoda is a sacred place, where the criminals of the surrounding countries may live unmolested. Like the ministers, however, they live at a fairly great distance, as the god will not allow the proximity of any man or woman not perfectly chaste" [5]), which last remark is confirmed by Raper [6]). Though considerable every year, the concourse of pilgrims is largest every twelfth year. This was the case last year (1630), when along those terrible mountain roads more than 80,000 pilgrims went thither. A troop of 8,000 jogis, "the greatest loafers of India," went up to the shrine carrying arms, but as the

[1]) Azevedo, MS. fol. 28. *Appendix I.*

[2]) Raper, p. 536.

[3]) *Asiatic Researches*, XVI (Calcutta 1828); quoted by Ritter II, 994.

[4]) Gazetteer of India, VI, 180.

[5]) Azevedo, MS. fol. 28. *Appendix I.*

[6]) Raper, p. 539. — Dr. Boeck gives some details about Badrinath (*Gletscherfahrten*, p. 356–361), but he was refused admittance into the temple.

rajah of Srinagar did not care for such a regiment of vagabonds, he ordered them to deliver up their weapons. On their refusal the whole troop was dispersed by force, so that with less joy and more haste they had to return to the place from which they had come, leaving many dead behind. For more than six months Badrinath is uninhabitable through cold and snow [1]).

Adolf and Robert Schlagintweit, who reached this famous spot in August 1855, also refer to this great periodical concourse of pilgrims. "The greatest number of pilgrims is drawn hither every twelfth year, when the planet of Jupiter enters the Water-bearer, and the Daloka Mela, 'the Fair of the Water-bearer', is held at Hardwar. The number of Hindus visiting Badrinath in those years is estimated at 40,000 to 50,000" [2]).

As regards Mana, it is a wretched hamlet, the population of which subsist on their sheep, which are used as beasts of burden to carry rice into Tibet, bringing back loads of salt. The neighbouring woods are the home of large numbers of muskdeer, from which is obtained the purest and most precious musk that is known [3]). At Mana Marques stayed behind, as the sheep he had hired to carry his provisions had not yet been got together, and Azevedo set out by himself to try the pass. "Halfway among these mountains [the Serra do Candâ (Kamet?) as he has just called them] I discovered the pool from which the Ganges issues, according to the information I have received. The Ganges flows southward, the Indus northward, both for a great distance hidden below the surface, but traceable by a peculiar sound; small and hardly visible when they first appear, but soon becoming abundant and powerful through the number of feeders. The former descends into the plains of Hindustan, flows eastward and makes its way to the Ocean across the plain of Bengal. The Indus flows through the mountains northward to Chaparangue, close to which place it bends westward. Later on it flows by the town of Lahore and runs seaward through the country of Sinde. From Lahore onward it is a navigable river" [4]). After the long discussion of a very similar passage in Andrade's account there is no need of further comment

[1]) Azevedo, MS. fol. 28. *Appendix I.*

[2]) Schlagintweit, II, 353.

[3]) Azevedo, MS. fol. 29. *Appendix. I*

[4]) Azevedo, MS. fol. 30. *Appendix I.* Like Andrade he uses the word 'tanque' not 'lago'. "Do meo desta serra descobrij o tanque donde nasce o rio ganges." He says nothing about the source of what he calls the Indus.

here, and we only note Azevedo's mistaking for the Indus the small mountain stream which, according to Hedin [1]), takes its rise on the northern side of the pass and joins the Sutlej at Totling. The true Indus he is one day to meet at Leh.

On August 25 he joined his brethren at Tsaparang, and it is doubtless from their long experience that he obtained the matter for his notes on the people and the country with which this part of his journal abounds. "This kingdom is one of those which are classed together under the name of Pot [Bod], and it is not the smallest but one of the largest and richest. About a thousand years ago it was ruled over by a king called Chopado, 'the giver of the book', because it was he who brought them the book of the law from China on the other side of Uzangue [Utsang]. Hence he was held in such high honour by the neighbouring princes that they considered it a privilege to become allied to his family [2])." With remarkable accuracy Azevedo here gives the date of the introduction of Buddhism into Tibet. At the beginning of the seventh century the Tibetan King Sron-tsan-Gampo invaded China and compelled the Emperor Taitsung to subscribe to a treaty of peace by the terms of which he married a Chinese princess whilst retaining his Nepalese wife. With the princess the first elements of civilization entered Tibet. Both women being ardent Buddhists and zealots for their religion, Sron-tsan-Gampo was converted to their faith; he built temples and monasteries, founded Lhasa and sent to India and China for the chief Buddhist books [3]).

On Tsaparang Azevedo is very brief. The town is built against the slope of a mountain and contains some good dwelling-houses, but most of the inhabitants compelled by cold, live in mountain caves, which they call 'pugos'. The castle in which the king resides lies on the top of the mountain and on account of its situation and defences is impregnable [4]). His description of the people is not flattering [5]).

The position of their eyes is like that of the Chinese, but their

---

[1]) Hedin, *Transhimalaja*, III, 275.

[2]) Azevedo, MS. fol. 31. *Appendix I*. A little further on he says that 'Pot' means Land of Snow.

[3]) Sarat Chandra Dás, *Contributions on the Religion, History etc. of Tibet*. — Journal of the Asiatic Society of Bengal, Vol. L, Part I (1881) p. 218-221. Waddell, *Buddhism*, p. 20 ff.

[4]) Cf. Young's description of the town quoted above in Ch. II p. 64.

[5]) Azevedo, MS. fol. 31. *Appendix I*.

faces resemble more those of the Javanese. They are not beautiful, rather they are ugly, and so dirty in their person and clothing that they may be said to live in filth from birth till death. This is confirmed by the latest travellers. Drew writes of the Ladakhis that they "all have a rooted objection to washing.... Their clothes worn next them are never washed, but are affectionately kept around them until they fall to pieces" [1]). Their natural disposition is gentle and kind, but conjugal faith is not in high esteem, least of all among the men: they will lend their wives to others and not blush to ask the same of their friends. Of polyandry Azevedo says nothing; in fact none of the Tsaparang missionaries mentions this pernicious Tibetan practice, which is spoken of at length by Desideri. One practice which Azevedo mentions is a *ius primae noctis*. "When they marry, the person who has negotiated the marriage and arranged everything has a right to keep the bride in his house the first night, which in fact is generally done; the next day he gives her back to her husband." Divorce is of frequent occurrence The husband conducts his wife back to her parents, and each holding the opposite end of a woollen thread they pull, break the thread, and thus the separation has become an accomplished fact; both parties go their several ways, the father with the son, the mother with the daughter [2]). Father Donsen mentions a somewhat similar thread-ceremony still in existence to signify the dissolution of a polyandric marriage. "When a wife who has lost her husband by death does not want to continue to live with his younger brothers, she ties one end of a thread round the finger of her dead husband and the other end round her own. The breaking of the thread is a sign of her breaking with the younger brothers of the deceased" [3]).

The food of the people consists of roasted barley-meal, fresh or dried herbs, and meat, which is either raw or slightly roasted. They never visit without offering a present, no letter even is sent without its attending gift. The host on the other hand must offer his guest food and drink as frequently as possible. He who wishes to plead his cause before the king must accompany his petition by

[1]) Drew, p. 248. Monserrate also knew of this peculiarity. He writes of the inhabitants of Bhot, "qui lanae coagmentum, quale est petasorum, corpori quam proxime possunt, suendo annectunt; nec ante exuunt, quam aut putrescat sudore, aut usu teratur et solvatur ut decidat." Monserrate, p. 594.

[2]) Azevedo, MS. fol. 31. *Appendix I.*

[3]) Donsen, p. 456.

a present; if his claim is not allowed, the present is returned. The king, on his part, offers the plaintiff food, and it would be rude not to take home any remains that should be left.

The brief remarks on the religion and the lamas, with which Azevedo concludes, need not detain us here; they do not go beyond Andrade's statements, or else they are to be found at greater length in Desideri's narrative [1]).

The forlorn state in which he found the much-tried Christian community at Tsaparang soon convinced Azevedo that ordinary measures would not suffice and he resolved to take a bold step. It was impossible to do anything here, for the new governor, appointed by the king of Ladakh, who had returned to Leh taking with him the late king and leaving a garrison in the town, was very hostile to the mission; so Azevedo made up his mind to go to Leh and treat personally with the king. But fresh obstacles arose. Small-pox had appeared at Tsaparang, and fearing that the travellers might carry the scourge to Leh the governor refused the required permit. Some presents, however, soothed his fears and he consented. The missionary had hardly been three days on his way, however, when he was overtaken by an order to return at once on pain of death. He obeyed extremely vexed that the favourable season, which had advanced well into September, thus threatened to slip by. On September 28, however, he was suddenly informed that in a few days he would be allowed to start together with some horse-merchants of Utsang. Among the missionaries present he chose Oliveira as his companion and interpreter, and on October 4, 1631, the caravan took the road to Leh [2]).

Before chronicling in detail the particular events Azevedo first gives us some general information about this journey from Tsaparang to Leh, the first undertaken by any European. The journey took twenty-one days, travelling from sunrise to sunset. The route is little frequented and runs through snow-covered mountains. Not a green leaf or plant is to be seen, but there is much snow and an abundance of wild animals such as hares, mountain-goats, donkeys, hyacas (yaks?) wood-pigeons, big ravens, eagles &c. [3]), the

---

[1]) What Azevedo has to say about the disgusting amulets and medicines (MS. fol. 32. *Appendix I*) is in perfect agreement with Grueber's statements on the subject. (Cf. Ch. VI, p. 191).

[2]) Azevedo, MS. fol. 34. *Appendix I*. Before starting a letter reached him from Father Cabral at Utsang, about which we shall speak in the next chapter.

[3]) Azevedo, MS. fol. 34. *Appendix I*.

same fauna therefore which is found on the plateau at the present day [1]). These remarks at once show that the travellers did not, as might at first be expected, take the road towards the valley of the Indus and thus drop down into Leh, the reason of which may with some probability be conjectured. As Schlagintweit remarks, the valley of the Indus in Ladakh from the frontier of the province of Gnari Khorsum onward is hardly available for the purposes of commercial intercourse especially on account of the presence of narrow and deep gorges, which force the traveller first to climb the steep slopes of the valley carved out by the river and then to traverse the difficult cross-valleys [2]). For a caravan of horses such a road presents, of course, almost insuperable difficulties. But even the road they actually took must have been far from easy as is borne out by a comparison of the number of travelling-days and the distance between the two termini, which in a straight line is 360 kilometers. Besides the unavoidable delay attendant on the movement of a large caravan it is especially the season of the year and the condition of the ground, more particularly the latter, not described with any detail by Azevedo, which tell in these matters. The track led across the plateau situated between the Zaskar and Ladakh ranges, which reaches an average elevation of 4,500 metres and is of a very irregular and rugged character. Captain Rawling, who from Gartok explored the basin of the upper Sutlej, supplies the description which is wanting in Azevedo. He argues at length that this plateau must at one time have been an enormous inland-sea, which was silted up with the debris of surrounding mountains forcing the water thus pressed for room to break through the Himalaya, and then continues: "Since then rain and snow have continued the work of wearing away the softened lines in the strata and forming great clefts and chasms many hundreds of feet in depth, to the bottoms of which the rays of the sun never reach. Narrow, precipitous ridges, spire-like pinnacles and isolated plateaux rise on all sides. It is a weird and wonderful sight, but also a depressing one, for neither shrubs nor grass can grow and a death-like silence reigns supreme. Now and again, in the centre of the largest nullahs, a small crystal stream may be seen trickling over its sandy bed, but during the winter these are few and far between" [3]).

[1]) R. Strachey, p. 79.

[2]) Schlagintweit, III, 231.

[3]) Rawling, p. 281. See also H. Strachey, *Physical Geography of Western Tibet.* — Journal of the Royal Geographical Society, XXIII (1853) p. 18, 31 ff.

It was through this maze of troughs and ravines that the party had to pick their way. "In the evening of the first day we arrived at the village of Sanze, built for the greater part along the slope of a mountain, so that the inhabitants, not very numerous, generally live in the recesses and caves of the mountain-side. On the summit is a fortification with some cottages around it; a beautiful river passes close by [1]). This can hardly be anything else than the present Shangtse, a settlement at an altitude of nearly 4,200 metres, 40 kilometres north of Tsaparang, on one of the tributaries of the Sutlej. As it is difficult to believe, however, that the whole of this distance was covered in one day, it is probable that the caravan was formed not in the town itself but at some distance from it on the other side of the river, and set out from this starting-point. The curious custom of living in caves, which Azevedo also notices at Tsaparang, is still in favour in the Sutlej basin. "The inhabitants are very partial to living in caves, and although houses are to be found, yet these caves are by far the most popular residences" [2]).

The second halting-place was another small town on a river — perhaps Ragbyaling on H. Strachey's map [3]) or else Tchoktse visited by Dr. Hedin [4]) — the third was a shepherds' encampment, without any further specification. Meanwhile the winter made its approach felt, for during the third night the cold became more severe and in the morning there was a foot of snow. "The next seven days we traversed great mountain ranges deeply covered with snow, a desert region without any settlement, till at last we reached Alner, where the chief of the lamas lives on the top of a mountain. It consists of only six or seven small houses, which form something like a fortification [5])." Though the name of Alner does not occur on the maps, it may almost with certainty be identified with Hanle in the extreme south-eastern corner of the present territory of the Maharajah of Kashmir, for Azevedo's particulars clearly point to a Buddhist monastery, and from the fact that the caravan remained south of the Indus, they must neces-

---

[1]) Azevedo, MS. fol. 34. *Appendix I.*

[2]) Sherring p. 336. Cf. C. Ryder, *Exploration and Survey with the Tibet Frontier Commission and from Gyangtse to Simla via Gartok* — Geographical Journal, XXVI (1905) p. 390.

[3]) See the map illustrating his article just cited on Western Tibet.

[4]) Hedin, *Transhimalaja*, III, 309.

[5]) Azevedo, MS. fol. 35. *Appendix I.*

sarily have travelled in a north-westerly direction from Shangtse. Besides, Hanle lies on the ordinary route to Leh. Thomas Thomson, who visited it in 1847, found there "a Buddhist monastery inhabited by about twenty lamas, built on the summit of a steep hill, which rises abruptly out of the plain". Except the monks there was no settled population; a few stone huts without roofs, which were scattered about the foot of the rock, were untenanted [1]). It is one of the highest inhabited spots on earth [2]). Probably, therefore, Alner is a misspelling or rather a mishearing for 'Anler' if indeed the place did not go by both names.

From Hanle the caravan pursued its way across the bare plateau and through the more sheltered valleys, and soon came upon a shepherds' camp consisting of some thirty tents. Large flocks of sheep — the journal speaks of 18 to 20 thousand — found the necessary pasture on the level alongside some small rivers. The nomads provided Azevedo with milk, not in exchange for money, with the use of which these solitaries were unacquainted, but for three raisins of the size of plums, which the Father had brought with him from Hindustan. They were so keen on them that three shepherds had to share one fruit! The next three days, again through barren and lonely mountains, were very trying for the two Europeans. They were half dead with cold, says Azevedo, his face and hands were all chapped and the blood ran down them, whilst his feet were also very sore. Oliveira, too, though he had passed some years in the climate, had much to suffer. Even the guides could not bear up and were quite disheartened. Fire-wood was nowhere to be found, nor even dung, the ordinary fuel in those parts. Towards the evening of the third day a wide valley opened out before them, in which was a large salt marsh (*hua grande marinha*) with beautiful white salt. After stopping here for the night to rest as best they could, they resumed their journey through the inhospitable mountains the following day; another terrible three days' march brought them to the town of Guiar [3]).

Guiar, the present Gya, the third and last place-name between Tsaparang and Leh given by Azevedo, together with the

---

[1]) Thomson, p. 152 ff.

[2]) The height is variously stated, nor is it always clear whether the plain or the top of the hill is meant: H. Strachey gives 14,500 ft., Schlagintweit, (III, 157) 15,117 ft., Drew on his map 14,276 ft.

[3]) Azevedo, MS. fol. 35. *Appendix I.*

mention of the salt marsh sufficiently enable us to fix the missionary's route and to illustrate it from the data of other travellers. So we shall leave him for a while at Gya.

When Thomson had visited Hanle, he first went some distance through the Indus valley leaving it at Puga, a stopping-place some fifty miles north-west of Hanle. Here he turned to the left and struck the direct road from Hanle to Gya. From this point onward, therefore, his route coincides with Azevedo's. It led him across the Pulolanka La, 16,500 feet (5,016 metres) high, a deep depression in the Ladakh range, in the district of Rupshu, and then to the banks of the Thogji Chumo, which had already been visited in 1822 by Trebeck, Moorcroft's travelling-companion [1]). "After reaching the banks of the lake," Thomson writes, "the road kept its eastern shore throughout its whole length, which was about three miles, and we encamped close to its north end on the edge of a level salt plain. Our elevation was about 15,500 feet. The margins of the lake, which was intensely saline, were generally very shallow, and its banks often swampy and covered with saline plants" [2]).

That Azevedo's "large salt marsh" must be the Thoghi lake seems to be beyond dispute, and is borne out still more clearly by Drew's description of this Salt Lake Valley as he calls it. "This is the widest opening in the whole of Rupshu; the length, in a direction north-west and south-south-east, is thirteen miles, and along a considerable part of that length the valley is five miles wide; the level of it is 14,900 feet. It is a flat surrounded by hills, occupied partly by land and partly by water. The original outlet — an opening between the hills on the northwest—is now filled up some 70 feet above the plain, so that there is no passage for the waters that collect in the valley, which therefore with its enclosing hills forms a separate drainage-basin. The hills are for the most part low in comparison with the mountains we have met with, all are bare of visible vegetation; as a rule they are not rugged, but have smooth surfaces of loosened stones. The surface of the plain is varied; in

---

[1]) Moorcroft, II, 47. The name has various spellings: Schlagintweit (III, 155) calls it Cho Thogchi Chenno or Tso Kar; Drew (p. 293) Tso Kar only; Cunningham writes Cho Kahr, and also notes how the country far around the lake is encrusted with salt. *Journal of a Trip through Kulu and Lahul to the Chu Mureri Lake in Ladak during the Months of August and September 1846* — Journal of the Asiatic Society of Bengal XVII (1848) p. 226.

[2]) Thomson, p. 171.

parts there is sand and gravel, in other parts an expanse of white clay; this again is sometimes caked with a thin covering, still whiter, of salts, various in composition; lastly, a not inconsiderable portion is occupied by two lakes — about a square mile by one of them which has fresh water, and seven square miles by the Salt Lake" [1]). It is obvious that the cold in these high valleys must necessarily be extremely severe, and with a clear sky there is a night-frost even in midsummer. The same writer draws attention to another influence which renders travelling in those high altitudes extremely painful, and which must have greatly aggravated the difficulties of the journey for Azevedo, who had only passed a couple of months in the Tibetan highlands. "There is one characteristic of Rupshu that is always making itself felt by those who are used to dwell at lower altitudes. This is the rarity of the air. In the valleys water boils at about the temperature of about 187° [86° C], which corresponds to a barometer height of 17'8 inches [449 millimetres]. Hence the amount of air — and of oxygen — taken into the lungs with an ordinary inhalation is only $^{7}/_{12}$ths of what would enter them where one at the level of the sea" [2]).

From the Thoghi lake or Tso Kar the road to Gya runs in the direction of the Tunglung pass parallel with the axis of the Ladakh range, alternately topping its spurs or dipping down into the valleys between them. Thomson, who traversed this part towards the end of September, found the ascent very steep. "The road was very stony and rugged.... The wind still blew very strongly from the north, driving in our faces the still falling snow and opposing our progress towards the crest, which was very rocky, being composed of a mass of stratified quartz. The elevation of the summit was about 17,500 feet (5,320 metres). [3]). No wonder the Portuguese traveller had something to say of the terrors of this march. Then another fourteen miles through a narrow precipitous ravine widening out a little towards the end, and the houses of Gya, the first after Hanle, were in sight.

A hundred and ninety years were to elapse between Azevedo and Oliveira's passing visit and the arrival in 1820 of two other

---

[1]) Drew, p. 292.

[2]) Drew, p. 290.

[3]) Thomson, p. 175. Drew writes the name of the pass Toglung; Schlagintweit (III, 228) Takelang or Tung-lung, and states the altitude at 17,727 feet (5,389 metres); Franke writes Thag-lang (p. 62).

Europeans, Moorcroft and Trebeck. They describe Gya as "a town of small extent and thinly peopled" [1]), whilst Drew speaks of it as a village of some forty houses with a proportionately wide area of cultivation [2]). It is situated at about 13,500 feet (4,115 metres) above sea-level.

At the time of the visit of the two Portuguese town and country were governed by a ruler "whom the king of Ladac had deprived of the kingdom of Mariul. He is very friendly with us, as he proved before, when he received Father Andrade." They, too, met with a kind reception, and among other presents received a dozen big apples, much resembling the very large and good ones of Lisbon, which, Azevedo adds, "I had not seen during the last thirty-seven years" [3]). That fruit is grown in the severe Tibetan climate is known; apricots and peaches are even among the staple articles of export from Ladakh; apple-trees are numerous and of several kinds. "They bear freely," writes Moorcroft, "endure great cold and intense heat, require little rain and are very rarely attacked by disease" [4]). He, too, was presented with some apples at Marsilang half-way between Gya and Leh.

With fresh energy Azevedo continued his journey. "After two days we arrived at a station in the kingdom of Ladac, from where six small hamlets can be seen among the mountains at a mile's distance from each other and resembling those spoken of before. They lie in the greatest and longest valley which I have seen in those mountain regions and which also contains many fertile barley-fields. This barley is not like that of our country, its grain resembles more that of wheat, and as food it is very nourishing and pleasant to the taste. The next day we reached the royal town of Lee" [5]).

The course of the Gya or Mandur river points the way from Gya to the Indus valley, which, therefore, was the route followed by Moorcroft and many after him. The narrow ravine through which

[1]) Moorcroft, I, 231.

[2]) Drew, p. 285. See also Thomson, p. 177; Schlagintweit, III, 228.

[3]) Azevedo, MS. fol. 35. *Appendix I.* So he must have left Portugal at or before the age of fifteen. He does not tell us the name of the ruler of Gya. When Francke was there in 1909 he found on a wall below the town an inscription of about 1630 probably bearing the name of the reigning chief. Unfortunately he was prevented by want of time from taking a full copy of the inscription. (Francke p. 63—64).

[4]) Moorcroft, I, 297.

[5]) Azevedo, MS. fol. 36. *Appendix I.*

the river speeds is about fourteen miles long and reaches the Indus near Upshi. It took Moorcroft and Thomson two days to traverse, which agrees with Azevedo's time-notice. But what are the six hamlets seen by the latter near Upshi, "the first station in the kingdom of Ladac", it is hard to say. Thomson came across no settlements in the ten miles between Upshi and Marsilang in the direction of Leh. On nearing Upshi, however, the Gya ravine widens out according to the same traveller "into an open plain, well covered with houses and enclosures, with scattered poplar and willow trees.... and traversed by irrigation canals conducted from the little Gya rivulet" [1]). May not Azevedo have meant this valley?

Towards the evening of October 25, 1631, then, the first Europeans entered the capital of Ladakh. Not, however, without going through the necessary formalities. When they came near the town etiquette required them to light from their horses and standing to await the permission to enter. On receiving it they were by the king's orders assigned a residence and provided with the necessary fuel, water and some measures of barley. Azevedo devotes only a few lines to the description of Leh. "It is built on the slope of a small mountain and numbers about 800 families. Half a mile lower down but still quite visible flows the river that goes to Lahore. By the town itself passes a mountain stream which works a large number of water-mills; a few trees are also found here" [2]). As we shall have to return to Leh in company with Desideri we shall not enter on a description of the town here. Let it suffice to remark that, if Azevedo's figures are correct, the population has rather diminished than increased; in 1847 Thomson was informed that it was 5,000, at present it must be about 2,100 [3]). Schlagintweit on his visit saw the water-mills on the Leh river" [4]).

The boundaries of Ladakh are thus given by Azevedo: "The kingdom of Ladac borders in the south on that of Chaparangue or Goge [Guge], in the east on the kingdom of the three Moors, also called by another name Archande [Yarkand], the capital of which is Cascar [Kashgar]. It is from there that caravans carry into China the clay of which porcelain is made. Through this kingdom with

---

[1]) Thomson, p. 178.

[2]) Azevedo, MS. fol. 36. *Appendix I.*

[3]) *Gazetteer of India*, XVI, 90.

[4]) Schlagintweit, III, 278. In 1820 Moorcroft (I, 240) noticed "corn-mills worked by the stream" in the village of Changa close to Leh.

its white, strongly built and vigorous population, Brother Bento de Goes travelled. Cascar is not more than six days' march from the kingdom of Ladac. On the western side, finally, it is bounded by the kingdom of Baldys [Baltistan], a people which is not so white but of better physique and taller stature." [1])

The very first day after their arrival the king had the strangers sent for "less to see us personally than to receive our presents", Azevedo adds slyly. The presents consisted of some pieces of cloth, six large and small fire-arms, two Chinese targets, an inkstand from Diu and some other gilt trinkets, all of which were eagerly welcomed and accepted. With great accuracy of detail Azevedo describes his first audience with Senge-nam Gyal. "He is a man of tall stature, of a brown colour, with something of the Javanese in his features [2]), and of stern appearance. He wore a rather dirty upper garment of some red material, a mantle of the same, and a thread-bare cap. His hair hung down to his shoulders, either ear was adorned with turquoise and a large coral, whilst he wore a string of skull-bones round his neck to remind himself of death. He was sitting cross-legged on an ornamental carpet of crimson velvet of the time of Mathusala." The queen, a short stout personage with sore eyes, was dressed like her husband but she was less imposing. When everyone was seated Chinese tea was served, a sign of great favour on their part. This tea is made with water, some butter and a little milk, it is a dark liquid, which is drunk as hot as possible. One who serves tea freely is reputed a very generous host, but on account of the cost only the rich can afford to do so. After this they were presented with a piece of raw meat and a ball of husked barley, which they call 'zanem'. After the interview most of those present saw them to their residence [3]).

Tea is, indeed, still a favourite drink in Ladakh, but the poor people, that is, Drew adds [4]), nearly all the population, are rarely able to get it. Barley-meal is the people's daily food; it is, Father Donsen says, either baked into a sort of pancake, or made into dough and rolled into balls for more convenient carriage when travelling [5]). The only thing Azevedo has to remark of the palace

---

[1]) Azevedo, MS. fol. 36. *Appendix I.*

[2]) "nas feiçoes jao".

[3]) Azevedo, MS. fol. 36. *Appendix I.*

[4]) Drew, p. 247.

[5]) Donsen, p. 430.

where the interview took place is that it was full of cobwebs and should be called dirty rather than clean. This does not render it probable that Senge-nam Gyal had already built his palace of nine stories, the construction of which is ascribed to him by the Ladakh chronicles [1]).

During this first audience, which had been more of the nature of a formal greeting, Azevedo had not touched on the subject of his coming. Four days later, however, he thought he saw his chance and during a second interview he submitted his proposals. The king promised he would consider the matter with his councillors. A week later, the journal says, he sent us his decision; it was a firman authorizing us to continue to work as we had done during the reign of the late king, not only in the kingdom of Coge, but also in Ridocho and even in his own capital. He did not give us this answer personally that he might not be thought to bind himself to favour and expense, if we should actually settle at Lee. At the same time he presented us with a horse very much like Don Quixote's, four pieces of woollen stuff, two tails of hyacas (yaks?) together with the permission to depart [2]).

As a long stay at Leh had never been intended and Azevedo was anxious to return to India to report, the two Fathers resolved to set out the next day, although the cold was already intense. In three days they were back again at Gya with the late king of Mariul. It was November 10. Here they took counsel, and, probably on the advice of the rajah, Azevedo changed the plan of his journey. The cold was already very severe, he relates, and the eighteen stages separating Gya from Tsaparang did not tempt him at all. He would, moreover, have to traverse the Mana pass in December, which, if not impossible, could at any rate not be done without imminent danger of life. "But if I took the direct road to Lahore, it would, it is true, be a new route across uninhabited regions and through many little kingdoms, but it had this great advantage that we should thus escape the terrible winter in nine days. Finally I resolved to take this new route to Lahore that I might not without necessity incur the danger of having to winter at Chaparangue" [3]).

---

[1]) Dr. Karl Marx, *Three Documents* (1891) p. 124, note 101.

[2]) Azevedo, MS. fol. 36 ff. *Appendix I*. Nothing is said by Azevedo of the king of Tsaparang, who had been carried off to Leh. From Andrade's letter of February 1633 it is clear that the latter had seen him, but the strict guard that was kept over the prisoner prevented the missionary from getting into touch with him.

[3]) Azevedo, MS. fol. 37. *Appendix I*.

So they took leave of the ruler of Gya, who urgently entreated them to send him one or more missionaries, whom he promised to house and support properly, and on the same day, Monday November 10, 1631, they set out with an experienced guide on their new expedition to Lahore. One cannot but admire the undaunted courage of those two Portuguese priests, who insufficiently equipped and provided with but few aids dared undertake in the unfavourable and late season a journey across the uninhabited plateaux of Rupshu and Lahul and through the dangerous Himalaya passes.

For centuries the trade-route from Yarkand *via* Leh to the Punjab has run and still runs across the mountain districts of Rupshu, Lahul and Kulu. As late as 1868 the British government opened an annual fair at Palampur in the centre of the Kangra tea-district in order to attract the Turkestan and Leh traders. But the irregular arrival of the Yarkand caravans at Leh and especially the fact of the market being held in autumn, which prevented those attending it from returning before the winter, militated against its being a permanent success, and it was abolished in 1879 [1]). Though the route is regularly used by the native population, it remained closed to Europeans for many years after Azevedo had traversed it. No account of his journey has ever been published and it was not till 190 years later that Moorcroft and Trebeck starting from India penetrated into those mountainous solitudes. Though in summer this route may not be very arduous, and entails nothing beyond the usual labour attendant on a mountain journey and the hardship resulting from scarcity of food and fuel, things are far otherwise in winter. The temperature remains below freezing-point, the snowstorm sweeps the valleys, obstructs the passes and shrouds the roads; the snowfall begins in November, and till the beginning, often till the end, of May all the Himalaya passes at 16,000 feet — which is about the height of Mont Blanc — are practically inaccessible [2]). No wonder, therefore, that the travellers were several times in danger of life. "For nine days we travelled through a solitude of plateaux and mountain ranges without meeting a soul. Crossing frozen mountain streams and rivers we arrived in those parts where from the mountains issue a great number of springs, the water of which freezes immediately on

1) Drew, p. 536.
2) Schlagintweit, III, 224.

coming out. I saw one mountain on the slope of which within the distance of a gunshot I counted 127 springs, but not a blade of grass was to be seen on the whole mountain. The greatest difficulty we experienced in these wastes was when we climbed and descended a very steep mountain wholly covered with snow and in some places with ice. It took us a whole day the snow reaching above our knees; no road was visible and our advance was nothing but a series of falls and rises and slippings on the ice, on which it was difficult to retain or regain a footing. Thank God there was plenty of sunshine and no wind that day, otherwise we should have been frozen to death. On the top of this great mountain the snow forms a pool in which two hundred boats might easily move; at the moment, however, it was one huge sheet of ice glittering in the sun with a brilliance that blinded the eye" [1]).

Knowing that Azevedo followed the trade-route from Leh to the Punjab these details allow us to form a sufficiently accurate picture of his journey. From Gya, his starting point, the road led him back along rising ground to the Tunglung or Takelung pass. Thence one may either drop directly into the north-south valley of the Zarra, a feeder of the Zanskar, and then pass into that of the Sumkiel, or one may take the direction of the Salt Lake Valley, and striking out to the south before reaching it, enter the Sumkiel basin through the valley of Rukchin. Both routes, of which the last-mentioned is the more common, finally abut on the Lachalung pass, leading on to the Bara-Lacha pass on the frontier of Lahul. Schlagintweit puts the elevation of the Lachalung pass at 16,750 feet (5,092 metres)[2]). The slope on the Lahul side is described by Moorcroft as very steep, and the road on the side of Rupshu is "a rough, undulating ground intersected by rivulets and watercourses" [3]). The mountain so rich in springs mentioned by Azevedo may be the Lachalung, whose pass he must have traversed; in any case it cannot be the Bara-Lacha, which must have been the mountain that caused him so much trouble in climbing, as appears from the sequel of the narrative and the mention of the frozen mountain lake. No such lake is spoken of in the description of the passes in Rupshu, but it is given in that of the Bara-Lacha

---

[1]) Azevedo, MS. fol. 37. *Appendix I.*

[2]) Schlagintweit, III, 227. Drew gives 16,500 ft.

[3]) Moorcroft, I, 222. Schlagintweit on the other hand describes the slope as unusually gentle (*sanft ansteigend*) even for Tibetan formations (III, 227).

pass. Schlagintweit mentions the Nam Tso on the south-western slope at 15,570 feet [1]); Drew has such a lake on his map but calls it Suraj Dal, from which issues one of the tributaries of the Bhaga river. That Azevedo took a whole day crossing the pass will cause no surprise if due account is taken of the season and the altitude. Though the height is differently stated, it is certainly above 4,860 metres [2]).

Two days after this crossing, just as they were marching through a valley (the Bhaga valley), an icy storm, which all day long blew in their faces, threatened to freeze him to death. Quite numbed he had to be lifted from his horse to be revived. In the evening they encamped in a cave by a frozen mountain stream, where they sat over a fire and partook of their scanty provisions: a few pieces of black bran-bread, "blacker than the blackest bread that is to be found," and some barley-meal porridge. Their sufferings, however, were for the present all but over, for the next day, the ninth after their departure from Gya, the cold was less severe and the limits of the lonely wastes were reached. Towards eleven o'clock they saw in the distance four cypress trees on the bank of the river, and continuing their way they came across more trees and numerous clear springs, until towards four o'clock they entered the first settlement in the little kingdom of Carja or Caria. In the house of a lama the travellers were treated to toasted bread and milk, the dainties of these people. The next morning the journey was resumed in the direction of the kingdom of Culu, to which that of Caria is subject [3]).

The first settlement, so all travellers tell us, which one meets on the way from Gya to Kulu is the hamlet of Darcha in Lahul. In the list of the stages from Leh to Palampur given by Drew it is the ninth stopping-place after Gya [4]). "It may be observed," Cunningham writes, "that the whole of the country from Darcha in Lahul to the Chumureri Lake [in Rupshu] is a vast uninhabited desert, without a single tree or even a bush knee high, and but scantily supplied with water" [5]). Moorcroft also notes near Darcha,

[1]) Schlagintweit, II, 396; III, 223.

[2]) Moorcroft (I, 216) states it at 16,500 ft., Schlagintweit (III, 222) at 16,180 ft., Burrard at 16,407 ft.

[3]) Azevedo, MS. fol. 38. *Appendix I.*

[4]) Drew, p. 537.

[5]) A. Cunningham, *Journal of a Trip through Kulu and Lahul to the Chu Mureri Lake in Ladak during the Months of August and September 1846* — Journal of the Asiatic Society of Bengal, XVIII (1848) p. 230.

which he calls Labrang, "a number of cypresses much decayed and many quite dead" [1]). These details square so exactly with the points mentioned by Azevedo that there need be no doubt about the identity of "the first settlement in the little kingdom of Carja" and the hamlet of Darcha. But what about the name of Carja, which is not found on any map? Perhaps we may have to think of some mutilated form of Gara as the valley of the Bhaga is locally called in Lahul [2]). Darcha itself is situated on the Bhaga river, which flows through Lahul in a north-westerly direction and joins the Chandra at Tandi to form the important Chenab river. As regards the country itself, "the climate of Lahul", Harcourt writes, "may be considered a very dry and bracing one, but towards the sources of the Bhaga and the Chundra the winds are bitterly cold blowing like a hurricane all day and subsiding altogether at night. In September the winter frosts set in, and from the end of December till April the entire country is covered with snow and almost completely shut out from the rest of the world" [3]). The vegetation, not nearly so luxuriant as in the district of Kulu, is almost confined within the limits of the valley. Besides rich pastures some pines and willows are met with here and there. Barley and buckwheat are the chief crops, wheat being much rarer [4]). The people, not very numerous, still clearly betray their Mongolian origin and live for the greater part in small settlements not only on the lower Chandra but also in the Bhaga valley. When Moorcroft went up this valley from Barling, north of Mundi, he passed all day long through a succession of villages "each containing from ten to twenty houses" [5]). All these characteristics are mentioned in Azevedo's notes. Starting from their first resting-place, so he informs us, in the direction of Kulu, the road ran between two mountain ranges covered with trees and vegetation. They passed through several small villages, the people of which gained their living by agriculture and cattle-breeding. They were a fine people of sound natural dispositions and especially much

---

[1]) Moorcroft, I, 210–214; Schlagintweit, II, 396.

[2]) *Gazetteer of the Kangra District*, Part. III. Lahul, p. 2. — Possibly Carja may be a mishearing for Garza, by which name the Tibetans indicate Upper Lahul. (Cf. J. Hutchison and J. Th. Vogel, *History of Kulu State* — Journal of the Panjab Historical Society (Calcutta 1919) vol. VII. no. 2. p. 145).

[3]) Harcourt, p. 251.

[4]) *Gazetteer of the Kangra District*, Part. III. Lahul, p. 6; p. 43 ff.

[5]) Moorcroft, I, 203 ff.; Schlagintweit, II, 394–395; Harcourt, p. 250 ff.

cleaner than the Tibetans, although they are related to them [1]). The lateness of the season caused fresh difficulties. On the frontier of Lahul the snowfall began to be so heavy that the travellers were continually losing their way. Soaked to the skin and numbed with cold they reached the foot of a mountain, where they had to pass the night in the shelter of a cave. The prospect of having to climb the pass the next day under such circumstances seemed anything but tempting to Azevedo, the more so as his boots, which were never meant for such mountaineering feats, had succumbed in the struggle. But their rest was protracted for two more days as the snowfall during the night was so heavy that even the natives dared not venture on the passage. In the early morning of the third day the ascent was begun with the aid of some Lahulis. Azevedo had obtained from them a pair of shoes of twisted straw, such as Schlagintweit still saw in use among the Ladakhis [2]). The horses sank into the snow up to their bellies. "I shoved myself along with the greatest difficulty without being able to take any rest, for if I stopped for a moment I sank into the snow up to my chest." For five hours he struggled on but then his strength failed him before the top was reached. He thought he would die on the spot, and it was only through the efficient assistance of his companions, who had to carry him in their arms, that he was enabled to continue the journey. As they could not get to the foot of the pass before nightfall they bivouacked on the slope, whence the exhausted travellers looked down with admiration and longing on the magnificent cedar trees in the valley beneath [3]).

Though this Rotang pass, 13,500 feet high and connecting Lahul and Kulu, is neither difficult nor dangerous, yet the crossing may be attempted under circumstances which entail the loss of human life. Thus Harcourt narrates that in 1863 of a hundred labourers who traversed it during a storm seventy-two perished [4]). Azevedo did not fare so badly, but, he writes, I shall long remember that day, because my hands, which I sprained several times in my repeated falls, have remained partly deformed. In the course of his conversation with the guides he had also learned that their pagoda stood in the middle of a large pool, which was formed by

---

1) Azevedo, MS. fol. 38. *Appendix I.*
2) Schlagintweit, III, 296.
3) Azevedo, MS. fol. 38—39. *Appendix I.*
4) Harcourt, p. 248.

the winter rains close to the pass. Perhaps the little lake Serkund is meant, situated on the southern side, which Schlagintweit calls a small "lake-like pool".[1])

Three days more, the journal goes on to say, saw the party to Magar Sarâ, the capital of the kingdom of Cullu. The road took them along flourishing villages and fertile fields. The town is situated in a mountain-valley intersected by many rivulets and adorned with an abundance of splendid cedars. The population is very numerous and the houses are very comfortable. They are built of hewn stone, whilst the verandahs they have running round the four sides are, like the roofs, made of cedar wood. They are a people with fine features, the children with their golden hair are very charming, and some of the women are as white as those of Portugal. It is a curious custom there for everyone to wear flowers or odoriferous herbs in their head-gear. Azevedo was less pleased, when with smooth talk he was relieved of a horse and a few other little items by a kinsman of the king's, who for the rest had received him well during the absence of the latter. "But I let things be, that I might obtain permission to continue my journey" [3]).

Thus our Portuguese missionary was the first European [2]) to admire one of the most delightful districts of the Himalaya, "which for beauty of scenery is the rival of Kashmir" [4]). What he only hints at is fully and admirably described by A. Harcourt, who by a two years' residence as a Settlement Officer was enabled to appreciate the wealth of beauty of the Kulu scenery [5]). And if the reader wishes to enjoy a continuous hymn of praise of these enchanting valleys and mountains, he should take up *Kulu and Lahoul*, the latest work of the well-known Himalaya-traveller, Lieutenant-Colonel Bruce. In these writers, too, he will find back

---

[1]) Schlagintweit, II, 394, "*eine seeartige Wasseransammlung*". Moorcroft (I, 192) in connection with the Rotang pass speaks of two pools sacred to the deity Gepan, the patron of Lahul.

[2]) Azevedo, MS. fol. 40. *Appendix I*.

[3]) The town of Nagarkot, mentioned by Father Monserrate, S. J., in his *Mongolicae Legationis Commentarius* can hardly be other than what was then the capital of Kulu. But from his passing remark it is not clear whether he actually visited the town. "Est hic ager [the Nagarkot district] earum rerum ferax, quas Hispanicus et Italicus plerisque locis producunt, quibus reliqua India caret." (Monserrate, p. 593) He states (p. 538) the longitude at 116°, the latitude at 31° 53′ 30″, the latter, therefore, being not much short of the true determination, 32° 6′.

[4]) Burrard, I, 165.

[5]) Harcourt, p. 247 ff. Cf. K. E. von Ujfalvy, *Aus dem Westlichen Himalaja* (Leipzig 1884) p. 34 ff.

down to the smallest characteristics that were noted by Azevedo. The luxuriant vegetation [1]), the peculiar style of architecture of the houses, "made in alternate layers of timber and stone.... with its gabled roofs of slate and wood and overhanging verandahs, [2]) unconsciously calling before the mind the chalet of the Swiss mountains; the people's fondness of wearing flowers [3]), and lastly the enchanting site of Nagar". The capital of Kulu at the time of Azevedo's visit, Nagar, has had to resign this title to Sultanpur, to which the seat of government has been transferred, but it still ranks first both with the people and the British rulers [4]).

Difficulties of quite another kind troubled the two travellers on their four days' march from Nagar to the kingdom of Mandi: like their provisions, so their funds began to run short. Fortunately, when starting from Tsaparang Azevedo had taken among his luggage a supply of certain herbs, which he calls 'naruleys'. He describes them as a sort of root-plant growing under the ground and having great medicinal properties against fever and other ailments. These roots were eagerly exchanged for provisions and thus they were enabled to continue their journey.

For the rest everything went smoothly. Impracticable roads are no longer spoken of, for the Babu pass, 3,000 metres high, on the frontier of Mandil presents no difficulties. Azevedo's feet, however, had suffered so badly that they refused to carry him further and the last stages of the journey had to be made in a 'gemary' a kind of palankeen with four bearers. Of Mandi it is remarked that it was tributary to the Mogul, but for the rest it was like all the other states in customs, climate and vegetation. Taking a westerly direction from Mandi to get to Lahore the party reached Mellah (?), where they had some anxious moments on account of the fanatical hatred of some Mohammedans and of the greed of the governor, who robbed them of almost everything worth stealing. But after surmounting these difficulties as they had surmounted so many others they presently crossed the last spurs of the Himalaya and left behind them the mountains "among which I had

---

[1]) Bruce, p. 64 ff., 156 ff. *Gazetteer of the Kangra District*, Part. II, Kulu. p. 79 ff.

[2]) Harcourt, p. 253. *Gazetteer of the Kangra District*, Part. II, Kulu, p. 31.

[3]) Bruce, p. 12.

[4]) Bruce, p. 169—171; Schlagintweit, II, 393; Moorcroft, (I, 184) calls the ancient capital Makarsa.

passed five months without seeing much more than snow." On his arrival, in the kingdom of Baynara at four days' distance from Lahore and subject to it, Azevedo once more modified his plan and resolved not to go to Lahore, but to turn southward at once and strike the Emperor Jahangir's great high-way to Agra. Eight days later he was in the province of Delhi, and *via* Maturam (Mathura) arrived at his point of departure, Agra, January 3, 1632[1]). His travelling-tour Agra-Tsaparang-Leh-Agra had taken him six months and five days.

We may certainly wonder how it has been possible for this interesting account to remain unknown till this day, the more so if we remember the great interest and popularity enjoyed about this time by Andrade's narrative and witnessed to by its translation into five different languages. The question must also be left unanswered whether Azevedo in his later correspondence ever returned to the subject of his Tibetan expedition. None of his letters are known to be extant, although after his journey he spent more than twenty-five years at the various mission-stations of India, last of all at Goa, where he died August 12, 1660.

---

[1]) Azevedo, MS. fol. 41 ff. *Appendix I.*

CHAPTER V

STEPHEN CACELLA AND JOHN CABRAL

When Father Andrade during his second stay at Tsaparang in 1625 was actively engaged in gathering more accurate and detailed information about the extent and the state of Tibet he learned from merchants coming from China of the existence of a great country, Utsang, situated, it was said, at one and a half months' journey east of Tsaparang [1]). To him this meant a possible new mission-field, and he wrote to India suggesting that the attempt to reach those more easterly territories should be made from Bengal [2]). Though some few published records have made it sufficiently clear that this advice was acted upon [3]), and that two missionaries, Fathers Stephan Cacella and John Cabral ventured upon a journey to Utsang, the meagre details of those records and the lack of first-hand evidence have hitherto rendered a full description of the expedition impossible. For the purpose of the reconstruction attempted in the present chapter the author has availed himself of a number of unpublished documents, letters and reports, all in the possession of the Society of Jesus. The most important among them are three letters which throw full light on the whole undertaking. The first is by Father Cacella, the head of the expedition, written from Golim or Gulim (Hugli) on July 10, 1626, and containing little more than the statement that he has arrived there from Cochin and is full of hopes as regards the rest of the journey. Of far greater interest is the second letter by the same, dated October 4, 1627, from the kingdom of Cambirasi, in which he tells at length about his stay in Cooch Behar and Bhutan. The third letter written eight months later, June 17, 1628, from

---

1) Andrade, *MS. Letter of September 10, 1625.*

2) Barretto, p. 114.

3) Barretto, p. 114—117; Cordara, II, 132, no. 114. 115; Desideri, *Difesa*, p. 2.

CHRONOLOGICAL SUMMARY

	1578.	Francis de Azevedo born at Lisbon.
	1597.	He enters the Society of Jesus at Goa.
	1627.	He is appointed to the Mogor mission.
June 28,	1631.	Starts from Agra for Tsaparang.
July 31,	1631.	Leaves Srinagar (Garhwal).
August 25,	1631.	Arrives at Tsaparang.
October 4,	1631.	Sets out for Leh in company with F. de Oliveira.
October 25,	1631.	Arrives at Leh.
November 7,	1631.	Leaves Leh for Agra *via* Lahul and Kulu.
November 26,	1631.	Arrives at Nagar, the capital of Kulu.
January 3,	1632.	Back at Agra.
August 12,	1660.	Death of Azevedo at Goa.

Hugli, is by Father Cacella's fellow-traveller Father Cabral, who briefly states their further experiences in Tibet itself [1]. As a valuable addition may be considered the communication made by the same Cabral from Utsang to his *confrères* at Tsaparang. This letter, to which we referred in the preceding chapter [2], has not been preserved but has been embodied by Azevedo in his own narrative. Fortunate as we have been in these finds we cannot but regret the loss, or at least the disappearance, of another document referred to by De Queyros in his biography of Brother Peter de Basto. Touching on Cacella and Cabral's mission to Tibet he says: "It would be like an epic to hear the accounts of the difficulties, dangers and trials which they underwent; but from this I am excused by a detailed narrative of the whole journey by Father John Cabral, which was sent to Rome after being read in Portugal, where I heard it during my stay at the college of Coimbra" [3]. This document must have been in Portugal and perhaps in Rome before 1635, in which year De Queyros left for India, but all my inquiries have failed to bring it to light again.

Of the earlier life of the two missionaries very little is known. Stephen Cacella was born at Aviz in the diocese of Evora, became a Jesuit at the age of nineteen and sailed for India in 1614. On completing his studies he was at least for some years stationed in Cochin [4]. The companion of his Tibetan journey, John Cabral, was his junior by fourteen years; a native of Celorico in the province of Beira, he had joined the Society of Jesus in 1615 and went out to India in 1624 [5].

Of the two provinces which divided between them the vast Jesuit mission in India, that of Malabar served Bengal, and as this country had been suggested as the starting-base, it was natural that this province should undertake the expedition. On April 30, 1626, the two travellers set out from Cochin together

---

[1]) The second and third letters are printed a the end of the book as Appendix II & III.

[2]) Chapter IV, p. 101. Cf. *Appendix I*, fol. 33.

[3]) Fernão de Queyros S. J., *Historia da Vida do Veneravel Irmão Pedro de Basto, Coadjutor temporal da Companhia de Jesus* (Lisboa 1689) p. 222: "Seria fazer hũa Iliada, se ouvessemos de contar as dificuldades, perigos e perplexidades que padecérão; do que me escusa a copiosa relação, que de tudo escreveo o P. João Cabral, que depoys de se ler em Portugal, aonde a ouvi, estando no Colegio de Coimbra, passou a Roma."

[4]) Cf. Besse, p. 21.

[5]) Machado, II, 617.

with a lay-brother, Bartholomew Fonteboa [1]). Their first object was the present town of Hugli [2]) situated on a branch of the Ganges-delta, where the mission had an establishment, and where information for the further journey could be gathered. They were very sanguine at what they were told, Cacella writes in his first letter, July 10, 1626, to Father Albert Laertius at Cochin. The road to Cathay is much frequented and offers no serious hindrances, whilst the people are said to behave as if they were Christians. He will, therefore, go to Cocho by Siripur, where he hopes to meet the Cathayans and to join them on their return to their country in October. He will write again from Cocho. This he actually did, as is borne out by his message of October 4, 1627 [3]), though the letter itself has not been preserved; fortunately, however, the October message repeats briefly the contents of his former letter supplemented by some other items, a chronological summary therefore, which may be quoted here to give a general idea of the undertaking. "On August 2, 1626, we left Golim [Hugli] and arrived at Dacca on the 12th. We set out again on September 5 and on the 26th of the same month we reached Azo and Pando, where we stayed for a few days with Rajah Satargit. From Azo we moved on October 8 to Biar, which we entered on the 21st. Here we had to wait for four months before we could cross the mountain ranges, so it was not till February 2, 1627, that we took the road to Runate, the furthest of the dominions of Cocho, and on the 21st we entered the kingdom of Potente. On the 23rd we began the ascent of the mountains and after eighteen days' travelling, on April 10, we met the Droma Rajah, king and great Lamba of this realm.

---

[1]) This is the date given by the *Littera Annua Provinciae Coccinensis anni 1627*, which at the hand of reports that have come in, treats of Cacella's undertaking at some length. Though on the one hand it is probable that Cordora draws on this record, yet on the other hand he wrongly assigns the departure to the year 1627.

The *Littera Annua Prov. Cocc. anni 1626* mentions March 15, 1626, as the day of Cacella's departure. It would seem therefore that the exact date cannot be fixed.

[2]) Cacella and Cabral always write Gulim or Golim. The name is supposed to be derived from 'gola', a large warehouse of bamboo, erected by the Portuguese on the site of the present town in the second part of the sixteenth century; it should be noted, however, that even before 1600 Ralph Fitch writes 'Hugeli' (Fitch, p. 182); Bernier's spelling is Ogouli (p. 176, 439).

[3]) *Appendix II*, fol. 1. — The *Littera annua Prov. Cocc. anni 1627* mentions a few details which are not found in the letter of October 4, 1627, and must have been drawn from this Cocho-letter. It was probably written in Nov. or Dec. 1626.

From Cocho they also wrote to the missionaries at Hugli as appears from a letter addressed from this place on Jan. 4, 1627, to F. Nuño Mascarenhas at Rome.

This man is held to be the greatest scholar and the most learned of all the great Lambas, who are eight in number in all the realms of Potente" [1]). After this brief survey he begins his circumstantial account.

On their departure from Hugli it was deemed prudent to take measures to provide for the safety of the two travellers; for Dacca, the first object of this stage of their journey, was at the moment ruled over by the Mohammedans during the absence of the Nababo (Nawab) at Rajabol [2]). Disguised as Portuguese soldiers they travelled under the guidance of Father Simon de Figueiredo, who had some experience of Dacca. On their arrival at Siripur Cacella left his companions behind, and proceeded further, accompanied only by Figueiredo, in order to reconnoitre. Their apprehensions had not been at all unfounded. At Dacca the two travellers and their boat were seized at once. After twelve days, however, they were set free again, and Cacella sent the boat down to Siripur to fetch Cabral. In view of the difficulties to which the further journey might give rise, Fonteboa, who was fifty years of age, was ordered to return to Hugli: he would be sent for as soon as things had taken a favourable turn. But he had hardly reached Hugli when he fell ill and died on December 26, 1626 [3]).

Continuing their way by water for three weeks the two passed some sixty 'choquis', a sort of custom-house, at each of which they had to pay toll. They were now at Azo. "Azo is the most important town and the capital of the kingdom of Cocho, a large country, very populous and rich. It used to be the residence of Liquinarane, king of Cocho, who is now dead, and the Nababo of Mogor, to whom the country pays tribute, also resides there. We passed the town and arrived at Pando, where lives Satargit, Rajah of Busna, the pagan commander-in-chief of Mogor against the Assanes [Assamese]. Pando is not a very large territory but it is densely populated. It does not stretch far into the interior but

---

[1]) *Appendix* II, fol. 1.

[2]) This can hardly be other than Rajmahal on the Ganges opposite Maldah Town, the ancient seat of government of Bengal before its transference to Dacca between 1606 and 1612. Cf. Hunter, V, 67.

[3]) According to the catalogue of the Cochin Province, dated December 1605, Bartholomew Fonteboa was born at Florence in 1576. He entered the Society at the age of twenty-three and went to India in 1602. He had been a painter at Bandraginore and perhaps in other places also, when he was sent on this expedition. His death is mentioned by Rodrigues in his letter of Jan. 4, 1627.

extends along the beautiful river of Cocho, and is the cause of the war which they are always carrying on against the Assanes, who border on Pando, the last district of the kingdom in that direction" [1]).

For a right understanding and just estimate of the particulars given by Cacella both here and in the sequel we must take a bird's-eye-view of the contemporary history of Eastern Bengal. There are at the time two kingdoms, distinguished from each other as Koch Bihar (Cooch Behar) and Koch Hajo, from the names of their respective capitals [2]). At the beginning of the sixteenth century — many say in 1509, others in 1524 — one Visu Sing became king of Cooch Behar, where he founded a beautiful town. He was succeeded by his son Nara Narayana, who extended his possessions in every direction, conquered the whole of Kamrup and made even the Rajah of Bhutan pay tribute. At the close of his life he divided his dominions giving the western half (Cooch Behar) as far as the Ṣankosh river to his son Laksmi Narayana, and the eastern half (Koch Hajo) to his nephew Raghu Rai. The division proved fatal to both parts. Laksmi Narayana very soon came into conflict with the mighty Mogul Emperor Akbar, who conquered his kingdom and only left him to rule it as a tributary king. After his death in 1622 Bir Narayana came to the throne, but he died after five years and was succeeded by his son Pran Narayana in 1627. Raghu Ral, too, did not long enjoy his new dignity; he died in 1593 leaving his kingdom to his son Parikshit, who "mounted cannon at Pandunath to the west of the Kamakhya hill [in Kamrup] and built a town at North Gauhati, whose fortifications can still be traced for many miles even at the present day" [3]). He quarrelled with Laksmi Narayana, who, now a vassal of Akbar's, called in his liege-lord's help. Parikshit was defeated and fled. But the struggle was continued by Parikshit's brother, Bali Narayana (1614—1637), who found support with the savage Ahom king. The latter took Pando, a town near Gauhati, and besieged Hajo. Though he was repulsed from its walls the war dragged on with varying success in Lower Assam.

---

[1]) *Appendix II*, fol. 3.

[2]) Cf. Hunter, X, 405 ff.; Blochmann, p. 52 ff.; Allen, p. 26 ff.; E. A. Gait, *The Koch Kings of Kamarupa* — Journal of the Asiatic Society of Bengal, LXII, Part I (1894) p. 268—309.

[3]) Allen, p. 26.

Thus it was that Cacella and Cabral on their arrival at Pando or Pandu in 1626 met the mighty Satargit, rajah of Busna, the commander of the Mogor troops against Assam. They begged an audience, presented their letters and declared their intention of proceeding to Cathay. The rajah had inquiries made among his people, but "there was no one who had any knowledge of this country except a Moor, who told us that it lay beyond a town called Cascar [Kashgar], through which one passes into it. He knew of no road leading to it from Cocho, but we were sure to find one after crossing the mountains of Potente. When we wanted to know how we were to get to the kingdom of Potente, Satargit proposed that we should consult Liquinarane, king of Cocho, at Azo, who as ruler of the country knew more of it, and was well acquainted with that people, who came down into his country by several gates" [1]). This was resolved upon and Satargit insisted on conducting them personally to Azo. No wonder that Cacella is very generous in his praise of the helpfulness of the powerful commander, who, he says, "through his knowledge and position stands very high throughout the country, as we noted at Azo, where the people in the streets cheered him as if he was their sovereign. This was also in part owing to the great liberality with which he disposes of his income amounting to about 200,000 tangas" [2]). These particulars also serve to bring out the less honourable part which this high-placed personage played a few years later. It is thus briefly related by Blochmann from the *Pádisháhnámah*. "Satrjit was the son of Mukindra, zamindar of Bosnah, which lies three stages from Dháká [Dacca] 'on this side'. Shaikh 'Aláuddín' when Governor of Bengal, had sent him along with the army which then invaded Hajo; and as he distinguished himself in the war, he had after the conquest of the country and the return of the army been appointed Thánahdár of Pándú and Gauhattí, where chiefly through his numerous dependants he had obtained the friendship of the Assamese and had also, by his influence as zamindar of Bosnah, become quite intimate with the chiefs of Koch. The governors of Bengal, who succeeded Shaikh' Aláuddín, had often called him; but he made for ever excuses and neither paid his respects, nor did he send the customary perhkash". The end was that finally he made common cause with Assam against his own sovereign,

[1]) *Appendix II*, fol. 3.

[2]) *Appendix II*, fol. 3.

and in the subsequent war he was taken prisoner and executed [1]).

It was this Satrjit or Satargit, then, who in 1626 escorted the two missionaries to Azo, which is but another name for Hajo, in fact the usual one on older maps. Thus on the *New Map of Bengal* by Matthew van den Broucke and published by Fr. Valentijn the town of 'Azo' is given in the 'Kingdom of Cos Assam' [2]). And much more recently on Dr. Griffith's map appended to the account of his Bhutan journey in 1837 we find the town of 'Azo', though in the text he and Captain Pemberton "started from Hayoo" [3]). "The beautiful river of Cocho", on which the town was situated, is of course the Brahmaputra, which name, however, seems to have remained unknown to the travellers. At the present day Hajo is at some distance from the river, which must necessarily lead to the conclusion that the Brahmaputra has shifted its bed a good way southward, which is not very surprising in the case of a stream so turbulent and liable to incessant fluctuations [4]). Cacella has no details about Hajo. In 1837 it was "a picturesque place and one of considerable local note.... The village is a large one, and situated close to some low hills; it has the usual Bengal appearance, the houses being surrounded by trees, such as betel palms, peepul, banyan and caoutchouc" [5]). Allen in his *Gazetteer of Kamrup* has nothing to say on the condition of Hajo, only mentioning the remains of an old mosque and a still existing temple of Vishnu restored by Raghu Rai in 1583 [6]).

To gain access to the king the travellers had to pass through three courts enclosed by roomy verandahs and separated from each other by strong gates. They led into a large garden, in the middle of which stood a villa, where Liquinarane awaited them. After giving them a kindly hearing he advised them to take the road to Biar, where his son Gaburrasa ruled, and thence to proceed to Potente through Runate, the furthest part of his dominions. He gave them letters of recommendation to his son, and

---

[1]) Blochmann, p. 156—59. Cf. E. A. Gait, *The Koch Kings of Kamarupa* — Journal of the Asiatic Society of Bengal, LXII, Part I (1894) p. 299.

[2]) Cf. Fr. Valentijn, *Oud en Nieuw Oost-Indiën*, vol. V. Keurlijke Beschrijving van Choromandel, Pegu, enz. enz. (Amsterdam 1726). Van den Broucke was governor of Choromandel from 1658 to 1664. — Bernier (p. 172) also speaks of 'Azo'.

[3]) Griffith, p. 208.

[4]) Cf. Allen, p. 7.

[5]) Griffith, p. 208.

[6]) Allen, p. 93, 101.

both he and Satrjit provided very liberally for their travelling-expenses [1]).

On comparing Cacella's notes on Liquinarane, king of Cocho, with the data supplied by Blochmann, Gait and Hunter, he can only mean Bir Narayana, king of Cooch Behar, because after Bali Narayana's flight to Assam the part of the country where Cacella was had not a king of its own. Moreover, Bir Narayana we know reigned only for five years and died in 1627 [2]), and Cacella writing on October 4, 1627, of his audience with Liquinarane in 1626, says that he "is now dead" [3]). Bir's successor was his son Pran.

Setting out for Biar on October 8, Cacella and Cabral arrived there on the 21st. They were not the first Europeans to enter the territory of Cooch Behar, for as early as 1586 it had been visited by the London merchant, Master Ralph Fitch. "I went from Bengala", the latter says "into the countrie of Couche, which lieth five and twenty dayes journey Northwards from Tanda. The King is a Gentile, his name is Suckel Counse [4]); his Countrie is great and lieth not farre from Cauchin China; for they say they have Pepper from thence. The Port is called Cacchogate [5]). All the countrie is set with Bambos or Canes made sharpe at both the ends and driven into the earth, and they can let in the water and drowne the ground above knee deepe, so that Men nor Horses can pass. They poison all the waters if any warres be. Here they have much Silke and Muske, and cloth made of Cotton. The people have eares which be marvellous great of a spanne long, which they draw out in length by devices when they bee young. Here they be all Gentiles and they will kill nothing" [6]).

The town of Biar is described by Cacella with a fair amount of detail. It "is situated on the river [7]) and extends so wide in a very pleasant region that in length and breadth it measures several leagues. The low buildings, which are very much like those of the other kingdoms of Bengal, offer nothing that is striking. The town is very populous and plentifully provided both with the things

---

[1]) *Appendix II*, fol. 3.

[2]) Hunter, X, 409.

[3]) *Appendix II*, fol. 3.

[4]) Shukl Gosain, brother of Bal Gosain (Nara Narayana); cf. Blochmann, p. 53.

[5]) Chichakotá, north of the town of Cooch Behar in the Bengal Duars.

[6]) Fitch, p. 181.

[7]) "Situada junto a ganga." When on his river-journey to Azo Cacella also speaks of "gangas mui frescas."

which the country itself possesses and those which come from Patana [Patna], Rajamol [Rajmahal] and Gouru [Gaur?], by whose merchants it is visited. There are many bazaars, in which is to be found everything that is produced in these parts. Biar is famous for its fruit, which are better here than I have seen them in India, and especially for its oranges of every kind" [1]).

On their arrival in the town, however, the king was not there. "Disheartened by the many inundations which desolated his capital he had removed to the interior some weeks before and taken up his abode at a spot which before had been called Colambarim and which was situated on a tributary of the same river. The Biar merchants were so eager to please their king and to found the new town that on our arrival there it had already taken the lead of Biar in the regularity and size of its streets" [2]).

The following description of the present capital is drawn by Hunter from Captain Lewin's *Account of the Kuch Behar State* (Kuch Behar 1876). "Surrounded on three sides by two small streams, both called Torshá, which enlap the town in their sinuosities, the site of Kuch Behar still recalls the days when the dread of the Bhutiás caused the position of a town to be chosen more with a view to defensive than to sanitary or commercial considerations. The town consists of a congeries of mud huts surrounding the brick mansion, which is by courtesy called the palace of the Kuch Behar Rájás. The trade is not large and the few Márwárîs, who have their small brick houses in the bázár, confine their dealings for the most part to export traffic. The small rivers above mentioned which pass near the town are only navigable for boats during the rainy season, and consequently at other times there is no communication with Bengal, save by road. The palace is a brick building, dating from the year 1828" [3]).

This description evidently does not in all points tally with Cacella's, and since even the excellent District Gazetteers fail to provide a complete account of the minutiae of topography, I applied to Babu Harendra Narayan Chaudhuri, the author of *The Cooch Behar State and its Land Revenue Settlements*, the best

---

[1]) *Appendix II*, fol. 4. This abundance of fruit, especially of oranges, in Cooch Behar, is also testified to by Blochmann's notes (p. 26) from the *History of the Conquest of Assam in 1662—1663*.

[2]) *Appendix II*, fol. 4.

[3]) Hunter, X, 359.

authority on this Indian State. After comparing Cacella's notes with the past and present state of the district he was so kind as to supply me with the following answer. "The Torsa on which the present town of Cooch Behar stands did not at the time of the traveller's visit in 1626 occupy the positions indicated in Captain Lewin's *Account of the Cooch Behar State*, but flowed further west, and was of much larger dimensions than now or in Lewin's time. The description of the surrounding country as given by Cacella is still applicable to the existing state of things to a large extent. The country around is smiling and boats of burden frequent the river even now. The river trade carried on by the Torsa was considerable in former days; up-country boats from districts lying higher up on the Ganges used to come up to the capital and go even further up two generations ago. Captain Lewin was in Cooch Behar at a time when both the channels of the river had almost dwindled into small streams. There is ample evidence furnished by the dried beds and marshes which lie all over the country about the town of Cooch Behar that the Torsa was at one time a powerful river and occupied successive positions over a laıge tract."

A royal change of residence, such as is mentioned by Cacella, is not at all rare in the history of this Indian State [1]). Thus Bir Narayana (1621—1625) removed his capital to Atharakotha and also had a residence at Mandahawasha. Later on Rup Narayana (1693—1714) moved the capital from Atharakotha to Guriahati on the eastern bank of the Torsa. The site then occupied froms part of the present Cooch Behar Town [2]). The removal to Colambarim, however, is nowhere spoken of and the place itself is not to be found in any map. One peculiarity might perhaps be interpreted to point to a place not far away, namely the fact that Cacella generally very accurate in timing his journeys omits all mention of time in the present instance. But then, which is the exact spot? For an answer to this question I have to thank the same kind correspondent. "The town of Cooch Behar," he writes, "has occupied approximately the same position as it does now from a long time past. Of course, the king of the country moved his residence now and then, but in so doing the neighbourhood was not left altogether and the old capital does never appear to have been fully abandoned. The traveller of 1626 must have been here after one such

[1]) Cf. Chaudhuri p. 228, 236, 241, 275.

[2]) Chaudhuri p. 236, 241.

temporary transfer of residence had taken place. The place spoken of in the MS., Colambarim, is very near the present town and can be none other than Kalabari Ghat [1]), which has given the name to a Taluk of the State and below which the Torsa flowed at one time. Both Kalabari Ghat and Guriahati were on the same side of the river and lay only about a couple of miles apart. Atharakotha, too, is not for from the present town; so also is Dhaliabari [2]). These places like some others formed the principal seat of Government for some time. All these sites are almost contiguously situated, and occupy different positions in a tract of country about twenty square miles in area, near and about the present town of Cooch Behar. In this connection it may be borne in mind that the name Cooch Behar is of a comparatively recent date, Behar or Nij Behar being the older appellation."

Owing to the letters of the king Liquinarane and of Satrjit they were well received at Colambarim, so that they were soon able to depart to Runate, which as we saw above, formed the Cocho border-territory towards Potente. On their arrival they met eight natives of that country, and the travellers, of course, were very eager to gather what information they could. They were not a little disappointed, however, to learn that at this season, there was no possibility of crossing the mountains on account of the snow, wind and rain, and however much they insisted, the men could not be prevailed upon to try the passage; so they were obliged to wait for four months in the kingdom of Cocho [3]).

There was nothing for it then but to return to Biar, whence they

[1]) Ghat = landing-place along a river.

[2]) Guriahati, capital under Rup Narayana, Atharakotha under Bira Narayana, Dhaliabari under Harendra Narayana.

[3]) *Appendix II*, fol. 4. — This is one of the points on which the *Littera Annua anni 1627* supplies some further details. It informs us that Cacella arrived there on the feast of SS. Judas and Simon, *i. e.* October 28. He had a man with him who had served as a guide to Father de Andrade. This man spoke with three hill-men, who offered goods for sale and who promised to conduct Cacella to the capital of Cathay (in regiam Cathay civitatem). These men were called Bottias and their country, which is very large, Botenti, or as Andrade writes Potenti. A town called Chaparanga, in which Father de Andrade lived, was unknown to these men, but if he (Cacella) would but go to king Dromarajâ, the latter would certainly provide him with a guide.

According to Cacella, the Letter goes on to say, no one knew a country called Tibet. A Persian whom he met, thought that beyond the mountains there were two vast countries, one of which was called O, the other Uturum. Reinate was on the furthermost border of Cocho; then began the country of Botenti which stretched away very far, even beyond Nepal.

sent their interpreter with letters to Hugli, with orders on his return to bring Brother Fontebona, of whose death they were still unaware. The stay in the damp and malarious climate was anything but pleasant. Almost at the same time they were attacked by a violent fever and their boys were also taken ill. Cacella recovered fairly quickly, but things began to look very black when Cabral and the servants boys grew so ill that for days they hovered between life and death, while everything was wanting for their proper attendance. November and December passed and Cabral was still ailing. But the time of departure being near Cacella went to take leave of Gaburrasa. The latter gave him letters for the governor of Runate and the people of Potente, and in token of his good-will he even presented him with a horse. He was very concerned about their departure especially "because the Cochos are in great fear of those men on account of the unconcern with which they behave in Runate without fearing anybody". During the whole of January they waited at Biar for the arrival of Fontebona and the interpreter, and at last on February 2, 1627, proceeded to Runate to get everything in readiness for the departure. Tired of waiting they had already made up their minds to do without an interpreter, however embarrassing it might prove to be, and to start on the 20th, when on the eve of their departure the long-expected one arrived from Hugli bringing the news of Fontebona's death. On Sunday February 21 they set out from the kingdom of Cooch Behar [1]).

Of all these particulars there is not a word in the older works referred to at the beginning of this chapter. Cordara sums up the whole of the journey in the statement that the travellers had to encounter innumerable dangers which it would be too long to recount [2]). Barretto is almost equally laconic. After mentioning their embarking at Cochin for Bengal he continues: "Thence they sailed up the Ganges and after long journeying they came to the kingdom of Coccio, which is situated at the foot of certain high mountains" [3]). The name Coccio had already suggested to W. Rees Philipps the conjecture, now proved to be correct, that Cooch Behar might be meant [4]).

[1]) *Appendix II*, fol. 5.

[2]) Cordara, II, 132: "Post infinita itinerum ac latrociniorum pericula, quae recensere longum esset."

[3]) Barretto, p. 114.

[4]) Hosten, *Missionaries*, p. 19.

It was after four days' travelling across mountain ranges that the two Portuguese, on February 26, reached the first village of the new territory. Difficulties arose at once. For when at Runate, they had associated themselves with an important personage of Potente, who happened to be there on business. He had not gone with them, but had sent them on before together with his servants secretly charging the latter to retain the foreigners in the village till he should himself arrive. This was to be after six months! Accordingly the villagers refused to aid them in any way towards the continuance of their journey, so that the travellers found them selves practically prisoners. After spending twelve days in trying to come to terms Cacella grew tired of these insolent proceedings and resolved to act. Leaving Cabral behind he set out, undaunted by the most terrifying accounts of the dangers that awaited him and attended only by a Christian boy and two men of Cocho who had a smattering of the language. On his way he fell in with two soldiers, whom he joined, as they said they were going to the same country. But the next day when crossing a stream the two fellows together with the two Cochos robbed the missionary of all his possessions. Left alone with his boy without a guide and having no knowledge of the language Cacella was forced to retrace his steps. This he did on a dark March night in the midst of a snow-storm which compelled him to creep on all fours along the narrow mountain paths. It was lucky then, he humorously remarks, that my fine travelling-companions had only left me my stick and my breviary to carry! On his return to the village he found that by adroit manoeuvring Cabral had made the people relinquish their hostile attitude, and that they were willing to help them on [1]). Or was it that they counted on the impossibility of the two escaping them when they should have got further on their way?

They set out on March 16 and along the ups and downs of the mountains they reached, after six days, another village called Rintam; here they found the first of the king's houses, and in it they were entertained. They were overtaken by a relative of the deceitful person with whom in Runate they had settled for their journey. He said he had come to see them to Pargão, the principal town of that country, and thence to conduct them to the king. He did, in fact, bring them to the said town in four days

[1]) *Appendix II*, fol. 5–6.

"The town of Pargão", Cacella tells us, "lies in a beautiful, wide plain, which extends very pleasantly between two mountain ranges. Just then the fields were covered with very promising crops of wheat and rice. Two rivers divide the plain, and lend it freshness and beauty, especially through the large willow-trees and the many irrigation-canals that emanate from the rivers. The houses begin at the very edge of the plain, large, high buildings with very thick walls, generally of three, four and even five stories, greatly beautified by windows and verandahs. These houses, however, do not line up into streets, rather they are sprinkled all over the plain and along the foot of the mountains. Thus they form a town of such length that the part of it which we saw and traversed must be at least three leagues, and there still remained something to be seen. For the plain continues in the way I have said till it comes to a mountain ridge which splits it lengthwise, and from which on either side descend the streams that water it. The town creeps up these slopes in two large stretches, the ends of which pass a good way beyond the two rivers. The number of inhabitants cannot be counted, and I estimate that there dwell there at least 500,000 souls. This is made possible by the way in which they live in the houses, because in each of them there are many inhabitants divided over the different stories and tenements. We arrived in this town on March 25" [1]).

At the point they have now reached the travellers must be a good way within the borders of Bhutan. This is not only borne out by their line of route, which is from Cooch Behar State northward through the mountains, but by the name of Potente, which is repeatedly used by Cacella. For Bod, or in Azevedo's spelling Pot [2]), is the general name for Tibet, while Potent or Potente means 'the end of Pot'. "Bhotan was so called by the Bengalis in the belief that it was the end of Bot" [3]).

As far as the author is aware Cacella and Cabral were the first Europeans to penetrate into this mountain region which even to-day is little known. Ralph Fitch never went there in person, though, of course, he learned some particulars about it during his

---

[1]) *Appendix II*, fol. 6.

[2]) *Appendix I*, fol. 31.

[3]) L. A. Waddell, *Place and River-Names in the Darjiling District and Sikkim*. — Journal As. Soc. of Bengal vol. LX, Part I (1891) p. 56. Cf. Waddell, *Buddhism*, p. 44, note 3; Schlagintweit, II, 102.

stay at Cooch Behar. "There is," he says, "a Countrie foure days from Couche before mentioned, which is called Bottanter and the Citie Bottia; the King is called Dermain; the people whereof are very tall and strong, and there are Merchants which come out of China, and they say out of Muscovia and Tartarie" [1]. The first, therefore, to follow the two missionaries were Bogle and Hamilton, who went through Bhutan when in 1777 they were charged by Warren Hastings with a mission to Tibet. Six years later they were followed by Turner and Saunders on a similar errand. Then Manning, Davis and Kishen Kant Bose stayed there for a short while, till in 1837 Pemberton and Griffith traversed the whole country from east to west. Like the others it was but a passing visit. But as the Bhutanese never ceased to worry the border-districts of Bengal, Ashley Eden was sent as a political agent in 1863 to come to a settlement with the unruly mountaineers. Through the hostile attitude of the government the negociations miscarried and led to a war, which ended in Bhutan having to cede the so-called Bengal Duars. Owing to the thoughtful endeavours of Mr. J. C. White the relations between the two countries have of late years been greatly improved. Beyond the accounts and reports of these travellers we have practically no information about Bhutan, and it is to them, therefore, that we shall turn to check and elucidate Cacella's notes.

The next point calling for discussion is, where did the two travellers cross the frontier? Satargit's remark about the people of Potente coming down into Cocho "by several gates" at once suggests the border-district of Bhutan, whence a series of defiles — the so-called Duars — lead down into Bengal. "The Duars of Bhutan," Markham writes, "— literally 'doors' or approaches — embrace the strip of land extending along the foot of the Bhutan Mountains in Bengal and Assam, like the 'terai' or 'murung' of Sikkim and Nepal. There are eighteen of these duars or passes, eleven on the frontier of Bengal and seven on that of Assam.... Several streams and rivers flow over pebbly beds from the gorges the different defiles to the Brahmaputra. The most northern position of the duars presents a rugged, irregular surface, occasioned by the spurs which project into the plain, and is very malarious.... Above the duars up to the snowy ridge of the Southern

[1]) Fitch, p. 183.

Himalaya, all Bhutan is a succession of lofty and rugged mountains separated by gorges, and a few valleys somewhat wider than the generality of the ravines" [1]).

As Cacella and Cabral set out from Cooch Behar, it is only the eleven passes on the frontier of Bhutan and Bengal that come in for consideration, the Assam Duars being ruled out by their geographical position. As their starting-point is mentioned Runate or Reinate, and though the name is not to be found in any map, the place must have offered evident advantages to intending travellers, for the missionaries are at once directed tither by king Liquinarane, and his son Gaburrasa is evidently unable to suggest a better place to start from. It is here that a remark of Father Desideri's, whose geographical work will form the subject of a later chapter, occurred to the writer as it seemed to point to a possible solution of the problem. When treating of the Lhoba-tribes in Southern Tibet and Bhutan he writes: "It is to be regretted that they permit no foreigner to pass through their territory. If they did, one would be able in a few days to go from Tibet to Rongmati" [2]). And in another place he calls Rongmati a province of Mogol at the other side of the Ganges, into which the principal river of Tibet flows [3]). If only Runate could be taken to be identical with Rongmati we might not unreasonably fix on the present Rangamati in Bengal as the starting-point. When these conjectures were submitted to Babu Harendra Narayan Chaudhuri I was favoured with the following reply: "The travellers of 1626 evidently went north from Behar and passed through Rangamati, which lies in the western Duars about twenty miles north-west of the modern sub-divisional town of Alipur Duar in the British District of Jalpaiguri. The place goes by the name of Rangamati Ioygaon. The whole of the western Duars formed part of the old Kingdom of Cooch Behar, and was finally lost after the second Bhutan war."

By its situation Runate- Rangamati naturally points the way to Buxa Duar which, therefore, is most likely to have been the 'door' by which they ventured into the mountains as Bogle and Hamilton did after them in 1774. One circumstance only might be interpreted to indicate a more circuitous route, namely the fourteen days of actual travel, which seems to be rather long to

---

[1]) Markham, p. xxxvii.
[2]) Puini, p. 76.
[3]) Puini, p. 100.

cover the main-road of Rangamati-Pargão. The name of Rintam cannot help us here, as the place is neither mentioned by any later traveller, nor included among the hundreds of names given by the Bhutan Blue-book of 1865. It is the difficulty which Markham encountered in discussing Manning's expedition, when he found it impossible to identify several places mentioned by the traveller for lack of adequate maps [1]). Fortunately, however, we have a firm hold again in Pargão as it cannot be other than the present town of Paro.

Almost every one of the more ancient travellers has his own way of spelling this name [2]), some of which run the Portuguese pronunciation of Pargão very close. On comparing Cacella's wonderful picture of the town with the description of the Paro valley by other travellers, by Ashley Eden for instance, who traversed those regions in February 1864, the identity appears to be beyond doubt. After describing the fort, which also serves as a palace, a five-storied building with a tower in its centre of some seven stories [3]), Eden continues: "About a quarter of a mile from the fort are the town and market-place. The town has about thirty good three-storied stone houses. The market-place is a large, open, stony square near the river. Every evening some two or three hundred collect here, but, as far as we could see, they never had anything to sell except walnuts, pears and radishes.... Paro from its situation, should be one of the largest cities in the East; situated in a perfectly level plain, easy of access from the low country, surrounded by land capable of producing great quantities of wheat and rice, only two easy marches by an excellent road from one of the chief marts in Thibet, it ought to be the entrepôt of the trade of Thibet, Tartary, China and India.... The lower and level portion of the valley is richly cultivated with rice.... the higher portion of the valley grows a very fine, full-grained wheat and barley. We rode on one occasion down the valley some ten miles, nearly where the Parchoo [Pachu] joins the Thimpoo or Tchincho River [Chinchu], along the bank of which is the Buxa Dooar route, taken by Pemberton and Turner. The Paro valley is a perfectly level plain;

[1]) Markham, p. 214, note 4.

[2]) Bogle's spelling is Parogaund (Markham, p. 62, 65), Turner's Parogong (Turner, p. 177), Saunders's Paraghon (Turner, p. 397), Manning's Parojong (Markham, p. 215), Davis's Paragong (Davis, p. 513), Kant Bose's Paragang or Paragaon (Bose, p. 141, 146).

[3]) The building was destroyed by fire in 1907.

to this point the road was an excellently made grassride along the river banks, with an avenue of weeping willows; both sides of the river are well studded with pretty villages.... There must have been some 600 or 700 houses in the valley, all of three or four stories. Cattle were numerous and the people seemed, compared with the rest of the Bootanese, tolerably contented. Just above the palace, the Parchoo is joined by another stream, which comes from a little valley to the north" [1]). Later accounts show beyond question that Cacella's estimate of the population is far too high even if every allowance is made for a possible falling off through polyandry, sickness, war and emigration. Eden and Austen estimated the population in 1864 at 3,000 souls [2]).

The visit of our Portuguese began most unpleasantly. The man who had shown himself so very obliging and had conducted them to the town, locked them up in one of the houses, robbed them of all their equipment and finally told them that they were to remain prisoners till the person with whom they had treated at Runate should arrive. This was the second attempt to bully the two unarmed strangers; but yet again they had reckoned without their host. After two days, seeing that no strict guard was kept Cacella and Cabral walked out of their prison. At once a mob collected, Cacella stood firm; violence was threatened and weapons were raised, but he declared his resolution of going straight to the king. This intrepidity told on the people and at last even assured him the support and the company of the most influential lamas of the place, and on April 5, Easter Monday, they were able to proceed.

Cacella, at this stage, does not clearly divide off the different days of travel, but from the general outline of the journey premised to his account we know that he met the king on April 10; the journey, therefore, took five days. The only reference to the character of the country is that the road led across fairly high mountains. The king was soon informed of their approach and bade them welcome in four different ways. First, after three days, they were met by a lama bringing servants and horses for the further journey. Then came a second messenger with two horses beautifully capa-

[1]) *Blue-book*, p. 213. Captain W. Lance, who accompanied Eden, briefly states that "Paro consists of a castle and numerous clusters of five and six houses placed at intervals along the plain." He was much struck with the high houses with their "wooden balconies projecting from the side of the house." (*Blue-book*, p. 235). See also Turner, p. 176, 178, 182, and Griffith, p. 284.

[2]) *Blue-book*, p. 260.

risoned for the two Fathers. A little further they were treated to tea, a favourite drink with the king and his attendants. And lastly there were sent to meet them a band of young lamas on horseback, who in their honour had horse-races in the plain. "Immediately after this we discovered among the trees a large crowd of people waiting for us, and then there was a sound of clarions and trumpets, for to these the musical instruments they use at feasts have some resemblance. A hundred young lamas, from twelve to twenty years of age, in double file came to welcome us, whilst three smaller ones walked in the middle carrying burning perfumes, which is a royal homage. Thus they conducted us to our lodging, a well-made tent lined with Chinese silk and adorned with a canopy. After a little while we were summoned into the king's presence and ushered into another tent also richly ornamented with silks. The king was seated on a raised seat draped with red silk and embroidered with gold. Close to him on his right, on a similar platform, stood a statue of his father, in front of which a lamp always burnt. There were also two raised seats for us, whilst none of the lamas, however high in rank, had any seat except the mats that covered the floor. The reception was very kind and in reply to the usual questions as to where we came from and who we were, I told him that we were "Portuguese" for the name of Franguis, by which the Portuguese are known throughout the East, was unknown to them, because foreigners never enter these mountain regions and no one could remember having ever seen or heard of their passage" [1]).

The conversation, however, continually floundered, because the interpreter they had brought with them, though he knew Persian, Hindustani and Cocho, did not understand the language of this country. It was kept up somehow through a lama of Tsaparang, who happened to be at the court and had some knowledge of Hindustani, and as the king was very anxious to converse with the strangers the lama was appointed their instructor and had to give them daily lessons in the language of the country.

We are given a full portrait of the king. He is called Droma Rajah, is thirty-three years of age, and is at once king and great-lama of this realm of Cambirasi, which is the first of the kingdoms of Potente in this region, and is very large and populous. He enjoys great

---

1) *Appendix II*, fol. 8.

regard for his gentleness, and not less for his abstinence from rice, flesh and fish, for he lives only on milk and fruits. At one time he passed three years in solitude living in a hut on a large projecting rock of a mountain without seeing or receiving anybody. With the aid of two ropes he drew up the necessary food to his inaccesible dwelling-place. He gave his time to prayer and in his leisure moments he made some images, one of which he showed us, an image of the face of God (*Imagem de vulto de Deos*) carved in white sandal wood, small but excellently made. He was also very accomplished in the art of painting; when Cacella showed him a picture of the archangel Raphael, he wished to make a copy of it and set to work at once. He enjoyed a great reputation as a scholar, and as such he was greatly respected by all the other great-lamas; for the same reason he always retained about him lamas from distant countries. The fact that the missionaries met him in tents here among the mountains was explained by the fact that people used to invite him to visit their districts, on which occasion he received great gifts of horses, cattle, rice, clothes and other articles, which formed his chief source of income. He lived with his lamas in these parts, where he was within easy reach of the others. For two months the missionaries followed the king in his progress from place to place among the mountains, after which they lived in his own house, which stood on the same mountain as his hermitage. The rocky soil really rendered the place unfit for habitation, but it had been chosen by the king with a view to protecting himself against another prince, the greatest of Potente, who lived at eight days' distance and with whom he had been at war for some years. His name was Demba Cemba. The cause of their quarrel was that the Droma Rajah had refused to give him a bone of the body of his dead father, for which he had been urgently prayed. On account of this same war the Droma Rajah did not reside in his town of Ralum, which was only at five days' distance [1]).

On wishing to test and confirm Cacella's statements about this Droma Rajah by the data furnished by Bhutanese history we meet with the difficulty that so very few reliable facts of the sixteenth and early seventeenth centuries have come down to us. Moreover, what was still preserved in the ancient native chronicles, was, White informs us, in great part destroyed by fire and earth-quake

[1]) *Appendix II*, fol. 8—9.

during the last years of the preceding century[1]). For what little there is we have to turn to Kishen Kant Bose, Waddell and White.

Down to the present day the Dharma Rajah (Cacella's Droma Rajah) or Lama Rinpotche has been the spiritual head of Bhutan, but there was a time when the dignity did not exist. Buddhism was introduced as early as the middle of the eighth century, and as more Bhuddist sects gained a firm footing in the country many quarrels arose dividing the people into different parties. The man who put an end to this was, so White tells us, Dugom-Dorji, better known as Shabdung Nga-wang Namgyal. The date of his birth is supposed to be 1534. He first lived at the Dukpa monastery at Ralung, but left it and moved to Bhutan in 1557. There he soon rose to great influence, and till his death in 1592 he used all his endeavours to consolidate his temporal as well as his spiritual power. His task was an arduous one, for not only had he to conquer and keep in hand the internal situation, but also to hold his own against the Tibetans, who tried five or six times to subject Bhutan to their rule. He was the first Dharma Rajah. Being of the Dukpa monastery he naturally made the Red-hats supreme over all; his fame soon spread to India and even to Ladakh. That he might wholly devote himself to the interests of religion he appointed a regent for temporal affairs, called Deb Rajah. After his death three incarnations appeared: that of his body became the Dharma Rajah, that of his voice the Chole Tulku and that of his mind the Thi Rinpoche [2]).

Waddell does not take quite the same view. With Kant Bose he takes it that the class ruling in Bhutan up to the middle of the sixteenth century were related to the people of Cooch Behar. Then the country was invaded by Tibetan soldiers. A lama called Dupgani Sheptun gaining great influence over them rose to be the

---

[1]) White, p. 165.

[2]) White, p. 101 ff. According to Csoma de Körös (p. 5) Nga-wang Namgyal came to Bhutan as late as in the seventeenth century. Bonin (p. 83 ff.) gives the same version of these events. He adds that this first Dharma Rajah became so renowned that the kings of Cooch Behar, Nepal and Ladakh sought his friendship. Not only they, but even Europeans did so! For in the native chronicles it is said that envoys came from the Pardoukou (Portuguese) offering their services, which, however, were declined. White (p. 102) has a statement to the same effect, adding that those strangers carried with them "some guns and gunpowder of a new sort and a telescope". Are we to see in this a vague recollection of the visit of the two missionaries blurred and refashioned in process of time? Neither Bonin nor White cite any authority beyond the 'native chronicles', of the date of which we are not informed.

first Dharma Rajah; he promoted the Dukpa sect throughout the country to the exclusion of all rival sects, which he expelled from his dominions. After his death his spirit became incarnate in a child at Lhasa. The child was conveyed to Bhutan, and when he was grown he placed the temporal administration in the hands of a regent or Deb Rajah. Dupgani Sheptun was a contemporary of the Great Lama Sonam Gyatsho (1543—1589); he seems to have been married, but his successors are celibate [1]).

If then, as the best authorities agree in asserting, the first Dharma Rajah died at the close of the sixteenth century, Cacella's host may be taken to have been the second in the line of those dignitaries. In his letter the Portuguese missionary repeatedly speaks of the father of the king, of whom the latter had made several images, and whom he worshipped as a man of extraordinary holiness and almost as a god. Though it is not explicitly stated one cannot get away from the impression that by the king's father is meant the king's predecessor, which would break the continuity of the successive incarnations, of which all writers speak. A simpler solution made plausible by the unfamiliar situation of the narrator, seems to be that Cacella, unacquainted with this curious law of succession took the Dharma Rajah's words about his predecessor as naturally referring to his father. Whether the Dharma Rajah was at the time exactly thirty-three years of age, is difficult to verify. His long beard, which Cacella says came down to his waist, might incline us to think him an older man. This beard, by the way, also played its part in the royal reception given to the travellers, for whilst it was generally worn wrapped in silk, it was now, as on all festive occasions, fully displayed to the eye [2]). The particulars about his frugal diet find unlooked-for confirmation in an account by a Bhutanese of the year 1661. The man, Blochmann relates from the *Fathiyab i Ibriyah*, was taken prisoner at Kanthalbari at the foot of

---

[1]) Waddell, *Buddhism*, p. 242. Dupgani Sheptun's name as Dharma Rajah is given by Waddell as Nag-dhan rnam rgyal bdud' jomrdorje, that of his successor as Nag-dhan 'jigmed rtags-pa, the latter being quite different from the name of White's second Dharma Rajah.

Schlagintweit (II, 138) is of opinion that the first Dharma Rajah held only a spiritual authority, the reigning native princes retaining their temporal power, which was only gradually encroached upon and at length broken by the appointment of lamas to the most important posts.

[2]) *Appendix II*, fol. 15. According to White (*Journeys in Bhutan* — Geographical Journal XXXV (1910) p. 35) the Dharma Rajah is usually depicted with a long pointed beard.

the Bhutan Hills during the war of the Mohammedans against Cooch Behar. He said that the Rajah of Bhutan was over a hundred and twenty years old. "He is an ascetic, eats only plantains, drinks only milk and indulges in no pleasures whatever. He is famous for his justice and rules over a large people" [1]).

Next to the Dharma Rajah, King and Great-lama, all accounts mention the Deb Rajah or prime minister, who conducts the administration of the country. The name does not occur in Cacella's letter at all, whilst only once and as it were *en passant* he refers to a lama "in whose hands rests the whole of the king's administration" [2]).

The town of Ralum, the residence of the king in more peaceful times, is identical with Ralung, a little over thirty miles east of Gyantse; in it is the famous Dukpa monastery, the original headquarters of the Red-hat sect of lamas [3]), which is supreme in Bhutan. The temporary residence was, as we saw, at five days' distance from Ralung, and eight from the abode of king Demba Cemba, with whom he was at war. At the end of the letter the latter king is once more referred to, when it is stated that he lived at Guiance [4]). This name seems to refer to Gyantse, but if it does, the statement is corrected by Cabral in his letter of June 17, 1628, written after his visit to Utsang. He says that the residence of Demba Cemba, "of whom we wrote in our last letter" — Cacella's letter now under discussion — is the town of Gigaci (Shigatse) [5]).

The same letter of Cabral furnishes the solution of yet another difficulty raised by Cacella's letter: the whereabouts of Cambirasi, "the first of the kingdoms of Potente in this region," of which the Droma Rajah was king. The name is not known in history, nor is it found on any map, and has been a puzzle to many. Cordara refers to it as "one of the many kingdoms which the Tartars possess between Mogor and China; on its western border lies Tibet" [6]). Barretto omits its mention altogether. Hosten surmised that Gamba or Khambha might be meant, probably thinking of Khamba Jong north of Sikhim [7]). But Cabral's letter brings light. Speaking

[1]) Blochmann, p. 67.
[2]) *Appendix II*, fol. 10.
[3]) Waddell, *Lhasa*, p. 283.
[4]) *Appendix II*, fol. 14.
[5]) *Appendix III*, fol. 2.
[6]) Cordara, II, 132.
[7]) Hosten, *Missionaries*, p. 18.

of the inhabitants of Utsang he says: "The common people differ little or nothing from those of the first kingdom, of which we wrote to you, and of which we now know that it is called Mon" [1]). This then is Cacella's Cambirasi, which again vindicates Desideri's statement that in 1627 the two travellers were in the province of Mon [2]). Csoma de Körös remarks on the name as follows: "The hill people of India who dwell next to the Tibetans are called [by the latter] by the general name of Mon" [3]), to which Waddell adds that the Tibetans call the Lepchas Monbô (Mon-pô), 'inhabitants of the Mon valleys' [4]). South of the provinces of Yarlung and Zzethang (Tsetang on the Tsangpo) Desideri places, in his description of Tibet, the provinces of Breemegiong (Sikkim), Pari (Phari) and Mon [5]), thus attributing to this last country the north-western portion of Bhutan. Kant Bose, slightly differently, says that "the country of Bhutan is bounded.... by Mem [Mon], or the Lepcha country, on the West" [6]), which raises the nicer, and perhaps unanswerable, question whether or how far the boundary-line, as drawn on our present-day maps, differs from that of the seventeenth century [7]). The reader, however, will excuse us from entering upon this point, and permit us roughly to identify Cacella's Cambirasi and Cabral's Mon with the north-western territory of Bhutan in the direction of Phari Dzong, which Kant Bose mentions as in his time still belonging to Bhutan [8]). But what about the name Cambirasi, and how did Cacella come to use it? We can throw no light upon it, unless we may suggest some connection with Chumbi, the Tibetan territory between Bhutan and Sikkim, where we are to meet Cabral once more.

To return to our travellers. Their prolonged stay at the Dharma Rajah's court afforded them an exceptional opportunity of studying

---

[1]) *Appendix III*, fol. 2.

[2]) Desideri, *Difesa*, p. 2.

[3]) Körös, p. 2.

[4]) L. A. Waddell, *Place and River Names in the Darjiling District and Sikkim* — Journal of the Asiatic Society of Bengal, LX, Part I (1891) p. 55.

[5]) Puini, p. 38, 70.

[6]) Bose, p. 128.

[7]) White, (p. 1) thinks that modern maps need revision. "The northern boundary of Bhutan has hitherto been defined by an imaginary line drawn eastward from Chomolhari to Kulu-Kangri, but my explorations prove that Bhutan extends much further to the north, as far as the snow ranges east of Kala-tsho and south of the Nelung Valley with the Wagya-la situated on the frontier, and in my map I have shown the correct boundary."

[8]) Bose, p. 138.

the daily life of the lamas. The younger ones, to the number of about one hundred, who belonged to the king's retinue, formed a kind of monastic school, whose chief occupation was to learn the rites and ceremonies of their religion. "They are called Gueloĩs," says Cacella, "and are the most important among the lamas, because they do not marry, and take only one meal a day, before midday; after that they are not permitted to take any rice, flesh or fish. Moreover, they never drink wine, and through all these things they are distinguished from the other lamas, who are of less strict observance. Twice a day, in the morning and in the afternoon they go out in a body. A great part of the day is spent in prayer, and even during the night they rise at a given signal to pray for half an hour, which they also do in the morning, chanting after the manner of clerics in the choir" [1]).

In 1783 Turner saw almost the same sort of life in the monasteries. "The Gylongs [lamas] assemble in their chapels three times a day for the performance of religious service, in the morning, at noon and at night. We were regularly roused, at the earliest dawn by the clamourous noise of numerous instruments to whose sounds they chanted their orisons. The religious from their first introduction into the order are bound by its laws to celibacy". In the main therefore, the round of duties was the same as was observed by Desideri [3]) in Tibet, and as has been described at length by Waddell [4]). Cacella's description of the lamas' dress still applies to their present apparel; their hair is short and some few grow a beard. They are forbidden to carry arms [5]).

Though continually on the move the missionaries did not neglect the study of the language. But progress was slow from the want of a good teacher, for "with the one we had we found it difficult to get on, and as he was not of this kingdom but of Chaparangue, he did not know the language of these parts, which we needed most at the moment. For although these kingdoms have one language, yet there is a great difference in pronunciation and endings, and the corruption of these in some parts of the country makes it almost a different language, especially in this kingdom,

---

1) *Appendix II*, fol. 9.
2) Turner, p. 83. Cf. Bose, p. 143–144.
3) Puini, p. 306–310.
4) Waddell, *Bhuddism*, p. 212–220; 432 ff.
5) *Appendix II*, fol. 15.

where it had undergone many changes on account of its secluded situation with little communication or trade with other countries. All the lamas, however, and nearly all the people understand the language of the other parts, so that the language we knew fitted us for all these. At the same time we endeavoured to be well up in the language of this kingdom also." At the time of writing they had got so far that they were able to compose the necessary prayers and instructions in the vernacular, which they caused to be transcribed in native characters. They were also able to read the books of the lamas though it was still a difficult business, as they were written in the best and most polished language[1]). Cacella's linguistic remarks coincide with those made by Csoma de Kőrös, who noted that the peoples of Kham, Utsang and Bhutan all understand each other though they differ in their way of pronouncing the language, and while in Bhutan the people speak a corrupt dialect of the Tibetan language, pure Tibetan remains paramount in several religious establishments and in a large part of the literature [2]). According to Hermann von Schlagintweit, however, the difference between the language of Bhutan and that of Tibet at the present day is much greater [3]).

Cacella has a great many things to say about the religion of Bhutan [4]), but it need cause no surprise that he is not always correct when giving the results of the conversations he had on the subject with the king and the king's teacher, an old lama. Neither time nor circumstances allowed of a thorough study of the intricate Bhuddist doctrine and mythology, such as, at the beginning of the eighteenth century, was permitted to Desideri, who knew Tibetan and was settled quietly in one of the monastic universities of Lhasa. Cacella's mind, moreover, was strongly biased by the rumours ever afloat in India about the existence of Christian communities in the northern border-countries, and he had hardly learned something of their religious ceremonies when the great question was mooted whether they were Christians, which, of course, was answered in the negative. When, however, they went on to declare that they were not pagans, and to speak scornfully of them, when they declined all relationship with Mohammedanism, when on

---

[1]) *Appendix II*, fol. 9.
[2]) Körös, p. 5, 7. Cf. White, p. 20.
[3]) Schlagintweit, II, 44.
[4]) *Appendix II*, fol. 10 ff.

the other hand several of their religious ideas und beliefs appeared to have a superficial resemblance to some points of Christian doctrine, Cacella's ignorance of the Buddhist Pantheon easily allowed him to take and explain everything in a Christian sense, and to see in all this, not indeed Christianity *pur sang*, but at least the garbled remnants of a Christian faith once preached in these regions. Thus he would be led to think of one God in three Persons when the Buddhist triad Buddha, Dharma and Sangha was referred to, or of the miraculous birth of a son of God, when reference was made to the birth of Avalokitesvara or Padmapani, the spiritual son of Amitabha [1]).

About the origin of their country the lamas told him that six hundred years ago there was no living being in Potente. All was water, but after it had dried up, the land remained with trees and two apes (*bugios*); from these all the people of Potente are sprung [2]). This version agrees in the main with the Tibetan which is given by Markham from a document brought by Bogle from his expedition to Tibet. There, too, it is related that first the whole of Tibet was covered with water and subsequently became dry. Then a monkey and a Rakshasi (a female fiend) met and their issue consisted of six children. These multiplied into the people of Bhot [3]).

There are two more illustrations given by Cacella of the great reverence in which the Dharma Rajah, King and Great-Lama, is held. He is offered great presents by the people that at their death he may send them to heaven. When death draws near, the king is sent for, and at the very moment of death he pulls out some of the man's hair that he may help his soul to heaven. If he should pull it out before death, great harm would ensue [4]). Waddell relates a like Buddhist ceremony in Tibet, but after death. "On the occurrence of a death the body is not disturbed in any way until the Lama has extracted the soul in the orthodox manner. For it is believed that any movement of the corpse might eject the soul, which then would wander about in an irregular manner and get seized

---

[1]) Probably this same Avalokitesvara in his monstrous eleven-headed form was meant, when Cacella was told about the legendary king with twelve heads. *Appendix II*, fol. 11.

[2]) *Appendix II*, fol. 11.

[3]) Markham, p. 341. Cf. Körös, p. 6; Waddell, *Buddhism*, p. 19, note 1. Rockhill, *Land*, p. 355. Desideri (Puini, p. 39) gives a somewhat different account.

[4]) *Appendix II*, fol. 11.

by some demon. On death, therefore, a white cloth is thrown over the face of the corpse, and the soul-extracting Lama ('p'o-'bo) is sent for. On his arrival all weeping relatives are excluded from the death-chamber, so as to secure solemn silence, and the door and windows closed, and the Lama sits down on a mat near the head of the corpse, and commences to chant the service which contains directions for the soul to find its way to the western paradise of the mythical Buddha-Amitābha. After advising the spirit to quit the body and its old associations and attachment to property, the Lama seizes with the fore-finger and the thumb a few hairs of the crown of the corpse, and plucking these forcibly, he is supposed to give vent to the spirit of the deceased through the roots of these hairs; and it is generally believed that an actual but invisible minute perforation of the skull is thus made, through which the liberated spirit passes" [1]).

When a man dies, our narrator goes on to say, the things found about him are distributed among the people, that the soul of the deceased may prosper in the other life, and those who were not present at the death of one of their relatives bring the bulk of the property of the deceased to the king that he may pray for him. This may be refered to, when Captain Pemberton relates that on the death of any head of a family, however numerous, the whole of his possessions passes to the Dharma Rajah [2]). According to Schlagintweit, however, this practice only obtains in the case of lamas who have in some way been connected with the court [3]).

As at Pando so also here the missionaries made inquiries about Cathay, but the result was equally unsatisfactory; the name had never been heard. But there does exist a country, the writer remarks, very famous here, which is called Xembala and which borders on another called Sopo, but about its religion the king could give no information. I think this may be Cathay, because it is very large and its border-country Sopo is a Tartar kingdom, which answers the description of Cathay given in the maps. That the name of Cathay is unknown proves nothing, for neither China, nor

---

1) Waddell, *Buddhism*, p. 488. Della Penna says that this operation may also be performed on a dying patient "se è spirante o spirato l'infermo". Klaproth, p. 429.

2) E. Dalton, *Descriptive Geography of Bengal* (Calcutta 1872) p. 98. — Kant Bose (p. 133) writes in more general terms: "When people die he [the Dharma Rajah] receives something at the funeral obsequies."

3) Schlagintweit, II, 140.

Tartary nor Tibet go by these names here, China being called Guena, Tartary Sopo and Tibet Potente [1]).

The little he had learned about Xembala was enough to inspire Cacella with a desire to penetrate into that distant territory. The idea of leaving had already suggested itself to his mind, for with all the outward show of kindness on the part of the king it seemed evident that mission-work — and this remained the main object which was never lost sight of — had little chance of success. In fact, he had already proposed to the Dharma Rajah that they should leave the country and join Andrade at Tsaparang. But the king had been piqued at the suggestion, for did not all the neighbouring countries know that they were his guests and that he considered this a great honour? Their departure would cast a slur upon him. Feeling, however, he had to do something he had given them leave to preach Christianity, promising to build them a house and church at Paro. Cacella had acquiesced, but after some further experience he resolved to go, while Cabral was to stay if the king made good his promise; for through a house of prayer he hoped he might draw the people. "For temples", he says, "are very few here. During the sixteen days of our mountain journey we noticed but one, right on the top of a mountain on a prominent rock, and the only thing we saw at Pargão was a lama's small house that served as a temple". This, at first sight, would seem to traverse Bogle's statement that "there are numbers of temples on all the roads" [2]); but the two are reconciled by Davis's remarks on the subject. There are he says no special buildings set apart for religious services; they are only held before altars erected in large apartments in the palaces and castles where the Gylongs are lodged, and the people are under no obligation to attend; but there are many small temples by the road-side with some representation of the deity whether painted or sculptured [3]). These may be supposed to have been there in Cacella's time, but religious worship not being their object he saw no reason to class them with temples.

The reader may remember the missionary's remark about the king's proficiency in the art of painting and about the images he

---

[1]) *Appendix II*, fol. 12. Körös (p. 2) says that among the Tibetans the Mongolian territory is called Sokpo and China Gyanak.

[2]) Markham, p. 32.

[3]) Davis, p. 493–494.

had made. Later travellers have also been struck by the artistic sense evident among the Bhutanese. "The sculpture they possess," says Griffith, "would appear to be Chinese; some of the figures were really excellent.... These people certainly have an idea of drawing" [1]). Godwin Austen praises their art of clay-modelling especially in the representation of their deities [2]), and White their skill in making bronze castings and fine metal-works of all kinds [3]).

The last pages of the letter, to which we are now coming, must be counted among the most important, containing as they do an abundance of detail about the country and the people [4]), which find ample confirmation from the observations of all later explorers.

Remembering, no doubt, his illness in Cooch Behar, he says that the climate of his new place of residence is extremely healthy. "Never in India did I enjoy such good health, and this is the case with all the people. We rarely meet a sick man, and there are a great many old people who are still hale and hearty. We have been in this hill country for more than seven months and all the time the temperature has been very moderate, neither very hot nor cold. From November to February — the letter is dated October 4 — it is colder, but they are well protected by woollen clothing."

"The country is very rich in corn, rice and cattle, all which is very cheap. There is an abundance of fruit, many kinds of pears first of all, then peaches, apples, walnuts and quinces. Indian lemons, peas and very good turnips are also found." The plentiful crops of corn and rice are referred to, as we saw above, in Ashley Eden's description of the Paro valley [5]), and all visitors extol the abundance of the fruits enumerated by Cacella [6]), whilst Markham goes so far as to call the turnips of Bhutan the best in the world [7]).

"There is no fish here," continues the missionary, "but very good dried fish is obtained either from the salt lake, which is not far distant and which also furnishes salt, or from Cocho." What

---

1) Griffith, p. 288.
2) *Blue-book*, p. 259.
3) White, p. 297 ff.
4) *Appendix II*, fol. 14–15.
5) *Blue-book*, p. 213; Cf. Bogle quoted by Markham, p. 191; Griffith, p. 277–278.
6) Cf. Bogle apud Markham, p. 19–21; Turner, p. 61; Davis, p. 516; Bose, p. 145.
7) Markham, p. 21, note 1.

lake is meant here is hard to say, perhaps the Rham lake or, still more northward, the Pomo Ċhang lake. This use of dried fish is somewhat curious, for according to Griffith there is fish, and even a plentiful supply of it, in most rivers, so that it might really form a valuable acquisition to the miserable diet of the lower classes, but, he adds, "this would not suit the benevolent ideas of the priests, who, however, appear to eat stinking fish from the Plains with considerable sangfroid." [1]) This inferior article must be obtained, according to Bogle, in the Rangpur market in exchange for Bhutan products [2]).

"Some things which are not produced here are found in other places situated at no great distance, for example grapes, from which wine is made, and which are found in a town called Compo, at twenty days' distance". Compo may be supposed to refer to Congbo or Congpo, a Tibetan province extending along the Tsangpo on the border of Kham. Desideri ascribes to it a milder climate [3]), and Waddell notes among its products a wild grape, besides an abundance of wild peaches and apricots [4]).

"This country," Cacella continues, "is also well provided with Chinese merchandise such as silk, gold and porcelain, all which comes from the same town of Compo. From here men go down into those regions, whilst trade is also carried on by them with the people of Caximir [Kashmir] *via* Chaparangue. Many strangers come to Guiance [Gyangtse], where lives Demba Cemba, the most powerful king of Potente, and which is at eight days' distance from here. To Laça [Lhasa] also, the town where the temple of Chescamoni is, come many Jogues [jogis] and merchants from other parts. But to the hill country where we live, no stranger ever turns his steps, and the only thing within the recollection of the people here is the rare passage of some jogue or other. Nor does any one come here from Cocho except the slaves, who are got from there. When some years ago an uncle of the king of Cocho, from curiosity and love of travelling, entered these mountain districts, he was caught after a few days' journeying and put to the plough. On hearing of it the king of Cocho gave orders that all the

---

[1]) Griffith, p. 274. Bose, p. 147: "The fish in the rivers they do not allow any one to kill."

[2]) Markham, p. 34. Cf. Davis, p. 503.

[3]) Puini, p. 75.

[4]) Waddell, *Lhasa*, p. 437.

subjects of those kingdoms who resided in his territory, should be taken prisoner and condemned, if his uncle was not released. This worked and he was sent back" [1]).

"This country is situated a little more than a month's journey from the kingdom of Chaparangue; hence during our stay here we have occasionally had news about the Fathers who are there, not from themselves, for they still seem to be unaware of our presence here, but from lamas coming from thence; and three times already we have written to them through others who were going there; at the same time I sent them letters to be forwarded to you *via* Goa." This frequent intercourse between Western Tibet and Bhutan may be explained from the great prestige enjoyed in both countries by the sect of the Red-cap lamas. The fact of the presence of the latter at Tsaparang is sufficiently clear from Andrade [2]), though he does not mention them by name, whilst the existence of these friendly relations between the two countries is attested by an event related in Dr. Marx's *History of Ladakh*. Under Lha-ch' endelegs nam gyal, the second successor of Sengge nam gyal as king of Ladakh, "the Bhutan State and the Bodpa [Lhasa] had a dispute. Now (the pope of) Bhutan was the patron Lama of the king of Lhadakh. (Hence) the latter sent a letter to Tibet, saying that he was prepared to take up his quarrel" [3]).

Cacella is silent about the character of the Bhutanese, but from what he experienced at the very first village and during his stay at Paro we may safely infer that his description would not have been flattering. He is more diffuse about their appearance, dress, ornaments and arms. "Their skin is fair though they hardly look it on account of want of personal cleanliness. All wear their hair long, so that it covers the ears and part of the forehead. On the face there is no hair as a rule, and on their breast they carry two pair of small well-made tongs, which are only used to pull out the hairs that might appear. Their arms are bare and the body is covered from neck to knee with a woollen garment, whilst another large piece of cloth serves as a cloak. They gird themselves with a leather belt studded with neatly worked small plates; the bracelets and amulets too, which they generally wear, are cleverly made

---

1) In Desideri's time (1715—1721) this policy of seclusion was still maintained. Cf. Puini, p. 76.

2) Andrade, *Letter of Aug. 16, 1626. Lettere Annue del Tibet* p. 7.

3) Marx, *Three Documents (1895)* p. 96.

and engraved. As a rule they go barefoot, though they know the use of leather boots and woollen stockings especially when travelling. Their arms consist of bow and arrow, short swords and daggers of excellent iron and skilfully adorned."

Subsequent visitors have noted most of these particulars. According to Turner the colour of their skin is less dark than that of the Portuguese; but cleanliness is quite beyond their comprehension [1]) — evidently a family failing, for their Tibetan cousins are hardly better than they. But their hair is worn short, which is also remarked by Godwin Austen, who likewise notes the absence of bangles [2]). With reference to the arms, finally, we may mention Turner's remark that Paro is famous for the forging of arms especially of swords and daggers and the barbs of arrows [3]).

That Cacella having made up his mind to depart was not a man to be deterred by difficulties will by now be evident to the reader, and as he was quite aware that the Dharma Rajah would not grant him a gracious leave, he would dispense with it altogether and take the first opportunity to escape from his forced detention. The particulars that follow are not derived from any documents from Cacella's hand, for none are known to be extant. In the letter that has furnished the material for this chapter he promised another account for the following year, and he did in fact write from Utsang to the Provincial in Cochin [4]); unfortunately I have not been able to recover this message. So it is to Cabral that we have to turn for the particulars about the rest of the undertaking. They are found in the letter which he wrote from Hugli on June 17, 1628, and which has more than once been referred to above [5]).

The Dharma Rajah [6]), then, had promised to build a house and

---

[1]) Turner, p. 85. Cf. Griffith, p. 266. As White (p. 12) disagrees with Turner's statement, things would seem to be less bad at present than they used to be.

[2]) *Blue-book* p. 258–259. See, however, Blochmann (p. 68), where there is question of a Bhutanese with long hair hanging down over the shoulders. — I have not come across any reference to the tongs used to pull out the hairs of the face.

From the picture of the Penlop of Tongsa and his retinue in Waddell's Lhasa (p. 268) and from the portrait of the present Maharajah of Bhutan in White's book (p 234) it is at once evident that the regular use of boots and stockings is not yet established in Bhutan.

[3]) Turner, p. 180. Cf. Markham, p. 62; Griffith, p. 267–268.

[4]) The MS. *Annua Littera Prov. Cocc. anni 1628*, which treats at length of Cacella's letter of October 4, 1627, has at the end a brief reference to another letter of the same stating that he has left the country and has moved to Utsang.

[5]) Cf. *Appendix III*.

[6]) Cabral writes Droma Rajah, like Cacella, and sometimes Lama Rupa.

church at Paro. One day, when at length the king had gone out to survey the site destined for the erection, Cacella went to a lama who was not quite friendly to the king and who was acquainted with the king of Uçangue (Utsang). From him he obtained the necessary equipment and escort, and in twenty days reached Gigaci (Shigatse), where the king resided. Being kindly received he sent for Cabral backed by letters from the king to the Dharma Rajah. Very unwillingly the latter allowed the departure on December 18, 1627, but owing to some delay on the road Cabral was not able to join Cacella till January 20. No route is mentioned in either case; but taking Paro as their point of departure the obvious route would be by Phari and Gyantse, the same as that followed by Younghusband's expedition on the march to Lhasa.

When on the day after Cabral's arrival the two missionaries were admitted into the king's presence, he again showed himself quite pleased at their coming, and he had a proclamation issued through his Great-Lama permitting them to preach their religion without let or hindrance. Moreover, he offered them a suitable residence and made ample provision for their sustenance, and being unacquainted with their habits and needs appointed a servant to inform him if at any time they should be in need anything. This generous treatment was for some time the topic of the day among the courtiers especially as the king enjoyed no reputation for liberality, even towards persons of distinction [1]). We need be less surprised, since we know from his invitation to Andrade at Tsaparang in the course of 1627 how anxious the king was to have the strangers at his court [2]).

With all these happy beginnings difficulties, engineered by the Dharma Rajah and at his instigation by the lamas, were not long in coming. For there were two emissaries of the former at the court, so Cabal informs us, evidently with orders to make our stay impossible. They first endeavoured to see the king personally, but on failing in this they made use of go-betweens. The main object, however, was to rouse against us the numerous lamas of the town by giving out that the main object of our visit was to pull down their pagodas and destroy their religion. Fortunately, he continues, none of the Great-Lamas were at court at the moment to work upon the king; but things were bad enough as they were, for

[1]) *Appendix III*, fol. 1.

[2]) See Chapter III, p. 73.

enough reached his ears to make him more reserved towards us.

Though Cabral stayed but for a few days, he has a fair amount of information to give about king, country and people. His account is not meant to go beyond the limits of a first draft and in its brevity is here and there somewhat laconic, occasionally even disappointingly so, which renders the loss or disappearance of his full account the more regrettable.

The king [1]) is a young man of twenty-two, of a fair complexion, in good health and, above all, very religious and generous towards the poor, the last of which qualities comes as a surprise after the statement made above about the king having no reputation for liberality. The royal town, he continues, is Gigaci (Shigatse) at the foot of a mountain on whose top lies a fortress, the residence of the king and all his attendants, together with a guard of soldiers. The construction of the fort is after the plan of those of Portugal, the only thing that is wanting is artillery. The insides of the houses are gilded and painted, and the wing containing the king's apartments is really worth seeing, more especially some rooms full of trinkets, which he has of every sort, for being a rich man he has the best of everything from everywhere. Hangings are much used in all his rooms, the plainer ones being of Chinese damask, but the others are equal to the very best in Portugal. The king's retainers dress very neatly, but the common people differ very little in this respect from those of the other kingdom of which we wrote to you before, and of which we now know that it is called Mon [2]).

The kingdom of Uçangue is very large, and, from whichever side it is entered, the passage, it is said, always takes a month and a half. It is moreover so densely populated that during the twenty days of my journey from there to the kingdom of Nepal my route always lay by and through villages. The climate is cold. In January and February I have crossed several frozen streams on horseback, but the snowfall is insignificant. There are large corn-fields,

---

[1]) Cabral gives no name, but at the beginning of his letter he speaks of their departure from the Dharma Rajah "to the kingdom (o reino) of Uçangue, called Deba Camba, mentioned in our last letter." As, however, Demba Cemba, mentioned in Cacella's letter, is not a kingdom but a king, Cabral evidently meant to write "to the king (o Rei) of Uçangue, called Deba Camba."

[2]) It is unnecessary for us to dwell at any length on Shigatse. The town is well-known through later writers such as Chandra Das, Rawling, Sven Hedin and others. There is a plan of the town in Das, p. 58, and a picture of the castle in Hedin, ***Transhimalaja***, I, 201, n. 105.

and I have seen no country more like Alemtejo in Portugal than this. To the northward it is bounded by the territory of the Tartars, with whom the king is sometimes at variance; the religion of the two countries, many say, is the same. Towards the east is Cochinchina, from where much merchandise arrives as well as from China, which is to the north-east. The two latter countries border on Cam (Kham), from where the musk comes. Xembala is in my opinion not Catayo but what in our maps is called Great Tartarea; Catayo lies more to the north [1]).

In this kingdom of Uçangue reside the chiefs of all the sects of lamas, hence they call it the school of their religion. Their monasteries, which they call Compas (Gompas), are not like ours but each Great-Lama has his own town, where he lives only with his own lamas. The Compa of the lamas of Chaparangue is situated near the fort here, at two cannon-shots' distance, and on account of this we get tidings about our Fathers every day, though they are at a month's distance away from us. These lamas are not very favourably regarded by the king, because he says they are a bad sort. The Great-Lamas live in royal splendour, and among them the Lama Rupa (the Dharma Rajah), about whom so much has been written, ranks in the fifth place, from which you may conclude what the others will be like. Fortunately none of them as a rule are in attendance on the king [2]).

Though Cabral does not mention the name of the "Compa of the lamas of Chaparangue", he cannot mean anything else than the famous monastery of Tashi Lhumpo, which at the present time is the residence of the Tashi Lama or the Pantchen Rinpotche. The castle of Shigatse according to Turner stood "upon a prominent ridge of the same rock on which the monastery is built" [3]). Its situation is estimated by Rawling at "half a mile to the east of the town on the left bank of the river" [4]).

The stay of the two Portuguese at Utsang nearly coincides with the turning-point in Tibetan history. At the time a king still resided in the castle, and the temporal and the spiritual powers were still severed, but only a few years later the ambitious Ngavang Lobsang would be at the head of Tashi Lhumpo and revolutionize

---

[1]) Compare Cacella's ideas of Xembala on p. 147.

[2]) *Appendix III*, fol. 2.

[3]) Turner, p. 295.

[4]) Rawling, p. 178.

the whole system of government. For very soon, so we learn from Tibetan records, he came into conflict with a king of Tibet or of Eastern Tibet [1]) and defeated him with the aid of tribes from the Koko-nor territory. In 1642 he began the building of the Potala at Lhasa, visited Pekin and managed so well that the emperor invested him with the temporal and spiritual authority over the whole of Tibet. He was the first Dalai Lama, the Gyalba Rinpotche or 'Gem of Majesty', and created for the head of Tashi Lhumpo the dignity of Tashi Lama, second only to his. By establishing the successions of the Dalai Lamas and Tashi Lamas as they now exist, he made the turbulent Yellow-caps, the Gelugpa sect, paramount in Tibet. At the time of Grueber and d'Orville's stay at Lhasa in 1661 Ngavang Lobsang was at the zenith of his power.

That Tashi Lhumpo, like Bhutan, had relations with Tsaparang need not surprise us, for we know from Andrade's letters that besides Red-caps there were also Yellow-caps in the place of his residence [2]). The head of Tashi Lhumpo even went to visit the country of Guge in 1610 at the invitation of its rajah [3]).

Whereas Cacella when in Bhutan could not bring himself to see that those people with their curious religious ceremonies were pagans, Cabral now admits it. "I begin to believe that these countries are pagan, both because they say they are, and because I have found that they have the same pagodas as the kingdom of Nepal and some kingdoms of Bengal. They only differ from the latter in not having their superstitions of caste and food." Though he has already touched on Cathay, at the end of his letter he returns once more to this land of fable — how little has hitherto been the fruit borne by Goes' journey and Ricci's letters! "As regards Catayo the more we learn of that country the less we know of it. One of the king's lamas told me that there was a country called Cata, whose religion he did not know for certain, but of which he had been told that it was very old and that it differed from that of these countries. The road to it he said is by Coscar [Kashgar], a well-known town, which accords with the report of Father Jerome Xavier, in which the same town is spoken of [4]).

---

[1]) On this point the records are not decisive, and, for all we know, the adversary may have been the king of Shigatse himself, who, as Cabral informed us, was no friend of Tashi Lhumpo and did not sympathize with its lamas.

[2]) Andrade, *Letter of Aug. 16, 1626. Lettere Annue*, p. 7.

[3]) Sarat Chandra Das, *Contributions on the Religion, History etc. of Tibet* — Journal of the Asiatic Society of Bengal, LI, Part. I (1882) p. 26.

[4]) *Appendix III*, fol. 2.

Twice in these last pages mention has been made of Nepal, a name as yet unheard of in the West; indeed, as far as can be ascertained, Cabral was the first European to traverse this Himalayan state. The object of this journey together with its general outline are given in the same letter. "It [the object] was, in the first place, to discover this new route through the kingdom of Nepal, in order that the mission might be continued through it, as the road through Cocho is so dangerous and uncertain. I have also come [to Hugli] to settle some affairs in connection with this mission, which I think may become one of the most glorious of the Society of Jesus; it is the gate to the whole of Tartary, China and many other pagan countries." Returning to the subject at the close of his letter he says: "The road to those countries is not through Cocho but through Nepal, which borders on Mogor. In Patana [Patna] and Rajamol [Raimahal] the road is perfectly safe and is used by many traders. The king gave me a captain to conduct me to Nepal. The latter carried letters and presents for the king of Nepal requesting him to help me in whatever I might need, as he esteemed me highly. This was done by the king of Nepal and very kindly he directed me to Patana, where I fell in with some Portuguese, with whom I have come to Gulim [Hugli], from where I write this letter. About the kingdom of Nepal I shall write to you at greater length later on, as I hope to get news there from Father Cacella and about the events that have taken place."

With the absence of all detail about this winter journey the reader is left to imagine those paths and passes buried under deep snow at an altitude of many thousand feet, and in the midst of these the lonely traveller with his one or two guides, whose language he hardly understands, and thence to form his judgment of the grit and intrepidity required to undertake it and carry it through. As they were the bearers of letters for the king of Nepal, their road no doubt went by Katmandu, whither thirty years later the Fathers Grueber and d'Orville were to direct their steps on quitting Lhasa.

Here we should have to break off the discussion of this remarkable mission-journey and leave the reader in uncertainty about the further adventures of the two men, whom he has followed for a while on their wanderings through Bhutan and Tibet, but for another letter of Cabral's written from Utsang to the missionaries at Tsaparang, the contents of which have been preserved by Azevedo in the account of his own expedition [1]). Azevedo does not say when and where it was written, but since the contents show that it was written from Shigatse, as will I think clearly appear in the sequel, and since it was received at Tsaparang some days after August 26, 1631, it must have been despatched about the end of July 1631, for the two towns of Tsaparang and Shigatse are by Cabral's own statement at one month's journey distant from each other [2]). Three years therefore lie between this letter and the one discussed above.

Azevedo summarizes Cabral's letter as follows:

"Father Stephen Cacella and myself went to this mission from Bengal. The Rajah Mana Rupa retained us for seven months on the way, after which F. Cacella set out for Uzangue and despatched me to Bengal to fetch some things that were needed. I tried to find a road [3]) and reached Oguly [Hugli] just when the Indian fleet arrived [June 1628] and with it Father Manuel Diaz with orders from Father Alberto [4]) to go to the mission if Father Cacella should send for some Fathers. As the latter had not invited any one, I objected to the departure of F. Diaz, who had been sent by the Father Rector of Bengal with unconditional orders. These difficulties protracted my stay at Oguly so long that I missed the favourable season [moussam] to return to Nepal. So I went to Cocho, from where I sent word to Father Cacella requesting him to send me a royal escort that I might pass on; for as the country of Cumba [Chumbi between Bhutan and Sikhim] bordering on that of Cocho had no king, it could not be traversed without the protection of an escort. My letter arrived so late that Father Cacella had already left for Bengal, because he could not, on account of the snow, get through to Chaparangue, for which place he had first set out. Finding, when in Bengal, that I was in Cocho with Father Diaz, he came to fetch us at once, although he was so ill that he could hardly stand, and in September 1629 he set out with Father Diaz, leaving me in Cocho with some luggage and intending to send for me in January. The difficulties they had to contend with on their way were such that in consequence of them

---

1) *Appendix I*, fol. 33.

2) *Appendix III*, fol. 2.

3) "Fuy para via de palpo", or in modern Portuguese "fui ás apalpadellas."

4) Father Albert Laertius, Provincial of the Province of Malabar.

Father Manuel Diaz died on November 3 in the kingdom of Morongo [Morang] [1]).

"Father Cacella reached Uzangue in such a state of health that only seven days after his arrival, even before he had seen the king, God took him on March 6, 1630 [2]).

"The king was deeply impressed by his death and at once sent for me to Cocho, but as it was winter the summons could have no effect. This year, 1631, he repeated his request by sending an escort, upon which I resolved to go in order not to offend him and not to leave the goods of the church in his hands. For a month and a half I have been here and have met with a very kind reception on the part of the king. Father Provincial Gaspar Frz [Fernandez] does not show himself anxious to continue the mission, and he will relinquish it on hearing of the death of the two Fathers. I have asked him to place me under your authority . . . It will be for you to decide whether it is desirable to establish a permanent station here, to which the king will not object" [3]).

This last suggestion commended itself to Azevedo especially because it was in Utsang that the great schools of the lamas were found, and before setting out for Leh he may have instructed the missionaries of Tsaparang to communicate with Shigatse. Though we cannot attain to certainty on this point, we may quote here from a letter of F. de Castro written from Mogol on Aug. 8, 1632, in which with reference to the mission of Tsaparang he says: "According to letters received here the Superior has gone to another mission-station established by the Fathers of the Cochin

[1]) Manuel Diaz was born in 1592 at Alpalhão or Aspalham in the diocese of Portalegre, became a Jesuit in 1608 and left for India in 1614. He worked first in Cochin, then for one year he was Rector of the college of St. Thomas (1627–1628), after which he received orders for Cacella's mission. Cf. Besse, p. 22, note 1; Sommervogel, III, 44, and IX, 212, 1763. The year 1630, generally given as the year of Diaz's death, is here shown to be incorrect. According to A. Franco (*Imagem de Virtude em o Noviciado de Evora*, (Lisboa 1714), p. 495) his death occurred at a village called Oacho.

[2]) Cacella had only reached the age of forty-five. The remark that he had arrived in Utsang but had not seen the king allows room for Desideri's statement (Difesa, p. 3) that he died and was buried at Shigatse. He certainly did not die in Guge, Western Tibet (Besse p. 20, note 4), nor at Tsaparang (De Queyros, *Historia da Vida do Veneravel Irmão Pedro de Basto*, (Lisboa 1689) p. 222). The *Littera annua anni 1630* does not record the death of the two missionaries. All it has to say about Tibet is: "There are three Fathers in the Cathay mission". It is only in the report for 1632 that the death of Diaz and Cacella is officially noted. The annual letter for 1633 passes over the Tibetan mission in silence.

[3]) *Appendix I*, fol. 33.

Province in the town of Uçangue, whose king greatly favours the mission. Thus the Superior hopes to help his own mission, because all the kings of Tibet obey the great king of Uçangue".

Beyond these few lines there is nothing in any letters private or official referring in any way to this new enterprise; hence it may safely be assumed either not to have been started at all or to have had no appreciable result.

If we are to believe Cordara, Cabral's apprehensions that the Provincial might be unwilling to continue the undertaking were well founded, and he was recalled to Malabar [1]). But whether recalled or not, he was certainly back at Hugli in 1632, where he was an eye-witness and nearly a victim of the siege and sack of this settlement by Shah Jehan's army, as he himself informed his Provincial in a long letter written from Ceylon, November 12, 1633 [2]).

There is one more mention of Utsang, in the report, already known to the reader, which was drawn up at Tsaparang on the state and prospects of that mission by Father Coresma on August 30, 1635 [3]). From like premisses he arrives at a like conclusion; as in the case of the mission of Tsaparang, so also in that begun by Cacella and Cabral his verdict is: the risks are too great, the promise of success also is too uncertain, the king's only object is to obtain presents from the missionaries.... therefore let the mission be relinquished.

This settled the matter. There was only one who stood up for the continuance of the mission. In the annual report for 1643 Father Simon de Figueiredo, the same who in 1626 accompanied Cacella

---

1) Cordara, II, 132. Cordara's notes are incomplete and unreliable. After stating that the efforts of the missionaries in Cambirasi came to nothing, he continues: "Then they went to the neighbouring country of Urang with similar result. On hearing this in Cochin Father Laertius called them back to the Malabar province." Not a word is said about the death of Diaz or Cacella, whilst the mention of Laertius as Provincial is incorrect, as in 1631 that post was held by Fernandez as appears from Cabral's letter.

I have made no reference to Barretto's account (p. 115—118) as his information is of no special value for the right understanding and appreciation of the expedition. He is more detailed than Cordara and refers to Cabral's departure from Utsang, or Catai as he calls it, and to Cacella's death in the same country. On Diaz he is altogether silent.

2) Cabral's short visit to Tibet is only an episode in the long tale of his travels. For years after he was engaged in mission work not in one place but in Cochin, in Japan, in Tonkin, then at Malacca and at Macao, and lastly as Provincial once more in Japan from 1650 to 1654. On his return he remained in the province of Goa, and among others was stationed for four years at Salsette. He died at Goa on July 4, 1669. Cf. Sommervogel, II, 494, and VIII, 1956.

3) Cf. Chapter III, p. 84.

to Dacca, addresses an eloquent appeal to Europe in favour of 'Botente'. Want of men and money has compelled us to give up the mission, but we cannot leave the country entirely to itself. Great sacrifices have been made, Brother Bento de Goes has died in discovering it; after him Fathers Cacella and Diaz have passed away — let us not be less generous. The people is worth it, it is really good, and the state of things there is better than in Japan or Ethiopia. Let those who ask to be sent to these countries, not forget the poor 'Bottos'. "Ite angeli veloces, ite ad gentem exspectantem!"

Figueiredo's desire was not to be fulfilled. No more missionaries went to Utsang to take up Cacella's work and to pray over his lonely and forgotten grave beyond the mountains, whilst even the memory of his daring enterprise has grown dim and has almost sunk into oblivion.

CHRONOLOGICAL SUMMARY

STEPHEN CACELLA.	JOHN CABRAL.
1585. born at Aviz (Portugal)	1599. born at Celorico (Portugal)
1604. joins the Society of Jesus	1615. joins the Society of Jesus.
1614. leaves for India.	1624. leaves for India.

April 30	1626.	departure of Cacella and Cabral from Cochin.
July 10		letter of Cacella from Hugli to F. Alb. Laertius at Cochin.
Aug. 2		departure from Hugli.
Aug. 12		arrival at Dacca.
Sept. 5		departure from Dacca.
Sept. 26		arrival at Azo (Hajo).
Oct. 21		arrival at Biar (Cooch Behar).
Febr. 2	1627.	departure from Biar for Runate (Rangamati).
Febr. 21		arrival in Potente (Bhutan).
March 25		arrival at Pargão (Paro).
Oct. 4		letter of Cacella to Laertius from the kingdom of Cambirasi.
Nov. (?)		departure of Cacella for Shigatse.
Jan. 20	1628.	arrival of Cabral at Shigatse.
Jan. (end of)		departure of Cabral for Hugli *via* Nepal.
June 17		letter of Cabral to Laertius from Hugli.
?	1629.	return of Cacella to Biar from Shigatse.
Sept.		Cacella's second journey to Shigatse, starting from Cooch Behar in company with F. Manuel Diaz.
Nov. 3		death of Diaz at Morang.
March 6	1630.	death of Cacella at Shigatse.
?	1631.	second journey of Cabral to Shigatse.
June (middle of)		arrival at Shigatse.
June (end of)		letter of Cabral from Shigatse to the missionaries at Tsaparang.
May or June	1632.	return of Cabral from Shigatse to Hugli.

LIST OF MANUSCRIPTS [1]

Copia da Carta do Pe. Estavão Cacella pera o Pe. Provincial de Cochi', escrita de Bengala no Guli' a 10 de Iulho 1626 (1 pag. 29 × 20 cm.).

Letter of F. Anthony Rodrigues to F. Nuño Mascarenhas at Rome, dated Ogolim (Hugli) January 4, 1627.

Relação que mandou o Pe. Estevão Cacella da Comp.a de Jesu ao Pe. Alberto Laercio, Provincial da Provincia do Malavar da India Oriental, da sua viagem pera o Catayo, até chegar ao Reino do Potente. *in fine*: Deste Reino de Cambirasi, e casa deste Rei em 4 de Outubro de 1627. 15 pp. (29 × 20 cm.).

This MS. is not in Cacella's handwriting, it is a copy probably sent to the General at Rome.

Annua Littera Provinciae Coccinensis anni 1627 ad Adm. R. P. Mutium Vitelleschi, *in fine*: Coccini 5. Dec. 1627. Ignatius Lobo. $5^1/_2$ pp. (31 × 21 cm.)

Relação da Missão do Reino de Uçangue cabeça dos do Potente, escrita pello Pe. João Cabral da Comp.a de Jesu. *in fine*: 17 de Junho de 1628. $2^1/_2$ pp. (29 × 20 cm.)

It appears from the letter that it was written at Hugli. The handwriting is not Cabral's, and this copy was probably meant for the General at Rome.

Annua Littera Provinciae Coccinensis anni 1628 ad Adm. R. P. Mutium Vitelleschi. *in fine*: Coccini 2 Jan. 1629. — Ignatius Lobo.

Annua Littera Provinciae Coccinensis anni 1630 ad Adm. R. P. Mutium Vitelleschi. *in fine*: Coccini 5. Dec. 1630—Ignatius Lobo.

Annua Littera Provinciae Coccinensis anni 1632 ad Adm. R.P. Mutium Vitelleschi. *in fine*: Coccini 3 Dec. 1632. — Antonius Carvalho.

Annua Littera Provinciae Coccinensis anni 1643 ad Adm. R. P. Mutium Vitelleschi. *in fine*: Coccini 1 Dec. 1643. — Simon de Figueiredo.

---

[1] All MSS. are in the possession of the Society of Jesus.

CHAPTER VI

JOHN GRUEBER AND ALBERT D'ORVILLE

If a journey from Pekin to the Koko Nor and thence through Lhasa and the territory of Nepal to Agra in India would be a considerable feat even at the present day, and secure for the traveller a place of honour in the annals of Tibetan exploration, this claim would become the more urgent if the journey were made 250 years ago. Yet this was done by two missionaries, and what Ritter wrote in 1833 still remains true that, as Grueber and d'Orville certainly were the first, so perhaps they still are the only Europeans of modern times who have traversed this route [1]). Consequently their names do, indeed, find a place in every work of importance on Tibet [2]), but the remark made in the preceding chapters again applies here, that the details of their journey as given in those works are either exceedingly scanty or on several points incorrect. It was this neglect that led Richard Tronnier to publish an excellent article intended to set the two travellers in their rightful place and to draw attention to the scientific value of their expedition [3]). But however grateful one must be for the results obtained, more and in part unpublished documents enable us to give a still fuller and truer picture both of the men and of their work. How little they are known outside the small circle of specialists is sufficiently borne out by the fact that Grueber's name will be looked for in vain in the *Allgemeine Deutsche Biographie* and that his companion d'Orville has not been able to secure a place in the *Biographie Nationale de Belgique*.

---

[1]) Ritter, II, 453.

[2]) Cf. Ritter, II, 453 ff.; Von Richthofen, I, 671 ff.; Markham, p. lvi ff. & p. 295—302; Peschel-Ruge, p. 588; Launay, I, 31; Wegener, p. 11, &c. &c. The principal among these authors will be dealt with in the course of this chapter.

[3]) Richard Tronnier, *Die Durchquerung Tibets seitens der Jesuiten Johannes Grueber und Albert Dorville im Jahr 1661* — Zeitschrift der Gesellschaft für Erdkunde zu Berlin (1904) p. 328—361

At the outset it should be stated that there exists no complete account of the expedition allowing us to follow step by step the wanderings of the travellers. The record must be pieced together from data drawn from different sources of unequal value, — a process which necessitates a somewhat lengthy critical disquisition.

Four principal sources are to be distinguished: i) a number of letters from Grueber's hand — ii) a short account by Kircher in his *China Illustrata* — iii) an Italian notice embodied by Thévenot in his *Relations de divers Voyages Curieux* — iv) ten answers given by Grueber to as many questions proposed to him by the Archduke of Tuscany. About each of these a few words must be said.

1. Grueber's earliest letter was sent from Surat in India on March 7, 1658, to Father John Haffenecker, S. J., rector of the college and of the university of Gratz in Styria. A copy of the original Latin is in the state-archives of Brussels and was first published by H. Bosmans, S. J., in his *Documents sur Albert Dorville de Bruxelles* [1]. A free German translation had been given to the public by J. Stöcklein, S. J., in his collection of letters *Der Neue Welt-Bott* [2]. The second letter, bearing no date and addressed to Father John Gamans at Aschaffenburg, was written after Grueber's return from China, most probably in the beginning of 1664, in any case before his second journey eastward, since the closing words are: "This as regards China, to which with God's help I shall return shortly" [3]. For our present purpose this letter is the most important. It is to be found in Thévenot's book after the Italian notice, which will be discussed presently. The third letter, addressed to Kircher from Venice on May 10, 1664, at the beginning of the attempted second journey to China, may be found in *China Illustrata* [4]. The fourth and fifth letters were written during this

---

[1] Bosmans, p. 62—65.

[2] Stöcklein, I, 111—112.

[3] "Haec de regno Sinensi, ad quod Deo dante intra pauculum tempus revertar". In his *Bibliographie Historique de la Compagnie de Jésus ou Catalogue des Ouvrages relatifs a l'histoire des Jésuites depuis leurs origine jusqu'à nos jours* (Paris 1864) n. 1011, p. 141, Aug. Carayon, S. J., calls Grueber's correspondent 'Grammans' and remarks that the letter was written from Vienna. Holdich (p. 71) speaks of a letter dated "Rome 1664", of the existence of which the author is not aware; probably the letter to Gamans is meant.

[4] Kircher, *China Illustrata*, p. 222—224. From a collation with the original it appears that Kircher has omitted the first part of the letter dealing with the return-journey from Venice onward.

same return-journey to an unknown correspondent, who had evidently applied to him for detailed information on several points; they are dated "Danzig December 11, 1664", and "Breslau March 14, 1665". They are given by Thévenot after the second letter.

While looking for fresh evidence I was fortunate enough to obtain copies of nine other unpublished letters of Grueber to Kircher. They were written between 1664 and 1671, and though they are not of very great direct value for the purpose of a reconstruction of the journey, yet there are many small details contained in them which may serve to throw light on several obscure points. For a fuller account of these letters the reader is referred to the List of MSS.

Finally we must note two Latin documents from Grueber's hand. One is a eulogy on d'Orville, who after being his companion as far as Agra, had died at this town shortly after their arrival; it was written at Rome on March 29, 1664, and is given in full by Bosmans [1]). The other, likewise an obituary notice written in memory of Father Henry Roth, who accompanied Grueber from Agra to Rome, was composed on January 30, 1670, at Tyrnau in Hungary. It is among the state archives at Munich [2]).

2. Of far greater importance naturally is Kircher's account [3]) written as it was under instructions from Grueber and Roth, as is clearly stated in the introduction. [4]) Grueber himself touches on this point in his Danzig letter : "As regards the geography, although I have made a good many notes I cannot tell you anything at present having left everything with Father Kircher at Rome, who is engaged in publishing it.... All will be printed at Vienna by order of his Imperial Majesty and will soon see the light [5]).

---

[1]) Bosmans, p. 82—85.

[2]) *Jesuitica in genere*, Fasc. 13, n. 215.

[3]) Kircher, *China Illustrata*, p. 64—78. The remarkable illustrations are from drawings by Grueber.

[4]) Kircher, *China Illustrata*, Proemium ad lectorem, p. 2: "Qui [Grueber et Roth] dum haec scribo mecum continuo morantur eaque quae quovismodo profutura norunt, communicare non cessant."

[5]) Kircher's account, therefore, is not composed from letters as is thought by Von Richthofen (I, 672, note). In this he probably follows Markham, who on p. lvii of his Introduction asserts that the original account of the journey has been preserved in a small booklet by Carlieri; of this an extract is supposed to have been furnished to Kircher, whilst both the booklet and the extract were printed by Thévenot. Markham may have been led into this error by the heading *Ex litteris Grueberi Kirchero inscriptis*, under which Thévenot prints Kircher's account with a few alterations necessitated by the omission of the illustrations.

Why this order was not carried into effect and why the book should only have appeared in 1667, not at Vienna but at Amsterdam, I have not been able to ascertain. In Grueber's opinion, then, Kircher was his official editor, and bearing this in mind one can hardly understand why this learned writer should have left his work in so many points incomplete and incorrect, especially as he had Grueber so near him. Was it that he did not grasp the significance of the journey so that many topographical observations, and those of first rate importance, are entirely wanting in his account?.... Or may perhaps Grueber have to be made answerable for the shortcomings of Kircher's book, because he did not furnish full information to the writer? Did the preparations for the return-journey and other engagements absorb most of his time during his two and a half months' stay at Rome, so that his editor had to be satisfied with a rough and ready account of the expedition and a promise of further details at some later date? It would seem to be so. For in his letter from Görz February 26, 1666, Grueber informs Kircher, that he will shortly comply with his request and send the whole journal, together with the complete history of the kingdom of Barantola (Lhasa), which he will be free to dispose of at will. He will also try to add drawings of some remarkable things he has seen on his journey [1]).

Evidently therefore Kircher had applied for more details than he had at his disposal, that he might use them in the composition of his book. When the long-expected journal did not arrive and he was forced to go to press without it, he still hoped one day to have it for a possible second edition, for he goes on insisting on its being sent him, as is clear from all those of Grueber's later letters of which I possess a copy.

Grueber himself greatly regretted the deficiencies of Kircher's account. Thus on September 20, 1669, he writes from Tyrnau, that he has arrived at that town after an absence of two years as an army-chaplain in Transsylvania. On a trip to Leopoldstadt, situated in the neighbourhood, he had first come across the *China Illustrata*. Grateful for the honourable mention of his expedition he adds: "I wish you had at least sent me the headings of the chap-

---

[1]) Grueber, *Letter from Goritia, February 26, 1666*: "Proxime mittam Vestrae Reverentiae totum petitum itinerarium meum cum tota historia regni Barantolae; utatur his prout iudicaverit in Dño; conabor etiam delineationes aliquas addere aliquaram rerum curiosarum quas in itinere conspexi."

ters before going to press; I should certainly have supplied you with several data of no small importance. These I intend to send you at some future time, perhaps shortly, together with the whole of my journal, which as yet I have not been able to finish on account of my continuous work among the soldiers. There are certainly points in *China Illustrata* that need correction, especially the drawings, but it is better to leave things as they are, though I shall send you the emendations for insertion in case the work should be reprinted" [1]).

Shortly after on October 7 writing from Tyrnau he tells Kircher that he has ordered a copy of *China Illustrata* from Vienna at his correspondent's charge, and invites him to remit the price of it at once, if he wishes to continue in the writer's favour and to obtain possession of the marvellous things which he is engaged in writing, and of the important drawings and the corrections of mistakes already made [2]). To this Kircher must have replied at once for on December 13, 1669, Grueber informs him, that as he has again asked for the journal at the request of the Duke of Etruria, he sends him the first chapter; the second is to follow after a week. Want of time has prevented him from making the drawings, which he will send in sets. In a postscript he insists on Kircher letting him have his opinion on the plan of the journal, whether he is to continue on the same lines or not [3]).

A month later another letter goes from Tyrnau to Rome, but the tone is less friendly. He has received no reply to his last letter, so he will not send any more, before he has been satisfied that his letters and the first instalment of the journal have been duly received. He then continues: „An opportunity is not wanting, if I wish

---

[1]) Grueber, *Letter from Tyrnau, September 20, 1669*: "Utinam mihi vel saltem titulos ante impressionem misisset, certe plura suggessissem non parvi momenti, quae etiamnum reservo fortasse brevi Vestrae Reverentiae transmittenda una cum toto meo itinerario, quod hactenus ob continuas occupationes inter milites absolvere non potui. Sunt quidem aliquâ in Chinâ Illustratâ quae maxime quoad delineationem emendatione indigerent, sed melius est sic permittere, mittam tamen veram correctionem Vestrae Reverentiae, ut, si forte opus reimprimeretur, emendari posset."

[2]) Grueber, *Letter from Tyrnau, October 7, 1669*: "si alias invenire vult gratiam in oculis meis et obtinere mirabilia quae iam sunt sub manu et calamo cum correctionibus priorum male a me per Vram Revtiam intellectorum et cum delineationibus non spernendis."

[3]) Grueber, *Letter from Tyrnau, December 13, 1669*: "Mitto primum caput, sequenti septimana secundum; delineationes facere non potui, quia tempus non habui; mittam plures simul .... Circa modum itinerarii quem incepi Vestra Reverentia mihi suum iudicium transmittat utrum sic peragendum sit an non, ut me dirigere possim."

to use it, any more than draughtsmen and protectors, to have all my notes printed at Vienna" [1]). On march 17, 1670, there is a third letter from the same place: Kircher's reply has meanwhile reached Grueber, but it does not contain a word about the first chapter. Kircher would also seem to have applied for a contribution towards the expenses of the publication, for Grueber refers him to the Emperor, who has promised ample pecuniary support. Finally he gives his correspondent to understand that the portrait of the Emperor of China carrying a stick and accompanied by a dog, as given in *China Illustraia*, will be taken as an insult in that country. The Emperor should be represented standing or sitting at a table covered with books and mathematical instruments; so he requests Kircher to have this changed accordingly in the Italian edition [2]). He himself will protest against this representation in the journal he is going to publish. Kircher may have taken offence at these remarks, for in a letter of December 23 from Jaurin (Raab) Grueber reverts to the subject saying that the print will not do and that it shall be differently printed in his own account, which he hopes will be given to the public in the course of the following year [3]). These remarks would seem to point to Grueber's intention of keeping the publication in his own hand. Be this as it may, his hopes were not realised, for he writes from Trencsin, May 2, 1671: "Being engaged in laborious and incessant work among the soldiers I have, as yet, been unable to finish the work I have begun; but now that I have more leisure I hope with God's help to have the whole completed before the end of autumn" [4]). Did this expectation come true, or was this "itinerarium" ever finished at all? And if so, where did it get to? What has become of the first chapter, which Kircher must have received? These questions must remain unanswered, for the above are the last words on the subject in Grueber's extant correspondence, and my researches in other directions have led to no results. Though it is just possible that at

[1]) Cf. *Appendix IV*.

[2]) As far as the author is aware no Italian version has ever been published. It is not given by Sommervogel.

[3]) Grueber, *Letter from Jaurin, December 12, 1670*: "Quare adhuc iudico imaginem eam reformandam esse, quam certe aliter videbit delineatam et expressam in meo Itinerario, quod spero sequenti anno lucem aspecturum."

[4]) Grueber, *Letter from Trencsin, May 2, 1671*: "Ego interim maximis continuisque laboribus inter milites occupatus opus meum inceptum adhuc perficere non potui; spero tamen iam ubi maior quies mihi datur cum gratia Dei ante autumnum totum perficiendum."

some future time the journal may be unearthed from the depths of one of the European archives, for the present we shall have to make what use we can of the incomplete data which have been cited above.

3. As to the Italian notice, it is the outcome of a long conversation which Grueber had on January 30, 1666, at Florence with two Italians, only one of whom, Carlo Dati, is known by name [1]). This interview was put down in writing afterwards. From the account itself it is clear that it was not so much the journey as the manners and customs of the Chinese that the inquirers wished to be informed about; for the few things said of the expedition itself would hardly cover two of the seventeen and a half folio pages, which the account occupies in Thévenot. But who drew up this report? Thévenot, the first to print it in 1672 under the title of *Viaggio del P. Giovanni Grueber tornando per terra da China in Europa*, mentions no name, but at the end of his French translation, subjoined to the original Italian, he says: "Je croirais faire tort au public, si je ne luy avais donné la relation du P. Grueber dans la langue mesme dans laquelle elle a estée écrite; car l'on entend assez ici cette langue pour y reconnaîstre un style noble, propre et juste, et un charactère d'esprit, qui fera deviner aisément le nom de son autheur" [2]). The riddle, however, seems to have been somewhat hard to read, for no record of the author's name has come down to us. In his *Notizie varie dell'Imperio della China* [3]) Jacopo Carlieri only informs us that the account which he prints, and which in a few unimportant particulars deviates from Thévenot's *Viaggio*, had been written a few years before by a member of the University of Florence [4]). Degli Anzi [5]) relates that in 1670 a

---

[1]) The date given in the notice is January 30, 1665, but Tronnier (p. 338) remarks that at the time the year was reckoned at Florence "ab Incarnatione" i.e. Lady Day, March 25; hence in our style: 1666. Ritter (II, 453) places the interview at Constantinople.

[2]) Thévenot, IV, *Voyage à la Chine*, p. 9. For the connection of the different parts and the pagination the reader is referred to the notes given in the bibliography under the full title of Thévenot's work.

[3]) Published at Florence, 1697. The account is to be found on pp. 1–80.

[4]) The contention of Von Richthofen (I,672) and of Markham (p. lvii) as to Carlieri's book being our chief source is simply inadmissible. As a matter of fact it appeared twenty-five years after Thévenot's, and in a discussion of Grueber's journey it may be dispensed with altogether.

[5]) Degli Anzi, *Il Genio Vagante* (Parma 1692). In the third part (pp. 331–399) he gives extracts from letters of Grueber's and also a *Relazione*. Not having the book available the details regarding it are taken from Tronnier's article p. 332, 333.

manuscript containing many particulars about China was presented to Canon Pinchiari and Count Valerio by Magalotti, who had received it from a Jesuit in 1666. This fact is difficult to reconcile with the statements of Sommervogel [1]) and Puini [2]) who take it to be a composition of Magalotti's. What then, for our present purpose, is the value to be attached to the Italian document in question? The fact of its being anonymous, of its being perhaps third hand evidence, of its being put together after the interview with the aid, may-be, of a few short notes must needs call for caution; to which should be added the remarkable fact that there are particulars given here, and very important ones too, which are not touched upon either in Grueber's letters or in Kircher's account. Inaccuracies and mistakes, on the other hand, are of fairly frequent occurrence, though a misunderstanding of Grueber's replies, or incorrect jottings during the interview may account for some of them. But the particulars regarding the journey itself, at any rate, cannot have been invented, fitting in as they do admirably with the whole of the journey, and. . . . confirmed as they are by Grueber himself in his answers to the Archduke of Tuscany. Thus, though the Italian notice cannot supply us with any fresh and reliable material, it serves to confirm such data as have come to us from elsewhere.

4. To come to our last source. The French edition of Kircher's work, published at Amsterdam in 1670, under the title of *La Chine Illustrée*, has on pp. 316—324 "La briefve et exacte Response du P. Jean Grubere de la Société de Jésus à toutes les questions que lui a fait le Serenissime Grand Duc de Toscane." There are ten pointed questions with as many categorical answers, nearly all of them of primary importance for a right understanding of the journey, elucidating as they do several obscure points in Kircher's account, as will appear in the course of this chapter. When and where Grueber composed these answers is unknown, and the document is printed at the end of *La Chine Illustrée* without any indication of date or place of composition [3]).

---

[1]) Sommervogel, III, 1884. He gives Fabioni, *Vitae Italorum Excellentium*, as his authority.

[2]) Puini, p. xxxvii.

[3]) This French edition being somewhat difficult of access — Tronnier (p. 331, note 1) could not avail himself of it in the writing of his article — the ten questions are here printed for the convenience of the reader:

As regards d'Orville, who died in India from the fatigues of the journey we have nothing from his hand bearing on the present question. Everything referring to his life and work has been carefully collected by H. Bosmans in his booklet already referred to, *Documents sur Albert Dorville de Bruxelles*. I have come across only one letter not yet published; it was written from Macao February 1, 1659, and addressed to Kircher, but contributes nothing towards our subject.

As to the travellers themselves, John Grueber, the more prominent of the two, was born at Linz on the Danube, October 28, 1623, and after the usual preparatory studies entered the Society of Jesus October 18, 1641 [1]). Towards the end of his course of theology when he was preparing himself for the mission of Transsylvania, he was invited to join the China mission by F. Bernard

---

1. Quel degré de latitude septentrionale termine la partie du Royaume de la Chine, qui approche le plus du Nord.

2. Sçavoir I. Combien est longue la fameuse muraille de la Chine. II. Si elle s'estend jusques à la mer orientale. III. Combien elle s'avance en terre ferme, et si elle biaise enfin du costé du midy.

3. Comment est-ce qu'on appelle les peuples qui sont au delà de ces murailles de la Chine.

4. Sçavoir si cette muraille est à présent destruite, ou s'il y a une simple ouverture; afin de faciliter la communication entre les Chinois et les Tartares Septentrionaux, et comment est-ce qu'on appelloit le sejour du Grand Cham de Tartarie auparavant qu'il envahit la Chine.

5. On demande si le P. Jean est entré dans les terres du grand Mogor par la Tartarie ou par Usbek qui regarde le Septentrion, ou bien si ça estē du costé d'Orient, et s'il a enfin quelque connoissance des Regions de Thebet ou Thabut dont le P. Antoine de Andrada fait mention.

6. Sçavoir si le P. Jean a entendu parler de Chambelich ou Cambalu, comme d'une ville de Tartarie.

7. On demande si les Tartares Septentrionaux avoient des coustumes, des loix et une forme de gouvernement approchant de celuy des Chinois, avant qu'ils se fussent emparés de la Chine; ou bien s'ils estoient rustiques et barbares.

8. Combien de temps employa le P. Jean à venir depuis les murailles de la Chine jusques au Royaume de Mogor, et qu'elle est la premiere Ville de l'Inde sujette au Mogor, qu'il a veuē en suivant son chemin; et combien de temps il faut employer pour venir de cette mesme ville dans Agra, Delly et Lahor, qui sont trois villes Royales.

9. Sçavoir si le P. Jean estime véritable le chemin et l'histoire de Marc Paul Venitien et qu'est ce qu'il a trouvé de conforme ou de different par la propre experience à ce qu'il en a dit.

10. Sçavoir si le Père Jean descrira les Provinces et les Estats qui sont hors de la Chine et s'il en donnera au public des cartes Geographiques.

[1]) Huonder, p. 187. Bosmans (p. 8) gives October 19, 1641, Sommervogel (III, 1884) October 13. Markham (p. lvi) and Peschel-Ruge (p. 558) incorrectly assign 1620 as the year of Grueber's birth.

Diestel. He accepted and together they set out for Rome [1]). In the course of the same year 1656 they started for China. Before leaving Grueber was urgently pressed by Kircher to report to him everything worthy of note which he might come across on his long journey [2]). This request was only natural as Grueber was to strike out a new route and not to make the voyage Lisbon-Goa as had been done by all his predecessors. What precisely was the object to be achieved in thus leaving the traditional ocean-route cannot now be ascertained the written instructions of his superiors having been lost. Was it the hope of discovering a safer route than the long journey by the Cape, which what with storms, freebooters, sickness and starvation had proved fatal to so many; or a desire to get rid of the oppressive protection of the Portuguese Government who had prescribed this route for all missionaries of whatever nationality travelling to their colonies or the countries within their sphere of influence? Only in Portuguese ships the passage was to be made, and how strictly this regulation was pressed appears among other things from a letter of King Alfonso VI. of Portugal to Father Goswin Nickel, General of the Society of Jesus, written July 17, 1664, in which the former seriously remonstrates on the subject of its non-observance [3]). However this may be, in 1656 Grueber und Diestel sailed from Venice to Smyrna, and travelling through Asia Minor and Armenia reached Bender Abbas on the south coast of Persia, whence they crossed into the island of Ormuz. Though such an overland journey in the second part of the seventeenth century is a sufficiently remarkable performance, we do not intend to dwell on it, as it is known from several other books of travel [4]). At Ormuz they took ship for Surat on the Gulf of Cambay, north of Bombay, where they were detained for ten months as Grueber informs Father Haffenecker in a letter written

---

1) These details are taken from the eulogy on Grueber. Cf. *Appendix V*.

2) Kircher, *China Illustrata*, Proemium ad lectorem, p. 2. — Many erroneously place his departure in the following year.

3) Huonder, p. 214.

4) See for example the interesting little work: *Peregrinationes Apostolicae R. P. Francisci Rigordi S. J. qui XII Novembris anni 1643 Massiliae solvens per Mare Mediterraneum; per Syriam, Arabiam desertam, Mesopotamiam, Chaldeam, Persidem, sinum Persicum et mare Indicum Goam pervenit 18 Martii anni 1646. — Inde egressus 14 Septembris eiusdem anni per littus Mogolense, per mare Indicum, per Persas, Parthos et Medos: per mare Caspium, Tartariam, Asiaticam, Moscoviam, Poloniam, Hungariam, Austriam et Italiam rediit Massiliam in patriam 4 Iunii anni 1649.* (Massiliae 1652).

March 7, 1658, on the eve of his departure [1]). He utilized his enforced leisure to fix the latitude of the town, which he found to be 21° 10′. He calculated the longitude at the time of a lunar eclipse in December 1657, but the letter containing his results never reached its destination [2]). An English vessel took them directly to Macao, where they landed safely towards the end of July of the same year, 1658. This date must be maintained against any other, affirmed as it is by d'Orville, Grueber's future travelling-companion. In a letter from Macao, dated October 30, 1658 [3]) he writes that a few days after his own arrival (July 17, 1658), there had arrived at Macao Father Grueber and his travelling-companion, Father Bernard Diestel, likewise a German [4]).

Grueber's stay at Macao must have been very short, for in the same letter d'Orville expects him to be sent to Pekin to assist Father Adam Schall at the imperial observatory. To what degree mathematical and astronomical studies had fitted Grueber, when still in Europe, for this important work, we are unable to say, but that he must have been thoroughly grounded in these departments of science his subsequent labours leave no room to doubt. His regular work at Pekin, however, was not long to continue uninterrupted. Of late there had arisen various doubts and difficulties calling for an early solution; letters on the other hand were so inadequate to the clear statement of a case and their arrival so uncertain, so dependent on the countless dangers from the elements and from men; that we are not surprised to find that the Superior of the mission thought of despatching one of his men, nor that he fixed his eye on the intrepid German, whom his long journey had made an experienced traveller: so he made up his mind to send Grueber to Rome as his agent [5]). But, then, the road by

---

1) Bosmans, p. 62; Stöcklein, I, 111.

2) Kircher, *China Illustrata*, p. 222.

3) Bosmans, p. 71. The year 1659 is given in the *Catalogus Patrum ac Fratrum e Societate Jesu qui a morte S. Francisci Xaverii ad annum MDCCCLXXII Evangelio Christi propagando in Sinis adlaboraverunt* (Shanghai 1873) I, 12. Also by Huonder (p. 187), Sommervogel (III, 1884), Tronnier (p. 335) and others.

It should be remarked that the time-notices in Thévenot's Italian account are wholly unreliable. Thus the time allotted to the journey from Ormuz to Macao is seven months, while, as Grueber himself notes, the stay at Surat alone was protracted through even a longer time than this. Thévenot, IV, *Viaggio*, p. 1.

4) Bernard Diestel was born in 1619, entered the Society of Jesus in 1638 and died at Tsi-nang-fu Sept. 13, 1660.

5) Kircher, *China Illustrata*, Proemium, p. 2: "Jussu Superiorum Provinciae Sinicae negotiorum causa denuo Romam .... missus." In his letter to Gamans Grueber

sea was closed or very nearly so. Macao was still, indeed, a Portuguese stronghold, but their power in the east was rapidly crumbling away under the blows of the Dutch. It was especially Bort and Speelman, the enterprising lieutenants of Jan Maetsuiker, the governor-general of Batavia at the time, who harassed them incessantly. They blockaded every Chinese port and held up every vessel sailing from Macao, in the first place, of course, those of the Portuguese. Such being the situation the idea of travelling by land suggested itself. Would it be possible to reach India, and yet avoid the perils of the sea? The memory of Goes' journey was no doubt still sufficiently alive at Pekin, but his route must have been discarded as too long and impracticable. Another route through South-China, Tonkin, Siam and Pegu came up for discussion, but it was set aside on account of the great variety of peoples, languages and customs of the countries that would have to be traversed [1]). As the question of a Siberian route had never yet been mooted [2]), there remained only the border-country, Tibet, the goal of many caravans every year, which therefore might be worth trying.

Grueber's mission to and from China is viewed in quite a different light by Bosmans. Discarding the traditional interpretation he asserts that the definite object of Grueber's mission to the East was, first to go to China following an overland route as far as possible, and then, after a few months' rest, to return from China to India by land [3]). In support of his opinion he adduces a letter of F. Fr. de Rougemont, dated July 27, 1661, which says: "F. Joh. Bapt. Grueber sent to China by our Very Reverend

---

writes from Rome: "Nunc R. V. significo me ex voluntate Superiorum e Sinis huc missum ob aliqua negotia."

[1]) This is stated by Grueber himself. Cf. *Appendix IV*, where his letter of January 13, 1670 is printed in full.

[2]) The first to look in this direction was Father Verbiest, the director of the Pekin observatory. For him, too, the chief motives were the countless perils of the sea-voyage round by the Cape, and the menace from the Dutch, who made the journey in Portuguese ships practically impossible. When in 1676 Nicholas Spathar Milescu came to Pekin at the head of an embassy, Verbiest took the opportunity to write to the Tsar to secure his sanction of the project. Cf. Bosmans S. J., *Le Problème des Relations de Verbiest avec la Cour de Russie* — Annales de la Société d'Emulation pour l'étude de l'histoire et des antiquités de la Flandre (Bruges 1913) p. 193—223.

[3]) Bosmans p. 8. He returns to the question at some length in his able article *Ferdinand Verbiest S. J., Directeur de l'Observatoire de Péking 1623—1688* — Revue des Questions Scientifiques (Bruxelles 1912) p. 219. Cf. also Duhr p. 334. — Huonder (p. 187) and Hosten (*Missionaries* p. 32) are of opinion that Grueber was recalled by the General himself. The version of the case as given by Sandberg (*Exploration* p. 29) is entirely wrong.

Father General to try and find some overland route from Persia to China wants to have Father Albert [d'Orville] as the companion of his arduous undertaking" [1]). As against this we can only reaffirm that the land-route was tried *because* it was the only one that was open, thus taking our stand on Grueber's explicit statement to Gamans, that "as the sea-route was closed by the Dutch blockading the Portuguese ports I have, with the exception of a few days, made the whole of this journey by land" [2]). Thus it was only when the ocean-route proved impossible that the idea of a overland journey suggested itself. The same letter, moreover, states that he is sent by the Superiors of the Chinese mission, which would be meaningless if he had been sent to China by the General with the avowed purpose of returning almost immediately; for there could then be no question of either sending or not sending him on the part of the local Superiors. Lastly it is well-nigh impossible to suppose that, having been charged with a task of such unusual magnitude, neither Grueber himself in his letters nor Kircher in his account should have had a word to say on the subject.

The quotation from Rougemont's letter given above is of value in so far as it shows Grueber's anxiety to have a companion in his travels, a desire which was natural enough in one who could not be ignorant of the lonely death of Bento de Goes on the Chinese frontier. But who was this companion? Thanks to the strenuous researches of Father Bosmans we are at present sufficiently acquainted with the particulars of Father d'Orville's life.

Albert Le Comte was the third son of Louis Le Comte, seigneur of Orville, and of Anna Hellincx, and was born at Brussels August 12 or 20, 1621 [3]). There are different ways of writing the name. Kircher has Dorville, Albert's signature in two extant letters is de Dorville; according to the genealogy of the family, edited by Baron Isidore de Stein Altenstein, the correct spelling is d'Orville, which we have adopted [4]). Albert seems to have left his native

[1]) C. F. Waldack S. J., *Le Père Philippe Couplet, Malinois, S. J., missionaire en Chine, 1623–1694* – Analectes pour servir à l'histoire ecclésiastique de la Belgique (Louvain-Bruxelles 1872) IX, 19: "Sed ecce P. Joh. Bapt. Grueber in Chinas ab admodum R. P. nostro missus ad aperiendam quamcumque tandem terrestrem ex Persia in Chinas viam, socium sibi petit tam ardui operis P. Albertum."

[2]) "Quoniam iter per mare ab Hollandis clausum est, qui omnes iam portus Lusitanorum occupant, confeci hoc totum iter paucis diebus exceptis per terram."

[3]) Bosmans, p. 8 ff. Sommervogel (III, 149) gives the year 1622.

[4]) *Annuaire de la Noblesse de Belgique* (Bruxelles 1878) p. 105. It is no doubt a slip of the pen which makes Grueber write Bonville once in his letter to Gamans. Dr. S.

country at an early age, for after a six years' course of humanities we meet him at the court of the duke of Neuburg, which he quitted in 1646 to begin his Jesuit noviceship on October 30 or November 2 at Landsberg in Lorrain at the northern base of the Vosges. Having first studied for three years at Ingolstadt he was from 1651—1654 a theological student at Louvain. Here it was that in 1654 he saw Father Martin Martini [1]). Leaving China in 1651 to report on the mission at Rome Martini was long detained at Batavia, but at length reached Amsterdam. At Louvain his lectures on China made a great stir, and among the first to volunteer was d'Orville. Setting out almost immediately he was already on his way to Vienna and thence to Rome, when a letter from the General, Goswin Nickel, arrived at Louvain disapproving of and annulling his nomination to the mission. Meanwhile he arrived at Rome, where he finished his studies, and at last obtained the desired permission setting out with Martini in 1656 [2]). We may note in passing that Father Ferdinand Verbiest, who was to become so famous later on, was also one of the little band. They followed the usual route by way of Lisbon and the Cape. That the misery to be sustained through those dreary months was very great, and the conditions of life on board unpardonably wretched was a common experience of outgoing missionaries in those times, and may in the present case appear from the fact that, on landing at Goa probably at the beginning of 1657, of the eighteen companions of Martini's who sailed from Lisbon two had died, one had gone mad, another was totally paralyzed and near his death, whilst all of them were in a very weak state of health. No wonder that d'Orville complained bitterly in a letter from Macao to F.

Günther *Geschichte der Erdkunde* (Leipzig und Wien 1904) p. 137, germanizes the name into Dorfelder.

[1]) Martin Martini was born at Trent in the valley of the Adige in 1614 and entered the Society of Jesus at Rome, October 8, 1632. He was sent to China in 1638, where he did not arrive till 1643. Among his several works on China his *Novus Atlas Sinensis* is no doubt the most famous. Von Richthofen calls him the father of Chinese geography. For a complete list of his works see Sommervogel, V, 646 ff. Martini died at Hang-cheu June 6, 1661, not at Tokien September 11, 1662, as stated by Yule in the Geographical Magazine for July 1874. — It may be remembered that in 1655 the Dutch East-India Company despatched a mission to Pekin under the leadership of Goyer and De Keizer; this was chiefly due to the communications made by Martini in 1651 at Batavia about the opening of the port of Canton to all trading nations. Cf. J. Nieuhof, *Het Gezandtschap der Neerlandtsche Oost-Indische Compagnie aan den grooten Tartarischen Cham, den tegenwoordigen keizer van China* (Amsterdam 1693) p. 21.

[2]) Bosmans, p. 9—19.

Nickel, the more so as it was not the first time that precious lives had thus been lost [1]). After staying at Goa till January 30, 1658, they continued their journey to Macao, which was reached *via* Macassar [2]) July 17, 1658 [3]). At the latter port some of the missionaries were so broken down that further travelling was impossible and they had to be left behind. D'Orville's arrival at Macao was shortly afterwards followed by Grueber's, as we saw above. The former's stay at Macao would seem to have been of fairly short duration, for when Grueber applied to have him as his travelling-companion, he had been occupied in the province of Shan-si for over a year and spoke the language well, as Rougemont informs us in his letter referred to above. About the middle of 1660 he went to the Pekin observatory to be trained by Father Adam Schall [4]) in geographical determination and thus to be of service to Grueber in his travels.

As regards the composition of the travelling party, their equipment, their instruments (for in the course of their long journey they determined the latitude of several places) all available sources are silent. We only know that they had obtained the emperor's permission and enjoyed even the protection of an imperial passport both of which had been procured through the influence of Father Schall.

It was April 13, 1661, when the travellers had completed their arrangements and set out from the ancient city of Cambaluc on their adventurous wanderings to the unknown West [5]). In

---

[1]) Bosmans, p. 19.

[2]) Macassar is not found on Kircher's map, nor does Tronnier mention it or take account of it in his calculation of the length of the journey. The fact, however, of the ship calling at that port is certain from d'Orville's letter written from Macao October 30, 1658. Cf. Bosmans, p. 70.

[3]) Both d'Orville's and Grueber's arrival is placed in the year 1659 by the *Catalogus Patrum ac Fratrum etc.* I, 12.

[4]) John Adam Schall von Bell, born at Cologne in 1591, joined the Society of Jesus October 21, 1611. Eleven years afterwards he landed in China, where his wide knowledge of mathematics soon secured for him a position of eminence at the court. He had a share in the reformation of the calendar and for years was at the head of the Pekin observatory. Himself a worthy successor to the famous Ricci, he was as happy to find in the Fleming, Ferdinand Verbiest, an equally able continuer of his work. Schall died at Pekin August 15, 1666. For an extensive bibliography of his works see Sommervogel, VII, 705 *ff.*

[5]) Thévenot, IV, *Autres Pièces etc.* p. 18. Letter to Gamans: "Discessi e Sinis Pequino 13 Aprilis 1661." Launay (I, 30) dismisses the whole expedition in fifteen lines; its only object is imagined to have been the founding of a mission.

thirty days they reached Hsi-ngan the ancient capital of the country, crossing the Hoang-ho on their way, and after another month, in the second half of June therefore, they arrived at Hsi-ning or Hsi-ning-fu after recrossing the river [1]). The road they took is not indicated, which for our purpose need cause no regret, it being sufficient for us to know that after two months they stood at the Chinese frontier, which fact is, moreover confirmed by Grueber himself in his answer to the fifth question of the Archduke of Tuscany [2]). That this was the ordinary rate of travelling may be inferred from a letter of Verbiest's to Father Couplet, in which he relates how in 1660 he travelled from Hsi-ngan to Pekin in a month [3]). Markham [4]) demurs at the crossing and recrossing of the Hoang-ho between Hsi-ngan and Hsi-ning, but if Kircher's phrase be referred to the whole journey, as it well may, the difficulty will vanish; in the supposition, however, of Grueber mistaking a tributary, the Hsi-ning-ho, for the principal stream this double crossing would become a necessity. But of this presently.

A fortnight was spent at Hsi-ning in preparation for the further journey [5]). Grueber made use of the opportunity to determine the latitude of the town several times. His result was 36° 20' north, not so very different from Rockhill's 36° 41' 4" [6]). He describes the town as large and populous, and from its situation near the Great Wall, of special significance, it being the first gate, where the Indian traders have to wait for permission to enter the Middle Kingdom. The Great Wall was wide enough there for six horsemen to ride abreast, and he was assured that from there to Su-cheu,

---

[1]) Ritter (II, 453) and Markham (p. lvi), who seem to be unacquainted with the letter to Gamans, place the departure from Pekin in June 1661, being misled by an obscure sentence in Kircher, who wrote a somewhat peculair Latin. He says: "Ex Pequino itaque hi Patres anno 1661 mense Junio, in Siganfu triginta dierum et hinc Sining sive Siningfu, totidem fere dierum decursu transacto bis croceo flumine, quod Hoang vocant, transito, confecerunt iter." *China Illustrata*, p. 64. — The French translator has entirely gone astray. He not only makes the travellers start in June, but makes them arrive at Hsi-ning-fu in thirty days, leaving Hsi-ngan out of account altogether. *La Chine Illustrée*. p. 88.

[2]) Kircher, *La Chine Illustrée*, p. 319.

[3]) H. Bosmans, *Ferdinand Verbiest S. J.* — Revue des Questions Scientifiques (Bruxelles 1912) p. 216—217.

[4]) Markham, p. 295, Note 4.

[5]) This is distinctly stated in Grueber's answer to the second question. Kircher, *La Chine Illustrée*, p. 317.

[6]) Rockhill. *Diary*, p. 387.

the second gate, the length of the wall was eighteen days' travel [1]). This description compels us to face the fact that at present no Great Wall is to be seen near Hsi-ning. Von Richthofen and Markham simply pass over the statement as a mistake of Grueber's, and Tronnier takes no notice of it [2]). Yet it invites discussion; when a man like Grueber stays a fortnight in the town and describes its situation so fully one can hardly think of a mistake or a slip.

It is well-known that it is precisely the valley of the Hsi-ning-ho, situated at a high level but enclosed on the north and south by massive mountain ranges, which has suffered terribly through the repeated rebellions of the Dzungarians againts their Chinese masters, and the traces of their devastations are still visible [3]). That on account of these inroads an existing defensive wall must have suffered and in some places may have gone to ruin is likely enough, the more so as it must be conceived as a broad, earthen embankment rather than as a defence in brick and stone. Father Gerbillon, who visited the Chinese wall over nearly the whole of its length, writes of it as follows: "Having traversed nearly the whole of it and having passed through nearly all its most famous gates I may speak of it as one who knows.... The first part, from the eastern sea to the beginning of the province of Chan-si, is entirely constructed in stone and brick.... From the beginning of the province of Chan-si to the other extremity in the west it is but a mud wall, or rather it is a terrace in many places gone to ruin, which I have crossed and recrossed many times on horseback. It is true that at certain intervals towers are found which here and there are of stone or brick, but most of them are of mud. To make up for this there are forts along the whole length of the wall, on the inside and four leagues apart, which at the time of the Tai-ming dynasty held strong garrisons.... At present these garrisons are mostly small and consist of Chinese soldiers only; it is but at some points of importance such as Fouen-fou.... Sining and Sotcheou, that strong bodies of troops are maintained" [4]). Gerbillon, therefore, held Hsi-ning to belong to the Great Wall, meaning by this

---

1) Kircher, *China Illustrata*, p. 64, 66.

2) Von Richthofen, I, 672; Markham, p. 295, note 4. Tronnier, p. 341, note 2.

3) Prejevalsky, II, 55 ff.; Futterer, I, 253.

4) Du Halde, IV, *Observations Historiques sur la Grande Tartarie, tirées des Mémoires du P. Gerbillon*, p. 70.

either the main structure or one of its numerous branches. That the town was not situated against the wall itself, but at some distance away from it may be inferred from Grueber's answer to the second question of the Archduke, in which after speaking of the walls of the town he continues: "At a distance of three miles from the walls of the town there is a fort armed with three rows of guns, where foreigners must necessarily pass" [1]). The gate to the empire, therefore, lay outside the town in some such way as Chiaicuon is the gate to Su-cheu. That Hsi-ning was a fortified town at the time of Grueber's visit we also learn from Martini [2]). It is described in detail by Futterer. "Far below the town one sees for hours the long monotonous walls with a few turrets over the gates and at the corners. After passing the first wall the traveller enters upon the wide site of a suburb, covered for the most part with the ruins of houses and other buildings. . . . Through a second, strong wall one passes from the Dzungarian into the strictly Chinese inner town, where no Mohammedans are allowed to reside" [3]).

But, then, are there in the valley of the Hsi-ning-ho no traces of any such wall as is described by Grueber? When relating his visit to the monastery of Chobsen, forty miles north-north-east of Hsi-ning, Prejevalsky says that four and a half miles east of the monastery there was a mud wall with towers as on the northern frontier of Kansu. It was much decayed so they told him and extended from Hsi-ning through Tatung to Kan-chou [4]). Sven Hedin likewise mentions ancient walls. Travelling from the Koko Nor to Hsi-ning he traversed the fertile district of Yuan-sän. "Here a partly decayed wall lies right across the valley. It rises to the crests of the lateral mountain ranges allowing a free passage only along the river and having two watch-towers built at that spot. A few kilometres further south, near Cho-yüan, walls are built on either side of the valley on small prominences" [5]). On the map of O. R. Coales, *Compass Route Traverse between Hsi-ning Fu and Kanchou Fu*, there is also traced "an ancient wall and gateway, said to be part of the Great Wall" [6]). But the fullest justification

---

1) Kircher, *La Chine Illustrée*, p. 318.

2) Thévenot, IV, *Martin Martinius, Description géographique de l'Empire de la Chine*, p. 65.

3) Futterer, I, 256. Cf. Huc, *Souvenirs*, II, 53.

4) Prejevalsky, II, 73.

5) Hedin, *Ergebnisse*, p. 337. Cf. Futterer, I, 229.

6) *Geographical Journal*, XXXIX (1912) February.

of Grueber's description is derived from the researches of Dr. W. E. Geil. To the west of Hsi-ning he found several relics of an ancient wall which "does not date back to remote times"[1]). He adds that existing chronicles of the district do not speak of that wall, but only refer to more ancient histories which are no longer extant. The Rev. H. F. Ridley a missionary resident at Hsi-ning furnished him with a sketch-map of the probable run of this "Tibetan loop of the Great Wall", as Geil calls it. In this sketch the wall is shown with a sudden westerly curve encircling the town, though it does not appear at what distance. — We may, perhaps, here recall the principle which Grueber's sense of fairness applied to Marco Polo: "It is so long since he died, and as the passing centuries cause a total change in nature, we should not think it strange if we do not see the things in the way in which he described them" [2]).

After this fortnight's stay the journey was resumed and Grueber and d'Orville entered a practically unknown territory. On the details of this journey to Lhasa we are left in great uncertainty. Broadly speaking there is a choice between two roads. One is called "the old road" on Hedin's large map of Tibet, running from Hsi-ning in a south-westerly direction, skirting the Tsaring Nor and the Oring Nor, the two sources of the Hoang-ho, and joining the other road south of the Tangla Range. This second road leads from Hsi-ning to the Koko Nor, loops round the lake on either side, passes over the South Koko Nor Range and runs through the eastern part of Tsaidam basin across the Bajan Gol to the monastery of Dzun-Saysak. The branch running off this road further on does not concern us here. Be it enough to say that in the end all join the "old road" south of the Tangla Range [3]). Which of all these was the one taken by our party?

If we turn to our sources, the only statement made in the letter to Gamans is to the effect that the journey through the desert of Tartary occupied three months[4]). Kircher is almost equally laconic. "Soon after leaving the wall they came to a river abounding in fish, crossed the Hoang-ho and traversed the Kalmack desert,

---

[1]) Dr. W. E. Geil, *The Great Wall of China* (London 1909) p. 275 ff. There are photographs of some remaining parts of the wall.

[2]) Kircher, *La Chine Illustrée*, p. 322.

[3]) Hedin, *Ergebnisse*, Map 5. Cf. Futterer, *Geographische Skizze von Nord-Ost Tibet* — Ergänzungsheft 143 zu Peterm. Mitteil. (Gotha 1903) p. 7.

[4]) Thévenot, IV, *Autres Pièces etc.* p. 18.

the journey to Barantola [Lhasa] occupying three months" [1]). But here the Italian interview comes to the rescue with fuller details. "After leaving China he entered the Tartar desert and in a three days' march arrived on the banks of lake Kokonor. This lake resembles the Caspian. From it issues the Yellow River of China, which flows through China with a rapid current to join the sea on the eastern side opposite the island of Korea. It is the largest river of China. Kokonor means great sea [mar grande] in the Tartar language. Leaving its shores the missionary came to the country of Toktokai, almost a desert, which acknowledges no authority, whilst on the other hand no one lays claim to it on account of its great poverty.... Through it flows the river Toktokai, whence the country derives its name. The beautiful stream is as wide as the Danube, but it is so shallow that it can easily be forded on horseback" [2]). That this detailed description is due to Grueber can hardly be doubted the country being a *terra incognita* in Europe at the time; but whose are the evident mistakes? The comparison with the Caspian Sea, which is perhaps sixty times [3]) the size of the Koko Nor, is no doubt due to the brackishness of the latter, but the name means 'blue' not 'great' lake. But Grueber's imperfect acquaintance with the Tartar language, to which he himself confesses, may easily account for this [4]). Then there is the statement that the lake is the source of the Yellow River, whilst it is certain that it is not. Here, however, Grueber in part corrects himself. He mistakes the Hsi-ning-ho for the Hoang-ho. Tronnier thinks such a mistake impossible both because the Yellow River is a so much mightier stream than the Hsi-ning-ho and because Grueber's estimate of rivers is on the whole so remarkably accurate, as will appear further on [5]). Yet that he did make it Grueber himself will tell us. In the answer to the second question of the Archduke it is said: "Three leagues outside the town there is a fort.... where foreigners must necessarily pass in order to get across the mountains or across the Yellow River, which is called

[1]) Kircher, *China Illustrata*, p. 67.

[2]) Thévenot, IV, *Viaggio*, p. 1.

[3]) Authorities do not quite agree either on the elevation or the area of the Koko Nor. For the latter, statements vary between 4,000 and 7,000 square kilometres. "This largest lake in the heart of Asia is still awaiting its investigator." Hedin, *Results*, III, 578.

[4]) Thévenot, IV, *Autres Pièces* etc. p. 19—21.

[5]) Tronnier, p. 345, Note 1.

Hoâm-ho and flows past the town of Sy nîm". So no doubt can be left about Grueber taking the tributary to be the main stream. But even this does not clear up the whole difficulty, as neither river takes its rise from the Koko Nor, the lake having no outlet at all. As, however, Grueber does not inform us whether he had his information from personal observation or from natives badly informed or badly understood, there is no use in discussing this point further. In the answer just now referred to there is another statement, which is of value for the very reason that it is erroneous. After describing the wall it continues: "This wall extends from the town to the great lake or sea of Tartary, called Kokonor, from which the Yellow River issues" [1]). These words contain a very strong argument for the authenticity of the Italian report, a common error pointing to a common source, which in the present case would be Grueber. On the other hand it is also quite clear from this same answer that not all the errors in the narrative of the Italians should be placed to Grueber's account, for while they call Korea an island, Grueber declares that Korea "is a peninsula, not an island, as they wrongly would make us believe in the maps they make."

If, then, we are safe to assume that the travellers took the Koko Nor road, it remains uncertain which of the alternative loops they followed. Tronnier [2]) supposes it was the northern one, for Grueber in his fourth letter, so he argues rather ingeniously, declares never to have seen rhubarb in bloom [3]); yet this plant is of common occurence among the mountains south of the lake, and it was during its flowering season that Grueber traversed those parts. On this supposition, then, Grueber's route would coincide with Huc and Gabet's in 1845, Rockhill's in 1889, and Sven Hedin's in the opposite direction in 1896. Obroochev and Futterer skirted the southern border.

Having left the Chinese Wall on July 13, 1661, the two Europeans reached the lake after three days. [4]) No description is given. Prejevalsky, who saw it in 1872, describes it as follows: "Its shores are very flat and shelving; its water salt and undrinkable. But this saltness imparts an exquisite dark blue colour to the surface,

---

1) Kircher, *La Chine Illustrée*, p. 318.

2) Tronnier, p. 339, Note 3, and p. 345. Also Dutreuil, p. 119.

3) Thévenot, IV, *Autres Pièces etc.*, Letter from Danzig, December 11, 1664.

4) Kircher, *La Chine Illustrée*, p. 321.

which excites even the admiration of the Mongols, who have compared it not inaptly to blue silk" [1]). On the interior of Tibet we only get some generalities. "This desert-like territory is partly mountainous, partly flat, sandy and exceedingly barren, except for a few strips intersected by small rivers.... This desert has several names. Marco Polo calls it Lop.... the Tartars anciently Belgian, at present Samo, the Chinese Kalmuk, others again Caracathai i. e. Black Cathay. Animals are not found there except a species of big bulls" [2]). In the third answer it says: "As regards the country on the other side of the lake, it is so desolate that fields are nowhere to be seen from the town of Sȳ nîm to the kingdom of Barantola, although a road of three months lies between them" [3]). The Italian notice, as quoted above, adds only one item: it speaks of a country and river called Toktokai, which name does not occur elsewhere. It is not found on any map, and the only thing that may possibly guide us is the description of the river, which is said to be as wide as the Danube but very shallow. On the authority of Klaproth Markham supposes that the Toktonai-ulan Muren is here spoken of, one of the upper feeders of the Mur Ussa or Di Chu, as the upper Yang-tse-kiang is called [4]). In discussing this view Von Richthofen thinks there are no sufficient data for a decision [5]). Rockhill, however, when describing the Mur Ussa as "the gently flowing red river", adds in a note: "Father Grueber when travelling to Lhasa crossed this river where the Hsining-Nagchuka road cuts it" [6]). Tronnier cannot agree [7]). For when Prejevalsky in 1879 visited the Toktokai-ulan Muren at its junction with the Mur Ussa, he found a width of 10—12 fathoms by a depth of one or two feet at the ford [8]), whilst Grueber's river is as wide as the Danube though fordable on horseback [9]). The question is, of course, which point of the Danube the traveller had before

---

[1]) Prejevalsky, p. 140.

[2]) Kircher, *China Illustrata*, p. 65. The bulls in question are no doubt roaming yaks.

[3]) Kircher, *La Chine Illustrée*, p. 318.

[4]) Markham, p. 296, note 3.

[5]) Von Richthofen, I, 672.

[6]) Rockhill, *Diary*, p. 211.

[7]) Tronnier, p. 346. Nor can Heawood (p. 134, note 2) share Rockhill's view.

[8]) *Ueber den Oberlauf der Jang-tse-kiang und das Tanla-Gebirge; Südlichster Abschnitt von Oberst N. Przewalskis dritter Reise in Hochasien 1879—1880* — Peterm. Mitteil. (1883) p. 349.

[9]) "Bellissimo fiume è in sù l'andar del Danubio, se non che ha pochissimo fondo, e un uomo à cavallo lo passa francamente a guado". Thévenot, IV, *Viaggio*, p. 1.

his mind. Tronnier and Von Richthofen take it to be Linz, Grueber's native town, and the width there being at least 200 metres they suppose that not the Toktonai but the Mur Ussa itself is meant, which near its confluence with the Napchitai-ulan Muren, where it is crossed by the eastern highway of Tibet, was found by Prejevalsky to answer fairly well to Grueber's description [1]). But all this, even though the Mur Ussa should occasionally go by the name of Toktonai, cannot quite settle the question, if, indeed, it is capable of settlement; for it can never be more than probable whether, in fact, Linz was the point of the Danube Grueber had in view. Attention should also be drawn to a remark made by Prejevalsky. When giving the measurements of the Toktonai-ulan Muren he notes that in summer the width may not inconsiderably be increased by the high water flooding the low stretches of land alongside the river. Hence, as Grueber travelled in the summer, probably reaching the ford at the end of August, his description might still apply to the Toktonai [2]).

The experiences of later explorers must be consulted to give us at least some idea of the dangers and hardships which the travellers must have undergone on their way from the Koko Nor to the Tangla Range, and of which our sources leave us in complete ignorance. Crossing the South Koko Nor Range and descending into the salty marshes of the Tsaidam basin they traversed the Baian Gol and may have halted at Dzun Sasak to prepare for the climbing of the Burkhan Buddha Range, the east-wing of the Kuen-Lun. Huc [3]) and Prejevalsky [4]), though not agreeing in all particulars, are at one in describing the passage as very difficult, which is not surprising seeing that the Nomokhun Davan pass attains an elevation of 4,900 metres. But it was only after clearing the Shuga mountains that the travelling-party got into the thick of the terrors of the Tibetan desert. This plateau over 4,000 metres high and broken up by numerous cross-ridges, is strewn with the bones and bodies of beasts of burden and adventurous travellers marking the way for those who come after them, and warning

---

1) Dutreuil (p. 136) takes the same view.

2) Ney Elias refers Grueber's description to the Bajan Gol in the Tsaidam basin, as described by Prejevalsky, to which it applies very well. (Ney Elias, *On Captain Przhewalsky's Explorations in Mongolia and Northern Tibet 1870—1873* — Proceedings of the Royal Geographical Society XVIII (1874) p. 80).

3) Huc, *Souvenirs*, II, 210 ff.

4) Prejevalsky, II, 175 ff.

them of the fate that may befall them on these immense glacial heights. To add to these natural terrors there are wandering marauders, also complained of by Grueber, requiring incessant watchfulness on the part of the toiling wayfarers. The crossing of the Baian-Kara Range led them to the banks of the Mur Ussa or the Blue River, which they forded either at the point they had struck or at a higher and more convenient spot, skirting the river bank for some time and perhaps crossing the Toktonai-ulan Muren on their way. This brought Grueber and d'Orville face to face with the huge Tangla Range, which it took Prejevalsky fully eight days to cross, in the course of which he had, moreover, to beat off a fierce attack of plundering Tanguts. "Slowly," he writes, "the ground rises to one of the highest plateaux of Tibet, the southern edge of which, running from east to west, is formed by mountains covered with eternal snow, the Tangla range. The ascent and descent are very gradual, though the pass followed by the Mongolian caravans lies at an elevation of 4,990 metres. On the whole the gradient is slow enough for a railway line to be laid over the Tangla" [1]). Huc, who does not mention the name of the pass he followed, calls both ascent and descent difficult, especially the latter, which occupied four days [2]). It is possible that the more unfavourable impression left upon Huc's mind may in part be due to the exceptional circumstances under which the passage was made, his companion Gabet having been ill for some time past. At Nag Chu Grueber and d'Orville no doubt changed their beasts of burden, because the road to Lhasa is from this point onward impraticable for camels and horses, which are generally replaced by yaks.

After fording the Toktokai, the Italian notice informs us, they first came through the country of Tangut to Retink, a province with a fairly thick population, belonging to the kingdom of Barantola, and at last to the kingdom itself. In Kircher we read that Tangut is the vast territory of Tartary, not a small part of which

---

[1]) *Ueber den Oberlauf der Jang-tse-kiang und das Tanla-Gebirge* — Peterm. Mitteil. (1883) p. 350. See also N. von Prschewalski, *Reisen in Tibet und am oberen Lauf des Gelben Flusses in den Jahren 1879 bis 1880, in das Deutsche übertragen von Stein-Nordheim* (Jena 1884) p. 131 ff.

[2]) Huc, *Souvenirs*, II, 231 ff. There is no need for us to reply to the continually unfair and unworthy criticisms passed by Prejevalsky on Huc's descriptions; this has been done effectually by Ney Elias, Yule, Henry of Orleans, Rockhill and others.

was traversed by the Fathers [1]). According to Tronnier the name is, as a rule, only applied to the Koko Nor territory [2]), which is traversed by a remark made by Father Régis, S. J., "that the name of Tanguth, which is also found on our maps, is a general name for all the countries from that of the Tartars at the Kokonor.... to the sources of the Ganges" [3]). So there is no valid reason for inverting the order of the names of Toktokai and Tangut in the narrative as Tronnier suggests. As regards Retink, Markham surmises that Jang Raiting Gompa, a monastery eighty kilometres north of Lhasa may be meant [4]). All our present-day maps do in fact show Reting Gompa south-east of the Tengri Nor, the same name being also used to designate the whole territory. The "fairly thick population" must, naturally, be taken in comparison with the practically uninhabited plateau Grueber had just left behind.

Though the fact is not mentioned in the account of the journey we may just point out that the two Jesuits also crossed the towering Transhimalaya Range, probably by the Penpo-la (5,400 metres) [5]), if we are to judge from their line of travel through Reting. Later Jesuit cartographers in the reign of the Emperor Kanghi would learn the general and hazy outline of these stupendous mountain regions, which in 1733 were to find a place in d'Anville's famous map of Tibet or "Bout-tan" under the names of Tchimouran, Coiran, Tchompa, etc.. Sven Hedin was the first to determine on the spot the axis of these ranges. He makes honourable mention of his predecessors [6]).

At last, then, the wanderers had arrived in the kingdom of Barantola and in the capital of the same name, "which the Chinese call Cām, the Tartars Barantola and the foreigners Lassa" [7]). Since Oderico de Pordenone, who must have stayed there in 1328 [8]), no European had set foot in the holy city of the lamas.

---

[1]) Kircher, *China Illustrata*, p. 68.

[2]) Tronnier, p. 347.

[3]) Du Halde, IV, 575.

[4]) Markham, p. 297, note 1. The map referred to by Markham is probably the "Map of Great Tibet shewing the Route of the Trans-Himalayan Explorers round Lake Tengri Nor to Lhasa 1872"; it is appended to the article *Great Tibet; Discovery of Lake Tengri Nor* — the Geographical Magazine II (1875) p. 41.

[5]) It is the pass called Pampou by Huc, and described by him as very difficult. Huc, *Souvenirs*, II, 242 ff.

[6]) Hedin, *Southern Tibet*, III. 3 ff.

[7]) Kircher, *La Chine Illustrée*, p. 318.

[8]) This, as we remarked in Ch. II, is the view generally held. It is also advocated by

Much has been written about the time of Grueber's arrival, but all doubt is settled by the answer to the eighth question: they arrived October 8, 1661 [1]). Three months, therefore, had been spent in travelling from the Great Wall, July 13—October 8. According to Father Desideri Chinese envoys took four months to cover the distance from Lhasa to Pekin [2]), or one month less than our missionaries. Account should be taken, however, of the equipment and the manner of travelling. Thus a former ambassador to the Dalai Lama told Father Gerbillon that he had travelled from Hsi-ning to the Potala in winter in forty-six days [3]). Grueber's time agrees well with the time taken by Huc and Gabet, who from the end of October till January 29 covered the distance between the Koko Nor and Lhasa [4]). Sandberg is astonished at the rapid rate of travelling of the two missionaries: "The pair of travellers must have made unusually rapid progress; because, according to their scanty notes, they arrived at Lhasa only three months *after quitting Pekin*" [5]). This would indeed give cause for wonder.

The goal being reached the caravan was disbanded and an opportunity for continuing their journey had to be looked for, causing a delay of several weeks. Here Kircher and the letter to Gamans are again at variance: the former speaking of two months [6]), the other of one month [7]). Tronnier would like to suppose the number of days to have been rounded off, upward and downward, which would put their stay at about one and a half

---

Professor Cordier in his edition of Yule's *Cathay and the Way thither*. We must, however, mention an article by Berthold Laufer in T'Oung Pao, vol. 15 (1914) p. 405–418, entitled *Was Odoric of Pordenone ever in Tibet*, in which he arrives at the conclusion (p. 417) that "Odoric of Pordenone has never traversed Tibet proper, has never been at Lhasa, — a feat with which he has been unduly credited for so long, and to which he himself lays no claim. The honour of being the first Europeans to have reached Lhasa is justly due to the two Jesuit Fathers Grueber and Dorville, who spent two months there in 1661. "Waddell (*Lhasa* p. 425) is also very sceptical about Pordenone's visit to Lhasa.

1) Kircher, *La Chine Illustrée*, p. 321.

2) *Lettres édifiantes*, VII, 268.

3) Du Halde, IV, *Observations historiques sur la Grande Tartarie, tirées des Mémoires du P. Gerbillon*, p. 52.

4) Also the Buriat Tsybikoff, entered Lhasa after a three months' journey from Kumbum, the famous monastery of the Koko Nor. G. Ts. Tsybikoff, *Lhasa and Central Tibet* — Smithsonian Report for 1903 (Washington 1904) p. 729.

5) Sandberg, *Exploration*, p. 28; italics are mine.

6) Kircher, *China Illustrata*, p. 72, "ad integros duos menses."

7) Thevenot, IV, *Autres Pièces, etc.*, Second Letter of Grueber, "in hac civitate sumus morati uno mense."

months. Details about their temporary residence are not given by Grueber, and a regular description of the town such as Desideri will give us is entirely wanting. The latitude is given by Kircher at 29° 6′, about one half degree less than the calculation of Montgomerie's famous Pundit, Nain Sing [1]). About the government of the country he is a little more communicative and his statements are confirmed by later evidence. There are two kings in this kingdom; one, the Deva (Deba), of ancient Tartar stock, carries on the government; the other, who is worshipped as a deity, lives in seclusion within the precincts of his palace. He is the Great Lama. They did not visit him in person, because a Catholic priest could not conform to the prescribed ceremonial [2]). Grueber's portrait of the Dalai Lama was done after a picture hung up at the entrance of the palace. But among all his sketches of types of the people, idols etc., of which he made a good many as Kircher's illustrations prove, it is his drawing of the famous Potala, Bietala he calls it, that has obtained the widest publicity. It would be hard to say into how many works on Ṭibet this picture has found its way, with its curious vehicle in the foreground, which we may suppose is a play of Grueber's fancy or more probably of the designer's, wheeled carriages being unknown among the Tibetans. The curiosity of those interested in things Tibetan has had to be satisfied with this print till the beginning of the twentieth century when the first photograph of the Potala was given to the world by the Kalmuk, Narzounoff [3]). From a comparison of Grueber's drawing with the numerous later reproductions, especially by members of the British expedition under Colonel Younghusband, it appears that the former saw only the main building completed, and that the two wings are later additions. In the preceding chapter we had occasion to refer to the man who started the building of this palace in 1642. It was the energetic Ngavang Lobsang, who from being the head of the Tashi Lhumpo monastery had, with the aid of the Tartar prince Gushi Khan, worked his way up to be the ruler of Central Tibet. In recognition of services rendered Gushi Khan and his successors had been made military commanders at

---

[1]) *Records*, part. 1, p. 52. The average of his calculations was 29° 39′ 17″. Waddell (*Lhasa* p. 361) has 29° 39′, Landon (II. 376) 29° 39′ 16″.

[2]) Kircher, *China Illustrata*, p. 72; Thévenot, IV, *Viaggio*, p. 1.

[3]) J. Deniker, *La première photographie de Lhassa* — La Geographie IV (1901) p. 242.

to face p. 190.

Grueber's drawing of the Potala.
(Kircher, *China Illustrata*)

Lhasa with the title of King, but under Ngavang Lobsang's suzerainty. In 1652 the latter went to Pekin to wait on the Emperor, by whom he was acknowledged as Great Lama or Dalai (Ocean) Lama [1]). He is said by Grueber to be the seventh incarnation, which is also Markham's opinion [2]), though there are others who call him the fifth [3]).

Here at the focus of Buddhism Grueber and d'Orville were, of course, met on all sides by the religious formula "Om mani padme hum," although they were not the first to make it known to Europe as Tronnier supposes [4]), Andrade having brought to the knowledge of the West an even more correct transliteration than Grueber's "O Manipe mi hum." [5]). But the latter does seem to be the first to make mention of the prayer-wheel and to give a drawing of this curious instrument of prayer [6]).

[1]) *Lettres édifiantes*, XIII, *Mémoire sur le Thibet et sur le Royaume des Eleuthes*, p. 230. Waddell, *Buddhism*, p. 39.

[2]) Markham, p. xlvii.

[3]) Milloué, p. 190. Günther Schulemann, *Die Geschichte der Dalailamas* (Heidelberg 1911), p. 157. — In connection with the troubles that have arisen in Tibet of late years it should be remembered that in 1866 Nain Sing heard a popular saying at Lhasa that the Dalai Lama will transmigrate only thirteen times. The present dignitary is the thirteenth incarnation.

[4]) Tronnier, p. 348.

[5]) Kircher, *China Illustrata*, p. 71. The translation "Manipe, save us" given in Kircher, is, of course, wrong.

[6]) Kircher, *China Illustrata*, p. 68 and plate 67.

That Grueber's information was obtained by close inquiry appears among others from his knowledge of a secret concerning the Dalai Lama, or rather concerning the disgusting curatives and preventives of disease which in his name are distributed among the superstitious people. . . . . "beatum ille se reputet, cui Lamarum benignitate aliquid ex naturalis secessus sordibus aut urina magni Lamae obtigerit; ex huiusmodi enim collo portatis, urina quoque cibis commixta . . . . contra omnium infirmitatum insultus tutissimos ac probe munitos se fore stolidissime sibi imaginantur." (Kircher, *China Illustrata*, p. 74, 51. Also Thévenot, IV, *Viaggio*, p. 2; id. ibid., *Autres Pièces* etc., Letter to Gamans.)

These almost incredible particulars are witnessed to by many later testimonies. Father Desideri, thoroughly qualified by his long stay in the country, is as outspoken as Grueber. (Puini, p. 294) Writing about the Dalai Lama from Lhasa October 11, 1741, the Capuchin Friar Constantin says. "Chi puo con questo parlare ed avere di lui più fetidi escrementi si stima felice." (*Atti e Memorie del Convegno di Geografi-Orientalisti tenuto in Macerata il 25. 26. 27 Settembre 1910* (Macerata 1911) p. 148). Sarat Chandra Das was given two packets of pills after his audience with the Dalai Lama. (Das, p. 223) "By special enquiry on the spot," writes Austine Waddell, "I elicited that the present-day custom confirms the report published in the *Dictionnaire Infernal* by M. Collin de Plancy of Paris in 1825" (follows the text of the *Dictionnaire* agreeing in the main with Grueber's words); Waddell, p. 397, note 2. The difficulty Grueber must have experienced in getting his information may be inferred from a remark of the Japanese Buddhist Ekai Kawaguchi, who wrote about these medicines as late as 1909:

The day of departure came and probably towards the end of November the two Jesuits left the mysterious city, of which they had only slightly lifted the veil. After four days, Kircher says, they were once more confronted by a high mountain range called Langur. When engaged in its lofty passes, which it is almost impossible for animals and vehicles to traverse, they could hardly breathe the rarified air, while in summer the poisonous exhalations of certain plants endanger the traveller's life. After one month's journey they arrived at Cuthi (Kutti or Nilam Dzong), the first town of the kingdom of Necbal (Nepal) [1]).

About this Langur, which can only be the Himalaya range, Sylvain Lévi remarks as follows: "Langur is a class-noun meaning 'a mountain range' in the Parbatic language. In their ascent of the high mountain masses rising between Kutti and Lhasa both Jesuits and Capuchins heard, on opposite sides, the very same cry from the lips of their guides: Langur! the mountains!" [2]) And this is the name still in use; all the snow-covered mountains are still called Langur by the Nepal people on the southern face of the Himalaya. "The term Himalaya is not used by uneducated people, who only talk of the snowy mountains as Barfāni Langūr", was the report of the native explorer no. 9 to Montgomerie in 1871 [3]).

From the time-notice, four days, it appears that the travellers crossed the Kampa La (4,700 metres) south of the Tsangpo or Upper Brahmaputra — no river is mentioned — and thence probably bore westward to Shigatse and Dingri, following the more common yet difficult route to Katmandu. After Shigatse, therefore, where thirty-one years earlier their fellow-Jesuit Father Cacella had died, their route coincides in great part with that of the native explorer Hari Ram in 1871. Traversing the Thang-lang La or

---

"To do justice to this superstition I ought to add that the common Tibetans are kept entirely in the dark as to the ingredients of the pills; they are taken as medicines prepared by the Grand Lama himself according to a certain secret formula, and the shocking secret is known only to a select few who are entitled to attend the Dalai Lama's court." (Kawaguchi, p. 395).

1) Kircher. *China Illustrata* p. 65.

2) Lévi, p. 85. There are a few inaccuracies in Lévi's appreciating discussion of Grueber's journey, e.g. that from Agra Grueber travelled to Rome by himself, that the interview with the two Italians took place at Rome in 1665 (p. 81), that Grueber died in the same year 1665 on his way to China.

3) *Records*, part. 1, p. 119. Langur is repeatedly used both for ridge and pass by B. H. Hodgson, *Route of two Nepalese Embassies to Pekin, with Remarks on the Water-shed and Plateau of Tibet* — Journal of the Asiatic Society of Bengal, XXV (1857) p. 477, 479 etc.

Thung La pass, which he calculated to be 5,626 metres high, the latter reached Nilam (Kutti) at 4,236 metres above sea-level in thirteen days, and as late as October 10 he still found his way encumbered with last year's snow and ice, which may give us a faint idea of Grueber and d'Orville's experiences in December. These difficulties, however, were thrown into the shade by their five day's march from Nilam to Nesti. What this was like is apparent from the description which Montgomerie gives from the account of the above-mentioned pundit. "Between Nilam and Listi Bhansār he [the pundit] followed the general course of the Bhotia Kosi river [one of the principal affluents of the Sun Kosi] and though it is but some twenty-five miles direct distance between the two places, the explorer had to cross the Bhotia river fifteen times, by means of three iron suspension and eleven wooden bridges, each from twenty-four to sixty paces in length. At one place the river ran in a gigantic chasm, the sides of which were so close to one another that a bridge of twenty-four paces was sufficient to span it. This was just below or south of the village of Choksum. Near the bridge the precipices were so impracticable that the path had of necessity to be supported on iron pegs let into the face of rock, the path being formed by bars of iron and slabs of stone stretching from peg to peg and covered with earth. This extraordinary path is in no place more than eighteen inches and often not more than nine inches in width and is carried for more than one-third of a mile (775 paces) along the face of the cliff, at some 1500 feet above the river, which could be seen roaring below in its narrow bed. The explorer, who has seen much difficult ground in the Himalaya, says he never in his life met with anything to equal this bit of path.... There are several other smaller pieces of paths between Nilam and Listi Bhansār which are nearly so bad, but they are fortunately not continuous" [1]). Such being the circumstances it cannot cause surprise that the two Fathers took eleven days to negotiate the distance between Nilam and Katmandu [2]).

If Father Cabral has been the first European to penetrate into the mountain country of Nepal, Grueber has left us more information about this Himalaya kingdom, which down to the present day has remained in such seclusion that almost the only European who is free to enter is the British Ambassador to the

[1]) *Records*, part. I, p 118.

[2]) The same journey took Desideri a fortnight. Cf. Puini. p. 87–88.

Court of Katmandu. This town, the Italian report tells us, is separated from Baddan, the present Patan, only by a river by which the Baghmati is meant; Kircher, on the other hand, puts half a day's march between the two. As a matter of fact Patan is about three kilometres from the south-eastern point of Katmandu [1]). Grueber found the latitude to be 27° 5', which Hari Ram corrected in 1871 to 27° 43' 29" [2]). On their arrival the travellers found Nepal in the throes of war. The king of Katmandu had leaged his forces with those of his brother Nevagmal, the ruler of Patan. Led by the latter the allied army had taken the field against a petty king, Varcam by name, whose repeated raids were the scourge of the country. Grueber presented Nevagmal with a small spy-glass. Having first spied out the spot where Varcam had entrenched himself he handed the glass to the prince and made him look in the right direction. Seeing the enemy so close the general at once gave orders to advance wholly unaware of the optical illusion. Of these historical details, for which we are indebted to the Italian report [3]), Sylvain Lévi found confirmation in the ancient Nepal chronicles. Towards the close of 1659 Pratâpa Malla (Partasmal) and Nivâsa Malla (Nevagmal) joined hands to put an end to the inroads of Jagat Prakâça Malla, king of Bhatgaon [4]). In November 1660 there was a temporary suspension of hostilities, which were continued afresh a year later (November 1661). Jagat Prakaça Malla suffered defeat after defeat, till at last, January 19, 1662, the fortified town of Theni (Timi or Dimi) was taken; the day after the two allied kings returned to their respective capitals [5]). Hence Grueber and d'Orville must have arrived in those parts a few days before January 19 at the latest, which is in perfect agreement with the data of our authorities.

The presents, especially the spy-glass and some mathematical instruments, had so captivated the king that he was unwilling to let the two Europeans depart and in the end only acquiesced on condition of their returning. If we may anticipate, Grueber must have mentioned this undertaking to Father Roth, his companion

---

[1]) Boeck, *Indien*, p. 270.

[2]) *Records*, part. 1, p. 123.

[3]) Thévenot, IV, *Viaggio*, p. 2.

[4]) Bhatgaon is 15 kilometres east of Katmandu.

[5]) Lévi, I, 88. In Lévi's opinion there can be no doubt that Jagat Prakâça Malla is the same as Varcam, Prakâça sounding like Parkas (Varcam) in the mouths of the people.

on the way back to Europe; for writing from Rome in 1664 the latter intimates that, in case a sufficient supply of men is available, he intends to penetrate into Pettent (Potente) or Lassa, and to establish himself in the town of Nepal [1]).

About the rest of the journey from Katmandu to Agra our information is very slight and the data derived from our different sources do not complete each other. From Kircher we learn that in five days they travelled from Nepal to Hedonda, a settlement in the kingdom of Moranga, in eight days from this place to Mutgari, the first town in the empire of the Great Mogul, and thence in ten days to Battana on the Ganges [2]). The Italian report summarizes as follows: after leaving Nepal they traversed the kingdom of Moranga in five days, proceeded to Minapor, where they crossed the Ganges, which at that point had double the width of the Danube, and arrived at Patana [3]). It is, therefore, at the town of Battana, Patana (Patna), that according to both accounts the two travellers eventually arrived. But the twenty-three days over which the journey is distributed by Kircher, differ widely from the length of time stated in Grueber's answer to the eighth question of the Archduke of Tuscany. After leaving Katmandu, he says [4]), I skirted several terrible mountains and at last after twenty-three days I reached the kingdom of Moranga. I passed only through a part of it and the only thing I saw was one settlement, which is called Hetunda. Then I arrived in ten days in the kingdom of Mogor, that is to say in India on the other side of the Ganges, and at league's distance I saw the town of Hagiapor, which is the first one meets on coming from Moranga. It is not far from Minapor on the Ganges.... The next town was Batane (Patna). — Thus we have at least 33 days, 23 of which were spent on the route Katmandu-Hetunda alone. An error, therefore, there must be, and it is precisely in the time assigned to this last-mentioned stretch that it must be sought. For Hetunda or, as Kircher writes, Hedonda, can hardly be other than Hitounda, which is described by Brian Hodgson in the Bengal Selections [5]), and for which Sylvain Lévi [6])

---

[1]) Stöcklein, I, 113.
[2]) Kircher, *China Illustrata*, p. 65.
[3]) Thévenot, IV, *Viaggio*, p. 2.
[4]) Kircher, *La Chine Illustrée*, p. 321.
[5]) *Bengal Selections*, XXVII (1857) p. 22.
[6]) Lévi, I, 86.

and Kurt Boeck [1]) write Hetaura. Grueber determined its latitude at 26° 36′ nearly one half degree south of the capital of Nepal [2]). Hodgson notes that the distance between the two is 19½ kos, the Nepalese kos being 2⅓ miles [3]); which works out at 45½ miles or 72 kilometres. That 23 days should be required to cover this distance is inconceivable even in a mountain region. Travelling in the opposite direction Boeck went from Hetaura to Katmandu in 2 days, but he pressed forward as fast as he could making 50 kilometres in one day. Kircher's five days, then, may safely be taken to be correct[4]).

The kingdom of Moranga is, says Markham, probably the same as Muring or Taraï, the swampy region between the mountains and the plain. Lévi [6]) on the other hand identifies it with the kingdom of Makwampur, probably on account of a remark in Thévenot's report to the effect that the kingdom of Maranga had to pay to the Great Mogul a yearly tribute of 250,000 tallari and 7 elephants [7]). As regards the other stopping places, Minapor, which is mentioned both in the Italian report and in the eighth answer, cannot from its situation on the Ganges be otherwise than Dinapur. The discrepancy between Kircher calling Mutgari, probably Motihari, the first town of the empire of the Mogul reached by Grueber, and the eighth answer mentioning Hagiapur (Hajipur) as such, may be considered as of minor importance.

The two way-worn travellers no doubt spent a few days at Patna of which the ever active Grueber availed himself to determine the latitude of the town, which he found to be 24° 44′, the present determination being 25° 37′ [8]). It may be mentioned in passing that nearly all of Grueber's latitudes are too low by 30′ on an average. Already Fathers Régis and Jartoux noticed this deviation when making their cartographical determinations. Du Halde is of opinion that most probably his instruments were at fault, or else,

---

1) Boeck, *Indien*, p. 235.

2) Here the French translator of *China Illustrata* has quite gone astray. Hedonda is called "la principale et la métropolitaine du Royaume de Mogor." (p. 104).

3) B. H. Hodgson, *Route of two Nepalese Embassies to Pekin* — Journal of the Asiatic Society of Bengal, XXV (1857) p. 475.

4) Kircher's further remarks about Moranga are wholly unintelligible. "Starting from Nepal they reached the frontiers of Moranga, which is part of Tibet. The capital is Radok [Rudok], the terminus of a journey undertaken by Father de Andrade in Tibet at an earlier period." (*China Illustrata*, p. 77).

5) Markham, p. 300, note 2.

6) Lévi, I, 87.

7) Thévenot, IV, *Viaggio*, p. 2; his French translation has "250,000 richedales".

8) *Gazetteer of India*, XIX, 65.

perhaps, he did not take sufficient account of the sun's diameter [1]).

Another twenty-five days' march by Benares and Katampor (Cawnpore) saw the travellers to Agra, where they arrived in the second half of March and met with a warm welcome from the Fathers Henry Roth and Henry Busaeus, then in charge of the mission of that town consisting of a church and a small college [2]). Probably they also met here F. Manucci, who by his own testimony had many talks about Tibet with the two travellers, but has transmitted no information about their experiences [3]). This was to be d'Orville's last halt. He arrived very ill and the very next day he had to take to his bed, from which he was not to rise again. The hardships and privations endured during those months of travel through the rugged Tibetan highlands and among the gigantic Himalayan ranges had broken his health and drained his bodily strength. His end was fast approaching and in a few days Grueber stood by the death-bed of his faithful companion, the sharer with him of countless dangers and fatigues: it was on the afternoon of Saturday in Holy Week, April 8, 1662 [4]). "Midway on his journey between China and Europe he departed for his heavenly home" [5]). In the evening of the same day his remains were interred in the so-called Martyrs' Chapel on the Catholic cemetery commonly called Padritola, where in 1906 Father Felix, a Capuchin Friar of the Lahore mission deciphered over his forgotten resting-place the following inscription: [6])

AQUI IAZO PE
ALBERTO DOR
VILLE FALECEO
EM AGRA AOS
8 D'ABRIL
1662
BELGA.

---

1) Du Halde, I, Preface, p. xv.

2) Cf. Bernier, p. 286.

3) Manucci, II, 440.

4) This is stated in Grueber's Obituary Notice of Father d'Orville, cf. Bosmans, p. 85. — April 2, the date adopted by Sommervogel (III, 149), Hosten (*Missionaries*, p. 33) and others cannot be maintained.

5) Kircher, *China Illustrata*, p. 77.

6) *Catholic Calendar and Directory for the Archdiocese of Agra and its suffragan dioceses of Allahabad and Lahore, and of the prefectures apostolic of Rajputana and Bettiah; entrusted to the Order of the Friars Minor Capuchin.* For the year 1907. Simla — *General historical records* No. IX. Father Santoos' chapel, or Martyrs' tomb, p. 215. Cf. Bosmans, p. 23.

Through d'Orville's premature death the duty of giving an account of the journey devolved wholly on Grueber, and thus Albert d'Orville's name has in the course of this chapter remained much in the background. Yet the memory of this stout-hearted Belgian is for ever linked to that of his Austrian companion, and in naming one we must not pass over the other — they are inseparable as are the names of Huc and Gabet, the latter of whom met, two centuries later, with a fate similar to d'Orville's. Grueber's high esteem of his friend is sufficiently proved by the eulogy he wrote in memory of him, March 29, 1664, on his arrival at Rome. He pays tribute to his many gifts of soul and body, his holy life, his patience, and especially to his unfailing cheerfulness in the midst of the greatest trials of the journey, the success of which was in great part owing to him [1]).

The differences between Kircher's account and the Gamans-letter have so far prevented any agreement as to the duration of the journey from Pekin to Agra. The former calculates 214 days of travel between the two towns, but adds that the addition of the days of rest would carry the time to one year and two months [2]). In his letter on the other hand, while stating at the outset that he left Pekin April 13, 1661, Grueber concludes by saying, "Here [at Agra] some rest could be taken after eleven months spent on the way from China" [3]). The point that could not be settled was: were these months to be counted from Hsi-ning or from Pekin? A reference to the dates now known to us will furnish the solution. Departure from Pekin April 13, 1661 — arrival at Agra shortly before April 8, 1662, the day of d'Orville's death, most probably therefore in the second half of March [4]). Hence eleven months were spent in covering the distance between Pekin and Agra, to which, therefore, the Gamans-letter must be taken to refer. Kircher's 214 days may still be considered as the number of days of actual travel, provided, as Tronnier remarks [5]), there be added

---

1) Bosmans, p. 82—85.

2) Kircher, *China Illustrata*, p. 66. "Ex Pequino itaque Agram usque, iter est continuatum 214 dierum, si moram spectas Caravanorum, iter est unius anni et duorum mensium circiter."

3) Thévenot, IV, *Autres Pièces etc.*, Second Letter. "Hic post undecim a Sinis itinere positorum mensium spatium aliquantum quiescere licuit."

4) This date it should be noted falls in quite naturally with the time-notices of the Lhasa-Agra stage of the journey.

5) Tronnier, p. 350.

the month spent on the Lhasa-Kutti route, which is omitted in Kircher's calculation, and raises the number of days to 244. The statement about the one year and two months is unquestionably erroneous [1]).

At Grueber's earnest request Father Henry Roth now became the companion of his travels [2]). From a letter of Roth it appears that by the written instructions he carried with him Grueber was to take another companion, if he should lose the one he had through death [3]). Having travelled to Lahore by way of Delhi they descended the Indus in a boat down to the port of Tattah. Without stopping long the indefatigable Grueber took his companion through Mekran and Karman to the island of Ormuz. From this point onward the road by Bender-Abbas through Mesopotamia to Smyrna was known to him. About the exact date of their arrival there has been much uncertainty. In Roth's letter written from Rome in 1664 and already referred to, he writes that he arrived there a short time before the battle of St. Gothard [4]), and as Monte-

---

[1]) Holdich (p. 72) has the following somewhat puzzling passage: "From Lhasa to India was a journey of one or two months (Grueber speaks of one month, but Kircher makes it two, which is the more probable if Agra was the terminus)." For it is a fact that the journey from Lhasa to Agra took three months at least. Is it, perhaps, that Holdich has mistakenly referred the time of rest at Lhasa to the journey Lhasa-Agra? For Grueber does, indeed, speak of a month's stay at Lhasa, whilst Kircher speaks of two months.

[2]) Henry Roth was born at Dillingen, December 18, 1620, and entered the Society of Jesus October 25, 1639. He left for India in 1650 and was at Smyrna in 1651; hence he proceeded to Goa *via* Ispahan. Being first engaged in mission work at Salsette near Goa he was transferred in 1656 to the Mogor Mission, first to Srinagar in Garhwal, afterwards to Agra, where by the time of Grueber's arrival he had governed the Jesuit College since 1659. — Having arrived at Rome and settled his affairs he immediately set out with Grueber on his return-journey. When Grueber was compelled by illness to stay behind at Constantinople, Roth continued his way alone and was back in the Mogor Mission certainly before November 1667. For in the catalogue of that date his name has the following note appended: "Nunc destinatus ad auspicandam missionem Napalensem." His work, however, was well-nigh ended. He died June 20, 1668, at Agra being under forty-eight years of age. This date is certain, not only from the Catalogus Defunctorum but also from the epitaph in the Martyrs' chapel in the Padritola churchyard. He was one of the first Europeans to obtain a great mastery of Sanskrit as was noted already in the '*Relaçao da Missao do Mogor del 1668*' by F. Manuel do Valle. Between p. 162—163 of Kircher's *China Illustrata* there are inserted five full-page copperplate engravings containing the alphabet and elements of Sankrit, the originals of which were drawn by Roth himself. They are the first specimens of Sanskrit ever printed in Europe. — There is an able essay on Roth from the pen of Prof. Seb. Euringer in *Jahrbuch des Historischen Vereins* (Dillingen 1918).

[3]) *Letter to F. John Paul Oliva at Rome*, dated Messina January 18, 1664.

[4]) Stöcklein, I, 113.

cucoli gained his victory over the Turks near St. Gothard on the Raab August 1, 1664, these words might be understood to point to July or June. But there was the fact of Grueber being at Venice on his way back to China and writing from that place to Kircher as early as May 10, 1664, and of his eulogy on d'Orville being dated Rome March 29, 1664. Clearly, therefore, Roth's statement was not to be taken too narrowly, and Grueber's arrival in the Eternal City was generally referred to the beginning of 1664 or the close of 1663. Fortunately every doubt is settled by a letter written by one Father G. Kaut on February 23, 1664 and probably addressed to some one in Germany [1]). He writes that the two travellers arrived safely at Rome February 20, 1664. Grueber had brought with him a Chinese, Roth a native of Mogor eighty-five years of age. The former had been on the road for three years, and from his account the overland route he had taken, though longer, was much safer and healthier than the sea-route.

The tireless Gueber scorned all rest. Arriving late in February he was again on his way back to China in the following May. On the 10th of that month he wrote to Kircher from Venice. They (himself and Roth) had arrived on the sixth of that month intending to take ship for the East. Four ships were about to sail, so there was no time to make proper preparations; on account of the war there was, moreover, great danger of their falling into the hands of the Turks. These circumstances and the advice of others had determined them to go to Poland with the object of reaching Persia through Moscovia, thus avoiding Turkish territory [2]). By way of Breslau and Danzig he went to Kurland, but learning on his arrival at Mitau that the empire of the Tsars was distracted by domestic troubles and the road to Astrakan barred by Tartars, he modified his plans, and, still having Roth as his companion, returned to Vienna and proceeded to Constantinople. But even Grueber's iron constitution could not bear up against the excessive fatigues of these interminable wanderings. He was taken seriously ill, and while Roth continued his journey to India by himself Grueber had to sail back to Leghorn and Florence, in which latter town the much-cited interview took place.

---

[1]) *Munich State Library*, Cod. Lat. 26472, p. 71. The letter begins "Tribus abhinc diebus.

[2]) Grueber, *Letter from Venice*, May 10, 1664: "Quare sciat nos sexta huius salvos et incolumes Venetias appulisse etc."

There is no evidence to show whether or not Grueber had any personal intercourse with the Emperor during his stay at Vienna, while it is certain that Roth had two conversations with him on the subject of their journey. They found in him a generous patron and benefactor. Not only did he give letters of recommendation for the dukes of Kurland and Moscow, but writing to the General of the Society of Jesus, Father Paul Oliva, September 17, 1664, Leopold I. declared that as the Dutch patrolled the ocean highways — and, perhaps, also to break the Portuguese monopoly — he accepted the patronage of the new overland route, by which some Fathers had already safely travelled to and from China; and that he wished his yearly contribution towards the equipment of missionaries to be earmarked for this route [1]).

Of Grueber's subsequent career we know next to nothing. He did not return to the Far East; but why? Was he so broken down in health that it was feared he would not be able to bear the fatigues and dangers of a fresh journey? Or were there other reasons opposing his return? We cannot say. From Grueber himself we only learn that after his recovery he returned to the Austrian province of his order [2]), but no reasons are given. Drawing on one of his unpublished letters we stated above, that for two years he was engaged as an army-chaplain to the imperial troops in Transsylvania, and that from September 1669 he was at ſyrnau and Trencsin, from which latter place he wrote to Kircher May 2, 1671. After this, all information is wanting, whence the variety of dates to which his death is assigned. The year 1665, which has been adopted by many [3]), need not be considered. The Jesuit list of departed members gives 1684, which is also held by Tronnier and Heawood. But as against these there is Sommervogel, who corrected his first date of 1665 into September 30, 1680 placing Grueber's death at Patak. This was correct in all points though the writer cited no authority [4]). For the MS. *Necrologia Provinciae Austriae* assigns September 30, 1680 as the date of his death at Patak (Saros patak) in Hungary [5]). He was nearly fifty-seven years of age.

[1]) "Hisce nos Fundatorem ac Protectorem huius itineris terrestris ad illas missiones declaramus." The full text is given by Huonder (p. 212). — On the non-committal reply of Father Oliva to the Emperor cf. Duhr, p. 335. note 2.

[2]) This is stated in his Necrologium of Father Roth.

[3]) Markham, p. lvii; Peschel-Ruge, p. 558; Huonder, p. 187; Levi, I, 81 etc.

[4]) Sommervogel, IX, 443.

[5]) Cf. *Appendix V.*

After this exhaustive discussion our summing up may be brief. While grateful for what Grueber gave us we cannot but regret that there is so very much more withheld from us. Arid as Tibetan uplands is Grueber's story: there is no description of landscape worth the name, not a word of admiration for the majestic ranges of the Himalaya or Transhimalaya, no homely picture of the life of his companions on the way or of his own life at Lhasa — nothing but cut-and-dried facts, few and brief, enough to whet the appetite, not to satisfy it. It is this niggardliness that drew a complaint from Ritter and prompted Markham to write: "Indeed, it would appear that Grueber was not very communicative; he has not the gift of narration "[1]). But with all this the expedition of the two missionaries remains in the words of the same writer a "wonderful journey".

---

[1]) Markham, p. lvii.

CHRONOLOGICAL SUMMARY

John Grueber.

Oct. 28, 1623.	born at Linz on the Danube.
Oct. 18, 1641.	enters the Society of Jesus.
end of 1656.	sets out for China.
May 1657.	arrival at Surat.
March 7, 1658.	letter to F. Haffenecker.
July 1658.	arrival at Macao.
1659—1661.	engaged at the Observatory of Pekin.

Albert d'Orville.

Aug. 12 or 20, 1621.	born at Brussels.
Oct. 30 or Nov. 2, 1646.	enters the Society of Jesus.
1651—1654.	theological student at Louvain.
1654—1656.	stationed at Rome.
1656.	sets out for China.
Jan. 30, 1658.	departure from Goa.
June 17, 1658.	departure from Macassar.
July 17, 1658.	arrival at Macao.
1659—1660.	stationed in Shan-si.
1660—1661.	engaged at the Observatory of Pekin.

April 13,	1661.	departure from Pekin.
June (end of)		arrival at Hsi-ning.
July 13,	1661.	leave the Great Chinese Wall.
Octob. 8,		arrival at Lhasa.
Nov. (end of)		departure from Lhasa.
Jan.	1662.	arrival at Katamdu.
March,		arrival at Agra.
April 8,	1662.	death of d'Orville at Agra.
Febr. 20,	1664.	arrival of Grueber and Roth at Rome.
April (?),	1664.	Grueber sets out on return journey accompanied by Roth.
Jan. 30,	1666.	interview with Carlo Dato at Florence on returning from Constantinople.
Sept. 30,	1680.	death of Grueber at Patak (Sarospatak-Hungary).

LIST OF MANUSCRIPTS[1]).

Letters of F. John Grueber to F. Athanasius Kircher at Rome:

May 10,	1664.	Letter from Venice.
Oct. 9,	1664.	„ „ Breslau.
Febr. 26,	1666.	„ „ Görz.
Sept. 20,	1669.	„ „ Tyrnau.
Oct. 7,	1669.	„ „ „
Dec. 13,	1669.	„ „ „
Jan. 13,	1670.	„ „ „
March 17,	1670.	„ „ „
Dec. 23,	1670.	„ „ Jaurini (Raab).
May 2,	1671.	„ „ Trencsin.

Letter of F. Henry Roth to F. Paul Oliva at Rom, dated Messina, Jan. 18. 1664.

Letter of F. G. Kaut to-, dated Rome, Febr. 23, 1664.
(Munich. *State Library*. Cod. Lat. 26472 p. 71).

Eulogy on F. Henry Roth written by Grueber, dated Tyrnau, Jan. 30. 1670.
(Munich. *State Archives*. Jesuitica in genere. Fasc. 13, no. 215).

Eulogy on F. John Grueber in *Provinciae Austriae Necrologia* for the years 1615—1685. p. 937—938.

CHAPTER VII

HIPPOLYTE DESIDERI

Father Desideri travelled by Kashmir and Ladakh to the capital of the Dalai Lama and made a prolonged stay at the city: this, or very little more, was not so long ago the sum and substance of the Italian traveller's contribution to the literature of Tibetan travel. The curious reader might turn to the only reference supplied, the translation of a letter written from Lhasa, April 10, 1716, in the *Lettres Edifiantes* [1]), but he would rise from its perusal with an intense feeling of disappointment: not a word about the long journey through the Tsangpo valley, not a word, worst of all, about Lhasa itself. It was the tantalizing incompleteness in this as in other documents that drew from Yule's pen the complaint that "a fatality has attended the accounts of Lhasa that *should* have been."

This was in 1866. Ten years later, in his book on Bogle and Manning, Clements Markham surprised his readers with the welcome statement that a manuscript of Desideri had been discovered at Pistoja, which was soon to be given to the public by the Hakluyt Society. Circumstances, however, prevented this plan from being carried out and nothing was done till in 1904 it was edited by the learned Professor Carlo Puini [2]). So far it has not met with the acknowledgment it deserves. Perhaps it is the flood of light which of late years has been thrown on modern Lhasa, especially by the expedition of Sir Francis Younghusband, which has relegated the more ancient records into a temporary obscurity. This neglect has not been without its attendant loss of historical truth and scientific accuracy, which however excusable in earlier writings,

---

[1]) *Lettres* VII, 259–268.

[2]) *Il Tibet* (*Geografia, Storia, Religione, Costumi*) *secondo la Relazione del Viaggio del P. Ippolito Desideri.* (*1715–1721*). Memorie della Società Geografica Italiana, vol. X (Roma 1904).

can now only reflect discredit upon the works in which those errors are originated or transmitted.

The MS. edited by Puini is at present in the Bibliotheca Nazionale of Florence; it is addressed to an unnamed missionary whom Desideri had met in the Carnatic mission. It contains 630 pages running on without any break till suddenly towards the end the headings: chapter 13, 14, 15 appear. For more convenient handling the editor divides the narrative into sections, but unfortunately their criss-cross arrangement renders a continuous reading of the journal impossible. Though the Florence MS. is in many places less clear and full than those cited in the list appended to this chapter and used by the present writer, still, as it is the only one in print and it may suit the reader to check the author's statements and conclusions, a reference will be given whenever it parallels a quotation from the MSS. A. or B [1]).

What was the occasion of Desideri's journey, what was the reason of this renewed interest in the Tibetan mission? These questions which have often been asked and never been answered, can now be settled.

From the third chapter the reader will remember the extinction of the Tsaparang mission. Since the time when Manuel Marques was a lonely prisoner there in 1641 it had been forbidden ground, but the hope of a future return had never been extinguished. Things remained as they were, till the man of push and position required to take up the matter, was found in Father Michael de Amaral [2]). On March 30, 1704, he was appointed Visitor to the Goa mission-province, and on studying the situation he resolved to re-establish the Tsaparang mission. Father Manuel Monteiro was commissioned to inquire at Agra about the most suitable route and to gauge the chances of success of a fresh effort [3]). When he died in 1707 he had not done more than gather some information from Armenian traders about the most practicable roads.

As Amaral meanwhile had been relieved of his post in 1706, the whole plan seemed off. But when he was again appointed Visitor in 1707 two young Goa missionaries, Fathers Carvalho and Gill,

[1]) See p. 275—281. Ritter (Asien II, 434) used a MS. of Desideri's journal, but as he gives no particulars, it cannot now be determined which.

[2]) Michael de Amaral, who was born December 13, 1657, at Viseu in Portugal, entered the Society in 1677 at Coimbra, where he died December 14, 1730.

[3]) He is registered in the Catalogue of November 1705 as being there "ad Thibetanam missionem investigandum."

certain of Amaral's support wrote to the General and volunteered for the Tibetan mission [1]). Though they did not see their wishes fulfilled, the Visitor's influence continued to be felt. For on December 15, 1708, the Provincial Manuel Saraya informed the General that at the instance of F. de Amaral he had appointed John Carvalho and Peter de Torres for Tibet, but had been forced by the death of two missionaries in Maysore to send them thither to supply the vacancies. Rome favoured and even urged the return to the old mission-field as appears from a letter of the General F. Tamburini of July 6, 1709 [2]).

Probably before receiving this letter, on January 3, 1710, Saraya informed the General that Fathers Joseph Martinetti and Francis Koch had been charged to undertake a new venture from Agra — though in fact nothing came of it — and on December 28, 1710 he re-affirmed his diligence in the matter [3]). Such was the state of affairs when on September 27, 1713, Father Desideri disembarked at Goa.

Born at Pistoja December 21, 1684, Ippolito Desideri entered the Society of Jesus April 27, 1700. After his ordination August 28, 1712, he set out from Rome for Lisbon on September 27 in company with Father Hildebrand Grassi [4]). At Genoa they were joined by Father Francis del Rosso and about the middle of March the party arrived at Lisbon, where the three took ship for India April 6, 1713 [5]).

Was Desideri specially commissioned by the autorities at Rome to re-establish the Tibet mission? We have it on his own autho-

---

[1]) *Letter of F. John Carvalho*, dated Goa, January 15, 1708, and *letter of F. Peter Gill*, dated Goa, Febuary 2, 1708.

[2]) "Ex data occasione valde commendamus ut aperiantur novae missiones et ferventius agatur de reditu ad Tibetum. Nec deterreant ullae difficultates, nam causa Dei est, qui iam sternit viam per Mogolense imperium" — quoted in *Desideri's letter from Goa* November 15, 1713.

[3]) There is no need to dwell on the undertaking of the two last-mentioned missionaries. Writing from Daman to the General November 29, 1713, Martinetti sums up under four heads the reasons for giving up that mission. He concludes with an appeal for his recall to Europe "since he has deserved better than to live an exile in this strange land." Evidently this man was not the stuff of which missionaries are made and that he could be mistaken for a possible successor to an Andrade seems, to say the least, somewhat surprising.

[4]) Hildebrand Grassi was born at Bologna in 1683 and became a Jesuit at Rome January 23, 1699. After working in the Mysore mission he died at Pondichery May 22, 1731.

[5]) *Letter of F. Anthony de Paiva to the General*, dated Lisbon April 18, 1713.

rity [1]) that for some time before leaving Europe he had entertained the idea of working in that field, and his purpose to devote himself to that mission was approved of and blessed by Pope Clement XI. at a special audience granted to the two travellers, but neither Desideri's letters nor any other extant writing contain any hint, that he had a special charge with regard Tibet. His letters rather go to show that he had not. Thus when writing to the General on November 12 and 15, 1713, he informs him that he has been *chosen* and *destined* for the new mission by the Provincial and that he is delighted at the appointment. He then urges the General to address him a special letter confirming the appointment and ordering him (Desideri) explicitly to open the mission of Tibet and to act in all this under direct responsibility to Rome; thus he will be able to overcome all the difficulties that may be raised against the undertaking [2]). Six weeks later he returns to this point [3]).

A constructive reading, therefore, of Desideri's letters would point to this sequence: first the Provincial at Goa made up his mind that the mission should be re-established, after which Desideri very likely volunteered, as he had done already before leaving Europe, and was accepted; he then sought authority for his enterprise directly from Rome.

We might now set about examining Desideri's geographical work, but such aspersions have been cast on his name — and not on his only — that no writer of credit could pass them over in silence; he must repeat or repulse the charges, not indeed on hearsay but on historical evidence.

What then is the case? In 1702 Tibet had been assigned as a mission-field to the Capuchins and in 1707 two of them had reached Lhasa through Nepal. They left again in 1711 and on their return in October 1716 they found Desideri in residence, who had travelled by way of Leh and Gartok and had arrived there some six months before. The question, which naturally arose, as to which

[1]) Puini, p. 3.

[2]) *Letter from Goa*, November 12, 1713. "Si compiace S. D. M. per mezzo del P. Provinciale di chiamarmi e destinarmi alla nuova Missione del Tibet."

Letter from Goa, November 15, 1713.... "nella quale espressamente mi da ordine di andar' ad aprir la Missione del Tibet, e di andare con l'autorità e dipendenza immediata di V. P.[ta]". etc.

[3]) *Letter from Surat*, December 30, 1713.... "que si degni con la sua autorità di confirmarmi l'avviso di andar' a riaprire la Missione del Tibet, datomi in Goa dal P. Provincial." etc.

party was to cultivate this arid field, was referred for settlement to Rome. Desideri meanwhile stayed at Lhasa or in the Capuchin house in Takpo-Khier on the best of terms with his hosts. When in 1721 he received orders from Rome to leave Tibet, he went at once. At Rome meanwhile the affair had been placed before the competent ecclesiastical tribunal, and Desideri on his return urged the claims of his Order, who had been the first to missionize Tibet, till in 1732 decision was given in favour of the Capuchins.

These events have led some modern authors to ascribe the journey to motives frankly dishonourable. Thus Sandberg bluntly tells his readers that "an agent of the Society" was sent "in the hope of being able to discredit the same" [1]) i. e. the Capuchins. Which assertion Sir Thomas Holdich does not shrink from improving upon by saying that Desideri went "to inquire into the working of the Capuchin missions and to discredit them as far as possible" [2]). Landon, short and sweet, stamps Desideri and his companion "Jesuit spies", which is evidently the main thing his historical conscience prompts him to say on the subject [3]).

As against these asseverations we first of all plead the absence of so much as a shred of evidence for those sweeping condemnations; we secondly refer to the audience granted by the Pope, who gave his blessing over Desideri's enterprise; we thirdly point out that Desideri *was never sent to Lhasa at all*, so that it is beating the air for a writer to hunt for motives why he was sent there. He was commissioned to re-establish the mission of Andrade as is abundantly clear from the plans of Amaral and the letters of Desideri.

What then was it, that brought the latter to Lhasa? Desideri will tell us presently what finally decided him, but we may point out that both Freyre, the superior of the travelling-party, and Desideri had clearly but very vague notions of the place where Andrade's mission had been and of Tibetan geography in general, while at the same time it is antecedently improbable, from their line of travel through Kashmir and Ladakh, that from the outset Lhasa can have been their goal. The letter of Desideri alluded to above was written to the General August 5, 1715. In it he says that on reaching Ladakh he wanted to stay there [4]). But his com-

[1]) Sandberg, *Exploration*, p. 52.

[2]) Holdich, p. 78.

[3]) Landon, I, 9, the tangle of errors that make up the six-line account of Desideri may be left to be straightened out by the author himself.

[4]) Puini, p. 368 ff.

panion objected. Accustomed to the Indian climate and worn with fatigue and hardship the latter only desired to get back to Mogor at the earliest opportunity. He did not care to take the road he had come. On inquiring about the possibility of going back by way of Srinagar and learning that this would take him through the mountains, he cast about for other possible routes and these investigations led to the discovery that besides Little and Great Tibet there was a greater one yet, the capital of which was Lhasa. It would take three months to reach. Freyre knew there were Capuchins there, but he also knew that from that place Mogor was easier to reach than from where he was now. This made him resolve to go [1]).

Desideri is against it. He does not want to go back to Mogor, but to do mission work in Tibet; moreover, in that third Tibet there are missionaries already, so there is no need for others to go there [2]). Freyre does not insist but leaves him free to stay in Ladakh on his own responsibility; Freyre himself will go to that third Tibet, where Father Andrade was once, because such is the mind of the Superiors [3]). Thus placed before the alternative either to stay where he is or to go on and help to re-establish the mission of Andrade, Desideri gives way and resolves to go with Freyre.

Thus it was that the two travelled to Lhasa, and thus it is that the idea of espionage or discrediting the Capuchins was as far away from their minds as the pens of Sandberg, Holdich an Landon travelled away from historical truth when they wrote down their unfounded charges.

On receiving his appointment at Goa Desideri left for Surate November 13, 1713 [4]), where he learnt that Father Manuel Freyre was to be his Superior and travelling companion. The leisure left him by his preparations was made use of to obtain a smattering

---

[1]) "Il P. Superiore siccome non vuol restare in verun modo in questo Thibet, cosi si protesta di non voler rimanere nel terzo, ma di ritornare al Mogor", etc.

[2]) "Aggiungasi che costa di certo che là furono i P. P. di Propaganda, e perciò non vi è necessita d'altri Missionarj".

[3]) "Dipoi soggiunse, che egli in ogni caso voleva andar al terzo Thibet, dove anticamente era andato il P. Andrade, per esser tale l'intenzione de i Superiori".

[4]) In his *Letter from Leh*, August 5, 1715 he dates his arrival on January 4, 1714 (Cf. Puini, p. 361). This must be an error since he wrote to the General from Surate on December 30, 1713.

of Persian. Proceeding to Dehli March 26, he arrived at this place May 11. As the wet season rendered further travelling impossible for some three or four months he made a trip to Agra and was back at Delhi by the end of August. Meanwhile Freyre had also arrived here and on September 24 the two set their faces northward for Lahore, from whence crossing the Pir Panjal Range they reached the town of Caximir, the present Srinagar, November 13, 1714 [1]).

Desideri gives a detailed description of this town, the Venice of India, standing in its wonderful plain of the Jehlam with its belt of lakes and delightful gardens, thriving on its traffic in wool and its world-famous shawls. On his arrival winter was fast approaching closing up the mountain passes. His health, moreover, had been severely shaken by repeated haemorrage of the lungs. So there was nothing for it but to await a better season and his enforced leisure of some months was used to ground himself in Persian. Provided with the necessary passports and letters of recommendation for the king of Ladakh they resumed their journey on May 17, 1715 with three Christian servants and an interpreter; a twelve days' journey took them to "a very high mountain called Contel, on whose top the first or Little Tibet begins" [2]). The next day, being in that year Ascension-day, the ascent was begun amid a heavy fall of snow and it was night before they came upon the first settlement at the other side.

All later travellers are agreed that this mount Contel can only be the Zoji and that the pass they followed must, therefore, have been the Zoji-la [3]). Moorcroft who traversed this pass in October 1822 was the first to identify it. "It is this part of the pass to which the name of Zwaje-la is applied and which seems to be the same as the Baltal Kotal of Desideri". The name of the "first settlement" is not given by Desideri. It cannot be the "first fortified place" of which Desideri speaks in a letter written from Leh

[1]) Desideri, MS. A. Book I, ch. VII. p. 44. Cf. Puini, p. 6. A French translation of Desideri's letter dated Lhasa, April 10, 1716, (*Lettres Ed.* VII, 260) puts their arrival at Srinagar on March 10, but in MS. B. Book III, ch. XLII, p. 435, Desideri advises the reader of the untrustworthiness of this translation citing as a case in point the erroneous date of his arrival at Srinagar. Markham (p. 363) has noted this error.

[2]) Desideri, MS. A. Book I, ch. XIII. p. 47. In Puini's edition (p. 11) the name of the mountain is not given though it is mentioned in a description of Little Tibet further down (p. 26 & 363).

[3]) The height is set down at 11, 120 ft. in Dr. De Filippi's ***Expedition to the Karakorum and Central-Asia 1913–1914***. — Geographical Journal LXVI (1915) p. 87.

on August 5, 1715, when he says the route lay through snow and ice as far as Dias, the first fortified place of this country [1]). For here can only be meant what at present is called Dras. But between this and Baltal, the last halting-place before the pass in Kashmir, there is a difficult stretch of some thirty miles, which, according to Drew, it takes two long days to cover. The first stopping-place on the Tibetan side is the hamlet of Matayan, sixteen miles from Dras, where no doubt our travellers stayed for the night [2]).

This first or Little Tibet, Desideri continues, is called Baltistan in the vernacular. It is not very wide in extent. To the south it borders on Mogol, in the west and the north on some parts of Turkestan, towards the north-east it extends as far as Caxkar (Kashgar) and eastward it touches on the second Tibet, Lhata-yul (Ladakh). First divided into some princedoms it has these thirty years been under Mohammedan rule. Though the language differs somewhat from that of the third Tibet (Utsang), it is in all essentials the same. There are no towns, but villages and hamlets, and most of the houses are half sunk into the ground. The country produces only barley, wheat and some vegetables, but no fruit except apricots. At one time the people professed the same religion as the inhabitants of the rest of Tibet, but during the Mogul domination most have passed over to that sect. The administration is conducted by the governor of Kashmir [3]).

Desideri does not touch upon the question, still debated among ethnologists, whether the Baltis are of Arian or of Tibet-Mongolian stock [4]). The language is evidently Tibetan [5]), and only a few years ago the Reverend Donsen found numerous traces of the ancient Buddhism in the religious practices of the now Mohammedan population; there are, moreover, numerous ruins of ancient Lama-monasteries scattered about the country. The productivity of the soil has not improved, and wheat, barley and dried apricots are still the only articles of commerce of Baltistan [6]).

A few days' travel carried the missionaries into the second Tibet

---

[1]) Cf. Puini, p. 363. Ujfalvy (p. 262) describes this town as a group of houses scattered about a stronghold.

[2]) Drew, p. 225; Moorcroft, II, 94.

[3]) Desideri, MS. A. Book I, ch. VIII p. 48. Partly in Puini, p. 26.

[4]) Cf. Ujfalvy, p. 244; Ratzel, III, 333.

[5]) Ujfalvy, p. 212.

[6]) Donsen, p. 431, 423.

or Lhata-yul. "One some maps it is called the kingdom of Ladak, Rudoc and Coghe. It extends over a fairly large distance eastward and westward. On the former side it borders on Baltistan, towards the north on Caxkar and some parts of the kingdom of Sokpo, also called Giongar, that is to say, independent Tartary. Towards the east it extends as far as the great desert, of which I shall speak later. In the south it touches on the territories of Collahor [Kulu], Sirenagar [Garhwal] and others. The language and religion agree with those of the third Tibet. Having first consisted of small kingdoms, such as Coghe [Guge], Redoc or Retôa, Lhata and others, the whole of it is now subject to Lhata [Ladakh]. The whole country is mountainous, fairly unproductive, and has but a scant population. It produces plenty of barley, little wheat, and as regards fruit, chiefly apricots. Trade with other countries is very insignificant, and is limited to a very fine wool, a small quantity of gold-bearing sand and musk. . . . Trees and wood-fuel are scarce, cattle plentiful. The staple food is roasted barley-meal and meat, whilst the popular drink is Ciang [Chang], a kind of beer made from barley [1]). Tea, however, is drunk several times a day. Their wearing apparel is of wool. Their natural disposition is not proud, but docile, polite, cheerful and kind. There are numerous monasteries with many monks, all of whom live under a chief lama. To attain to this dignity, however, study in one of the universities of the greatest Tibet is necessary, which, indeed, is required of every one who wants to rise. . . . There are no large towns, but only villages, farmsteads and castles, with the one exception of Lhe or Lhata, the capital both of the King and of the Chief-Lama of this kingdom. This town, situated in a wide plain entirely surrounded by mountains and studded with villages, is built up the slope of a mountain up to the residence of the Chief-Lama and the palace of the King, large and fine buildings. The whole is crowned with a large fort close to the summit, on which there is another fort. Below and on the flanks the town is surrounded by walls and defended by gates" [2]).

Down to the smallest details this description of land and people is confirmed by later visitors: quotations from Thomson, Drew, Hedin and others might be multiplied, but it may suffice to refer

---

[1]) "Chang" is "a light beer made without hops". Drew, p. 247.

[2]) Desideri, MS. A. Book I, ch. VIII. p. 49—51; Puini, p. 30—31, with some minor discrepancies here and there.

the reader to the elaborate description given by Moorcroft [1]), who after the lapse of a century was the first European to visit Ladakh and Leh.

The route followed from Baltistan to Leh is not accurately traced by Desideri. The first places in Ladakh were ruled, we learn, by a petty independent Mohammedan prince, who received them well in his fortified hill-top town. He even gave them an escort to send them safely across one of those rope bridges of plaited willow twigs, which is minutely described by Desideri, for though we are at present amply acquainted with these kind of structures, to him it was something unique [2]). A few days later they reached an important town, where the son of the Longbo, or first minister, of Ladakh was governor. The names of these two places cannot be more than guessed at. Puini supposes them to be the fortress of Dras and the monastery-town of Lamayuru, but whatever be said of the last conjecture, the first can hardly be maintained as Desideri considers Dras to be a town of Baltistan. In the writer's opinion Kargil in the Mohammedan part of Ladakh would be a likely halting-place [3]).

Forty days after their departure from Srinagar the party entered Leh. The many hardships of such a march on foot along frightful roads had exhausted Freyre's endurance, and no sooner had he arrived than he tried to find out if there was any possibility of returning to Mogor by another road. When the answer was in the negative, it was resolved to push on to Lhasa [4]).

They met with a very kind welcome, which extended from June 26 to August 17 and if at the end of these two months [5]) the king

---

[1]) Moorcroft, I, 259—346.

[2]) Desideri, MS. A. Book I, ch. VIII. p. 51—52. Cf. Puini, p. 28. In Book II, ch. IV. p. 18—20 this kind of bridge is again spoken of at length.

[3]) When in 1822 Moorcroft visited Pashkyum, a town south-west of Kargil, on a tributary of the Suru River, the rajah showed him a book, which he had inherited from his grandfather. "It was an edition of the Old and New Testament from the Papal press, dated in the year 1598. It was bound in morocco with the initials IHS surmounted by a cross, stamped on each side of the cover. How it had come there no person could inform me, but it might possibly have been given to the former rajah by Desideri who visited Ladakh, although it is very doubtful if he reached Le". (Moorcroft II. 22). The device on the cover of the book evidently points to its Jesuit origin, but from the date 1598 it can hardly be supposed to have been carried out to Tibet by Desideri in 1715; it would rather have been left there by Father Azevedo during his visit to Leh in 1631.

[4]) Desideri, *Letter from Leh*. August 5, 1715. Puini, p. 366.

[5]) Desideri, MS. A. Book I, ch. IX. p. 54; not three months, as stated in Puini, p. 32.

had had his way, they would have settled there. Only once the harmony threatened to be disturbed when it was given out by merchants from Kashmir that those two poor foreigners were disguised traders carrying large quantities of precious pearls. An inquiry, however, soon settled these stories.

In his *Relazione* Desideri does not mention the name of the king, but in his Lhasa-letter to Grassi he calls him Nima Nangial [1]), the same therefore as Nyi-ma-nam-gyal, the great-grandson of Seng-genam-gyal, as appears from Dr. Marx's Ladakh documents [2]).

On August 17, 1715, they proceeded again on their great journey, this time on horseback and with guides. Soon they entered upon the wide plains called in the vernacular Ciang-Thang or 'northern plain'. They are covered partly with dead and foul water, partly with veins of sulphur and pools of sulphurous water. The rotten water and tainted air are very dangerous both for men and horses and cause such violent swellings of the gums and lips as sometimes to endanger life. Relief and cure for man and beast can only be obtained from the chewing of various herbs, especially aloë. On the evening of September 7 the caravan took up its quarters at Treêscy-Khang "Casa dell'Allegrezza", the first strongly fortified frontier-town of the third or greatest Tibet [3]).

Ciang-Thang or Chang-tang 'the Northern Plain', is the general name comprising the whole of the table-land of northern Tibet. "This is the region of highest elevation too high and too cold for anything but pastoral use, where salt-lakes are scattered at intervals amidst vast sterile flats, where grass is scanty and trees are absolutely wanting" [4]). The mere mention of this plain, however, still leaves a considerable choice of route. It is unlikely that our travellers have taken the direct road through the Indus valley judging from the distance and the time of actual travel; for the road from Leh to Treêscy-Khang, the present Tashigong, some five miles below the point where the Singh-gi and Gartang Rivers join to form the Indus, is only 275 miles, which it would have taken them three weeks to cover. Now Hedin was told on good authority that the journey from Leh to Gartok, about 70 miles beyond Tashigong, is reckoned at only 22 caravan-days [5]). Since, moreover, no

[1]) *Lettres*, VII, 263.
[2]) Marx, p. 99.
[3]) Desideri, MS. A. Book I. ch. IX. p. 56—57; Puini, p. 32—33.
[4]) Holdich, p. 35.
[5]) Hedin, *Transhimalaja*, III. 30.

traveller mentions bad or sulphurous water close to the valley road, we may safely conclude, that Desideri has followed a circuitous route, and that possibly from the Indus-valley he crossed over to Tankse through the Ke-la; thence skirting the southern shore of the Pangong Lake he may have made for Thangra on the Indus, his route thus partly coinciding with the one that was to be followed by Littledale [1]).

With a view to the dangerous journey through the sterile wastes that lay before them, they now looked about at Tashigong for a caravan which they might join; luck served them beyond all expectation. At a distance of two days, Desideri tells us, in a large plain called Cartoâ a strong, permanent force of Tartar and Tibetan soldiers was stationed not only for the defence of the frontier-fortress of Treêscy-Khang and the surrounding settlements, but more especially to watch all those who from that side entered the country. The commander, a Tartar prince, had died and his widow had taken over the command till a new governor should arrive. When about to return to Lhasa, she came for a last inspection to Treêscy-Khang. Our travellers at once applied for permission to travel under the protection of her numerous retinue, which was readily granted, and starting on October 9 they arrived two days later at Cartoâ [2]).

That Cartoâ is the present Gartok there is no doubt. Though Desideri connects the name only with the plain, there can be no difficulty in admitting one name both for a settlement and the surrounding country, or rather for a two-branched settlement and the intervening tract of country. For as Rawling tells us, "Gartok in reality consists of two different places situated forty miles apart. The one we visited is known as Gar Yarsa or Summer Quarters and the other which is also on the Indus but at a lower altitude Gar Gunsa or Winter Quarters" [3]). These topographical remarks will also settle any doubt as to the feasibility of covering in two days the seventy miles that separate Tashigong from Gartok; to reach Gar Gunsa or the "Winter Gartok" they only had to travel thirty miles.

In a few days the new caravan was ready to move and the two

---

[1]) Hedin, *Southern Tibet*, I, 272 makes the loop somewhat too deep by supposing Desideri to have gone round by Rudok.

[2]) Desideri, MS. A. Book I, ch. X. p. 58 – 59. Puini, p. 43.

[3]) Rawling, p. 272.

missionaries set out for Lhasa along a road where no European expedition was to follow them till that of Rawling and Ryder in 1904. On the 9th of November they reached "the highest region we have traversed during the whole of our peregrinations. It is a complete desert, called Ng-nari Giongar, and is held in the highest veneration on account of a certain Urghien, the founder of the Tibetan religion. Away from the road there stands an enormously high mountain, very wide in circumference, its summit hidden among the clouds, covered with perpetual snow and ice, and most terrible on account of the icy cold. In a cave of that mountain, according to the legend, there lived the above-mentioned Urghien in absolute retirement and uninterrupted meditation. In his honour this cave has been changed into a temple, which has a rude unshapely monastery attached to it, the residence of a lama and some monks of the sect, who serve the temple. Not only do the Tibetans visit the cave, where they invariably leave some presents, but with very great inconvenience to themselves they make the round of the whole mountain, an occupation of some days, by which they gain what I might call great indulgences" [1]).

For the first time from the pen of a European we have here mentioned and described one of the most sacred spots of Buddhist Tibet. For this "mountain of Urghien" is the Kang-Rinpoche or Kailas, 22,028 feet high, the seat of the gods for the religious world of Central-Asia, around whose base foregather weary pilgrims from the farthest corners of the Tibetan uplands and the Himalayan fastnesses, that by a visit to the monastery and a round of the mountain they may be protected from all evil for the rest of their lives [2]).

For the most complete and best-illustrated description of this mountain the reader should turn to Sven Hedin's third journey in 1907 [3]). Personally he made the circuit along the pilgrim road, which it takes an ordinary pedestrian two days to complete. If a man should wish to obtain the merit of thirteen such rounds at once, he must measure the whole of the sometimes dangerous mountain road with his own body, till after many thousands of

---

[1]) Desideri, MS. A. Book I, ch. X. p. 60. Puini, p. 44.

[2]) See, among others, Kawachugi, p. 167. ff.

[3]) Hedin, *Transhimalaja*, II, p. 164—177; for the illustrations see Nos. 267, 269 ff; Cf. also *Southern Tibet*, II, *passim*.

these prostrations the round is completed [1]). As regards Urghien, whose memory is venerated here, he is better known by his Indian name of Padmasambhavâ 'the Lotus-born one', or by that of Guru Rinpoche, 'the precious Guru' given him by the Tibetans. He is the founder of Lamaism and was given the surname of Ugyan or Urgyan, because he was a native of Udyana or Urgyan, which term, according to Yule not only denotes Udyana north of Peshawar but the whole hill region south of the Hindu Kush between Chitral and the Indus [2]).

Desideri is perfectly correct in describing the parts he was now traversing as the highest of his journey, for by the Jer-ko La, a pass 16,200 feet high but not difficult of access, he had entered upon the inhospitable wastes of the province of Ngari, where the proud Kailas rears its giant height. Rawling, who traversed this region in the beginning of December, describes it as a barren and desolate country. "Grass undoubtedly grows in great profusion during the summer months, though at the time of our visit it was all dead and withered, herds of goats picking up here and there their scanty sustenance of the shrivelled blades. As grass decreased in quantity so the prickly scrub proportionately increased, covering the lower slopes of the mountains and the hollows in the plains and growing at times in such profusion as to almost obliterate the track" [3]).

Continuing their route across this high plateau the caravan reached a sandy plain called Toscioa [4]), with some roaming herds of yaks and horses belonging to the Great Lama and the King. After a two days' rest in the first days of December, the party drew near another holy spot, the sacred lake of Mansarowar, famous in Hindu mythology. The journal dwells on this part at length. "A little further we traversed a plain called Retôa, in which is situated a large lake, some days' march in circumference, from which the Ganges is supposed to take its rise. If, however, I am permitted to give an opinion from my own observations and from what I have heard asserted by persons who know both these regions and the

---

[1]) According to Rawling (p. 263) the ordinary round takes about three days, the extraordinary one three weeks.

[2]) Cf. Waddell, *Buddhism*, p. 25—26. In his chapters on Buddhism Desideri returns several times to the subject of Urghien, e. g. MS. B. ch. 35 & 36, p. 357—381.

[3]) Rawling, p. 264.

[4]) Hedin, *Southern Tibet*, I, 274, conjectures Tokchen, but this is east of Mansarowar lake, while in the journal Toscioa is reached before the lake.

kingdom of Mogor, I should think that this mountain system of Ng-nari Giongar is the source not only of the Ganges but also of the Indus. For as this is the highest spot from which the land sinks down on both sides, the water, whether from rainfall or thaw, which runs down the western slopes, flows towards the secord Tibet [Ladakh] as experience most clearly shows. Thence it goes to Baltistan, breaks through the mountains of Kashmere and at last reaches Little Guzzarat, there to form the broad and navigable Indus. In like manner the water that flows down the eastern side of Ng-nari Giongar, first enters lake Retôa, thence takes its course downwards and thus gradually becomes the Ganges. To this a conjecture may be added [1]). Famous in the writings of our forefathers are the gold-bearing sands of the Ganges. But the supposition that this river has its source elsewhere would take away all ground for their statement and make it into a fabrication, since in no other part of the river the slightest vestige of such sand is to be found. If, on the other hand, my view be accepted, that the origin of the Ganges is to be sought in the Ng-nari Giongar mountains and in the lake Retôa — also called Redok — [2]) their assertion is in accordance with the truth.

"For it is known — I may say all over the world — that on the shores and in the sands of this lake large quantities of gold-dust are found, which is carried down by the drainage of the Ng-nari Giongar and other intervening mountains. Tibetan and other merchants come to the lake from time to time to search for and collect the gold, which brings them a good profit.

"This lake, moreover, is held in high veneration by the superstitious people. In consequence they sometimes go there on pilgrimage and with great devotion walk round it, thinking thus to gain great indulgences, if I may so express myself" [3]).

It is at once clear from this first description [4]) of the Mansarowar lake (for no other lake can be meant), whose hydrographic import has raised so many discussions, that Desideri had not broken away from the tradition of the ages as regards the origin of

---

[1]) "S'aggiugne a ciò una conjettura." In the Puini MS. "confirmasi ciò da una particolarità".

[2]) This parenthesis is not in Puini, where there are also some other minor discrepancies.

[3]) Desideri, MS. A. Book I, ch. X. p. 60—61; Puini, p. 45—46.

[4]) A first brief mention was made by F. Monserrate as early as 1591. Cf. Monserrate, p. 560.

the Ganges, on which enough has been said in the chapter on Father Andrade. The Sutlej River was the Ganges and for the honour of antiquity it must remain so, though Desideri's opinion may also have been influenced by the name Ganga or Nganga, by which the channel joining the Mansarowar lake and Rakas Tal is still known at the present day. But no one has a right to reproach Desideri with this error. "Who could require of him, that in two days' time he should have fully investigated those wonderful watercourses on which explorers and travellers have been at issue for two centuries afterwards. I have spent more time exploring the country about the lakes than any of my predecessors, and to me it gives a sense of restfulness and refreshment when in Father Desideri's old journal I again come across 'il lago di Retôa' " [1]).

But whence the name Retôa? Hedin remarks that "Retoa or Redoc is Rudok, a name which he has heard and either misunderstood or misplaced when writing his narrative "[2]), which is plausible and may be correct. Perhaps a hint for another solution may be found in the name Reta-puri [3]), which is given by Ekai Kawaguchi as the name of a place in the upper-Sutlej, and which may be supposed to have had reference in Desideri's time to the whole of the lake country.

To take up again the trail of the travellers, they now proceeded for several weeks through a desert-like and fornlorn region, which however, he warns us, should not be considered as entirely valueless. Both the King and the Great Lama derive great profits from it. In the first place tolls are taken from all passing travellers [4]). Then, there is fairly large quantity of gold found and the numerous herds, that find their sustenance on those plains, yield an abundance of excellent butter. Nain Singh observed that "from the Manasarowar to Ralung, 400 miles, there were no villages and no cultivation of any kind. The mountains had a very desolate appearance, but still numerous large camps of black tents and thousands of sheep, goats and yaks were seen. The fact being that the mountain sides, though looking so arid and brown, do produce a very nourishing coarse grass" [5]).

[1]) Hedin, *Transhimalaja*, III, 178.

[2]) Hedin, *Southern Tibet*, I, 275.

[3]) Kawaguchi, p. 159.

[4]) On arriving at Lhasa he was requested to pay a sum of 120 rupees, due to the Cartôa customhouse, but was he let off on entering a protest. (MS. A. Book II, ch. XII. p. 75).

[5]) *Records*, I, 11.

On January 4 the desert-like country lay behind them and they reached the first habitations of the third Tibet, "a large settlement called Ser-kia, a well fortified place, the residence of a great Deva, governor and chief of the province of Zzang-to" [1]). As the Tartar princess was taken ill here and the missionaries were not permitted to proceed by themselves, their journey was not resumed till January 28, when it was continued through a better country with many small villages and with only two large towns, Secchia and Giegazze, at each of which they stayed a few days. At length ten months after their departure from Srinagar the roofs of the mighty Potala loomed before the eager eyes of the travellers and on March 18, 1716, they set foot within the holy city of Lhasa [2]).

Having reached his goal Desideri, quite naturally, casts a look back on the long and laborious journey and recounts at length the tale of his experiences: the difficulties of supply, the want of fuel, life in a tent, the unbearable cold, the difficult, sometimes impracticable roads through snow and ice, the care of the horses, of which he lost five out of seven between Leh and Lhasa — all this and much more is passed in review [3]). But these need not to detain us here; narratives of like experiences are accessible to the reader in any modern book of Tibetan travel, though it should never be forgotten that through their ignorance of mountain-travel, its conditions, its difficulties and dangers these two pioneers had to struggle against far heavier odds than the well-read, well-equipped and often well-experienced mountain-travellers of modern times. Nor should we forget another feature, which even in the case of the present-day explorer is singled out for special mention. In the discussion following Ryder's lecture at the Royal Geographical Society Sir Francis Younghusband and other speakers specially emphasised how much more arduous Ryder's journey had become on account of this fact alone that it had been performed at the beginning of the cold season, Gyangtse being left on October 10 to arrive at Gartok on December 10 [4]). What then to say of our travellers who from the second part of October to the middle of March bore up against the pitiless severity of a Tibetan winter.

---

1) Desideri, MS. A. Book I, ch. X. p. 62. Puini, p. 47.

2) Desideri, MS. A. Book I, ch. X. p. 62 and ch. XI. p. 69; Puini, p. 47, 50. Serkia, Secchia and Giegazze will be treated of at a later page.

3) Desideri, MS. A. Book I, ch. X. pp. 62–69; a more succint account in Puini, p. 51–54.

4) Ryder, p. 392.

One more remark remains to be made on this part of Desideri's journey. For weeks on end his route has lain along the southern base of the Transhimalaya mountains, yet he has practically nothing to remark on this huge range. He knows the Kailas, mentions the mountains round Lhasa, but never even hints that the whole of his route from Mansarowar to Lhasa is bordered by mountains on its northern side; it is only the Himalaya, Langur as he calls it with Grueber, which he thinks worth mentioning. Is not this strange? Not so to one who has traced Desideri's steps, is Sven Hedin's answer. The difficulties of its crossing stamp the Himalaya on the mind beyond all possibility of effacement. But with the Transhimalaya things are otherwise. It is only from two points down in the deep river-valley that it is specially impressive, along the rest of the route the nearest mountains which shut off the main ridge are not remarkably high, and one may pass alongside of them without even a suspicion of the gigantic range beyond [1]).

Father Freyre meanwhile had not given up the plan of which he had been frustrated at Leh. Closer acquaintance had not reconciled him to the climate, and the intense cold and the thin air of the Tibetan highlands proved too much for a constitution already weakened by a stay of many years in the tropics. On reaching Lhasa he hardly allowed himself a few days' rest before he returned to Hindustan through Nepal [2]).

Thus Desideri was left behind the only European at Lhasa [3]). This fact stated in Desideri's journal and in his letter corrects Sandberg and Holdich, who assert that on his arrival at Lhasa he found three or four Italian Capuchins [4]). There were none. In 1707,

[1]) Hedin, *Transhimalaja*, III, 113. *Southern Tibet*, III, 10. Nain Singh's few remarks on the northern mountain-range between Lhasa and Mansarowar may be seen in *Records*, I, 11.

[2]) Manuel Freyre was born at Ancião in Portugal in 1679 and entered the Society at Goa October 7, 1694. In 1710 we find hem engaged in the Agra mission, to which he returned after his Lhasa journey. After 1719 his name disappears from the yearly lists. There can be no doubt that he left the Society, for in a letter to the General written from Goa Dec. 10, 1724, he petitions for his re-admission. The reply is not known, but the catalogue of 1728 has a note appended to the effect that the name of Manuel Freyre has not been entered because he will not be able to present himself till after a month. Nothing seems to have come of the affair, for his name is not seen either in the catalogues of later years or in the *Catalogus defunctorum*.

[3]) Desideri, MS. A. Book I, ch. XI. p. 69—70; Puini, p. 51. Cf. also his *Letter to the General*, Lhasa, February 10, 1717, printed by Puini, p. 370.

[4]) Sandberg, *Exploration*, p. 57; Holdich, p. 79. I am at a loss how to explain the

indeed, two such missionaries [1]) and in 1709 a third, the well-known Father Dominic da Fano, had arrived at Lhasa through Nepal, but want of the necessaries of life had compelled them to return. On October 1, more than six months after Desideri's arrival, another party of three reached the capital of Tibet *via* Nepal, where they were received by him and instructed in the language of the country [2]).

In a summary of some twenty pages Desideri gives a general survey of his stay and activity in Tibet; the chief points of which may find a place here before we pass on to a discussion of the detailed geographical notes furnished by the rest of the journal [3]).

Within a few days after Freyre's departure he was summoned to the palace by an order of the king and cross-questioned by the commander-in-chief, Zze-ring-ton-drup as to the object of his coming. About a month later, May 1, he had a personal audience with the king, and was granted permission to preach [4]). He was

---

scant and almost cavalier treatment of Desideri by Sir Thomas Holdich, the more so as the latter can see and appreciate true merit. After he has discredited the object of the journey, to which we have referred at the beginning of this chapter, it almost looks as if he wishes to "damn with faint praise" the performance itself, for he continues thus: "Desideri entered Tibet by Ladakh and as he was something of an observer and a writer, we have some most interesting records from his pen of the nature of the now well-known route to Leh." The journey beyond Leh, the stay at Lhasa, the description of Utsang are hardly mentioned, yet Puini's book with Desideri's extensive journal is noticed in the bibliography. Surely it would argue a poorer mind than Sir Thomas's which could disengage from these remarkable pages only this feature, that their author "was something of an observer and a writer".

Again in 1911, after Dr. Arthur Neve had read a paper at the Royal Geographical Society on *Journeys in the Himalayas and Some Factors of Himalayan Erosion*, Sir Thomas Holdich paid a warm tribute to the geographical work of the missionaries especially with regard to Central-Asian topography. Yet of all those pioneers of the seventeenth and eighteenth centuries only one name, Father d'Orville's suggests itself to his memory, after which come those of later travellers Huc, Gabet, Desgodins, Della Penna. (Cf. *Geographical Journal* XXXVIII (1911) p. 361—362) It is no disparagement of the merits of these men to say that the omission of Desideri's name in this connection is an injustice; his title to be ranked with them cannot be questioned and the position taken up by Sir Thomas Holdich can to my mind only be explained from insufficient acquaintance with the missionary's writings.

[1]) Cf. Giorgi, p. 331. *Missio Apostolica*, II, 4. The date, generally but wrongly, assigned is 1708.

[2]) *Missio Apostolica*, II, 48. Desideri, *Letter of February* 15, 1717. Cf. Puini, p. 372—373. In this letter the writer discusses the question of priority at issue between the Jesuit and Capuchin missionaries, to which reference has been made at the beginning of this chapter.

[3]) Desideri, MS. A. Book I, ch. XI—XVI. p. 70—92; partly given by Puini, p. 61—65.

[4]) Etiquette required presents to be offered. Most of these Desideri bought at Lhasa

also authorized to buy a house at Lhasa, from which foreigners were generally debarred; they could only rent houses. He thus became the owner of a residence conveniently situated in the centre of the town and in the principal street, the Khoràstreet.

With undivided zeal Desideri now addressed himself to the study of the language. "From that day to the last which I passed in that kingdom I studied from morning till night". Nor without success, for by the end of December of the same year he had finished an *exposé* of the Christian religion in Tibetan, which was presented to the king at an audience on January 6, 1717. Acting on the advice of the latter to study the religion of the lamas in their own writings, Desideri stayed from March 25 to the end of July at the monastery of Ramo-cce, where he was chiefly engaged in the study of the Kaâ-n-ghiur, "gli oraculi tradotti", a collection of 115 volumes [1]). But since the best insight into the doctrinal part was to be obtained in the Universities, where lamas not only from Central Tibet, but from Ladakh, Tartary and China thronged the lecture-halls, Desideri moved in August to the University of Sera at two miles' distance from Lhasa. Here he was comfortably housed and could say mass in his private oratory; he had the free use of the libraries and could converse with the most learned among the professors [2]).

His plan was to write in the Tibetan language a refutation of the errors of their doctrine and a defence of the Catholic religion. But he had hardly set to work when it was interrupted by a violent catastrophe. The Tartars invaded the country, Lhasa was taken and sacked, and December 3 the king and his ministers were murdered. Not thinking himself safe at Sera Desideri retired to the province of Takpó-Khier at eight days' journey from the capital, where he found time and opportunity to finish his book. His retirement lasted till April 1721 with the exception of a few months

---

from foreign merchants, but added from his own store *due Pietre di Belzoar di Goa, un Cocco di Balsamo del Brasile e un vasetto di Balsamo apopletico*, with directions for their use written by himself in Tibetan.

[1]) "The Kang-gyur, or properly the Kah-guyr, the great code or "the Translated Commandment" is so called on account of its text having been translated from the ancient India language and in a few cases from the Chinese" .... "The code extends to one hundred and eight volumes of about one thousand pages each, comprising one thousand and eighty-three distinct works." For these and other details cf. Waddell, *Buddhism*, p. 157—158.

[2]) He took a great deal of trouble to understand the subtle and intricate treatises that go by the name of Tongba-gni (*il Vacuo*).

at Lhasa. In one of his visits to the capital he gave his book to read to his former teacher of Tibetan, one of the cleverest among the lamas. It consisted he tells us of three volumes. The first argued against the migration of souls as taught by Buddhism, the second attacked the main error into which the Tongba-gni falls, the denial of an Absolute Being (*Ens a se*), Creator of the world, Itself uncreated. The third volume was constructive and in the form of a dialogue gave an exposition of the Christian doctrine.

The work caused a great stir and "my house suddenly became the scene of incessant comings and goings by all sorts of people, but chiefly learned men and professors, who came from the monasteries and universities, especially from those of Sera and Breê-bung, the principal ones, to apply for permission to see and read the book" [1]).

While he was still staying at the hamlet of Trong-g-nêe in the province of Takpo-Khier, he received orders from Rome to leave Tibet [2]). At the request of the Capuchin Father Guiseppe da Morro he translated into Italian the book Lam-rim-ccea, which is a kind of digest of the two great works Kaa-n-ghiur and Tongba-gni; this translation was to assist da Morro in his study of the Buddhist doctrine. Then in April he set out for Kutti on the Nepal border; it was five years and one month after his entrance into Lhasa [3]).

Father Desideri devotes the second book of his account to a detailed geographical description of Tibet. Frontiers, morphology, climate, fertility, products, rivers, everything is reported on, thus making the missionary's journal the most complete account on Tibet that we possess [4]). A detailed discussion and comparison with the findings of modern travellers would weary the reader and

---

[1]) Desideri notes (MS A. Book I, ch. XV. p. 91) that he took the book away with him when he left Tibet. I surmise it is the third of the Tibetan MSS. mentioned on page 275 but this must be left for Tibetan scholars to settle. It consists of 704 pp. and bears the initial date of June 24, 1718. The second of the above-mentioned MSS. dated Dec. 8, 1717, must have been begun immediately on his arrival at Takpo-Khier. See p. 275.

[2]) The letter is dated Rome January 16, 1719; the text is given by Launay, II 378.

[3]) Books swarm with inaccuracies concerning Desideri's Lhasa journey. Here are some. Very generally the length of his stay is put at thirteen years (1716—1729) e. g. Markham, p lviii; Rockhill, *Diary*, p. ix; Günther, p. 164; Wegener, p. 11; Waddell, *Lhasa*, p. 10; Landon, I, 9; Launay, I, 34; Heawood, p. 142. Then Rockhill places his route through Sikkim, Schlagintweit (III. 11) through Nepal, etc., etc.

[4]) See the titles of the several chapters in the list of MSS.

overpass the limits of this book; only such points, therefore, will be dwelt upon as may call for special notice.

Speaking of the boundaries of Tibet Desideri remarks as follows: "Looking from west to east, that is from Treêscy-Khang and Cartoâ to Sciling [Hsining], the most western extremity of the Great Chinese Wall, this country is so vast that six and a half months of uninterrupted travel are needed to cover the distance between the two extreme points. From north to south the extent varies greatly. Between Cartoâ and the beginning of the province of Zzang-to, that is, a distance which it would take two and a half months to travel over, the country extends far to the northward and only slightly to the south: for in the north it has as its frontier the rugged and inaccessible rocks that reach as far as Yarkand. In the south the country touches the kingdom of Collahor and other countries situated at the same latitude as Sirenagar.

"From the beginning of the Zzang-to province to Lhasa, one month's travel, the country extends much further soutwards, much less northward. From the province of Chieê-rong it borders on the dominions of the king of Patan, the second prince of Nepal, and near Nesti, where the realm of the king of Kattmandu—the highest of the three Nepalese princes — begins, the frontier descends to 28° N. The city of Lhasa lies at about 30° N. Taken at that point the country does not extend far northward. But to the south the provinces of Mon, Pari en Bree-me-giong [1]) border on Altipari, Porania and Negricot, all subject to the Great Mogul and situated at the other side of the Ganges. From Lhasa to Sciling, that is to China and Lower Tartary in the direction of Coconor, a distance of three months, the country extends far northward, for it reaches as far as Sciling, which is situated at 36° 26′ N. And to the south, where the provinces of Lho-ro, Zze-ri, Cong-tó and Cong-mè have as their neighbours certain tribes called Lhobà, that is 'Southern Peoples', the territory of Tibet descends to the 25th degree" [2]).

From these latitudes it is also apparent, says Desideri, that the intense cold of Tibet is not due to its northern geographical position

[1]) Desideri includes Bree-me-giong or Sikkim among the Tibetan provinces. It probably means that just now Tibetan influence was paramount at Sikkim, which had recently been liberated by Tibetan arms from the domination of the Bhutanese. (Cf. White p. 16). In 1730 Della Penna writes: "Il Regno di Bregiong" bordering on the Tzang-province (Klaproth p. 188).

[2]) Desideri, MS. A. Book II, ch. I. p. 2—3; cf. Puini, p. 37—38, where there are some discrepancies. Desideri pushes the southern limit about 2° too far south.

but rather to the thinness of the air in a country which is nothing but mountains in every direction, and to the prevailing winds, which carry down the glacial cold from their ice-bound tops. From October to the middle of April or the beginning of May the cold is most intense, then the weather grows milder, and in June, July and August, but for the cooling effect of the rains, the heat would be quite unbearable intensified as it is by the reflection from the naked mountain sides. Thus vegetation is rendered possible. September is a dry season and up to the middle of October the temperature remains moderate. Because the air is dry, the cold, however intense, does not affect one's health, and I never took any harm from sleeping in the open as I often had to do on my journeys [1]).

The numerous scientific observations that have been taken of late years have greatly enlarged our knowledge of the climatic conditions of this highest table-land on earth [2]). In consequence, the views generally prevalent concerning the utterly arid nature of the Tibetan climate have had to be thoroughly revised. Desideri's observations have special reference to the Tsangpo district, with which he had been in touch. On this territory Sandberg remarks: "In Central districts rain-showers occur on very many days in July and August, the monsoon effects not reaching the North-western Central region until about July 20th. From the middle of June to the end of August, in the provinces of Tsang and Ui, including Yarlung, Yamdok and Lhobrak, nearly every day the sky is cloudy and frequently heavily overcast" [3]).

From the British expedition staying at Gyantse and Lhasa in 1904 we have some maximum temperatures for the summer-months of that year. These statistics work out for Gyantse (13,200 feet) from June 26 to July 14 at an average maximum of 95° F (35° C.) with a highest maximum of 105° F. (40° C.) on July 11; for Lhasa (12.290 feet) from August 3 to August 31 an average maximum of 86° F (30° C.) with a highest of 95° F. (35° C.) on August 3; for Sept. 1 to 22 these figures were 80° F. (26° C.) and 89° F. (31° C.) respectively, the last being registered on 1 and 3 Sept. With reference to Desideri's remark regarding the summer-rains it may be noted that at Gyantse rain was recorded on 6 days

[1]) Desideri, MS. A. Book II, ch. II p. 6–7; Puini, p. 38–39.

[2]) Cf. Sandberg, *Tibet*, p. 21–27.

[3]) Cf. Sandberg, *Tibet*, p. 28.

out of the total of 18, and at Lhasa on 14 out of the 29 days in August [1]).

The produce of the soil is but scanty in this rocky, cold and barren country, where moreover no water can be had for irrigation except at the foot of hills and mountains. Barley is an important crop as is also rice in the southern districts; the most important, however, are root-crops, especially turnips, radish, garlic and onions. Fruit also is scarce. Walnuts and peaches are met with in every district, pears only in Thakpó-Khier and in Kham, where even the vine manages to keep alive [2]).

The presence of gold and silver all over Tibet, especially in Kham, one of the points brought out by Desideri, has been amply confirmed by later travellers. Thus Nain Singh speaks of a rich silver-bearing hill-district four miles north of Lhasa. But the government prohibits any mining operations because the country would be impoverished and the population degenerate, should the metal be worked [3]). A different policy is followed with regard to the gold-fields of Thok Jalung about 100 miles north of the Kailas Peak. There under the supervision of a special gold-commissioner appointed by the government at Lhasa, the gold-bearing soil is dug up and washed [4]). To this effect, Desideri informs us, they use a wooden structure, something like a gun-carriage or the conduit of a water-mill. On the bottom of this machine large square sods covered with thick coarse grass are placed and on these the dug-up earth is spread out. From the top large quantities of water are poured in, which rushing down with force carry away the lighter earth and small stones, leaving a black substance with the heavier gold between the blades of grass. After this the sods are taken out of the tray and again washed and shaken over bowls, which operation is repeated till the pure gold of the size of coarse sand remains behind [5]).

---

[1]) Cf. Waddell, *Lhasa*, p. 463—466.

[2]) Desideri, MS. A. Book II, ch. 2. p. 7; Puini, p. 96. Desideri makes special mention of Reopontico (*Rheum rhoponticum L.*) and of the Zedoary called Nirbisi by Nain Singh and other. About vine-growing in Takpo Della Penna writes "Vi sono alcune viti incolti, che fanno un poco d'uva" (Klaproth. p. 275).

[3]) Cf. *Records*, I, 22. According to O. Coales (*Economic Notes on Eastern Tibet* — Geograph. Journal, vol. LIV. (1919) p. 246) the Tibetans have a superstituous objection to removing precious metals from the earth, believing that they contribute to its fertility.

[4]) *Records*, I, p. 82.

[5]) Desideri, MS. A. Book II, ch. II. p. 8; given less fully in Puini, p. 97.

Besides salt, in which Tibet is so rich that it can supply Nepal and the southern border states, there is found a very fine, white powder, called Putoa in the vernacular. It is used in making tea, in order to change its natural colour into that of red wine by which they set great store. It also takes the place of soap and is used to clean articles of clothing [1]. Sherring has a different account to give of the red colour and the stimulating effect of the Tibetan brick-tea. That it was the result of an admixture he says was well known, but the secret was very carefully kept by the Chinese manufacturers. "It was accidentally discovered by one Kumaon firm, the Berenag Tea Company, as a cake of Chinese brick-tea opened by them was found to have a leaf of the herb utilised left in it by an oversight. This leaf was carefully examined and was traced to be a wild plant which grows very generally in many localities in our hills, and as soon as experiments produced the red colour and the stimulating effect in the beverage it was known for certain that the whole secret was discovered" [2].

Desideri does not fail to notice the thermal springs of sulphurous water and the use made of their healing power by sick people, though he does not specify, as Sandberg does, that one of the main purposes of those baths is "the efficacy of the sulphur in the destruction of vermin," by which all Tibetans are plagued on account of their loathsome dirtiness [3].

Among the curiosities of Tibet Desideri mentions a curious kind of springs. "In some localities there are other mineral waters of somewhat acid taste and of a peculiar quality which I would not have believed possible if I had not experienced it. The springs do not work all the year round nor have they that peculiar quality except at a fixed season. Towards the end of the severest cold, that is about the end of March, when the peaches begin to bloom, the springs suddenly begin to flow. The water has the taste of peach blossom, and as long as the blossom continues on the trees, so long does the water retain this taste, and during the same period it has the wonderful property of purging the stomach,

---

[1] Desideri, MS. A. Book II, ch. II, p. 9. Puini, p. 98. Della Penna also mentions "una specie di terra candida minerale corrosiva che serve per sapone, per tirar fuori il colore e far cuocere sollecitamente le vivande." (Klaproth p. 275). This Putoa is probably a calcium carbonate. Das (p. 136) says that "a kind of wood-dust called sug-pa" is used as soap, whilst Waddell, (*Buddhism*, p. 214) refers to the use of "saline earth".

[2] Sherring, p. 318.

[3] Sandberg, *Tibet*, p. 72.

either by vomiting or defecation. Hence the Tibetans throng those springs at that season and take their waters for some days till they are satisfied with their purge. About the end of April the blossoming season is over and with it the working of the springs, and if in some case the latter do continue to flow they have lost their pungent taste and purgative property" [1]. Are we to take this merely as a reference to the thawing of the springs at the beginning of the mild season? or must we here recognize geysers with their intermittent character, which are frequent in some parts of Tibet [2]? But even then, what about the wonderful taste and the curative properties of these waters?

Turning to the animal kingdom Desideri now describes the Tibetan fauna, the musk deer, the parrots of Takpo and Congbó, and especially the yak, after which a chapter is given to rivers, boats and bridges [3]. The reader who should expect a minute description of the Tsangpo, would be disappointed; there are a few general remarks on it but the name is not mentioned. "The mountainous nature of the country has allowed the formation of only one large river besides inconsiderable mountain streams; flowing from east to west [*sic*] this river divides the whole of this third and principal Tibet into a northern and southern territory. Then after traversing the whole province of Lower Congbó it turns east and south, enters the country of the Lhobàs and thence descends into Rongmati, a province of Mogol, finally to reach and join the Ganges." This is all.

On the other hand there are the boats of yak or cow hides and the hanging bridges, which engage a great deal more of his attention. Thus all the bridges span the river without any support, except the iron bridge east of Zze-thang, where the river is so wide that it requires three spans resting on two stone piers built in the stream [4]. "From sheer necessity I have twice made use of such a bridge, in all other cases I have been able to avoid them", which concluding remark seems to show that Desideri did not consider these bridges the safest mode of transit.

---

[1]) Desideri, MS. A. Book II, ch. II. p. 10; not found in Puini.

[2]) Sandberg, *Tibet*, p. 69—71.

[3]) Desideri, MS. A. Book II, ch. III p. 11—17 (partly in Puini, p. 89, 99 f.) & ch. IV. p. 17—20 (Puini, p. 100—102).

[4]) This bridge is no longer extant. Pundit Kishen Singh, who was at Tsetang October 8, 1882, crossed the river three miles below the town, where it was 299 paces wide. "There was formerly an iron bridge at this place which I was told was destroyed by lightning". *Records*, II, 286.

Desideri now resumes again the geographical description of the Tibetan territory, some stray remarks on which he had recorded in the diary of his journey from Leh to Lhasa. He starts with Serkia, the capital of the province of Zzangto, where the Tartar princess in whose escort he had travelled, had been taken ill. The enforced leisure had allowed him to look about him. "Serkia is built in the form of a crescent on the side of a high mountain, whose slope it covers till a large and populous monastery is reached. Right at the top lies a fort. Down below flows a river across which a fine bridge has been thrown, not of iron, but of brick and wood. Many houses and villages are seen scattered about the surrounding plain. In the town itself reside a governor and many officials" [1]).

Serkia can I think only be identified with the Saka Dzong or Saka Fort of modern maps. (Sometimes Sarka, cf. Stieler 1901). It is situated at about 85° E and 29° 30′ N, a mile or so north of the Chaka River, a tributary of the Charta, which joins the Tsangpo some ten miles to the west. The place is described by Rawling as "a straggling village of about twenty-five mud brick houses built under the shelter of a low ridge and on a mound lying just above the level of the plain." Not a town, therefore, in any real sense, nor is any mention made of a gompa or of a fort. Yet it is a place of considerable importance not so much from its size as from the fact that it is regarded as the centre of a very large district [2]). Nain Singh, who was there in September 1865 and in May 1866, calls it "a large village containing numerous houses built of sun-dried bricks. It is ruled by a Jongpon" [3]). A fort standing at the east end of the village is also mentioned by him but no monastery. Very likely the place has fallen into decay in the course of time. Perhaps we may see a relic of former greatness in the fact that the whole district from Tra-dom to Sang-Sang-Kau, a distance of about 160 miles in a straight line, is under the jurisdiction of the Jongpon or governor of Saka.

"The two other provinces of the most western part of this Tibet", Desideri continues, "are those of Chieê-rong and Kutti, both of which border on Nepal. In the first the Zedoaria is especially found, which is exported to Nepal and chiefly to Hindustan and sometimes fetches an exorbitant price. By the Chieê-rong route

---

[1]) Desideri, MS. A. Book II, ch. V. p. 21.

[2]) Rawling, p. 221. Ryder (p. 381) only speaks of "a dozen or so houses very dirty."

[3]) *Records*, I, 17, 33, 70. Kawaguchi in 1900 only speaks of the castle (p. 227).

it is possible to ride to Nepal and thence to Mogul on horseback, not so by that of Kutti. This last province, which is not very large, has a capital of the same name, also called Gnee-lam. It begins near Kciusciam and Nesti, the first frontier-towns towards Nepal, and ends in an immense mountain range, called Langur, about which later on. Not long ago the town and country of Kutti were subject to the Ragia of Kattmandu, but for several years it has formed part of this Thibet. If there is but one governor in other important places of this kingdom, here at Kutti there are three, forming one governing body or law-court. The reason is that the king wants to make sure of their fidelity, not only because it is a frontier town where many strangers come and go, but more especially because every year this region furnishes considerable sums to the treasury. For in the first place these parts supply the whole of Tibet with iron. Then because the above-mentioned desert [Ngari Giongar] renders travelling very irksome, there are always passing through Kutti caravans of Armenian merchants, and traders from Hindustan, Caximir and Nepal. The merchandise arrives in uniform and well-closed packages, each bale weighing two *Man di Pattna*, which if I remember right is about eighty pounds. Those packages called in Hindustani *Baccu*, in Tibetan *Thobo*, are not opened or examined as to their contents, but for each two *Man di Pattna* several *Trang* are paid. Each Trang is 13½ Roman paoli [1]) or 3⅓ Hindustani rupees. The import duties are not the same for every one. Nepalese merchants pay less by a privilege granted them by a Great-Lama of Tibet who was born in their country, and by a Nepalese princess who became queen of Tibet; all others pay the full amount. In case the wares are not conveyed in large packages but in small parcels payment is made according to estimate. The outfit necessary for the journey is duty-free. Those who pass from Kutti into Tibet pay no personal toll, but those who go out of the country pay four Roman paoli, i. e. two *Mandermali* of Nepal or one rupee of Hindustan. All goods going from Kutti to Nepal must be carried on the shoulders of men, but in the opposite direction everything is done by horses or mules, and this constant commercial intercourse is of great pecuniary profit to the inhabitants. Another good custom is the following. The import duties having been paid on entering Kutti one is free to traverse the whole

---

[1]) The paolo is an ancient silver coin worth nearly fivepence.

of Tibet without being liable to further payments. Many rich Nepalese merchants live at Kutti. It is a cold country and in winter the snow often lies very deep" [1]).

In the province of Chieê-rong we easily recognize the Kerum Shahr district, where in 1865 Nain Singh had so many obstructions put in his way before he could proceed on his great journey to Lhasa and the upper-Tsangpo basin [2]). Hari Ram, who visited it in 1885, calls it Kirong [3]). The capital of the same name lies (9,100 feet) on the left bank of the Jongka Changbo River, about 50 miles in a straight line from Katmandu. Both explorers call attention to an article of commerce, a plant called Nirbisi or Jadwar, growing wild in great plenty, which Montgomerie specifies as the Zedoary, "a spicy plant somewhat like ginger in its leaves, but of a sweet scent". Its root is held in very great esteem throughout India, as possessing great healing power when applied to cuts, scars, bites of venomous serpents and insects. Large quantities of the root are gathered from July to October, and after being dried in the shade they are ready for export [4]). Hari Ram also points out the advantage of the Kirong route over that by Kutti or Nilam, because it is practicable for ponies.

Kutti or Gnee-lam, the present Nilam Dzong on the Bhotia Kosia River, as well as Nesti (Listi Bhansar) have been spoken of in the preceding chapter, and the mention of the former by Grueber as the first town of Nepal gives indirect confirmation of Desideri's statement that not so very long ago it had been part of Katmandu. In 1871 Hari Ham found not three, but two Jongpons exercising joint jurisdiction within their district "so as to be a check on one another," which institution he also found at Kirong[5]).

"Whether from the upper district of Ser-kia or from the lower district of Kutti", Desideri goes on, "the journey to Lhasa, the centre of this Tibet, requires a full month; the road lies continually through well-inhabited regions in which especially three places are of importance and well known. The first is Chiang-ze, the capital of a province and the residence of one of the principal governors. It has a large, populous monastery and there live many

---

1) Desideri, MS. A. Book II, ch. V. p. 21–23; Puini, p. 85–86.

2) *Records*, I, 13 ff.

3) *Records*, II, 392.

4) *Records*, I, 16, II, 397–398.

5) *Records*, I, 118, II, 392.

foreign merchants. Certain woollen goods manufactured here are in great demand in Tibet, so that the sale throughout the kingdom is very great.

"The second place is Secchia, the capital of a fairly large principality. The land and people of this district are under the suzerainty of the king of Tibet, but they pay no tribute and render him no services in ordinary circumstances. They are governed by a Lama, a feudal vassal of the king. He is not like other lamas bound by the law of celebacy, but may marry to secure the succession. This having been secured he must separate from his wife, and on his death he is succeeded by his son both in his spiritual and his temporal office. This prince lives at Secchia in the large, populous monastery in the middle of which stands his splendid palace. There is also another, still larger, monastery for women. Besides the temple connected with those monasteries, there is outside the town yet another of extraordinary size and wealth, where now and then services are conducted by the monks, the nuns and the Lama himself. The town is situated at the foot of a high mountain, against which the houses gradually rise in the form of a semi-circle. The whole is walled in and in the plain round about stand many fine houses.

"The third place of importance is Giegazze, once the capital of the former kingdom of Zzang, now of the province of Zzang-mè... After Lhasa this is the most important town of Tibet. It is the residence of a Lama, very powerful and rich, who is second in dignity to the Great-Lama so that, if the latter should be a child, the Lama of Giegazze must teach and educate him. The Lama who lived there at the time of my stay was held in such high esteem both in Tibet and outside, that when the late Emperor of China sent an embassy to his kinsman Ginges-Khang, king of Tibet, he also despatched one to this Lama. Every one admired his firmness and courage when he offered heroic resistance to the conquerors of Lhasa, who after the sack of this town marched on Giegazze to make the fabulously rich temple and the monastery share the same fate. In a short time he fortified both with a new wall, armed his people and forced the enemy to retreat. He has numerous subjects, enjoys huge revenues and is enormously rich. He lives in a splendidly built palace and is the owner of the rich temple with its gold idols and costly ornaments. The large and finely ornamented monastery adjoins the palace; and as this is one of the principal universities of Tibet, monks flock to it from many places and different nations. Nor is a large nunnery wanting, subject to his authority. In it lives the Tartar princess who so greatly facilitated my journey through the desert of Ng-nari Giongar.

"The town of Giegazze lies in a wide plain, close to a mountain. It has a numerous population and harbours a great many foreigners: Tartars, Chinese, merchants from Kashmir, Hindustan and Nepal. In it resides one of the principal governors of Tibet with his whole staff of officials. In 1720 the damage sustained during the siege was repaired and the town enlarged. Across the large river that flows by the city, a long and strong bridge is built, one of the best of the whole of Tibet. The plain round about is studded with farmsteads and villages" [1]).

Gyāntse or Chiang-ze (13,120 feet) situated on the Nyang River an affluent of the Tsangpo was visited by Nain Singh in 1865 and by others after him, and has been well-known since Sir Francis Younghusband's expedition, a party of which had to sustain a regular siege at this place. A full description of the flourishing, large town is given by Waddell, who like the Pundit before him makes special mention of the woollen cloth referred to by Desideri, for which the town has remained famous till the present day [2]).

Far less known is Secchia or Sa-kya, which for ages has been the headquarters of the semi-heretical Sa-kya school of Buddhists, who were paramount in Tibet till their power was broken by the Gelugpa-sect [3]). Della Penna dates the independent position of its Great Lama from the year 790, when the Chinese Emperor created this dignity [4]). The town lies at an altitude of 13,900 feet on the right bank of Sa-kya Chu about at 88° 10′ E and 28° 55′ N. When staying there in 1871 Hari Ram learned that the great monastery at the foot of which the town is situated, counted 2,500 inmates ruled by a Great Lama called Sa-kya Gangma. His are the only lamas in this part of Tibet who are allowed to marry. Sarat Chandra Das discusses several points in the history of the Sa-kya principality. A few months before his visit in 1882 the Prince-Lama had died leaving five sons out of whom a successor was to be chosen [5]). Ekai Kawaguchi felt so disgusted at the

[1]) Desideri, MS. A. Book II, ch. V. p. 23–26; Puini, p. 47–50.

[2]) Waddell, *Lhasa*, p. 196–244; *Records* I, 18.

[3]) Waddell, *Buddhism*, p. 69 ff.

[4]) *Missio Apostolica*, I, 30.

[5]) *Records*, I, 117. Das, p. 312–316.

degeneracy of the sect on his arrival in 1900 that he declined to prolong his stay at the monastery[1]). According to the testimony of Ugyen Gyatso and Das the people of Sa-kya bear no high character in Tibet [2]).

There is no need to dwell on Giegazze or Shigatse (12,850 feet) on the Nyang River not far from the Tsangpo, where in the famous monastery Tashi-Lhumpo the Pantchen Riponche or Tashi Lama resides. The particulars given by Desideri and many more have become generally known especially after Sven Hedin's inquiries during his seven weeks' stay there [3]).

Desideri was now at the heart of Tibet, Lhasa, the mystic city, which was to remain shrouded from the eager West for nearly two centuries more. When in 1866 with the most diligent search Yule had gathered together whatever evidence was available, the poorness of the result drew from him the complaint referred to at the beginning of this chapter: "A fatality has attended the accounts of Lhasa that *should* have been". Nor where the additions made to our knowledge in subsequent years by Pundits, by Das and others of a nature to satisfy the desire for accurate and detailed information that stirs the modern mind. The turning point came with the famous expedition of Sir Francis Younghusband in 1904, when at a sweep the veil was torn away behind which the golden roofs of the far-famed city had gleamed so mysteriously. In the palaces of the great the hated foreigner made his home for weeks, in the splendid apartments of the wonderful Potala he deliberated upon the fate of Tibet, even within the precincts of the Jo-kang he set his foot when the doors of the sacred treasure-house and Kaaba of all Lamaism were thrown wide. Lhasa had yielded up its secrets, and the reader who may wish to wander in imagination among the monuments of its past, need but turn to the splendid volumes by Austen Waddell and Percival Landon.

Nearly two centuries before, Desideri wandered in those same streets, a lonely traveller. What he noted down of the sights he saw was never known to Yule, nor is it mentioned by either of the two writers just referred to. Desideri's account does, indeed, lack finish and detail, it is silent on points of importance, it wants the indispensable aid of drawing and photography, yet its historic-

---

1) Kawaguchi, p. 241—245.

2) Das, p. 278, 313.

3) Hedin, *Transhimalaja*, I. 264—363. See also Kawaguchi, p. 249 ff.; Das, p. 59.

al value cannot be denied, the more so as its author saw the city before it was swept by the devastating storm of the revolution [1]).

Two principal personages are always mentioned by Desideri, the Great-Lama and the King. The dignity that goes by the latter title was created by Kushi Khan, who in 1642 conquered Tibet. Retaining the sovereignty himself, he appointed by the side of the Dalai Lama, a Desi or Governor. The Desi is commonly called regent (gyal-tsab) or king (gyalbo), and the extent of his power and influence is at any time greatly dependent on the personal character of the Dalai Lama. At present the office is elective, though the candidate must be a lama from one of the four great Lings, the royal monasteries of Lhasa [2]).

Without venturing on any estimate of the population Desideri only notes that it is very numerous and contains among its numbers a large proportion of foreign merchants, which is still true of the modern city [3]). The houses are described as built mainly of stone, three stories high and having large and comfortable apartments and rooms with floors made of a kind of mosaic gleaming like mirrors. There is, moreover, a domestic oratory with lamps burning before the images of the gods, whilst offerings of water, rice, corn and fruit are displayed in dishes of porcelain or other material. Evidently only the dwellings of the well-to-do can have answered this description and even these cannot, at the present time, be said to come up to this standard. Speaking of modern Lhasa Waddell says that "the houses of the citizens are substantially built of stone or sun-baked bricks; the walls neatly white-washed and the woodwork picked out in colours, with charms against the Evil Eye pasted over the doorway, give a general look of comfort from the street. But a glance within dispels the illusion and shows the interior to be quite as squalid and dirty as those of the wretched hovels in the country, and reflects the general poverty of the place. The more well-to-do also live in a curious mixture of squalor and dirt. Their larger houses have similar mean and untidy interiors, although some of the more wealthy, imitating the Chinese have sufficient taste to ornament their interiors

---

1) Desideri, MS. A. Book II, ch. VI. p. 26–32. Puini, p. 54–61.

2) Cf. Das, p. 228–230; Waddell, *Lhasa*, p. 334, 375.

3) There is great variety in the later estimates: Tsybikoff (p. 735) rates the civilian population alone at about 20,000; Landon (II, 376) puts the whole at 10,000, of whom 3,000 are monks. Waddell (*Lhasa* p. 345) similarly at 30,000, of whom in the city and suburbs at least 20,000 are monks.

with paintings, frescoes and better furniture, and a few may have one or two glazed windows, a great rarity in Lhasa" [1]). Desideri refers neither to dirty interiors nor to wretched dwellings of the poorer classes, though we may fairly suppose them to have been no better than they are now. The condition of the streets he has also passed over in silence, though every modern visitor has pronounced them to be unutterably wretched, being unpaved and converted into regular mud pools, or rather cesspools in the rainy season, since they also serve the purpose of sewers. But then, the European notion and practice of cleanliness and comfort had not reached the level which we now consider normal, and in Desideri's opinion this feature did not call for special mention [2]).

In the centre of the city, we are further told, is a fairly large square, in which market is held every day till the evening. Its nothern side is occupied by the luxurious Trussi-Khang palace, the residence of the king. "On the west-side of this square stands an ancient and very rich temple, called Lha-Brang, palace of the Lha. In the porch are fine pictures. Within there are many recesses, like chapels, which are dedicated to the several gods of those peoples and in which many large lamps, fed with yellow butter instead of oil, burn night and day. Like the other temples of Tibet it is covered with a flat roof. From this roof rise a number of pillars arranged along a large, oblong opening, and supporting a canopy made of bronze or brass plates ornamented with bas-reliefs, the whole being beautifully guilt. The sun shining on it makes it luminously resplendent and proclaims afar the majesty of the temple. Small bells which tinkle at the slightest breath of air are hung up at the edges especially near the corners. This superstructure is not quite flat but rises towards the middle like a roof the sides being covered with figures and arabesques of guilt metal. Through the screen light has access to the temple. Round the flat roof of the building runs a cornice and an imposing frieze of very beautiful bas-reliefs all in guilt metal. Daily services in the temple are conducted by a great number of monks, who live in a vast monastery close by, and the people flock to them in great

---

[1]) Waddell, *Lhasa*, p. 349. See also Huc, *Souvenirs*, II, 247; Landon, II, 205. The latter's reference to an "original description of the place by Father Andrada", can have no meaning, since Andrade never went to Lhasa any more than to Tashi-Lhumpo. (Landon, I, 6).

[2]) Cf. Tsybikoff, p. 734; Kawaguchi, p. 407 ff. "a metropolis of filth". Waddell, *Lhasa*, p. 351.

numbers and in a religious spirit. The temple is surrounded by a wide street with very important buildings, and it is along this street that the Tibetans make their Khora or circuit of the temple in such a way as always to have it on their right; great remission of punishment is they think thus secured. No one, not even the king, may pass through this street on horseback; every one must dismount and lead his horse by the bridle or leave it at the entrance. Some even traverse the street measuring the whole length of it with their bodies."

Waddell has only a passing reference to the "chief market-place in the great square surrounding the Cathedral" [1]), by which, of course, the wide street of the Khora is meant, as also appears from the plans of Lhasa given by Waddell and by Landon, though these plans do not agree in every detail.

The Pundit Kishen Singh, who stayed at Lhasa for some months in 1879, is the only one to mention that the temple and its three adjacent buildings — the court-house, the police-station and the treasury — are surrounded by a street thirty feet broad; he, too, is the only one when speaking of the sacred roads to include the circuit round the temple [2]). When describing the temple Waddell does indeed refer to a sacred road round it, the so-called Middle Circle "an alley by which pilgrims circumambulate the main building" [3]), but this cannot be the "wide street". Has the sacred rite of walking round the temple fallen into disuse? It is certainly strange that, whereas every visitor reports on the Lingkor, the principal circular road, the *via sacra* of Lhasa, that girdles the town, Desideri seems to be unaware of its existence.

The great temple Lha-brang, the house of the gods, — the name of the city has the same meaning and was originally the distinctive name of the temple — commonly called Jo-kang, was of course an object of interest during the English occupation. The descriptions by Waddell and Landon are far more complete than Desideri's, for they could procure admission to the innermost parts, even to the great golden statue of the principal god Jo, which is meant to represent Buddha as a young man [4]). The two writers diverge widely in their appreciation both of the architecture and

---

1) Waddell, *Lhasa*, p. 340.

2) *Records*, II, 240; 222.

3) Waddell, *Lhasa*, p. 367; see also on p. 365 his "Ground Plan of Lhasa Cathedral".

4) Waddell, *Lhasa*, p. 362—371; Landon, I, 301—314.

the statue; thus while Landon impressively states that "this beautiful statue is the sum and climax of Tibet", to Waddell's cooler judgment it is "a repellent image, about a man's size, seated with goggle eyes and coarse, sensual face, and [it] is of very rude workmanship. So inferior is it to anything that I have seen in China and so unlike in feature to any type of Buddha's image there, that I doubt the story of its foreign origin. Nor does it resemble any Indian ones, nor have I seen anything so uncouth in Buddha's images in Burma, Ceylon or Japan." Equally incompatible are the descriptions by these two writers of the Doring, the ancient monument before the main entrance of the temple [1]).

Whether the outward appearance of the temple has been much tampered with since Desideri's time it is hard to say. He clearly mentions but one canopy, Giorgi refers to five [2]) and Kishen Singh to four, while Waddell counts "three so-called golden pavilions of Chinese pagoda shape". Tinkling bells are not referred to by any later travellers.

"There are at Lhasa", the narrator continues, "three other idolatrous temples and monasteries of the same sect [the Gelugpa or Yellow-caps]. One is situated in the north-eastern quarter and is reserved for the Tartars. The other two lie towards the east, one near the town-limit, the other just on it, both called by the same name Ramo-cce. In the former there live many monks, mostly children, who start their first studies here, later to pass into the university-monastery to take their degrees. The second is dedicated to Sciacchià-Thubba [the Tibetan appellation of Buddha Sakya Muni], whom the Tibetans acknowledge as their founder. The legendary tales current about him can be read in the rich paintings of a large monastery near the temple. It is especially the Nepalese merchants, with whom the god is held in great honour, who come here to perform their devotions; therefore the abovementioned Nepalese princess on becoming queen of Tibet, had it constructed for their convenience" [3]).

Supposing the site of Desideri's "Tartar" monastery to be correctly given, it must be identified with the establishment visited

---

[1]) Cf. Waddell, *Lhasa*, p. 341. Landon, II, 292 ff. and the photos. Landon mistakes the Doring for the so-called small-pox edict.

[2]) Giorgi, p. 413; his plan is totally different from Waddell's.

[3]) Desideri, MS. A. Book II, ch. VI. p. 29. Puini's text (p. 61) mentions only one Ramo-cce, temple and monastery, situated in the northern part of the town. No mention is made of the Nepalese princess.

by Waddell and described by him as the "wealthy monastery of Muru at the north-east corner of Lhasa, famous for its teaching of the occult and black art" [1]), though no mention is made of its being specially reserved for Tartars. As to Ramo-cce, which lies to the northward, the site assigned to it by Desideri is quite wrong, while in no modern writer any hint can be found of there being two distinct establishments of the same name. Opposite the Ramo-cce temple Waddell in his Plan of Lhasa marks an "Upper School of Mysticism", which is probably Desideri's scholastic establishment. Temple and school would make one monastery, which is also the appellation applied to Ramo-cce by Nain Singh [2]) and Kinthup [3]). The temple itself, after the Jo-kang the most venerated of all temples in Tibet, impressed Landon as "a mediaeval building of an undistinguished type, the guilded roof is the prettiest thing about it" [4]). Sarat Das was much disillusioned when he saw it. It has been built by the Chinese princess Konjo, while the *rôle* of the Nepalese queen is reduced to the placing of the oldest images [5]).

In ancient times, our missionary goes on to tell us, Lhasa was an open place, Ginges-Khang being the first to protect it at various points with gates and fortifications [6]). Situated in a plain the town is enclosed by mountains so as to leave only four approaches each of them defended by a fortification. Through the middle of the plain, close by the town, a large river flows from west to east. Coming from Giegazze one meets, on approaching the plain between two huge mountains, a fort situated at a great height. Failing other means, stones would suffice to stop a whole army. Not far from it there is a vast university-monastery, called Breebung, inhabited by many lamas, doctors and professors and some thousands of undergraduate monks. Coming nearer to Lhasa one passes some pleasure-grounds and thickets, and also the cemetery of the Mohammedans, who come here to carry on trade. North of the road lies a large garden with a delightful country-house con-

[1]) Waddell, *Lhasa*, p. 402.

[2]) *Records*, I, 19.

[3]) *Records*, II, 335.

[4]) Landon, II, 192; 220.

[5]) Das, p. 206. See also Sandberg, *Tibet*, p. 182.

[6]) Ginges-Khang is not the famous Mogul despot but a Tibetan king, of whom more will be said later on. The defences mentioned here were constructed, according to Koeppen (p. 333), towards the close of the seventeenth century and pulled down again in 1722 by order of the Chinese Emperor Kanghi. Some gates and fragments of the old wall are still to be seen (Waddell, *Lhasa*, p. 339).

taining beautiful paintings. It was built by the same Great Lama who constructed the Trussi-Khang palace. Still closer to the city-gate on the right there are another fort and a monastery on a high and steep mountain, while on the left the mountain-side is connected with the town-gate by a short wall. Then, entering the town, one approaches the famous Potala, a splendid sight, the magnificent residence of the Great Lama of Tibet [1]).

The situation of Lhasa in its fairly level plain (11,831 feet above sea-level) surrounded by mountains has been known for some time from the explorations of the Pundits. Barring the slip which makes the river Kyi flow from west to east, instead of the opposite direction, Desideri's account agrees on all points with Waddell's journal. When the British expedition had crossed the Tsangpo by the iron suspension-bridge of Chaksam, the Kyi valley lay open before them. But the entrance "narrowed into a strong trail along which we had to pass in single file over masses of rocks fallen from above, threading in and out amongst giant rusty boulders and climbing giddy staircases hewn across the face of the granite cliffs overhanging the rushing swirling tide of the muddy Tsangpo, a few yards below.... This defile was nearly two miles long, and about the most formidable natural barrier we had yet encountered. The strongest part of all was at its lower end, where it joined at right angles the valley leading up to Lhasa. Here the rocks rose up in almost sheer cliffs into colossal columns and aiguilles, owing to the massive cristalline granite splitting sharply along its lines of cleavage, and on the topmost pinnacle, nearly half a thousand feet above us, outlined against the sky, stood looking down upon us the old castle of Chu'sul and its lower fort on a knife-edge ridge much nearer. These two forts, although now more or less ruinous, had evidently been of enormous strength,.... this marvellously strong natural position.... luckily was not held against us, although an immense heap of newly collected stones at its lower end showed that the Lamas had intended to hold it" [2]). The aptness of the quotation will, it is hoped, atone for its length since it would hardly be possible to afford a more vivid illustration of Desideri's somewhat jejune statement concerning the natural strength of the approach to the Lhasa valley.

The university of Breebung with its thousands of students is

---

[1]) Desideri, MS. A. Book II, ch. VI. 29–30; partly in Puini, p. 55–56.

[2]) Waddell, *Lhasa*, p. 316–317.

the still famous Drephung monastery [1]), whose numerous inmates exercise no small influence in the political circles of the capital [2]). The royal country-seat with its large park northward of the road is the Lha-lu palace, one of the five beautiful things of Lhasa, where the British mission took up its quarters, and which is fully described by Landon as a typical Tibetan house [3]). The monastery on the right close to the town-gate Pargo Ka'ling, the chief gate of Lhasa, is that of Kündeling, one of the four royal monasteries or Lings, from which the Regent used to be chosen during the minority of the Dalai Lama.

The residence of the foremost personage in all Tibet is, of course, not passed over in silence. But after seeing the illustrations in Waddell and Landon the want of them in Desideri is only the more regretted [4]). "The Potala is a mountain or rather a rock of large circumference but not very high. To the south of it lies a fine square, which like a fortress is shut in by heavy walls with gates and outworks, and on the inside is beautified with fine porticos. From this square, by broad stairs with balustrades of extraordinary architectural beauty, there is an easy ascent up to the top of the rock, where stands a splendid palace covering its whole length and breadth. It has five stories and at the top a cornice in the same way as the above-mentioned Trussy-Khang palace. In the centre, where the principal apartments are situated, the symmetry of the palace-front is perfect and well-proportioned. The two wings do not possess the required harmony and proportion, the left wing especially being out of keeping with the rest, yet the whole is splendid and in good taste. The riches of the palace are not to be described, especially in the apartments of the Dalai Lama and in the Lha-khang or temple dedicated to Cên-ree-szy. In former times it was not so vast and splendid as can be seen in the drawing made of it by the Fathers Dorville and Grueber and published by Kircher in his "La Cina Illustrata", plate 18. It was enlarged and embellished by the same Great Lama who built Trussy-Khang and the country-residence [Lha-lu palace]. On the northern side

---

1) The name varies with every writer; it is given as Dăpung, Daipung, Dabung, De-bung, Brebung, Rebung etc. Its distance from Lhasa is also subject to various estimates, of which four miles may be taken to be a fair average.

2) In Giorgi's time (p. 453) the number of immates was 5,000, while 40 years before it must have been 10,000. At present it fluctuates between 5,000 and 7,000.

3) Landon, II, 236–245.

4) Waddell, *Lhasa*, p. 387–399. Landon, II, 279–286.

of the rock there is another wide road leading to the top, of such easy ascent that one can ride on horseback right to the point where the rooms begin. At some distance north of the rock there is a large lake surrounded by trees and woods. In the middle of this lake stands another palace, Lu-Khang, a well-built circular edifice with a splendid open gallery running round it. The paintings inside are very good" [1]).

To what extent the Potala has had to suffer from the catastrophe that befell it in Desideri's time cannot now be determined. Waddell still found much to admire, whilst Landon declares "that cheap and tawdry are the only possible adjectives which can be applied to the interior decoration of this great palace-temple. Part of it is fine in design, most of it is commonplace, all of it is dirty" [2]).

After the town Desideri naturally undertakes the description of the environs and of the central provinces of Tibet beginning with the famous university of Sera, where for four months he led the quiet life of a student till he was driven thence by the great revolution. This university is situated about two miles from Lhasa, and its heavy walls, its streets and squares, palaces and two large temples together with its population of thousands of monks make it almost a town in itself. Moreover, on the slope of the mountain against which it is built there are a number of hermitages for the convenience of those who want to pass some time in solitude. East of Sera on another mountain lies a nunnery and between the two mountains runs the road to Dam, where the eastern desert begins. This desert extends as far as Coconor and China, a journey of three months, after which one reaches Sciling (Hsining-fu), the first town at the commencement of the famous wall [3]).

The monastery-town of Sera "with regular streets and lanes, some of which recalled those of Malta" [4]), was visited by several members of the British expedition, and before them by others, such as Huc, Nain Singh and Kawaguchi. Huc seems to exagge-

---

[1]) Desideri, MS. A. Book II, ch. VI. p. 30–31; Puini, p. 57–58.

[2]) Landon, II, 284. Younghusband thus sums up his impressions of temples and monasteries at Lhasa: "Outside they were solid and massive, though hardly beautiful. Inside they were weird and quaint and sometimes grotesque". *Geographical Results of the Tibet Mission* — Geograph. Journal. XXV (1905) 492.

[3]) Desideri, MS. A. Book II, ch. VII. p. 32; Puini, p. 66. The latter omits the name of Dam in this place, but on p. 15, note 1, Puini identifies it with Tsaidam, which is not correct. Dam is the territory to the north of the province of Reting and shut off from the Tengri Nor by the Ninchin-thang-la Range.

[4]) Waddell, *Lhasa*, p. 372.

rate in his estimate of 15,000 lamas, since all other reports speak of about 6,000 [1]).

Besides the northern road by Sera, Desideri resumes, two others issue eastward from the Lhasa valley both protected by fortifications. One traverses a very high mountain and leads to Sa-m-yeê, the other, more to the east, narrows down between two mountains on one of which the monastery-university of Kaa-n-den is situated. The head-lama ranks so high, that when the Great Lama is absent, he may supply his place on solemn occasions. If now you take the road that skirts the mountain on which Kaa-n-den stands and then turning to the left strike for the north, you come upon a province, still uncivilized, called Hor, the inhabitants of which, mostly farmers and herdsmen, call themselves Ciangba or Horba. From this region one enters the eastern desert, in the direction of China, called by geographers Lopo. If, turning to the right, the southern route is taken, one is led to the province of Taze and other provinces situated on the northern bank of the large river that traverses the whole of this Tibet and divides it into a northern and southern half [2]).

In Kaa-n-den or Ga-den [3]) we meet with the third large monastery-town and university of the Tibetan Yellow-caps. It is situated close to the Kyi River twenty-five miles from Lhasa and was founded by Tsongkapa [4]), who is interred there. When visited by Nain Singh in 1866 its inmates numbered 3,300. Its head, according to Waddell, exercises spiritual authority over the three great state-monasteries and over the whole of the Yellow-cap order [5]). It was he, too, who at the time of the British expedition officially negotiated with Colonel Younghusband after the flight of the Dalai Lama.

---

[1]) Huc, *Souvenirs*, II, 283. Cf. *Records*, I, 19, 42; Landon, II, 272. etc. Desideri explains Sera to mean 'hail'. Waddell does the same in *Buddhism* (p. 269) but in his later work *Lhasa* (p. 372) he interprets it as "hedge of wild roses". Landon (II. 266) prefers to derive it from 'ser', gold, in which he is supported by Huc (Souvenirs II. 378) and Koeppen (p. 343). Any of these interpretations is etymologically admissible according to Puini (p. 66). since Sera can be a derivation of the Tibetan se. ra (rose), Ser. ra (hail) or gser. ra (gold).

[2]) Desideri, MS. A. Book II, ch. VII. p. 33; partly in Puini, p. 66—67, where the details on Hor are wanting.

[3]) Kaa-n-den is a local pronunciation according to Puini.

[4]) Huc, *Souvenirs*, II, 277. The year of foundation is 1409 according to Koeppen (p. 345).

[5]) Waddell, *Lhasa*, p. 400. See also Kawaguchi, p. 336.

Hor or Sokpo is according to Csoma de Körös the Tibetan name of the northern Mongolian territory[1]) and on the map "Tibet and adjacent Countries", published in 1914 under the direction of Colonel Sir S. G. Burrard the name "Hor or Bod-yul" is marked north of the thirty-second parallel. Della Penna places the home of the Hor tribes between Tartary and the provinces of Ciang or Ngari[2]), while Nain Singh thus expresses himself: "The province of Hor is also inhabited by nomads, termed Horpas.... This province is bounded on the south by the snowy range north of Brahmaputra, on the west by Ngari Khorsum, on the north by Eastern Turkestan and Sokpohuil or the country of the Sokpos or Kalmucks. Eastward this country extends beyond the Nam Lake to the frontiers of the Kham province" [3]). Sven Hedin, however, would erase the name Hor from every map of Tibet. "For the Tibetans call the Turks Hor or Horpa and the Mongolians Sok or Sokpa. There are no Turks until you come to the northern side of the Kwen-lun mountains. But in spite of almost all modern maps, there is not a single Turk in the heart of the Tibetan plateau-land. And there is nobody else either, for the part of Tibet which is generally called Hor on our maps is not inhabited" [4]).

As to the province of Taze I am unable to identify the name. Puini surmises Dechen, a town on the Kyi or Lhasa River, from d'Anville's spelling Tetsi, but while improbable on other grounds this identification implies an unsupported use of the name for both town and province.

The second eastern route, so Desideri told us, led across a high mountain to Sa-m-yeê, thus indicating the Gokhar La, 16,680 feet, half way between Decken and Sa-m-yeê. Sa-m-yeê is famous throughout Tibet. There is an ancient, magnificent temple, the first that was built in Tibet, really something extraordinary not only on account of the seize and architecture of the building but of the number and variety of its images and its great wealth. Joined to it is a large library with a vast number of books among which are the manuscripts of the first Tibetan translations of the books which in distant ages were brought from India at enormous expense. Then there is a large and rich monastery and several

---

[1]) Körös, p. 2.

[2]) Klaproth, p. 196.

[3]) *Records*, I, 194.

[4]) Hedin, *Southern Tibet*, III, 11.

palaces, some of which are simply magnificent, especially those of the Great Lama, of the king and of the local head-lama. From all parts the Tibetans flock to this temple to celebrate the memory of a certain Urghien, the founder and propagator of their religion, of whom I shall speak later on. The locality is frightful, for on the north and west it is hemmed in by high mountains and to the east and south stretches a sandy plain, in which very cold winds are prevalent [1]).

After Nain Singh in 1874 Sarat Chandra Das stayed a few days at Samaye [2]). The town is situated, he says, 35 miles south-east of Lhasa, cut off from the northern bank of the Tsangpo by a sandy belt of over two miles. These shifting sands constitute a real menace and a large portion of the town including some of the temples has already been buried under them. The principal temple is that of Wu-tse; this, however, is not the ancient edifice referred to by our missionary, which together with the library was destroyed by fire in the early years of the nineteenth century. Urghien or Padmasambhava we have had occasion to speak of in connection with the Kailas Peak. He is worshipped in a temple erected outside Samaye over the cave which at one time was his dwelling-place. Precisely on account of its sacred character the large monastery now serves the purpose of state-treasury, to which circumstance Desideri does not allude.

"At a day's journey eastward of Samaye across the river, on its southern bank therefore, lies the town of Zzé-thang, the capital of the province of the same name. It is the residence of several governors and officials, some Tartar, some Tibetan. The town is known for its manufacture of woollen stuffs, especially serge, which is made so fine as to look like silk. There is also a large monastery with a temple, while the trade causes many merchants to settle in the town. To the west the province of Zzé-thang touches on that of Yarlung, known for its large pieces of fine rockcrystal. To the east lies the large province of Yee the most populous of all; whose ruler consequently takes precedence of all other provincial governors. Gold is found there in greater plenty than elsewhere, not in small grains but in nuggets of considerable size" [3]).

---

[1]) Desideri, MS. A. Book II, ch. VII. p. 33–34; Puini, p. 67–68. Desideri, MS. B. book III, ch. XL, p. 415, treating of tempels again, mentions the large library.

[2]) Das, p. 292–297. Cf. *Records*, I, 175–176; 187. Ugyen Gyatso was in Samaye in 1883. Cf. *Records*, II, 349.

[3]) Desideri, MS. A. Book II. ch. VII. p. 34; Puini, p. 70.

As no European has set foot in this eastern part of South Tibet, we have only the scanty reports of some Pundits to go upon. The town of Tsetang is placed by Nain Singh, who was there in 1874, about twenty miles east of Samaye on the right bank of the Yarlung Chu, a considerable southern affluent of the Tsangpo [1]). The explorer Lala was struck by the open-air market where all sorts of goods from Calcutta, China, Kashmir and Nepal were sold [2]). No visitors report on Tsetang as specializing in serges, though Tsybikoff notes, that it is famous "for the production of cloths, knitting and the yellow monk hats" [3]). While Nain Singh speaks of two monasteries, Lala and Kishen Singh mention only of one with about 700 inhabitants [4]). Since Nain Singh seems to make a point of mentioning all the gompas or monasteries that lie along his route, his report seems the more reliable.

As to Desideri's province of Yarlung, or geographically the Yarlung valley, Nain Singh, the Lama Ugyen Gyatso and Chandra Das are one in extolling it as one of the most fertile and populous regions of Tibet [5]). Wheat and barley are abundant as well as peas and many other kinds of vegetables. Fruit-trees, especially apricots and pears, are very common. Das specially notes west of Yarlung the "Shetag Mountains, or Black Crystal, thus called from the glistening black rocks exposed to view along the road", Desideri's rock-crystal. Even with the additional data of Desideri, we can throw no light on the more eastern province of Yee. No Indian explorer supplies information. Beyond mere mention of "a wealthy district" east of Tsetang by the Lama Ugyen Gyatso there is nothing in his report, nor is there in Lala's or Nem Singh's. Gold in this region is referred to only by Kinthup, who records two mines near Lhagyaro, about twenty-five miles ESE of Tsetang and two more near Laringbu [6]).

"South of the province of Zze-thang and Yarlung", the survey continues, "lie the two districts of Mon and Pari. It is from these that all parts of Tibet receive rice, which is grown in great abundance, and certain red flowerets from which the red pigment for cloth-dyeing is obtained. There is also an enormous export-trade

[1]) *Records.* I, 177; 187.

[2]) *Records*, I, 203.

[3]) Tsybikoff p, 740.

[4]) *Records*, I, 286, 317.

[5]) *Records*, II, 347; Das, p. 302–307.

[6]) *Records*, II, 329; 336.

in gum for the manufacture of dyes and sealing-wax. Moreover, the two districts supply white cloths of various descriptions and other textiles resembling silk, and others again that are called wood-silk [seta d'alberi]" [1]).

This southern border-tract of Tibet, enclosed between Pari in the Upper Chumbi-valley in the west and Mon-Yul in the east, called for some discussion apropos of Cacella and Cabral's journey [2]). The exact frontier between Tibet and Bhutan in Desideri's time cannot now be determined, it certainly did not coincide with the present boundary line, for no district in Southern Tibet grows rice, not even the fertile Lhobrak country, as Ugyen Gyatso expressly notes [3]), and all the supplies are imported from Sikkim, Bhutan and Assam. The same holds for the other products mentioned by Desideri, as far as the reports of the Indian explorers on the subject allow us to judge. Thus at Tsöna Dzong, some thirty miles north of Tawang in Mon-Yul, Nain Singh came on an important market, in which Tibetan articles were exchanged for rice, spices, dyes, fruits, and coarse cloths (a kind of silk) from Assam. Rice is even a state monopoly and at Tsöna is a De-Rang or rice house in charge of a Lhasa official who buys up all the imports [4]). Something of the kind is reported by Rinzin Nimgyl for Chhampa village in the Punthang valley in East Bhutan. There the exports from Tibet, especially salt and wool, were either sold for cash, in Tibetan currency, or bartered for *bure* (a kind of silk), *khamar* (coloured silk), *yultha* (a cotton cloth), rice etc. The same traveller briefly notices a plant from which a scarlet dye is obtained. South of Chumbi in Bhutan he found "a scandent plant, called *chud*.... It is found growing wild in these parts entwined round the trunk of trees and it is a most important article of trade. The people gather it in the jungles, cut it up into small pieces and carry it away into Tibet, where a rich red dye is extracted from it, when dry. This dye is in great demand throughout Tibet" [5]).

---

[1]) Desideri, MS. A. Book II. ch. VII. p. 34; Puini, p. 70—71.

[2]) Supra Ch. V, p. 143.

[3]) *Records*, II, 345. The Lobrak River is found at about 91° E, on Bhutan territory it is called Kurn in Burrard's map.

[4]) *Records*, I, 177.

[5]) *Records*, II, 373; 365. White (p. 201) likewise classes rice, madder and stick lac among the principal articles of export from East Bhutan to Tibet. In the marketplace of Lhasa Landon (p. 393) bought some sealing-wax, which he praises as one of the best products.

"From Yee", Desideri continues, "one passes into regions with a somewhat more temperate climate, which are called Takpó. This territory is divided into several provinces, the principal is Takpó-Cignì with the large town of Cignì as its capital; then there are Takpó-tŏ, Takpó-rŭ, Takpó-trù-lung and Takpó-Khier, each administrated by their own governor. All these have abundant supplies of fruit and wood. On the mountains grow the *Reopontico*, the *Assenzio Pontico*, the *Melilotus* and the *Spigonardo* in great plenty, besides the juniper and the pine-tree, which yields an excellent gum. There are more and better fields, hence the wealth of a household consists in its stock of cattle and yaks, while large quantities of excellent butter are the staple article of export of those parts.

"Takpó produces the best kind of writing-paper, which is used throughout Tibet and is exported to Nepal. It is made of the inner bark of shrubs. In Takpó-Khier also, the wine needed to celebrate Mass is manufactured, but it must be boiled to keep, in which process one third of it is lost. The Tibetans do not understand the art of making wine, nor do they drink it, their only beverage is *Ceiang* a kind of beer.

"There are two places of special importance in the Takpó districts. One is a rugged, high mountain with a plateau about half way up. On it stands a splendid temple, which is held in such high veneration by the people, that both men and women come to live as hermits up and down the mountain-side, some in monasteries, others in hermitages. Two palaces are the residences of two lamas, one of whom belongs to the class which is permitted to marry to secure the succession, whilst the other has to remain single and will be succeeded by a re-incarnate lama. The top of the mountain consists of many clefts and crags on one of which stands a building which serves as a retreat to the lama and is connected with the other crags by long wooden bridges. Many come to this place to present their offerings and many make arrangements for their bodies to be carried hither to be devoured by the ravens and eagles.

"The other place of importance and also greatly venerated is a wide tract of very high and wild mountains, which form as it were a kind of stairs. They are constantly visited by hosts of pilgrims who make their rounds there, with this restriction, however, that women are only permitted to climb the lower mountains and must not cross a certain limit under pain of death at the hands of the

Khaa-n-dro-ma, a kind of guardian spirits. The men may climb to any height and in their ascent they observe several stringent usages. The highest parts of these mountains are covered with ice and snow all the year through and several visitors perish there, but they think themselves happy to be allowed to die in this way. Even in these forlorn region hermits are found living here and there, who are sought out by the pilgrims" [1]).

The whole of Takpó country still belongs to the *terra incognita* of Tibet. It has been traversed by only two Pundits: by Nem Singh in 1878—79 and by Kinthup in 1880—1884, neither of whom was a trained explorer while both worked under difficult circumstances. Hence Kinthup's information can only be treated as a *bona fide* story of his travels [2]).

From the reports of both Takpó has good soil and rich pastures with thick woods in the higher parts, but there is nothing about a division into provinces, of which Desideri puts the number at five and Della Penna at seven [3]). A wild grape is only reported for the more eastern Congbó, yet its presence, confirmed by Della Penna[4]), was a reason for the Capuchin missionaries to establish their station of Trong-g-neê in Takpó-Khier [5]).

Desideri is very vague in locating the two sacred spots, but, his mention of the lama who is not bound to celibacy affords some clue. For in MS. B. when speaking of the lamas who are free to marry he mentions three such: those of Secchia, Takpó and Lungar [6]). Now Nem Singh mentions 88 miles from Tsetang "the large and fine fort of Gyatsa Dzong and the Takpó monastery" [7]) without any further details. Some help towards the identification of the second spot is given by the name Çe-ri. D'Anville's Map of Tibet has, in the district of Tac-pou-y, a place called Dsiri south

[1]) Desideri, MS. A. Book II, ch. VIII. p. 35—36; Puini, p. 71—75. The latter has several omissions and additions: thus the first sacred spot is situated on the border between Takpó Cigni and Takpó Khier and has four gompas near its temple; the second is called Çe-ri and is situated in the extreme east of Takpó near to the Congtó border.

[2]) Thus Col. Tanner in *Records*, II, 329.

[3]) Klaproth, p. 192.

[4]) Klaproth, p. 275.

[5]) *Missio Apostolica*, II, 187.

[6]) MS. B. Book III, ch. XIX. p. 184; Puini, p. 299. Lungar I cannot identify; elsewhere in the same MS. (ch. XXI. p. 208) it is described as situated on a high rock surrounded on three sides by a large river; Desideri was on such friendly terms with its lama, that during the Tartar revolution the latter was helped by him to effect his escape.

[7]) *Records*, I. 210.

of the Dsiri mountains and the later sketch-maps of the Indian Survey, on the authority of the two above-mentioned Pundits, show a settlement named Tsari. The same name is to be found on the Tibet-map of the Royal Geographical Society brought up to date in 1906; it is on a southern affluent of the Tsangpo at about 29° N and 93° E. It does not show in Burrard's map of 1914, perhaps on account of its uncertain position. Nem Singh narrates that at "125 miles from Tsetang [he] crossed the Tsāri Chu which comes straight from Tsāri only two days off to the south. It is said to be not a large town, but there are many villages in its vicinity and plenty of bamboos and woods. One and a half day to the south of Tsāri is a country of wild tribes: the district is called Gimuchen, literally the "naked men country". There is a rise of five miles on to the ridge called the Hongbo Nga La, which forms the western boundary of the Kongbo district" [1]). No temple or pilgrimage is mentioned here. Kawaguchi referring to Tsari as "a peak in the Himalayas in the south-east which forms the frontier of Assam" calls it a place of pilgrimage and the second sacred place in Tibet, but he furnishes no further details [2]). Sandberg has this: "In Takpó is the famous place of pilgrimage named Tsári T'ugka, and nearly forty miles SE of this Tsári is the great snowy peak of Pal Tsári, which is the *ultima Thule* of Tibetan pelgrimage, involving a fortnight of hard travel from the banks of the Yeru Tsangpo. Tsári peak is said to be covered with thick pine forests at its base. The chief risk of journeys in Takpó and Tsári arises from the savage tribes dwelling across the ranges in the south of these districts,who appear occasionally to make raids on pilgrim bands" [3]).

As regards the curious restriction that at the second sacred spot women are prohibited under pain of death from crossing a certain limit, may it not be connected with a legend heard by Kinthup on his way to Tsari? Near Mipa he traversed a high pass (15,960 feet) from which all women were warned away under heavy penalties on account of an offence once committed by a woman against the goddess Drolma. From this same goddess is was said to have been called the Drolma pass [4]).

---

[1]) *Records*, I, 210–211; discussing Nem Singh's data Lieut. Harman wants to identify Tsari with D'Anville's Chai, which in the latter's map is shown in Takpó, but somewhat more to the east than Dsiri.

[2]) Kawaguchi, p. 593. [3]) Sandberg, *Tibet*, p. 85. [4]) *Records*, II, 335.

The other territories now described by Desideri are as unknown as Takpó. "South of the province of Takpó-trù-lung on the northern side of a very steep range, lies the province of Lho-ró, where gold is found in fairly large nuggets. On the south it borders on the so-called Lhobá-peoples, with whom trade is carried on, but very cautiously, as they are exceedingly wild tribes.

"Setting out eastward from Takpó, one first passes through the small province of Nang, which terminates in an enormously high mountain very rich in woods; then one enters the Congbó-country. It is divided by the river into Cong-tó and Cong-mê, or upper and lower Congbó, each of which is again divided into provinces. The climate is less rigorous, but the soil is less fertile because too sandy. Yet these territories are better populated and richer because the infertility has made the people apply themselves to trade. Pine-trees and cypresses are of frequent occurrence in Congbó as well as other sorts of large vegetation, which render so pleasant the mountain slopes and the banks of the river which traverses all this part of Tibet and divides Congbó into an upper and a lower part. To the south of Congbó live the Lhobá or southern peoples.

"The Lhobas are savage tribes. They mostly live in woods and in wretched cabins, and their only occupation is hunting all sorts of game, the flesh of which is eaten raw or ill-roasted. They sometimes feed on human flesh and do not scruple to kill a man when he appears to be healthy and plump. They always go armed with bow and arrow and are excellent archers. One very barbarous custom obtains among them: when a man sees one of his kinsman or a beloved friend at the point of death he consoles him in his extremity with the promise that he shall not leave this world alone, but he will give him so and so many companions, saying a definite number. If the man dies, he kills the number stated, and as an authentic proof of the faithful discharge of his promise he wears a collar of as many teeth as he has killed men.

"These peoples do not allow any one to pass through their country, whosoever the stranger may be, and for this purpose they watch the roads and keep them in an impracticable state. If a passage were possible, one might travel in a few days from Tibet to Rongmati and from Bengal to Tibet. But even their neighbours and business friends, the Tibetans of Congbó, are not permitted to cross the frontier, where they bring their merchandise consisting chiefly of large quantities of excellent yellow and white honey, wax, cinnamon, cardamon and many other medicinal herbs. From the province of Lho-ró and from Cong-mê I have ventured to within half a day's journey of their country.

"The rest of this 'Thibet da Ponente' in its lower tracts, in so far as they resort under Tibetan authority, loses itself in impenetrable and inhospitable forests and jungle" [1]).

"The small province of Nang" very likely is the tract of land surrounding the large monastery of Nang Dzong, at 123 miles from Tsetang, and probably extending as far as the Congbo-Nga pass, which is marked by Nem Singh as the western boundary of the Congbó district [2]). Kinthup describes Nang Dzong as a building with fortified walls whence all the roads to Congbó branch off. No one can go to Congbó without passing this Dzong, to which a monastery is attached [3]).

On the Congbó territory we are very ill-informed. Nem Singh, who traversed it, only notes a low stone wall near the Kyimdong River to mark the boundary between Upper and Lower Congbó [4]), while Kinthup's wanderings along both banks of the Tsangpo only prompt him to some general remarks on the fertility of the soil and the abundance of live stock and of wood. One feature Waddell learned from him was that peaches and apricots are so plentiful that pigs are fed on them [5]).

Nor is our information about the Lhobá tribes much more satisfactory. The name here used for the southern neighbours of Congbó is of much wider application and may include all the tribes living in this southern part and even Bhutan itself. For Schlagintweit notes that the people of this country call themselves Lhopas [6]), and even before him Körös takes Lhopato and Bhutan to be synonymous. White has not this name, but he divides the Bhutanese people in two parts, the boundary line being the Pele-La, about halfway between Punakha and Tongsa. The eastern group he says is not of Tibetan descent nor do they speak Tibetan [7]).

The first to get into more intimate touch with these tribes was Nain Singh in 1874. On his march down the valley of Dirang,

---

1) Desideri, MS. A. Book II, ch. VIII. p. 36–38; Puini, p. 75–77.

2) *Records*, I, 210–211. 3) *Records*, II, 330. 4) *Records* ,I, 201.

5) Waddell, *Lhasa*, p. 437.

6) Schlagintweit, II, 45; cf. Bonin, p. 78.

7) White, p. 9; 13.

south-east of Tawang, he was overtaken by a party of fifteen of these savages. "He was much struck with the appearance of these men, and especially noticed the enormous development of their arms and the calves of their legs, which far exceeded in size any he had seen elsewhere. They wore cylindrical-shaped hats made of bamboos; their only garment was a long blanket folded somewhat after the fashion of a Scotch plaid and fastened round the waist by a cloth girdle which is used as a quiver for their arrows, which all carry as well as a bow slung over the left shoulder. The greater part of their arms and legs were bare. They wore no boots, but ornamental rings made of rope were fastened very tightly both on their wrists and on their legs below the knee. They had high cheek-bones and Chinese-looking eyes, wore no hair on their faces, but allowed that on the head to grow to a great length; this was drawn together behind the head and then allowed to hang down"[1]). Nem Singh applies this name Lhobá to the people of the Pemako country near the great elbow of the Tsangpo [2]), where Kinthup also met them and found them the same as Nain Singh. They were fond of hunting and left the cultivation of the soil to the women and old men [3]). Lama Serap Gyatsho likewise speaks of them and distinguishes three different kinds; he was also told of a case of cannibalism [4]). The funeral slaughter mentioned by Desideri is not confirmed from any other source.

"Upper Congbó", thus Desideri concludes the chapter, "borders in the north on the country of Kham. This a very vast territory, once an independent state, now a Tibetan province. Throughout Kham there live many thriving merchants, among whom foreigners, a result partly of the trade-connections with China, partly of the great quantity of gold and silver found there. As it is too far away from Lhasa I did not visit it, but only went as far as the frontier" [5]).

The name Kham or Kam includes the whole of eastern Tibet, according to Oliver Coales [6]) even the whole territory from the Tanta La north-east of Lhasa to the Chinese border. It is inhabited by tribes of very varied characteristics and under various forms

---

[1]) *Records*, I, 187—179.
[2]) *Records*, I, 212.
[3]) *Records*, II, 337.
[4]) *Records*, II, 327.
[5]) Desideri, MS. A. Book II, ch. VIII, p. 38; Puini, p. 77.
[6]) *Eastern Tibet* — Geographical Journal, LIII (1919) p. 228.

of government. Della Penna mentions that there are twelve provinces, eight of which he knew the names of [1]). Huc traversed it on his way back from Lhasa to Batang and after him it has been opened up by the travels of Kishen Singh, Rockhill, Bower and others. It owes a great deal to its trade-route from Darchendo or Ta Chien Lu to Lhasa, the main line of the tea-traffic, the indispensable daily drink of the Tibetans.

Desideri's long stay naturally furnished him with a large amount of information on the people. — As a rule strangers meet with a kind welcome in Tibet and thus Desideri was well treated everywhere, while his permission to have a house of his own argues exceptional kindness. Only Mohammedans did not share in this generous hospitality. Thus whereas in the second Tibet they were allowed their own mosques and burial-grounds, in the third Tibet they were forbidden to have them, and they had to give up the cemetery which they anciently had at Lhasa and to transfer it to the interior, to some waste tract of country. This aversion is at least partly based on religious grounds as appears from the nickname *Mutekba*, 'unbelievers' [2]).

The caste-system is unknown and mutual intercourse is free and unhampered; only butchers are avoided because they slaughter animals, which is a crime in the eyes of the people. This is another reason why Mohammedans are looked down upon.

Till October 1720 Tibet was a monarchy under an absolute and independent king. From that time, however, all power has passed into the hands of the Emperor of China [3]) and the actual government consists of a body of ministers appointed by him, some of whom are Chinese, some Chinese Tartars, others again Tibetans. All decrees must be promulgated in three languages Chinese, Tartar and Tibetan.

The highest dignity after the king under the old regime, and after the imperial ministers under the new, is that of the four Kaa-lung-scià, who preside the civil and criminal law-courts. They sit in the Lha-brang and decide in common matters; in more important affairs they advise the sovereign with whom the decision rests.

---

1) Klaproth, p. 194 ff.

2) Though there was a mosque at Lhasa in Huc's time, the Mohammedans were not held in high esteem. Huc, *Souvenirs*, II, 266.

3) This change of government will be treated of at the end of this chapter.

At the head of each province is a governor or *Deba*, who is directly responsible to the sovereign, who also appoints some of the lower officers. The Deba is appointed for life and generally the office passes from father to son. Within their province they exercise absolute authority even in matters of life and death. They collect all taxes and tributes, and forward them to the royal treasury. Every year at the beginning of the *Daà Tangbo* or of the first moon at the time of the *Lo-sar* or New-year's feast they must present themselves at Lhasa and disburse their receipts. In a similar manner the king of Bree-mè-giong (Sikkim) is bound to send ambassadors.

Administration of justice. — As a check on petty law-suits it is the rule that on the first hearing each party has to disburse a sum of money varying with the importance of the case. As a natural result the parties will be more inclined to settle the dispute by private agreement. For the rest the case is very conscientiously and expeditiously treated.

The oath, however, which is administered in some rare cases, is barbarous and unreasonable. Yet it is practised not only in Tibet but in Nepal and other parts of India. The procedure is the following: two stones, one black, the other white are placed in a vessel of boiling oil; the accused is then ordered, if he is conscious he can swear to the truth, to put his hand in the vessel and draw forth one of the stones, with the warning that his taking out the white stone without hurting himself will show forth his innocence. Another way of administering an oath is this: a piece of iron is made red hot and the party in question is ordered to lick it three times with his tongue, being told that he will be considered innocent if he takes no harm. The third and more common way of making a man take a solemn oath is to conduct him to some mountain or other, and there he swears by the Lha or guardian spirit of the place or by other suitable sacred objects invoking their vengeance on himself and his family if he be forsworn.

The way in which a capital sentence is carried out varies according to the quality of the criminal and the malice of the crime. Some are beheaded, some drowned in the river, some bound to a stake and pierced with arrows. Robbery with murder, a rare occurrence, is punished with death by arrow; it might be called a kind of crucifixion as the culprit is bound to a sort of St. Andrew's cross, called Chiang Scing. Smaller thefts entail restitution and a public whipping, while in more serious cases the thief has his hand cut off or is branded on the forehead and exiled. In grave cases a man may be punished, though he had no part in the crime, for the mere fact of knowing of the plan and not revealing it. Not only murder and injury but altercation and menace are treated as criminal affairs and punished. Hence one never hears of a man being killed in a brawl, and even cases of injury are rare. In all crime the Tibetans have the greatest fear of the law. Simple fornication is not amenable to punishment, but the father is bound to provide for the child, who remains with the mother. Adultery is punished rigorously. But the severity of the law is softened by the custom of releasing some prisoners at the New-year and other important dates.

The land is the king's and the people have only the use of it. Each settlement has its own limited territory, of which the agricultural land is shared among the households while the pastures and woods are reserved for common use. Out of the produce of these lands each family pays a certain tax in money or kind into the royal treasury. Moreover, all are liable to compulsory labour, the so-called Ulla, by which a man places his own person, or a substitute, with his beasts of burden at the disposal of the prince or of whomsoever the latter may have given a written authority or Kaâ-scioa. The musk-deer is fair game, while gold may be dug for a small consideration to the local governor.

A peace-loving country, Tibet has no standing army but only a kind of bodyguard to the king and a few troops at Cartoâ and Nga-ri Giongar to guard against possible raids by the Tartars of Giongar-Yul or Independent Tartary. In the event of war each household has to provide one soldier and if none among them are able to carry arms they must provide the cost of one. Pay, arms, commissariat, horses are at the charge not of the prince but of each province or settlement. Being hardy and tractable they make good soldiers. Among their arms are a few iron canon, but even unarmed they could easily defend themselves with stones in their strongholds on inaccessible mountains [1]).

Desideri's notes on wearing-apparel, head-dress and orna-

[1]) Desideri, MS. A. Book II, ch. XIII. p. 60—68; Puini, p. 175—181 with a few discrepancies. There are many points of agreement with Desideri's remarks, especially on

ments both for men and women [1]) are in so entire agreement with the descriptions and illustrations in books on modern Tibet, that they need not detain us, any more than their pens made of bamboo and their strings of a hundred beads made of a Chinese yellowish wood. Perhaps their habit of not sleeping on their backs but entirely huddled up is just worth mentioning.

Their diet and their cooking lie under no restriction, religious or otherwise [2]). Besides various kinds of meat: mutton, pork, beef, goat's flesh, fowl, they have dairy produce and fish, eggs, rice, carrots, radish and other vegetables. Bread they have none, but in its stead there is the *Zzamba*, roasted barley-meal mixed with warm water. There is nourishment, too, in their favourite drink *Cia*, a mixture of tea, putoa (the white powder with its resultant claret colour), milk, butter and salt, all boiled in water; highly esteemed by every Tibetan, it is drunk throughout the day and no friend or guest can be welcomed without it.

Though the grape-vine grows in Tibet, wine is unknown; not so *Cciang*, a kind of barley beer, the whole brewing-process of which is described by Desideri. Of the four kinds only the two milder ones are drunk by women and children, the others two are reserved for men. Though they often drink deep and sometimes too deep, their drunkenness issues at the worst in singing and sleeping, and though their drinking-bouts at weddings and other festivities are sometimes protracted through three days or more they never end in brawls. Monks are forbidden to drink it, but the water being so unwholesome they take it privately [3]). The use of arrack distilled from this beer is much more restricted.

Before every meal a small offering is made to the gods. When on more solemn occasions, such as a wedding or leave-taking, tea or beer is served to persons of distinction the rim of the cup is slightly buttered in three or four places in token of esteem and not for the purpose alleged by Father Ath. Kircher in his

---

the jurisprudence, in Della Penna's *Breve Notizia* (Klaproth p. 288—296). — Quarrels with Nepal and Britain have now led Tibet to maintain a standing force. Cf. Kawaguchi, p. 549.

[1]) Desideri, MS. A. Book II, ch. XIV. p. 68—72; Puini, p. 113—116 is not so detailed.

[2]) Desideri, MS. A. Book II, ch. XIV. p. 72—77; Puini, p. 116—120 falls a good deal short in minor matters.

[3]) Nain Singh's report (*Records*, I, 10) says: "The good-natured Tibetans are constantly brewing *chang* and they never begrudge any one a drink.... The Pundit stoutly denied that this custom tended to drunkenness among his Tibetan friends" etc.

China Illustrata [1]). At table they know the use of cups and plates, not of forks and the rest; they take their food with their fingers.

Their fuel consists of wood and dried dung, and where nothing better can be had, of a kind of dried sods [2]). The chapter concludes with a remark on the pine-wood torches used outside at night in some parts of the country, which practice he had also seen observed in Nepal.

The next chapter opens with a long lesson in the elements of Tibetan grammar, a discussion of its symbols, thirty in number, its vowels and consonants, its pronunciation and spelling. [3]). There are repeated references to a separate sheet of drawings, but this has parted company with the manuscript.

The complete mastering of the language, he says, would not be so difficult, if they did not write before, behind, above and below the characters which they pronounce, other characters which they do not pronounce; while the difficulty is increased by each of their four vowels, e, i, o, u, having a fourfold value [4]).

His remarks on books, libraries and studies he reserves for the part of his work where he will treat of Buddhist monasteries and universities. The Tibetan people, he goes on, are of a lively disposition and an acute mind, while they are cheerful and industrious. Everyone as a rule can usefully employ himself in various ways, in spinning, weaving, sowing, rope-making; Desideri runs up a list of fourteen industries. Hence it is natural that artisans proper, skilled in but one handicraft, are rarely met with. But painting, sculpture, and casting are not so generally practised. Their works in the first two arts are not of the highest order, though on the other hand they are not to be despised. But in casting statues, vases and musket-barrels they are very proficient. The Nepalese,

---

1) This is a stricture on a statement of Kircher's on p. 75, when he is discussing Grueber's journey. "Mos huius gentis est ut mulieribus propinantes potum Cha vel vinum alii viri aut foeminae ter eisdem infundant et inter bibendum tria butyri fragmenta ad amphorae limbum affigant unde postea bibentes accepta fronti affigunt"

2) Cf. Kawaguchi, p. 253.

3) Desideri, MS. A. Book II, ch. XV. p. 77 – 82 Of this chapter Puini has only a few lines on handicrafts and one page on medicine. Cf. Puini, p. 120 – 121.

4) Kawaguchi states expressly (p. 256) that there are but four vowels as against others mentioning five. Desideri, too, speaks of four vowels, though he mentions besides two a's, one the twenty-third, the other the thirtieth letter of the alphabet.

too, are masters of this craft, as they are of sculpture; this is why many of them make a good income in Tibet.

Medicine is a much sought profession. While well-acquainted with maladies and their causes they diagnose the disease without much questioning; they merely feel the pulse, first right and left alternately, then together. Their medicines, mostly in the form of pills or powders, are not numerous; the few they have are derived partly from their own country, partly from Nepal, China, Hindostan and the Lhobá country. Before the curing of a disease is undertaken, an agreement is made as to the charges [1]).

The climate, Desideri continues in the following chapter, is healthy, hence there is little sickness. In the larger towns, however, many people suffer from venereal diseases, for which they have excellent remedies, though as a rule the cure is but temporary. Almost every ten years a large part of the population is infected with smallpox and the death-rate rises enormously. For though an infected person is at once carried from his house and quarantined, a great number perish from the wretchedness of their shelter and the insufficiency of the attendance [2]).

As soon as a man falls ill a Cciŏ-Kiong, a kind of sorcerer, or a lama is sent for to decide what doctor must be consulted and how the patient is to behave; which decision is scrupulously carried out. Should the patient get worse, a band of monks gather in the house to hold the *Corim*, that is, they make offerings, while singing prayers to the accompaniment of musical instruments. They fill the rest of the day with reading aloud and together, from some of their books which are called Kaa-n-ghiur. Such a Corim may last one or two or even more days. If the patient's means allow, money is sent to one or more monasteries for a Corim to held there for his benefit. Friends and relations likewise present offerings and make the Khora, or solemn circuit. On recovery another

---

[1]) Kawaguchi (p. 487 – 488) does not think highly of the Tibetan medical men, "who are utterly incompetent for the important function assigned to them". From Waddell (*Lhasa*, p. 377) it is clear that feeling the pulse is still the cardinal point in medicinal art.

[2]) Nearly every writer mentions smallpox, the most deadly disease in Tibet. Thus Huc, *Souvenirs*, II, 345; Das, p. 167, 206, 225 etc.; Tsybikoff, p. 730 estimates the deaths due to this cause in 1900 at Lhasa and the neigbouring monasteries at ten per cent. of the population. On the curious smallpox-edict see Waddell (*Lhasa*, p. 362); it is inscribed on a stone tablet near the entrance of the chief temple of Lhasa, and contains prescriptions to be followed when the disease makes its appearance.

Corim is held in thanksgiving, but it also takes place, if he dies [1]).

Desideri then dwells at some length on their games, among which is a kind of draughts, their cattle-breeding and their agriculture with its irrigation system that recalls the method of the Spanish huertas. He has words of approval for the character and the religious sentiment of the Tibetans which he thinks would fit them to receive the Gospel [2]).

One of the serious obstacles, however, is polyandry, which, though not the rule, is quite common. If the husband has younger brothers, each takes his sister-in-law as his wife and they make one family. The issue that is born is the eldest brother's, and the children are treated as the nephews and nieces of the brothers-husbands. The causes of this custom are two: the meagreness of the soil which on being parcelled out into small lots would not support a family; and the small number of women [3]). When the bride is being conducted to the house of the bridegroom, she resists with all her power, and the ceremonial welcome with which she meets there is not attended by her parents "thus keeping up the fiction that she has been carried off and has married without their consent" [4]). No marriages are permitted among the descen-

---

[1]) Desideri, MS. A. Book II, ch. XVI. p. 84–85; Puini, p. 121–122. Cf. Kawaguchi, p. 486; Tsybikoff, p. 732.

[2]) Desideri, MS. A. Book II, ch. XVI. p. 86–90. Puini p. 123–126. Strange to say Desideri has not a word on the unutterable filth of the Tibetans, which renders them so offensive to all foreigners and which has been most cuttingly remarked on by the Japanese Kawaguchi (p. 264–267; 407–409). Nor does he refer to the curious fashion of women painting their faces with a black paste before appearing in public, a custom noted by Huc, Rockhill, Kawaguchi and Hedin. According to Huc (*Souvenirs*, p. 254) this custom dated from some two hundred years back, while Rockhill (*Land*, p. 214) would suppose it was made compulsory only towards the end of the eighteenth century. Desideri's silence would seem to favour the latter opinion. Landon (I 6.) it is true cites Grueber's name as bearing witness to this custom; but the nearest approach to any such testimony which the present writer has been able to find has quite a different bearing; let the reader judge for himself: "Foeminae horum Regnorum adeo deformes sunt, ut diabolis similiores quam hominibus videantur, nunquam enim religionis causa aqua se lavant, sed oleo quodam putidissimo; quo praeterquam quod intolerabilem foetorem spirent, dicto oleo ita inquinantur, ut non homines sed lamias diceres". Kircher, *China Illustrata*, p. 76.

[3]) Cf. Rockhill, *Land*, p. 211, from which it appears that polyandry is practised among the agricultural population, not among the pastoral Tibetans. Cf. also Das, p. 327, and on Ladakh Drew, p. 250. Kawaguchi (p. 373) looks for the origin of these abominable practices in the old Bon religion.

[4]) Though Chandra Das and Kawaguchi describe wedding-ceremonies at length, Waddell (*Buddhism*, p. 553) is the only one to hint at something like the sham marriage of capture described by Desideri.

dants of the same father at any remove[1]), but affinity, as a rule, creates no impediment except in the first degree [2]).

Desideri winds up his sketch of country and people with some notes on funerals and their entirely unchristian character [3]). As in the case of sickness so in the case of death the sorcerer plays an important part since his advice is generally taken and acted upon. Taking account of the social and financial position of the family he will order people of wealth and dignity to cremate the body, a costly affair in a country so badly off for fuel as Tibet. Those who are not so well-to-do may carry the corpse to some holy mountain top, where it is gashed in several places and left a prey to eagles and vultures. Religious are generally thus disposed of. Those who can afford no expense at all carry the body to a certain spot, called Tur-tro, where it is cut into small pieces as food for the dogs which wander about there in great numbers. Lastly there is the method of throwing the body into a river as food for fish.

"When, however, Father Kircher writes," Desideri continues, "that the custom of leaving the dead to wild beasts is due to their opinion that it is the highest honour to have as one's last resting-place the belly of living animals — his theory is more ingenious than true [4]). For the reason is quite different; it has a religious basis, and is a consequence of one of their cardinal points of belief: sympathy with all living things. One of the most sublime expressions of this belief would be to give oneself to them as food; it being too heroic a thing to do so during their life-time, they prefer to put it off till their death. Thus also they are afforded a means of attaining to the most difficult degree of sympathy, for they voluntarily return into the cycle of innumerable transmigrations in order to deliver others out of it. Yet there is nothing unreasonable in the bodies of the principal lamas being preserved in urns and venerated; for by their powerful protection they benefit all. Their repeated incarnations, too, for the sake of teaching and guiding others are proofs of sympathy on their

---

[1]) According to Das (p. 326) this is still the case up to the seventh degree.

[2]) Desideri, MS. A. Book II. ch. XVII. p. 90–96; Puini, p. 129–133. Desideri errs in thinking that Tibet is the only country where polyandry is practised. Cf. E. Westermarck, *Origine du Mariage dans l'Espèce Humaine* (Paris 1895) p. 425–433.

[3]) Desideri, MS. A Book II, ch. XVIII. p. 96–103; Cf. Puini, p. 157–174.

[4]) The reference is clearly to the following passage: "Dum hoc unicum gloriosae mortis monumentum esse sibi persuadent, intra vivorum animalium ventres sepulchrum obtinere." *China Illustrata*, p. 76.

part. The cremation may be taken as a mere inconsistency".

These details have also been recorded by Andrade [1]) and Della Penna [2]). Rawling witnessed such a funeral [3]), while a full account of one is given by Kawaguchi.

In the note on the manuscripts, appended to this chapter, it is adverted that the third book of MS. B. is especially taken up with the religion of Tibet [4]). This being Desideri's subject of special interest he enters into it at great length and he has thus given to the world what is probably the most complete survey of the whole Lamaistic system composed by any European, who lived on the spot. As such, however, it falls outside the scope of this work; for the text the reader may be referred to Puini [5]).

Space must be found, however, for one passage not given by Puini. In the course of his discussions Desideri remarks on the passage where Kircher makes Grueber say that the Tibetans worship the god Manippe with the invocation. "O Manippe mi hum" meaning thereby "Manippe save us" [6]). For, he says, there is no god bearing that name and the prayer which Grueber has in mind "Om mani pêmé hum" has quite a different meaning.

The reader will remember that Andrade did not venture on an explanation of those obscure words, while Della Penna also prefers to keep on the safe side: the explanation would be too long, he says [7]). Later writers, among whom such scholars as Koeppen and Grunwedel translate: "O, Jewel in the lotus, Amen," and Waddell, "Om! the Jewel in the Lotus! Hum"; this formula the latter adds, is addressed to the Bodhisattva Padmapani (Avalokitesvara or Chrenresig) the patron-god of Tibet and

---

1) Andrade, *Lettere Annue*, p. 14.

2) Klaproth, p. 430–432.

3) Rawling, p. 200 ff. Sherring, p. 121. According to Waddell (*Lhasa*, p. 233) the scarcity of wood for cremation and the difficulty of digging the soil for graves are in part accountable for this revolting method of disposing of the dead. Interment only takes place in case of death of smallpox. Cf. Kawaguchi, p. 388.

4) He makes an end of the legend, so often told by earlier travellers concerning ancient Christian settlements in Tibet. Neither history nor tradition among the Tibetans affords the slightest ground for such a supposition (MS. B. Book III, ch. XLII p. 424–425). He also withdraws, as entirely erroneous, the statements on the religion of the country contained in his Lhasa letter to Grassi of April 10, 1716. (ch. XLII. p. 435).

5) Puini, p. 185–334.

6) Kircher, *China Illustrata*, p. 71.

7) Klaproth, p. 426.

controller of metempsychosis[1]). The most recent rendering is von Ow's: "Praised be thou Om, Jewel in the Lotus! Hum!"[2])

What, then, may be Desideri's interpretation of the cryptic saying? "The word *Om,*" he writes, "is not a significant term but a mere ornament of style, the common opening-word of every charm. The second word *Mani* means a jewel, such as a pearl, diamond or other precious stones. The third word *Pêmé* is a compound of the two words Pêmà and E. Pêmà means a flower, that grows in the water, in ponds and lakes; in Hindostani it is called *Câmêl pul.* The E is a particle of address or invocation as with us the particle O. The last word again, *Hum,* is not a significant term, but a mere ornament, the termination of every magic saying. This being premised, it is necessary for the proper understanding of this puzzling formula, which does not construe, to remember the Tibetan god Cen-ree sy; he is generally represented carrying a jewel in his hand and seated on a flower, which in their language is called Pêmà. Hence this Tibetan prayer is nothing but a simple invocation of their god and great protector Cen-ree sy and it means: O thou, who holdest a jewel in thy hand and art seated on the flower Pêmà. The Tibetans say that anciently such a prayer had been taught and recommended to their forbears by the same Cen-ree sy as very acceptable to him, and conducive to their happy and early salvation in the long and toilsome process of metempsychosis" [3]).

At an earlier page in this chapter passing reference was made to a political event of the last importance which took place during Desideri's stay in Tibet: the temporary Tartar domination of the country and the subsequent annexation of it by the Chinese. It broke up his stay at the university of Sera and compelled him to provide for his own safety by withdrawing to the province of Takpó-Khier. His full account of those convul-

---

[1]) Waddell, *Buddhism*, p. 148.

[2]) A. von Ow, *Religionsgeschichtliches aus Sven Hedin's Transhimalaja*, Anthropos (1910) p. 1063.

[3]) Desideri, MS. B. Book III, ch. XL. p. 418–419; this is wanting in Puini. The latter interprets the formula as follows: "Gloria (om.... hum) alla Religione (mani) sulla terra (paamê = nelumbium speciosum). Nella cosmografie buddiste, la terra è di frequente raffigurata dentro un fiore sbocciato di questa pianta." (Puini, p. 259 note 1) Kawaguchi (p. 261) stands quite apart with his interpretation: "All will be as we will".

sions is of special value as being that of an eye-witness and must needs be represented here at least by a brief summary [1]).

The military commander or king of Lhasa, Ginghes Khang [2]), to whom Desideri paid his respects on his arrival in 1716, had been in power since 1705. In that year he had violently usurped the supreme power by murdering the ruling governor, and had greatly strengthened his position by obtaining the approval of his kinsman the Emperor of China. Naturally he was not on friendly terms with the Dalai Lama. The latter was a dissolute young man, whose conduct offended Ginghes Khang. Friction and trouble were unavoidable. At last the king pretended that the Emperor Kang-hi had invited the Dalai Lama to visit him. The thoughtless youth never suspected the trap laid for him; he set out with a large retinue, and after a couple of days' travelling he was murdered. Before his death the unhappy young man declared he would soon be back; on the Chinese border he would be re-born; they would have to look out for him there.

The immense stir that was created in the monasteries by this crime was but increased when the king on his own authority installed a new Dalai Lama. It was only by exerting the greatest severity that this intruded dignitary could enforce compliance, and the number of malcontents among the lamas was ever on the increase. Plots were formed to oust the two usurpers and the aid of the king of Independent Tartary, who was offered the crown, was secretly solicited. These advances were well received, and to conceal his plans the king proposed a marriage between his daughter and Ginghes Khang's eldest son, who was to come to him to receive his bride. He also asked Ginghes Khang to lend him some troops in a war against Muscovy and for the suppression of a rebellion in Jarkant; all of which proposals were agreed to by the Lhasa king [3]).

Meanwhile the rumour spread abroad that on the Chinese bor-

---

[1]) Desideri, MS. A. Book II ch. IX—XII. p. 39—60. Puini, p. 338—358. The same events are spoken of in the *Mémoire sur le Tibet et sur le Royaume des Eleuthes* — Lettres Edifiantes, XIII, 230 ff.; also in Koeppen, II, 185 ff; Waddell, *Lhasa*, p. 32. ff; Günther-Schulemann, p. 168 ff.; Haenisch, p. 197. ff. etc.

[2]) All writers call this ruler Latsa or Latsang Khan, Koeppen (II, 189) being the only one to note that the name Gingkhir Khan is also found.

[3]) These circumstances are confirmed by an edict of the Emperor Kanghi in 1717, which says that Tsewang Rabtan (the Tartar king) has forcibly retained the son of Latsang Han (Ginghes Khang) Cf. Haenisch, p. 209.

der, near Hsi-ning, the murdered Dalai Lama had become re-incarnate and had revealed himself in the person of a young child. Fresh hopes were aroused among the people of Tibet, but at the instance of Ginghes Khang the child was kidnapped and shut up in a fortress by Kang-hi[1]). This second outrage against the sacred person of their spiritual chief was beyond human endurance and the secret machinations became open rebellion. The movement was headed by the three principal monasteries of Breebung, Sera and Shigatse. At their instance the Tartar king crossed into Tibet in 1717 with an army of 6,000 men under the command of General Zze-ring-ton-drup [2]), while a second army was directed towards the Chinese frontier to liberate the re-incarnated Lama.

Ginghes Khang who as usual was spending the summer months in the country of Dam north of Lhasa, was taken wholly unaware by this sudden attack. His second son succeeded in hurriedly mustering some troops and beating off the first attack. For three months the king held his ground in Dam and it was not till the end of October that he fell back on the fortifications of Lhasa. About a month later the Tartars appeared before the town; their arrival had been delayed because they had first awaited the arrival of the troops sent off to liberate the young Dalai Lama. Though this army had been defeated by the Chinese, Zze-ring-ton-drup was careful to keep the depressing news to himself and to give out a glorious victory. The monasteries of Sera, Breebung and Kaa-n-den supplied the Tartars with victuals, and when in the night of November 30 a general assault on Lhasa was delivered the gates were thrown open by their confederates. In a couple of hours there was nothing left for Ginghes Khang but to seek safety in the Potala Palace. For two days Lhasa was given over to a pillaging soldiery. Desideri was at the Sera monastery so that his belongings were safe except for a few things which he had left with the Capuchins at Lhasa; their house did not escape in the general loot and one of them even sustained personal injury. On 3 December the Potala was assaulted and taken, but the king got away with his son and some grandees through a secret passage. Hotly pursued his horse stumbled, he was taken and killed. The rest of the fugitives likewise were shortly afterwards caught by the governer of the pro-

---

[1]) Waddells version (*Lhasa*, p. 32) departs considerably from Desideri's as well as from Koeppen's or Haenisch's.

[2]) Ssereng Donduck (Koeppen), Cering donhob (Haenisch).

vince of Taze, delivered up and executed. The first minister, Targum-treê-sey was the only one to make good his escape; he reached Gartok where he collected the frontier troops, who had remained loyal and barred the way back to Independent Tartary.

The death of his kinsman Ginghes Khang and the raid of the second Tartar army into his own dominions offered a welcome opportunity to the Emperor Kang-hi to assert himself in Tibetan affairs. His first attempt in 1718 failed; the expedition from Hsining across the plateau to Dam came to nought through lack of provisions and discord among the leaders [1]).

The second was better planned. "Had I not seen it with my own eyes I would not have believed it", Desideri narrates; "but no sooner had the Chinese penetrated into Tibet than the country literally ran over with silver. To supply his wants every soldier had received advance pay for five years in bits of uncoined silver of various sizes. The Tibetans were at a loss how to dispose of this abundance, and sent most of it to Nepal to exchange it by weight for the currency of the country, out of which transaction the Nepalese made a handsome profit".

In this second expedition, moreover, the Emperor played his highest card. He released the youthful Dalai Lama and sent him with the army. This at once changed the whole face of the situation. Having their religious sentiments satisfied the people sided with the Dalai Lama, and therefore with the Chinese; almost everywhere they took up arms against their recent allies, the Tartars. Desideri himself, who at the time resided at Trong-gnêe in Takpó-Khier, one day received orders under pain of death to join the Chinese army within twenty four hours. He was to appear provided with a horse and arms, and accompanied by two of his followers also armed. The local governor, however, succeeded in getting the order countermanded by the general in command.

The Tartar occupants were not to be cowed by a mere martial show. They understood that they had to stake all on the seizure of the Dalai Lama. For three nights running they stormed the Chinese camp, but had to retreat after a great carnage without attaining their object. The fourth night, however, they were in their turn attacked on two fronts by the best among the Chinese troops and

[1]) According to Haenisch (p. 205) the whole body of troops was cut to pieces near Kara usu about the end of August.

were almost exterminated in the furious struggle that ensued. The survivors fled with Zze-ring-ton-drup in the direction of Gartok. Another massacre followed among those who had befriended the Tartars, but at last the storm subsided and in October 1720 the new Dalai Lama ascended the golden throne of the Palace of Potala. The temporal sovereignty, however, had passed into the hands of the Chinese for ever.

But few words remain to be said about Desideri's journey back, for we do not mean to follow him far out of Tibet [1]).

In the early days of 1721 when staying at Trong-g-neê a letter reached him from the General of the Society. It was dated Rome, January 16, 1719 and ordered him to quit the Tibetan mission at the earliest opportunity. Returning to Lhasa April 16, he left the holy city twelve days later and took the road to Kutti in Nepal. He was accompanied by the Capuchin Friar Joseph Felix da Morro whose destination was Katmandu. Though the usual route was *via* Shigatse and Sakya, they went by Gyantse, because after the recent upheaval things had not yet settled in those parts. "On this journey one passes a very high and trying mountain, called Langur. Such a mountain has the peculiarity that every one who crosses it will infallibly feel a great discomfort, especially a severe head-ache, shortness of breath and difficulty of respiration; in addition to this some are taken with fever as I was during the whole day which it took us to cross the mountain, and the night which we passed on it. Though it was towards the end of May that we traversed it, the snow was still very deep, and the cold was so intense and the wind so piercing that notwithstanding my thick clothing I was quite numbed and feared I might not live through it. A common remedy against these discomforts of mountaineering is to chew roasted rice or sugar-candy, or cloves, cinnamon and a kind of Indian nuts, called arecca by the Portuguese. It being impossible to cross the Langur in one day there is a large house where travellers can pass the night. The difficulty of respiration, however, makes it impossible for many to stay indoors and they sleep in the open. The head-aches and other inconviences come to an end together with the crossing. There are many who think that all these discomforts

[1]) See the headings of the 20 chapters of the 3rd book of MS. A, which is entirely taken up with the return journey. Only the first few chapters concern us here.

are due to some volatilizing minerals that may be hidden within the mountain; but since no trace of them has so far been discovered I am inclined to ascribe those phenomena to the extreme thinness and keenness of the air" [1]).

The name Langur as another name for the Himalaya Range is familiar to the reader from Grueber's account. What is more remarkable is Desideri's suggestion as to the cause of the mountain sickness, which more than a hundred years later is still ascribed by Huc, when on the heights of the Burkhan Buddha Range, to the action of carbonic acid [2]).

After thirty-two days of continuous travel on horseback, on May 30, the two arrived at Kutti or Nilam Dzong. While da Morro soon proceeded on his journey to Katmandu, Desideri resolved to prolong his stay at Kutti till the winter, because otherwise the change from the Tibetan to the Nepalese climate might be too sudden, and "because during those summer-months influenza is prevalent at Katmandu every year with a very high death-rate". Moreover he would have to stay on at Katmandu till the end of December before he could proceed further [3]). Hence it was not till December 14 that in company with the Capuchin Father Felix da Montecchio he set out again taking his route *via* Nesti. As his notes on the abominable mountain road are in complete accord with Hari Ram's characteristics of it [4]), given in the preceding chapter, it is sufficient to state that he traversed it safely and was hospitably welcomed at the Capuchins' house of Katmandu on December 27.

The political organization of Nepal with its three royal cities of Katmandu, Patan and Bhatgaon is set forth with the customary fulness, while the character, religion, language and dress of the people are likewise passed in review [5]). He also expatiates on the "influenza", called *Ol* by the natives, a sickness which every summer debars travellers from the country. Not on the mountains but in the plains the disease is contracted, during the night rather than during the day. It is all due to the intense heat and the foul evaporations of stagnant water, which is abun-

---

[1]) Desideri, MS. A. Book III, ch. I. p. 2—3; Puini, p. 82—83.

[2]) Huc, *Souvenirs*, II, 210.

[3]) Father da Morro died within two months after his arrival at Katmandu.

[4]) *Records*, II, 118.

[5]) Desideri, MS. A. Book III, ch. III. p. 8—18; Puini, p. 88—90; 94—95.

dantly present everywhere as a result of rice-growing in flooded fields, while at this season there are hardly any air currents to carry off the noxious emanations. The vapours arise during the day to descend again upon every valley and plain during the night; hence this is the time of danger. The disease is practically incurable save by native remedies, the secret of which is jealously guarded by the people. They take a drink called *Bang*, drawn from dry leaves, hemp-leaves one might say or something very like them, but even so a great number perish [1]).

With long intervals at Patna, Benares and Allahabad the traveller at last arrived at Agra; it was April 22, 1722, sixty years after Grueber and d'Orville had terminated their toilsome wanderings in the same city. Like the latter Desideri was taken seriously ill, which he ascribes to his rapid transition from an arctic to a tropical climate. But he recovered in the old capital Dehli, where he stayed till 1725, when he left for Pondicherry. Tireless as he was he was just engaged in the study of Tamil to make himself useful in the Carnatic mission, when he was told off in January 1727 to carry to Rome a collection of papers and documents concerning another great missionary, Blessed John de Britto. Following the sea-route he passed the Cape of Good Hope, St. Helena and Ascension, but a few days after leaving the last-mentioned island an accident compelled the ship to sail to Martinique of the Lesser Antilles for repairs. There were no further mishaps, and August 11, 1727, he landed at Port Louis, a small port near Lorient in Brittany. By way of Paris, Marseilles and Genoa he reached Rome, January 23, 1728. It was here that he completed his *Notizie Istoriche del Thibet*; here, too, he died suddenly April 14, 1733 at the age of forty-nine.

In conclusion we may quote the words with which Desideri winds up his account: "All this I have written after traversing all three Tibets and living in those parts continually for several years; after obtaining, moreover, a knowledge of the language fairly wide and deep, and after reading and examining with pro-

[1]) Desideri, MS. A. Book III, ch. III. p. 18—20. Puini has nothing on this point. The subject is referred to by Georgi in his *Alphabetum Tibetanum*. Cf. Levi, I, 121. Kawaguchi relates that at the present time Katmandu is visited by large numbers of pilgrims between September and February, a season which at first sight seems quite unfavourable for travelling. But he adds that they are liable to catch malaria fever if they come through the Himalaya passes during the summer months. (p. 36).

tacted study and serious application a great number of the principal and also very abstruse books of that people" [1]). He meant his narrative to be a solid piece of work and every page we have examined bears witness that it is. As such is has been dealt with by Sven Hedin in his *Southern Tibet* and after bringing out Desideri's great merits as a contributor to our knowledge of Tibet he concludes: "Add to this the general merit of his narrative, the absence of fantastical speculation, the quiet matter-of-fact way in which he gives his observations, and nobody will call it an exaggeration if I regard Ippolito Desideri as one of the most brilliant travellers who ever visited Tibet, and amongst the old ones, by far the most prominent and the most intelligent of all" [2]). No candid reader of the preceding pages will demur at this tribute.

We have thus come to the end of our task: there are no conclusions to draw beyond those that have, at every turn, suggested themselves to the reader. Both the character of the men and of their work have been submitted to searching, if sympathetic, criticism, and have, we venture to think, stood the test. The work remains the work of pioneers, scrappy, irregular, imperfect, but granite blocks by their very rudeness speak of the immense labour of fashioning them into any shape at all.

If the names of those forgotten pioneers, on almost every page, appear side by side with those of the greatest among modern explorers, this in no way detracts from the greatness of the latter. Nay, it lends a new importance to the discoveries of these latter days, since it is only by the light of modern research and exploration that the work of those who preceded them by centuries can be duly appreciated. And it is thus that the old achievements, undertaken in silent obscurity and carried through at the cost of gigantic personal effort, are dragged forth from the dimness of their remote past, and by the very splendour of modern results are lit up with a halo of tragic greatness.

---

[1]) MS. B. Book III, ch. XLII. p. 443. Puini, p. 273.
[2]) Hedin, *Southern Tibet*, I, 278–279; cf. III, 13.

CHRONOLOGICAL SUMMARY

Dec. 21.	1684.	Hippolyte Desideri born at Pistoja.
April 27.	1700.	He enters the Society of Jesus.
Sept. 27.	1712.	Leaves Rome for India.
Sept. 24.	1714.	Accompanied by F. Man. Freyre he set out from Dehli to Tibet.
Nov. 13.		arrival at Srinagar (Kashmir).
May 17.	1715.	departure from Srinagar.
June 26.		arrival at Leh.
Aug. 17.		departure from Leh.
March 18.	1716.	arrival at Lhasa. -- Return of Freyre to Hindostan.
March 25-July 30.	1717.	stay at the monastery of Ramo-cce.
Aug.-Dec.		stay at the university of Sera.
Dec. 1717— April 1721		stay at Trong-g-neê in the province of Takpó-Khier.
April 16.	1721.	return to Lhasa.
April 28.		departure from Lhasa.
May 30.		arrival at Kutti.
Dec. 27.		departure from Kutti.
April 22.	1722.	arrival at Agra.
January	1727.	departure from India for Rome.
January 23.	1728.	arrival at Rome.
April 14.	1733.	death of Desideri at Rome.

LETTERS OF F. DESIDERI

Letter to the General of the Society, dated Goa, November 12, 1713. MS.*

Letter to the same, dated Goa, November 15, 1713, MS.*

Letter to the same, dated Surat, December 30, 1713. MS.*

Letter to Father Francis Piccolomini in Rome, dated Agra, August 21, 1714; published by the present writer in: *Atti e Memorie del Convegno di Geografi-Orientalisti, tenuto in Macerata*. (Macerata 1911). p. 30–39.

Letter to the General of the Society, dated Delhi, September 20, 1714. MS.*

Letter to the same, dated Leh, August 5, 1715; published by Puini p. 361–370.

Letter to Father Hildebrand Grassi in Mysore, dated Lhasa, April 10, 1716; published in *Lettres Edifiantes et Curieuses*. (Lyon 1819) VII. 259–268.

Letter to the General of the Society, dated Lhasa, February 15, 1717; published by Puini p. 370–376.

Letter to Father Felix da Montecchio, dated Takpó, March 12, 1718; published by Puini, p. 376–377.

Letter to the same, dated Trong-g-neê, August 4, 1718; published by Puini p. 378–382.

Letter to the General of the Society, dated Lhasa, December 21, 1719. MS.*

Letter to the Pope, dated Kutti, September 21, 1721; published by Puini p. 382–383.

Letter to the General of the Society, dated Kutti, September 21, 1721. MS.*

Letter to the same, dated Kutti, October 5, 1721. MS.*

LIST OF MANUSCRIPTS *

I. Four MSS. written in Tibetan.

1) MS. of 54 pp. dated on first page July 1, 1717, on last page June 29, 1721.

*) In the possession of the Society of Jesus.

to face p. 274.

Desideri's Tibetan Manuscripts: first page of MS. 2

2) MS. of 117 large oblong pages, bearing as its date on the first page December 8, 1717, on the last page the words: "B. Aloysii Gonzagae festus dies huic tractatui finem imposuit. 1718", (i.e. June 21).
3) MS. of 704 oblong pages, 33,5 × 18,5 cm., having 35 lines to the page. Its opening date is June 24, 1718.
4) MS. of 128 narrow strips, 33,5 × 13,5 cm., with 7 lines to the page, undated.

The MSS. very probably contain Desideri's refutation of the Buddhistic doctrine and his defence of the Catholic Religon, which writings he is known to have carried away with him from Tibet; but the author must leave it to Tibetan scholars to decipher the text. Specimen pages are given at the end of this chapter.

II. Italian MSS.

MS. of 430 pp., 27 × 30 cm., in a very clear handwriting, not Desideri's. It has title-page and preface, and is divided into three books, each subdivided into chapters; it seems ready for the press.

In the preface Desideri states that at first he had no intention of publishing anything, but now does he so at the instance of others. The last page of the MS. is dated June 22, 1728, the title page 1733; did he hesitate all these years till his sudden death in 1733 prevented the publication?

This MS. is cited as: Desideri MS. A.

Its contents are as follows:

Notizie Istoriche del Thibet
e Memorie de' Viaggi e Missione ivi fatti
dal P. Ippolito Desideri
della Compagnia di Giesu.
Dal medesimo scritte, e dedicate
1712—1733

p. 3—6. AL LETTORE

LIBRO PRIMO

Memorie del Viaggio da Roma sin' a Lhasa, citta capitale del terzo Thibet, e missione ibi intrapresa

Capitolo	I. p.	1—4.	Partenza da Roma e viaggio sin' a Lisbona.
„	II. p.	4—10.	Navigazione da Lisbona sin' all altura del Capo di Buona Speranza.
„	III. p.	10—16.	Continuazione del viaggio di mare sin' a Mossambiche e dipoi sin' a Goa.

Capitolo IV. p.	16–28.	Partenza da Goa e Viaggio sin' alla citta di Delly, capitale del Imperio del Mogol. Brevi Notizie di qualla corte.
„ V. p.	28–35.	Delle Chiese e Christianita, che ha in Delly la Compagnia di Giesu e d'alcuni insigni Christiani ivi abitanti.
„ VI. p.	35–42.	Dimora nella citta d'Agra, e notizie della Missione che quivi ha la Compagnia di Giesu.
„ VII. p.	42–47.	Partenza da Delly; arrivo a Cascimir e dimora in quella citta. Alcune notizie di quel luogo.
„ VIII. p.	47–54.	Partenza da Cascimir e viaggio sin' al Lhata, capitale del secondo Thibet.
„ IX. p.	54–57.	Dimora in Lhata, citta capitale del secondo e Gran Thibet. Partenza e arrivo a Trêescy-Khang.
„ X. p.	57–69.	Viaggio del Gran Deserte di Ng-nari Giongar e ajuto ricevuto dalla compagnia d'una Principessa Tartara.
„ XI. p.	69–75.	Entrata nella prime popolazioni del terzo e massimo Thibet. Continuazion di viaggio e arrivo alla Capitale. Visite al Re, e a' primi Ministri. Principio di Missione in quel Regno.
„ XII. p.	75–80.	Protezzione del Re. Soccorso dato al medesimo, e al Primo Ministro in un pericolo. Dimostrazioni di Gratitudine da medesimi usate. Rifuito de loro doni e offerte.
„ XIII. p.	80–85.	Primo Libro composto dall' Autore in quella lingua e solennemente presentato al Re in una publica Udienza.
„ XIV. p.	85–88.	Studio de' Libri e degli errori di quelle Genti.
„ XV. p.	88–92.	Altri Libri composti dall' Autore in quella lingua.
„ XVI. p.	92–101.	Ragguaglio della Missione che la Compagnia di Giesu ha avuto nel Thibet, dalla sua fondazione fin' a tempo dell' autore.

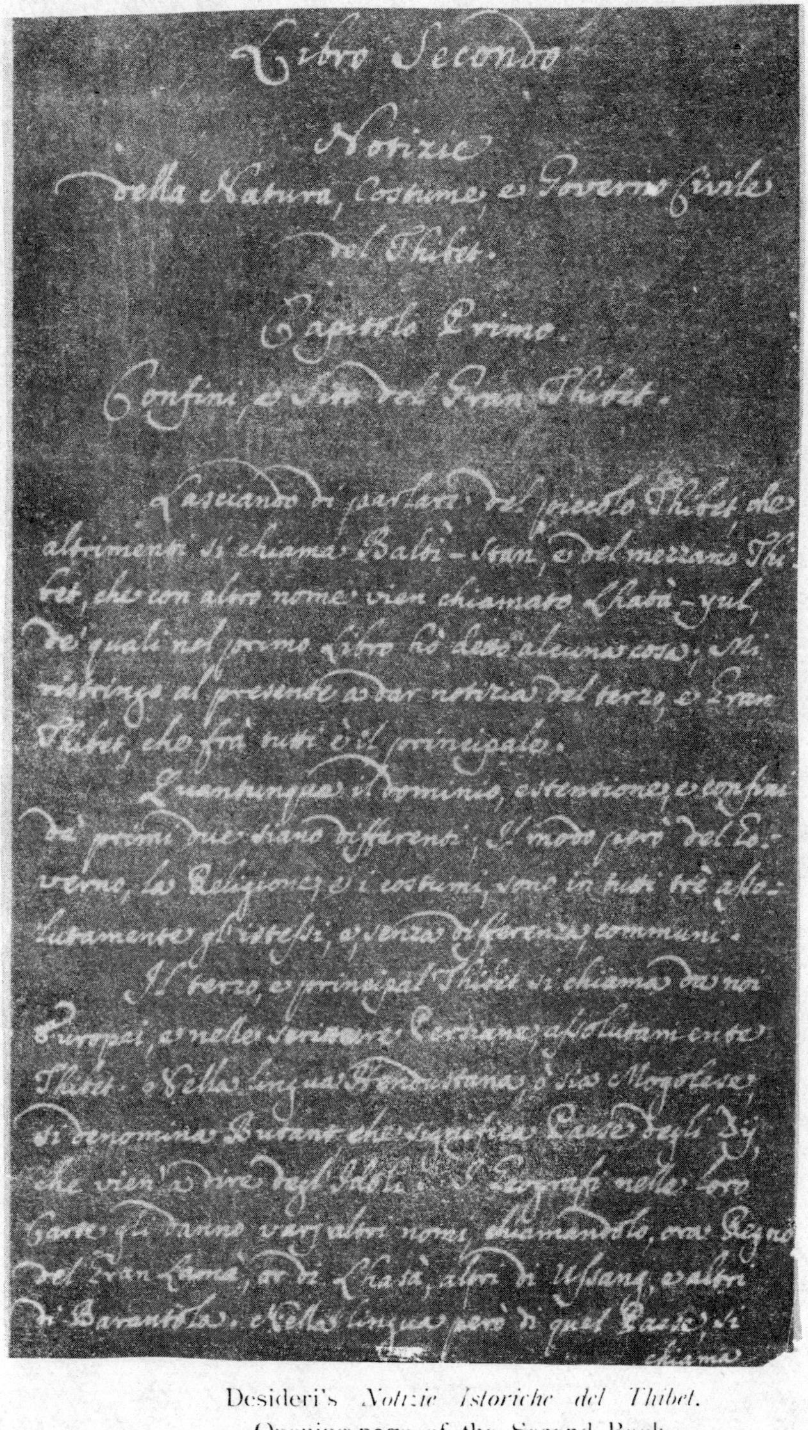

Libro Secondo

Notizie

della Natura, Costume, e Governo Civile

del Thibet.

Capitolo Primo.

Confini e Sito del Gran Thibet.

Lasciando di parlare del piccolo Thibet, che altrimenti si chiama Baltì-stan, e del mezzano Thibet, che con altro nome vien chiamato Lhatà-yul, de' quali nel primo Libro hò detto alcuna cosa; Mi ristringo al presente a dar notizia del terzo, e Gran Thibet, che frà tutti è il principale.

Quantunque il dominio, estensione, e confini de' primi due siano differenti; Il modo però del Governo, la Religione, e i costumi, sono in tutti tre assolutamente gli stessi, e senza differenza communi.

Il terzo, e principal Thibet si chiama da noi Europei, e nelle scritture Persiane, assolutamente Thibet. Nella lingua Hindustana, ò sia Mogolese, si denomina Butant, che significa Paese degli Dij, che vien' a dire degl' Idoli. I Geografi nelle loro Carte gli danno varj altri nomi, chiamandolo, ora Regno del Gran Lama, altri di Lhasà, altri di Ussang, e altri di Barantola. Nella lingua però di quel Paese, si

chiama

Desideri's *Notizie Istoriche del Thibet.*
Opening-page of the Second Book.

LIBRO SECONDO

Notizie della Natura, Costume e Governo Civile del Thibet

Capitolo	I. p.	1—6.	Confini e sito del Gran Thibet.
„	II. p.	6—12.	Clima e fecondita della terra del Thibet.
„	III. p.	12—17.	Dell' animale del Muschio e d'altri animale che sono nel Thibet.
„	IV. p.	17—20.	Del Fiumi del Thibet e loro Barche e Ponte.
„	V. p.	20—26.	Della Parte Occidentale del Thibet e d'Alcune sue Provincie e Citte.
„	VI. p.	26—32.	Della Citta di Lhasa, capitale del Thibet e suo contorno.
„	VII. p.	32—35.	Delle vicinanze di Lhasa e Provincie intermedie di questo Thibet.
„	VIII. p.	35—38.	Delle Provincie della parte Occidentale del Thibet.
„	IX. p.	38—42.	Del Dominio del Thibet passato ne'i Tartari.
„	X. p.	42—47.	Rivoluzioni del Thibet, prima che il suo Dominio da' Tartari passasse ne' Cinesi.
„	XI. p.	47—53.	Fine infelice del Re Ginghes-Khang e della sua Famiglia.
„	XII. p.	53—60.	Del Dominio del Thibet, da' Tartari passato ne' Cinesi.
„	XIII. p.	60—68.	Del Governo civile del Thibet.
„	XIV. p.	68—77.	Delle vesti, e de' Cibi, che s'usano nel Thibet.
„	XV. p.	77—83.	Delle Lettere e Alfabeto de' Thibettani, e abilita di quella Genti agli Studj e alle Arti.
„	XVI. p.	83—90.	Delle disposizioni corporali, occupazioni, ginochi, agricultura e inclinazione de' Thibettani.
„	XVII. p.	90—96.	De Matrimonj de' Thibettani.
„	XVIII. p.	96—103.	Costumi de' Thibettani circa i Defonti.

LIBRO TERZO

Partenza dalla Missione de' Regni del Thibet; passagio ad altre Missioni e ritorno in Europa

Capitolo	I. p.	1—8.	Partenza di Lhasa. Dimora fatta in Kutti. Partenza dagli ultimi confini del Thibet, e arrivo al Regno di Nepal.
„	II. p.	8—18.	Si danno alcune notizie del Regno di Nepal.

Capitolo III. p.	18—27.	Viaggio da Nepal sino al Gange e sino alla Citta di Pattna.
„ IV. p.	27—36.	Alcune notizie della Citta di Pattna.
„ V. p.	36—43.	Partenza da Pattna, e viaggio sin' alla Citta d'Agra. Notizie delle Citta di Benares e di Allahabad e del Gange. Dimora fatta in Agra.
„ VI. p.	43—57.	Missione fatta in Delly, Citta capitale del Mogol.
„ VII. p.	57—66.	S'espongono le cause delle turbulenze che nel Mogol insorsero tra l'Imperatore e il suo Vazir Nezam-em-muluk.
„ VIII. p.	66—77.	Si continua a descriver le turbulenze del Mogol tra l'Imperatore e i Grandi di quella Corte.
„ IX. p.	77—85.	Partenza da Delly. Ritorno a Pattna. Passaggio a Bengala. Navigazione a Pondiscery.
„ X. p.	85—91.	Notizie della Citta di Pondiscery. Andata alla missione del Carnat.
„ XI. p.	91—102.	Notizie della missione che la Compagnia di Giesu fruttuosamente esercita nel Regno di Carnat.
„ XII. p.	102—106.	Partenza dalla Missione di Carnat. Notizie della Citta di Meliapur, e delle memorie, che quivi si conservano dell' Apostolo S. Tommaso. Notizie della Citta di Madrassa.
„ XIII. p.	116—123.	Partenza dall' Indie. Navigazione per l'Europa. Malattia mortale avuta in mare. Grazia ricevuta per intercessione del V. P. Giovan de Britto.
„ XIV. p.	123—132.	Continuazione della Navigazione dopo il Capo di Buona Speranza. Isole di S. Elena e dell' Ascenzione. Passaggio della Linea e arrivo all' Isola della Martinica nell' America. Arrivo a Porto Luigi.
„ XV. p.	132—137.	Viaggio da Porto Luigi a Parigi, e da Parigi a Marsiglia.
„ XVI. p.	137—146.	Viaggio da Marsiglia a Genova. Passaggio per la Toscana e arrivo a Roma.
„ XVII. p.	146—157.	Sentimento dell Autore intorno alla Dottrina, che si richiede ne Missionarij dell' Indie; e primieramente quanto grande ella debba essere.

„ XVIII. p. 157—165. Qual', e in qual genere particolarmente convien que sia la Dottrina, che indispensabilmente si richiede ne' Missionarij, che si destinano alla conversion degl' Infedeli nell' Indie.

„ XIX. p. 165—175. In qual modo la sopra esposta e necessaria dottrina possa promoversi ne' Missionarij, che per l'Indie si destinano.

„ XX. p. 175—210. Si mostra la grave obbligazione, che a ogni Christiano indispensabilmente corre d'aiutar', e promover' le Missioni da farsi tra gl' Infedeli; e in qual modo possa da ciascuno nel proprio suo stato adempirsi una tal' obbligazione.

DIE 22 JUNIJ 1728

Another MS., 27 × 19,5 cm., to be cited as MS. B. seems to be a first draft on account of its many erasions, corrections and additions. It contains much of what is found in MS. A., but it has, besides, a great number of chapters dealing with the religion of the Tibetans. These chapters are, naturally, beyond the scope of the present work.

The sequence of Books and Chapters in MS. B. is somewhat puzzling: Book I covers 138 pp., and its division into 16 Chapters corresponds to that of Book I in MS. A.

Book II from p. 1—124 parallels the chapters 1—13 of MS. A. Book II. They are immediately followed by some chapters that form part of Book III, which treats of the religion of Tibet; the headings are:

Capitolo I. p. 135—140. Del Gran Lamma, Capo della Religione.

„ II. p. 140—156. Ragioni che persuadono la riferita incarnazione del' nuovo Gran Lamma essere opera immediamente del' Demonio.

„ III. p. 156—169. Risposto gl' argumenti di chi stima che l'inganno riferito sia artifizio degl' huomini e non del' Demonio.

„ XIX. p. 175—185. Si proseguiscono le notizie intorno al Gran Lamma e altri Lama inferiori del Thibet.

„ XX. p. 185—203. De Religiosi, e Religiose del Thibet; de loro conventi, abito, instituto e consuetudini.

„ XXI. p. 203—214. Diversi specie di Religiosi che sono nel Thibet.

Leaving one blank page there now follows from p. 216 to 260 the rough copy of chapters 14—18 of Book II MS. A. After another blank page these are followed by 16 chapters, not assigned to any Book; the headings are subjoined:

Capitolo XXVII. p. 262—276. Si comincia a trattar degli errori e della Religione de Thibettani. E primieramente si spiega il systema della Metempsycosi ò sia Transmigrazion Pittagorica conforme da' medesimi è asservita e creduta.

„ XXVIII. p. 276—288. Opinione de Thibettani intorno agl' animale, e a certi Viventi da loro chiamati Itaa che coso credino e affermino in ordine all' Inferno.

„ XXIX. p. 288—301. Si proseguiscono le notizie d'altre cose, che affermano e credono i Thibettani concernenti allo spiegar il loro systema della Metempsicosi.

„ XXX. p. 301—317. Si propone e si spiega im altro enormismo e primario errore della Setta de' Thibettani, che consiste in negar, che vi sia alcun' Ente a se e incausato, e alcuna causa primaria di tutte le cose.

„ XXXI. p. 317—324. Se, negando i Thibettani l'existenza del vero Dio, amettano alcuna favolosa Divinita, o se siano absolutamente senza cognizion di Dio.

„ XXXII. p. 324—337. Di tre classe d'oggetti di culto e d'invocazione che amettono i Thibettani. Se ne spiega la qualita e si fa vedere, che nessuna Divinita in essi riconoscono.

„ XXXIII. p. 337—347. Di cio che contiene la Religione de' Thibettani in ordine alla morale, o sia in ordine alla virtu e ai vizi, e in ordine a regolar' i costumi.

„ XXXIV. p. 347—357. Del Legislatore de' Thibettani, e alcune favole che del medesimo descrivono.

„ XXXV. p. 357—371. Di due altri Idoli principali de' Thibettani. L'uno detto Cen ree sy, e l'altro chiamato Urghien.

„ XXXVI. p. 371—381. Si riferiscono altre favole da' Thibettani credute, e spacciate intorno al sopradetto Urghien.

„ XXXVII. p. 381—388. Il Thibet anticamente senza legge. Il Re Si-Kiong-teuzzen cerca alcuna Religione. Invia per tal fine Ambasciatori a diversi parti, e una scelta di Giovanni all' Hendustan.

Capit.	XXXVIII.	p. 388—402.	Da chi fosse introdotta nel Thibet la falsa Religione. Primo tempio in quel Regno fabricata; libri tradotti in quella lingua; Conventi di Religiosi quivi instituiti e altre industrie usate per quivi disseminar gl' errori.
„	XXXIX.	p. 402—413.	D'Altri oggetti inferiori de venerazione invocati e riveriti dai Thibettani.
„	XL.	p. 413—422.	D'Alcuni luoghi tenuti in venerazione da' Thibettani e di cio che verso di essi osservano. Della loro corona e loro diguini.
„	XLI.	p. 422—433.	Si soddisfa a alcuni dubbii e quesiti, che sopra le materie sin qui trattate potrebbera occurrere.
„	XLII.	p. 433—443.	D'Alcuni Relazioni e autori che hanno trattato del Thibet; e guidizio intorno a esse.

APPENDIX I

AZEVEDO'S ACCOUNT OF HIS JOURNEY TO TIBET. SECOND PART.

DE AGRA PERA O TIBET

fol. 18. Huma sexta feira 27 de junho me passou o Padre Matheus de Payva da outra banda do Rijo de Agrâ aonde estava a carreta que me avia de levar com algumas couzas de sagoate pera o novo rajâ de Chaparangue; não na pudemos arrumar em modo que se pudesse aquelle dia fazer jornada, pelo que nos fomos recolher da calma a quinta da Rainha Nurmal que fica de longo do Rio. He este muy largo e fermozo, de boa Agoa. Pera a passagem de gente innumeravel, e animaes, tem grande numero de barcas e barcaças, algumas tão capazes que levão 600 e mais peçoas, outras que tem em sy cazas de madeira repartidas pera homens e molheres, muito bem lavradas em que se vão recrear grandes pessoas. Nasce das serras do Tibet, e vay pagar tributo ao mar de Bengala pelas fozes do Ganges. Vão e vem de lá muitas e grandes embarcações carregadas de mantimentos e roupas; vem em 60, e vão em 15 dias. He tão abundante de peixe vario, e muito bom, que sempre se acha no bazar fresco, e tão barato, que pelo mesmo preço o dão aquy pera duas porções que em Goa por todo mar, pera huma.

Cingeo por huma parte a cidade de Agrâ assento e corte destes monarcas que em suas ribeiras veo fundar Elrrey Acabar. Junto dellas edificou seus passos dentro[de] huma fortaleza tão capaz que cabem nella mais de des mil cazas, he verdade que so as delrrey tem algum geito, singida de muros muito altos e bem feitos de pedra vermelha, casta de jaspe. fermosos a vista, mas de pouca rezistencia a qualquer boa espera. As munições e guarnição são seis mil molheres delrej tão arranjadas [?] que sô o ouro e joyas pudera ser tezouro grande de qualquer Rey. Estende-se a cidade a vista do Rio bebendo nelle por quasi duas legoas, engrossando pera o sertam proporcionadamente. Nisto que he pouvo e gentes he Lixboa muito inferior. Mafamede com as largas licenças que lhe deu he cauza de tanto numero de abitadores que so tratão de propagar o genero humano. Porem falta-lhe o primor da raynha das cidades Lisboa, a Magestade de seus edificios, [a] magnificencia e grandiosidade de seus templos, a fermosura de suas ruas, a ordem, o primor, a policia etc. Todas as cazas quasi, são terreas. No meo della se ve sito o collegio de nossa Senhora do nacimento de nossa Companhia de JESUS com sua não muito grande mas linda igreja tã o fermosa e bem ornada que como a tal a vem vizitar grandes Senhores e nâvabos como tambem quando vivia, el Rey Jangir, | aonde publicamente fol. correm nossos christãos com suas obrigações a sino tangido muy desabafadamente ouvindo suas missas; assistindo aos divinos officios como se em nossas terras estiverão, apezar de Mafoma, com grande gloria e reputação de nossa santissima ffeê catholica. He collegio de seis e mais religiosos aonde rezidem ordinarjamente dous ou tres alem de muitas vezes que se ayuntão de varias partes em que em missões estão espalhados. Serão em numero os christãos que frequentão esta igreja quasi quatroçentos em que entrão muitos armenios que nesta cidade assistem, alem de outros que vão e vem da Perçia mercançiar e de alguns europeos, italianos, francezes etc. criados delrrey e purtuguezes. O mais delles são naturaes novamente convertidos a nossa santa ffeê. Não tenha V. R. o numero por pequeno nesta corte, em que Mafamede he o que manda tudo. No Reino de Gozepor vinte jornadas pera as partes de Bengala assistem de prezente o Padre Jozé de Crasto millanes grande santo e o Padre Francisco Morando bolonhes em companhia de Dom Gonçalo Mirijâ que governa aquellas Provincias da mão delrey, aonde tem bom numero de christãos a sua conta. Em Sambar que he parte do Reino de Asmir pera o ponente témos alguns outros christãos a que se acode do collegio de Agrâ todos os annos com hum Padre que na coresma e noutros tempos do anno os vaj vizitar e consolar. O mesmo se faz com outros que vivem no Reino de Lahor, aonde temos a huma fermoza igreja que os Reys passados Acabar e Sargir de boa memoria [?] edificaram [á] nossa Companhia de JESUS etc.

Tem ao longo da ribeira boas cazas de Principes, de Navabos, alguns serralhos de molheres dos Reys passados em que ficão fechadas com tão boa comedia como vigias sem sahirem, verem, nem serem vistas a vida toda, que pera casta de gente tão apetitoza de apareçer, tão barata de se comunicar he na vida o mesmo inferno. Os capados são os porteiros e o seu Mafoma que as deve de consolar com frequentes revelações.

Fazem seus edificios ainda que terreos, ou pouco levantados, muy acomodados ao viver humano; porque como a terra he descomedida nas calmas e disconforme nos frios, pera acudirem a ambos os exçessos, ou extremos, como meo neçessario edificam [de] fejção que no mor rigor das calmas tem cazas muj frescas e regaladas e no mayor dos frios, quentes e abrigadas como logo veremos.

Pella outra banda vem beber a borda deste rio fermozas quintas tambem com soberbos edificios e de grandes despezas. So tocarei a V. R. nesta da rainha Nurmal que nos agasalhou aquele dia muito bem. Fella ella com muita curiosidade pera trazer e ter nella a elrrey Jangir, mais frequentemente. He mayor que o terreiro do passo em quadro bem murada, repartida em varios quadros iguaes, o pavimento das divizões de marmore muito lizo, no lugar em que se vem unir os quadros fermozos tanques cobertos de mimozo arvoredo; por meo do pavimento dos terriplenos por hum vão de 8 palmos direito vaj agoa regando seu compaço grandes fileiras de siprestes, pessegueiros, larangeiras etc. e pelo pê destas por bella ordem cravos, lirios, jasmins, com toda a mais variedade de flores.

Dos quadros huns são [de] parreiras, outros de laranias pequenas muito boas, como e milhores que as de Salçete de Goa tão estimadas, outros de maçeiras e outras fruitas de qua; outros de fermozos rozaes; he aly muito pera ver a fermozura dos tanques, as invenções dos canos de agoa com que se refrescão no rigor daquellas calmas que nos fizerão recolher então mais çedo do que dezeiavamos, a humas cazas que cahem sobre o rio de abobada obra real, no meo de cada qual se vê hum tanque de agoa do rio muito fresca. Estas são as que fabricam pera fugir da calma, então tam frias que he summo regalo estar nellas. Assy vive esta çega gente buscando emquanto pode as mores deliçias do corpo, como se nem suas almas nem Deos lhe mereçerão alguma lembrança.

No andar da quinta se vêem huns passos pera Elrej, pequenos mas bem feitos, dourados, curiosamente pintados. Entre varias imagens se vê aly a de nosso Salvador, da Senhora, da Madanella e outras de capitães famozos no mundo, mas não a de Mafoma que lhe não tinha Elrrey devação alguma. Entre esses passos abreviados, e outros que lhe respondem pera molheres, do mesmo tamanho e bondade, se metia hum fermozo e grande pateo, em que se via hum tanque de alabastro couza fermoza em roda do qual fazem os fidalgos achouquy, quando Elrrey está prezente; a hum canto delle se vê huma charola grande de pedra, muy bem lavrada e dourada, donde Elrrey apareçe hum dia de somana aos seus grandes que lhe vem fazer do rio e embarcações a tascelima.

Ao sabado de madrugada, em aparecendo a aurora, offerecendo a Verdadeira tão comprida, trabalhoza e arriscada peregrinação, partij so acompanhado de alguns frecheiros por arreceo dos ladrões que não faltão neste caminho. He a terra daquella banda plaina nada inferior em bondade e fertilidade a toda a que tenho visto, e muito barata; mas não nos faltarão invernos pera este verão.

Passados dous dias fuy entrando pelas terras do rajâ que tirou ao Rey Jangir das unhas do leam. Tinhao ferido elrrey de huma pilourada, arre-
fol. 20. mete a quem o ferio, e quando todos fogem, este fidalgo | gentio põe as costas em Elrrey e o peito no leam abraçandose com elle; com os dentes se andarão por espasso de tempo ferindo os dous leões, athe que chegandosse hum lascarym perto, o leão subitamente largando a este fidalgo, arremeteo ao lascarym, e fazendoo em pedaços ambos cahirão mortos cada hum pera a sua parte. Ficou tambem este fidalgo ferido de morte; chega elrey, levao nos braços, deitao nas suas andas, manda levar a sua tenda, com grandes promessas aos surgiões, se o dessem vivo. Emfim viveo, e elrrey o fez capitam de sinco mil cavalos que são de renda em cada anno mais de trezentos mil cruzados. Salâdij se chama este esforçado fidalgo.

Por muito perto do meu caminho ha nesta terra huma mina, ou salyna de salitre que os rebeldes a seu rey comprão aly, sinco mãos por hum rupiâ, e lhe sahe purificado em duas maõs [?], que fazem sinco mãos das de Goa. Quá no publico dizem elles que neste salitre de hum fazem dez na sua terra, e quando estão borrachos, tempo em que, se falam verdade, dizem que de hum fazem 30.

Em Agrâ val huma mão de salitre purificado, de hum rupiâ pera dous; bem pudera o estado, ou a companhia mercantil ter nesta cidade de Agrâ hum feitor que lhe faça alem de outros mil proveitos este que he de grande importancia e com isso muita guerra aos inimigos. Elles o levão em tanto pezo e numero com formão delrrey a Surrate em cafila de camelos, e nós o poderiamos levar a Damão, ou dentro a Goa nos mesmos, com licença dos Reys; não sey quem nos cega, que nos vay a mão.

Passados outros dous dias, dey com muitas ortas de Anil, que por extremo deseiava de ver. Nam se dá este em todo lugar, aquy neste pedaço de terra sy, naquelle daquy a hum tiro de mosquete, não. Pode bem ser que mande a V. R. a semente que tenho; pera que negala se a nossa terra o cria, porque esta he como essa temperada.

Lavrasse a terra com a primeira chuva, e logo outras duas vezes; nella, assy lavrada tres vezes se lança a semente como qualquer outra; logo brota em humas vergonteas de ate 4 palmos que todas rompem em gomos de folhinhas da cor e tamanho da losna. Passados dous mezes que ja se mostrão maduras, cortãose rentes com a terra as varas, as rayzes ficam; aquellas assi com as folhas se metem em hum tanque alto cheo de agoa pondolhe encima grandes pezos de pedra. Assi estão 24 horas, no fim das quaes tirão fora todas as varas e folhas que nellas ficaram, logo abrem o tanque grande sobre hum mais pequeno em que se recolhe toda aquella agoa com o summo de sustancia das folhas; logo nella entrão 4 homens esforçados que por meo dia batem e revolvem aquella agoa até ficar muito negra e grossa; passado o meo dia botão sobre ella cantidade de mea canada de azeite de gergilim, com o qual todo o summo e grossura das ervas vay fazendo pee, o outro meo dia e a noite toda; pola menhã vão tirando a de leve toda aquella agoa até chegarem ao groço e Papas negros que no fundo estão, as quaes são o Anil, e então as tomão, e as vão botando em hum pano que está sobre hum pequeno sumidouro aonde ellas fição sem agoa; e dahi as põem ao sol aonde se secão sô por tres dias, porque, se secão por mais, pezão menos. Quando he barato, val huma mão nas aldeas que são duas de Goa 25 e 28 rupias; quando he caro, val 30 e 35; quando o vendem por hum dia ynteiro o põem em lugar humedo, pera que peze mais. O que o falsifica tem pena de morte.

Afora a primeira brotão as raizes nos tres invernos seguintes, e dellas se colhe o mesmo fruito, sem no tempo do verão lhe fazerem beneficio algum; este he o anil, assi se faz, aquelle quá seu preço, assy o levão estes estrangeiros com que fazem grandes proveitos, e fazem muito bem, pois não prestamos pello menos pera fazer qua alguns pera que nossas naos não vão vazias; pois as destes mouros dependem tanto de nós pera os seus cartazes, não cuido que devem de nos negar [a] assistencia de hum feitor nosso aquy se são bem aconselhados.

Ao quinto dia que foi da vizitação ao romper da manhã, depois de me fol. 21.
encomendar á divina, partimos. Tres legoas andadas demos nas ribeiras do afamado Ganges tão venerado de toda a gentilidade Indiana como buscado de muitos e muitos centos de legoas pera se lavarem nelle de suas culpas. Vem a este rio algumas vezes magote de 10 e de 20 mil devotos gentios receber a sanctificação de suas agoas por mãos de muitos Bramenes centenarios que cozidos em devação se deixão ficar por aquellas praias, ou aldeas vizinhas, já limpos de toda a culpa como os pobretes cudão, por não tornarem a ver mais mundo cantando alegres nunc dimittis servum

tuum quia viderunt oculy mej, pera que quando ouverem de entrar nos campos elizeos suas almas vão Purificadas por agoas tão Sanctas. O que aquy as não tocou, não he tido por bom Bramene, nem por religioso Gentio. He o Rio largo, fermozo, de excelente agoa sempre fresca e fria por ser nascido da neve, mas tem tal calidade que se tirada logo se não bebe, logo aqueçe; na corrente tão manso por estes campos como pellos de Coimbra o nosso Mondego, passando estes da outra banda com tanto alvorosso a se meter sofregos nelle como se entrarão no paraizo, entrão e sahem mil vezes porque tem que toties quoties ganham indulgencia plenaria.

Passando o Rio fuy tirando a terreiro o que nos governava a carreta por ser Bramene que prezumia em suas patranhas até que mais singelo do que eu cuidava se veo a esborroar na fabula seguinte, que de hum dos primeiros homens ficarão cento e hum filhos, que ocupada grande parte da terra fizeram muitos possos; oprimida com isso a terra queixousse a Deos; e este lhe dice: quando cavarem outros, deixate cahir sobre elles, com o que os pobres ficarão esmagoados penando aly suas Almas Junto [a] esta ganga sem poder passar ao ceo. Hum so filho que daquelles ficou pedio[a] Adão de merce que o servio doze annos que lhe dece a salvaçam pera seu Pay e tio. Adão lhe disse: leva esta Ganga que em lhe tocando os ossos com suas agoas, suas almas limpas entrarão no Ceo. O Gange que sabia que em lhe tocando com suas agoas avia assy de acontecer, e juntamente sabia que em aquellas cento e huma almas purificadas entrando no ceo se avia logo de acabar o mundo, por se não acabar tam depressa, se desviou do lugar em que estão as ossadas e as almas penando, mas o rio ficou com a vertude de sanctificar que Adão lhe deu, e tambem os corpos; donde se segue terem pera sy que se não salva o gentio a quem não tocou a agoa deste rio, mas que todo o tempo que lhe toca os ossos ou aquy ou aonde lhe levão algumas gotas, consegue a salvação. Pergunteilhe como agora não falava o Ganges? e porque a terra estava muda. O pobre se embaraçou tam depressa que se fechou a banda na materia mais mudo que o Ganges, e so lhe tirej por fim o que a cartilha manda fazer e dizer aos meninos, que sua ley tinha Doutores que me saberião responder.

Naquelle mesmo dia sinco coicez alem do Rio vij a primeira vez ao longe as altas serras do caminho do Tibet com grande consolação minha reprezentandoseme na memoria aquella divina donzella quando de pouco mais idade que 13 annos, tenrra e delicada sobindo com toda a preça pellas montanhas de Ebron por alumiar huma alma, mostrando Ella o fervor, e alvorosso que a levava mais correndo e voando que andando por tantas dificuldades e trabalhos. São por estes campos inumeraveis as povoações, os animaes sem conto, o vaqum, que he o mais, quasi todo branco, os canaveais de Assucar muitos. Fomos fazer manzel a Ambruâ aonde se vê o quintal de Bugios afamado. Hum mouro pera que ficasse aly sua memoria, nelle criou dous pequenos, e quando morreo, [se] sepultou nelle deixando com que se sustentassem os Bugios que ia então erão muitos e agora mais de cento que aly se criarão, vivem e vos vem a mão comer o que lhe dais com muita festa, e familiaridade, com que não pouco recreão os passageiros e renovão a lembrança de quem os criou naquelle lugar.

Na manhã sequinte partimos buscando a pouvoação de Ambruâ em

cuio caminho demos com grande copia de bichinhos do tamanho de huma unha polegar como carangueios todos de cor encarnada; a casca de cima era hum veludo carmezim tão soberanamente obrado pellas mãos da natureza que se não fartavão os olhos; e estavão os campos semeados delles, fermosos rubins entre | esmeraldas. Criãose estes com as primeiras agoas do fol. 22.
Inverno que avia tres dias levavamos comnosco. La pello meo dia cheguej a hum rio que por vir com o Inverno crecido e furioso o não pudemos passar a vao. Estando não pouco cuidadozos do remedio, vimos da outra banda 3 negros, Acherontes sem barca, sem remos, que logo contentes do premio trouxerão huns calõis sobre que no rijo tecem huma rede de bambus, assento pera huma pessoa e nella nos forão passando pouco a pouco por huma corda que tinha as pontas em terra, com não pequeno risco por amor da corrente tão furiosa que nos levou por hum pedaço a carreta. São descontos do caminho. Pouco alem deste rio dos calões fomos repouzar da molestia passada não pequena a outro dia na cidade de Ladinhar, e desta partij pera os limites do Reino com as serras, a huma aldea que fica dellas 8 legoas. Foi neste dia a chuva tanta que me danou o que levavą, e a outro dia que foi Domingo me fes parar, e não foy este o mor mal, como direy.

A segunda as 11 party metendome por aquelle mato aonde se dividem os Reinos do Mogor e os das serras que por isso he hum perpetuo covil de ladrões em que roubão os de qua e os de lâ a seu gosto, desculpandose com o mato aonde querem que todos os gatos seião pardos a toda hora. No meo delle fuy dar com o Rio dos calões que passamos duas vezes aquelle dia com a agoa pellos peitos, que com a pressa que levava, se não foi medo, se me enxugou muito depressa, e pera falar verdade ella foi tal que em menos de 4 oras me poz a pe no fim da jornada que foi de 12 coices que são 8 legoas. Não faltão por este espesso mato elefantes, leões, tigres, Badas, Bufras, ussos, pello que he necessario passalo acompanhado e com cautela.

Estas serras estão, a respeito dos que nos metemos por ellas com o rosto no norte, de ponente a levante; pera o ponente se vão metendo por Laor, Casmir, Cabul, pera a Persia; pera o levante vay a outra ponta buscar o mar de Bengala. Tanto que entrei por Cordoar huma pouvoação de poucas palhotas ao pê de huma pequena serra sobre que a pouvoação está, me puz de joelhos Bejandoa, e dey muitas graças a nosso Senhor por me fazer digno de por a boca aonde com tantos trabalhos, tantos servos seus de sua Companhia de JESUS puzerão seus pes com tanto zelo da conversão das Almas.

Veme Vossa Reverencia ja posto em salvo sobre a primeira serra? Pois saiba que de novo me deu nosso Senhor hoie a vida, que tão arriscada a tive pouco antes de chegar. O não partir ao Domingo antes mo empedir a muita chuva, deu lugar aos daquella pouvoação donde party, pera virem dar por alvitre aos desta serra que estivessem alerta porque hun fringuy lhe avia de cahir nas mãos e comigo grande preza. (Hâ Vossa Reverencia de saber que o mesmo he dizer por qua fringuy, que o homem cheo de pedraria e de riquezas). A cubiça deste lanço pos em silada no mesmo dia e hora em que passamos naquelle caminho e mato a hum bom numero de cavaleiros ladrões. Mas nosso Senhor que não desempara os seus, e sua santa Mãy a quem o perigo de tal caminho me fes peitar com a pobreza de minhas devações mil vezes nelle repetidas, moveo a lhe fechar os olhos de maneira que quando iá tiverão vista de nos, hiamos sobindo a serra pera entrar na pouvoação, quando bem alheos de sua danada tenção forão entrando comnosco esbofados e bem magoados por perderem a ocazião. Ja então estavamos seguros, posto que em sua caza, aonde o Rajâ não concente furto em forma alguma. Se nos tomavão ainda no baixo, aly ficavamos, porque estes pera lhe ficaremos digo ficar o furto sem sobroço, matão aos passageiros.

São tantas as serras neste sertam de Asia que parece que nelle depositou o autor da natureza o mor numero e pezo dellas; mais de sinco mezes caminhej pera o norte e no fim pera o levante sem nelles verem meus olhos mais que serras tão altas e fragosas como na sua as pinta o Padre Antonio de Andrade primeiro descobridor evangelico dellas, as mais impinadas ao ceo, as mais alcantiladas ao baixo que virão os olhos humanos; e com se-
fol. 23. rem estas, não deixão de ser fertilissimos campos, | porque as mais dellas se lavrão e semeão do pé até a cabeça, tudo pode a arte, a tudo se atreve o trabalho e industria dos homens, pois nhuma serra que se vay a pique não so as nuvens, que muitas lhe ficão sempre por baixo, mas ao ceo, vay cavando terriplenos em redondo de huma, de 3 e de mea braça, aonde leva os boes, lança a somente, e colhe copiosos fruitos duas e tres vezes no anno em grande abundancia, com que enriquecem ao reino muito mais do que se dentro de suas balizas todo fora plaino. São estas serras hum perene tizouro de toda a casta de mantimentos, hum pumar de todas as fruitas, hum fermoso jardim de huma infinita variedade e de huma varia infinidade de flores, tão prenhes de bonissimas agoas que por partes sem numero se desentranhão em candelosas ribeyras e fontes frescas.

O Natural da gente he brando, ella pouco polida, a ordinaria menos bem feita, não assy a gente limpa muito mais delgada nas feições, as crianças lindas. Ha nella poucos siumes porque o matrimonio dura emquanto se não enfadam, donde nasce que 4 Irmãos comprão ao Pay a filha pera todos, que concertados no numero dos dias a tem cada qual em caza pro rata, e quando lhe vem a vontade lhe dão com a licença a liberdade. A que he cazada com hum, se se enfada delle, offerece ao Rey sinco rupias, e fica juntamente sua captiva, e livre daquelle marido; e quando depois quer ia outro, offerece ao Rey 15, e o vai tomar. O mesmo fazem ao Bramene do Pagode Badrj pera se descazar e cazar; a que quer ser solteira, com huma espada nua na mão, da 50 voltas a caza do Pagode, com o que fica sua cativa, e livre pera toda a mâ ventura. Emfim he a carne nestes ares (com serem excelentes) tudo o que pode ser, de podre, e as almas no que toca ao Ceo, tão ignorantes como emperradas na segueira de seus pagodes.

Dando as costas aos fermosos campos industanos huma segunda feira, comecey a sobir a primeira serra, que da sobida me levou até as duas da tarde sempre com os olhos aonde se poem os pés porquanto nisso nos vai a vida, assi por ser o caminho pelo recosto da serra estreitissimo, como porque se olhais pera sima pasmais, se pera baixo perdeis com muito perigo o lume dos olhos. O mato dellas muito fresco, cheò de muita Sylva; e de bem meudo mangericão; depois por outras, ate que o fim do dia nos fes fazer manzel em huma Aldea despovoada; ao dia sequinte em que fomos dar com o Rio dos calões no fundo de altissimas serras, mas tão atenuado e humilde que nos não deu molestia aquella vez.

He bem verdade que caminhando hum bom pedaço por elle me deu huma dezatinada dor de ouvidos que me deu bem que sentir por 3 dias. Acodiome nosso Senhor com o remedio naquelle mato, quando eu menos o cudava; foi que vendome gemer hum serrano, e sabendo a cauza se compadeceo, e me offereceo hum pé de pavão de fumo seco que logo moeu e me lançou em humas gotinhas de agoa no ouvido, com o que sentij dentro grande frialdade e logo a dor quebrada.

Fomos outro dia entrando por grandes pinhaes que emramão estas serras. São os pinheiros infinitos, muito altos, e muito apraziveis, a figura he differente nos de câ porque o mesmo reprezenta aquy o pinheiro com seus ramos do que a pinha na figura. Se por lá os ouvera nesta conformidade pode ser que os estimarão mais nas quintas que [os ci]prestes por terem na figu.a mais graça. Estes lhes fazem grandes aberturas ao pê, e no tronco, por onde recolhem grande cantidade de Rezina branca pera muitas couzas, e de suas rachas emsopadas nella fazem candeas que alumião como se de cera forão.

Ao outro dia fomos ao Rio dos cabaços (chamase assy porque nelles se passa, assy como o outro em calões) aonde hum alcavalista nos fes algumas perrarias, e nos não deu aviamento até não tomar de nos o que quis. Passeio ja tam tarde que não pude deixar de fazer manzel no alpendre de hum pagode sito na outra banda em hum lugar sobranceiro ao mesmo Rio.

He este pagode chamado o Deos da fortaleza deuvij cotta e por isso nestas serras de grande reputação, devação, e de muita romagem; a caza he humilde, triste e pequena, cayada com bosta que tem muita devação por ser de vaqua, dentro mal cheirosa, escura, medonha emfim o diabo; a curiosidade me levou dentro; acheo a hum canto suio, no cham, como merece, de 4 palmos, | negro nas cores, desbarbado mas bem afeiçoado, na fol 24.
mão esquerda hum escudo; o terçado estava na cinta do bucho, do braço dereito lhe saya huma espada nua, com morrião na cabeça. Logo hum pouco pera dentro estava hum tumulo quadrado cuberto com dorcel de seda, a roda muitos buzios com que os Bramenes tangem e alguns defumadouros [?].

Em sahindo aparecem ao longe decendo hum monte hum magote grande de serranos e serranos que com grande traquinada de tambores vinhão na volta do pagode; la pararão em me vendo, e logo emviarão a hum Bramene a descubrir terra; chegou, prostrousse, e beiou muite devoto o lumiar da porta, logo me dice que toda sua aldea em forma vinha fazer aquelle Pagode festival e solenne sacrificio pera que lhe não fizece mal.

Se he vosso Deos, como vos fas mal? Embaraçado me tornou que não fazia mal de coração, mas so se agastava, e assombrava a quem lhe não fazia a vontade; mais que com algum bode sacrificado acabavão as merencorias passadas e se amigava logo. Nam me quis deferir a mais perguntas; então deu seu sinal aos que o esperavão, que logo arrancarão do posto com toda a fragalhota de tympanis, sistris, cimbalis e outros mil trupizupes pera o pagode com muita soma de fugareos, homens, e molheres em fileiras, pelo meo 8 façanhosos cabrões, e huma Bufara que os Bramenes trazião por cordas emramados; todos se hião prostrando, e beiando o batente do negro pagode.

Má noite me deu aqui o Diabo com a horrenda matinada que estes fazião; o mal hera que eu não tinha outro lugar, por ser ia noite, o não podia buscar, e assi me foi necessario prestar paciencia. Logo os devotissimos serranos em procissão com ramos verdes e omne genus muzicorum em procissão tres vezes lhe rodearão a caza; depois ficando todos fora entrou o perro do Bramene, e fingio que consultava o Pagode em que gastou huma hora estando os de fora em silencio. Ella passada, com hum buzio grande deu sinal como o pagode estava contente de se lhe fazer o sacrificio e que disso lhe fazia mercê. O valhame Deos, que Alvoroço, que alaridos, que diabolica matinada.

Então ordenão e fazem de novo em reconhecimento do novo beneficio a quarta procissão levando demais nella muitos yssopes com que hião derramando não sei que agoa pellas paredes do pagode, e muitos turibulos com que as incençavão. Por fim della em hum momento cortarão as cabeças aos bodes a porta, e logo tingirão seus degraos com o sangue, o que feito se prostrarão todos com o rosto no cham por bom espaço em silencio, até que passado elle, o cão do Bramene com o Buzio fes sinal que estavão as amizades feitas. Então se levantão, entrão e vão beijar es pés do pagode polla mercê, e logo se sahem os Bramenes a cozinhar e comer os bodes, cuja carne he sõ pera elles. Isto passava de mea noite, e o pobre de mym com a cabeça aberta sem pregar olho; cuidava eu que com o passado punham fim a suas doudices e tregoas a meu trabalho senão quando começam na mesma forma de procissões, e matinadas, o sacrificio da Bufara em nome dos servidores da aldea que depois a comerão. E isto quasi manhã que avia de ser? Como quer V. R. que o Demonio me agazalhace? Não he elle pessoa de quem se mais espere. Rompeo a manhão e com ella me pus ao caminho em companhia de toda aquella canalha por huma impinada serra que da sobida nos levou até o meo dia, dandonos liberalmente aquy e aly de copias de agoas de huma fresca ribeira que de seus cumes despenhada a vinha banhando. Aquy dei com muitas Arvores de canela no cheiro das folhas muito viva e aquellas muyto queimativas.

Vingada aquella grande serra fomos decendo e sobindo por mil outras todas encadeadas sem daremos em plano algum consideravel. Por meo nellas de[i com] Alguns matos de grandes sovereiros carregados de bolotas amargozas de que fazem azeite; tambem se achão algumos doces. Assi fomos dar em hum fundo vale sem pouvoação alguma, medonho com o grande numero de pinheiros, aonde nos foy necessario fazer manzel por ser tar-
fol. 25. de. Quando aly começavamos | a descanssar nos cansou muito aparecerem por entre o mato sinco soldados Patantes digo patanes por casta e por isso conhecides ordinariamente por ladrõis. A verdade he que me não fizerão bom estamago que logo começarão a cortar ramos pera dormir, e lenha pera cozinharem. A vizinhança não parecia muito sadia; por fim os sobresaltos com que a noite toda se passou Deos os sabe que sabe o muito que sua sanctissima mãy e os sanctos lhe rogaram por nos; quebrou-lhe Dêos o animo porque a quererem levavão o fatinho quando de barato nos quizessem perdoar as vidas. Todes tinhão armas e entre nos so avia huma espada

pera o pião, e outra pera mym que devia andar muy destro nella, e dous bichinhos nossos em lugar de armas somente pernas pera que te quero.

E pera que V. R. não atribua tudo a medo saiba que assi nos preservou Deos Nosso Senhor de huma boa em aquelles não terem noticia alguma da morte do Rey daquellas serras na guerre, como a tivemos a outro dia ao meo dia, por ser costume quando o Rey morre, lançaremse todos a pilhagem emquanto não ha outro a quem respeitem. Ainda o trabalho e sobroço foi mayor a outro dia quando nos tomou no meo daquelles matos tal nova; restandonos ainda pera chegar a cidade o que do dia nos restava, fizerão os amaés comigo o possivel por eu não hir dormir nella atemorizandome que era entam menos segura, as revoltas mayores, os furtos mais certos. Vyme duvidoso, emcomendeime a nosso Senhor e a sua purissima mãy pondolhę entam diante a primeira vez sua sacratissima pureza de quem ella sabe que deseio ser devoto; logo o concelho dos sobreditos me começou a parecer mal, e com a mor pressa que pude comecei a decer huma alta serra em que gastei o mais do dia, até a boca da noite chegar a cidade aonde tive alguns dias bem que descanssar; achea triste, mas muy quieta sem revolta, sem furtos.

He esta cidade de Siranagar cabeça do Reino, isso quer dizer o nome, Cidade Cabeça; aprazivel, sita nhum plaino dezabafado ao longo das ribeiras do Rio Ganges, que aly vay muy fundo, e furioso, de ambas as partes acompanhado de altas serras. E estava ella então como orfão sem Pay, ou como viuva triste, as buticas fechadas sem se comprar nem vender; logo se lançou bando que ninguem trouxesse touca, que rapacem as cabeças e barbas, que se não matace pera comer couza viva, nem ainda ervas sob graves pennas, o que assi se guardou a risca, de modo que tambem eu em que me pez estive por ella, so podião comer arros cozido, com leyte ou com manteiga. Como a terra he dos gentios tudo quanto querem lhe metem na cabeça os bramenes, e durou isto até se levantar novo Rey que forão 20 dias em que nem mainatos podião lavar roupa; tambem se empedirão os caminhos até o Rey novo tomar posse que não passace estrangeiro algum por amor dos ladrões.

Crea V. R. se quizer que mais senty isto que comer arros e leite somente como bramene, porque me forçou a ley a ficar aly quinze dias de remolho com grande penna minha. Veio a V. R. apetitozo de saber como morreo este Rey, e pois em que me pes me dão tempo pera isso, quero satisfazelo. Trazia elle continua guerra com o Rey de Camau vizinho seu, serrano como elle, que ainda que com menos campos e forças lha mantinha com esforço e brio fiado não sô em serem os seus melhores soldados, que tem por primor não fugirem na guerra sob penna de quando assy vem fugidos lhe sahirem suas molheres a porta descarregandolhe nas barbas com huma panela dagoa, e de lhe dizerem fechandolha, ide que assi se fas as vaquas que fogem da guerra, ide buscar outras ao mato, por aquella que diz que de fora dormirdes, com o que ficão tão descazados como afrontados; não so como digo, em serem os seus esforçados, mas tambem em ter por ssy a rezão; sem embargo da qual respondeo aos honrados partidos que lhe o outro fazia, que sem sua cabeça não voltaria atras, e assi lhe foi soberbo entrando muitas povoações na serra. O de Camau lhe mandou fazer doação dellas com

tanto que concentisse na paz. Não esta por isso, vay entrando, o outro se retira até que o teve num estreito em que não puderão os seus valerlhe; aly de huma frechada no olho e de huma pelourada cahio sua muita sober-
fol. 26. ba. O vencedor emviou o corpo a rajxâ viuva | e ao minino filho dizendo que seu Pay fora o que quizera morrer, que em sinal disto lhe offerecia pazes emquanto elle foce minino atê que querendo pudesse vingar a morte de seu Pay.

Foy o corpo trazido aquella sua cidade 2 dias depois que a ella cheguey; e sobre hum bem feito cadafalço da lenha cheirosa aguilla brava, sandalo etc. nas prajas do Ganges foi queimado com não poucas lagrimas dos seus; no mesmo forão queimadas quasi vivas 60 comcubinas suas; digo quasi vivas porque alem de serem queimadas muito contra seu gosto, por força e as pancadas as meteram no fogo. Passados 15 dias, antes de o menino que he de sete annos se coroar, me deu licença pera passar quando ja o Irmão. Manoel Marques tinha vindo de Manâ com muita consolaçao minha e grande alegria que receby com as boas novas dos Padres, Posto que agoadas com o novo e trabalhozo estado da missão.

Toquei a V. R. neste Rey mal logrado porque alem de me tomar sua morte não so no caminho, mas em sua cidade merecenos elle alguma lembrança pellos muytos favores que nella fes ao Padre Antonio de Andrade e grande deseio que lhe mostrou de nossa assistencia naquella sua corte offerecendose pera nos dar sitio ao longo do Ganges junto de ssy, caza feita, aldeas pera a sustentação e toda a liberdade (que he o que queremos) pera naquellas serras propagaremos a verdadeira ley.

Bem vy aly nas emformações do Irmão a mudança das couzas do Chaparangue com a mâ fortuna do chodo pa Rey: rey que foi nosso grande amigo agora ja não rrey, mas captivo de outro fino idolatra, e que as prosperidades com que nosso Senhor fundou aquella nova christandade, sobre a extraordinaria benevolencia daquele Rey estavão algum tanto quebradas; mas não foi isso parte pera deixar de continuar no caminho pera me ver e consolar com os Padres como se me tinha ordenado.

Dia de Nosso Padre Sancto Ignacio nos partimos confiados nelle que nos alcançaria os favores necessarios pera o restante de viagem muito mais trabalhosa; como o caminho he comprido sempre sobindo, ou descendo e por pedragulho foi forçado sentiremno os pês de alguns de nos, renovandoselhe feridas velhas com novas chagas, de modo que nos foi necessario caminhar algumas jornadas descalsos por aquelles não sofrerem sapatos (isto he, o Padre meu, contar hum amigo a outro com confiança de amigo trabalhos padecidos pello ceo, que agora alegrão e então não entristecião).

Esta naquelle caminho huma serra entre mil outras afamada por sua altura que chamão a de Barochy que em algumas partes se sobe de gatinhas mas muito fresca assi em arvoredo e verdura como em bellas fontes e levadas de agoa com que a cada passo nos refresca e alivia do excessivo cançasso da sobida que nos gastou das sinco da manhã até a huma; ao cume della cheguey tão canssado que não cuidei que chegasse, e o mesmo foi chegar a elle que entrar com pequena decida por fermozos rozaes de huma e outra parte, com huma caudelosa ribeira de longo do caminho as serras de hum e outro lado cheas de boninas, de flores e muitas outras her-

vas cheirozas, o que tudo nos foi acompanhando ate bem perto de pouvoação. Na serra passada e nas que se vão seguindo he muito pera ver os cedros que as vestem, os aciprestes que as ornão quasi sem numero, aonde vy sipreste tão grosso no tronco que tinha de nove pera 10 braças; delles he a lenha que os serranos gastão tão cheirosa que quando arde, rescende e enche tudo de suavidade. Sedros não vy tão grossos, mas alguns de 4 e de 6 braças de grossura no tronco, tão altos como os mais altos pinheiros com os quaes tem muita semelhança na folha que não he mais grossa, mas mais curta com es mesmos bicos muito mor na copa muito mais espeço e escuro; servemse os montanhezes em suas cazas das taboas com as quaes se cobre. Nãm faltão por esta paragem muitas nogueiras e aveleiras, muitos pessigueiros devrazios e mollares, entre elles vy hum de tres braças de grossura no tronquo; grande copia de castanheiros, mas são as castanhas rões na carne, na casca muito negras, assy as comem aquelles. Estas são as Arvores que o Padre Antonio de Andrade vio cheas de ramalhetes de flores vermelhas tão perfeitos pela mão da natureza como se as emvejas | de fol. 27.
arte, nellas se quizera mostrar, ao que acrecento por couza notavel que primeiro cria e aparece com o ramalhete de flores lindamente postas em seu lugar, e depois sacudidas aquellas fica em seus pés aparecendo com o fruto ou com outro ramalhete de castanhas na ordem, no concerto e conformidade de suas flores.

Antes que chegassemos ao manzel este dia em Jussy, aconteceo ao Irmão meu companheiro [o] que direy. Hiamos pola lombada de sua muy alcantilada serra a pique sobre o Ganges aonde em certo lugar a passagem hera por cima de Dous paos juntos encostados a ella com lama, os quaes com a muita chuva da noite atras tinhão caido no rio. Cometeo o Irmão o caminho pegandose de algumas raizes penduradas na rocha porque ja outros se tinhão arriscado; no meo lhe quebrarão as rayzes e assi foi cahindo, e com elle que o estava vendo o meu coração e a alma, tão sobresaltado que so tive acordo pera lhe chamar por sancto Ignacio; a rocha era tão limpa e dereita como huma parede e de 4 braças de alto ate o rio; indo assi escorregando, no meo della se lhe meteo nas mãos não sej como (Deus scit) huma rais bem delgada pela qual pegou, huma braça antes do Ryo, donde o tiramos por cordas que lhe forão botando ate que se segurou e o pos Deos Nosso Senhor em salvo a quem demos infinitas graças pello vida que de novo assy lhe deu. No como eu passej, e com que risco, pella mesmo lugar sabe nosso Senhor. Dirá V. R. porque passava com tanto risco? Se tiveramos outro remedio, diz V. R. bem; mas nem outro remedio nem outro caminho avia, salvo tornar pera tras ate em muitas somanas se concertar aquelle.

Esta a pouvoação de Jussy aonde chegamos, setuada no recosto de huma ingrime serra, a cazaria he boa, nella a gente muita, tem no meo hum pagode entre 4 torres de pedra de cantaria; de fronte de sua porta se ergue hum pedestal de 15 palmos sobre o qual se vê hum Anjo de bronze muito lustroso notavelmente bem feito na figura e nas feições, de joelhos com o rosto pera o Pagode como quem o reverenciava com as mãos alevantadas. Em hum de seus alpendres nos recolhemos aquella noite; a boca della veo huma procissão de homens e meninos com varias campainhas e defumadouros com que em mais breve tempo do que me eu ja temia, rodearão e defumarão ao senhor Pagode. Vy aquy dentro nhuma torrinha piquena que não tinha mais vão que 4 palmos, fazendo penitencia a hum venerando velho que acentado vivia e dormia sem poder al fazer, nem o lugar donde não sahia, lhe dava pera mais licença.

Pola menhã nos deu esta serra não menos trabalho em a decer do que outras muy impinadas em as sobir. Ao pê della passamos hum de quinze rios com que o Ganges se fas poderoso, e logo nos fomos metendo pello baixo de duas serras muy altas e tão estreitas que quasi se não vê o mesmo Ganges que as vay solapando tão escondido que escaçamente o vê o sol no meo dia, com tanto estrondo que se não ove huma pessoa a outra senão a orelha. No espaço daquella manhã por entre estas serras assy continuadas se vem os mayores perigos deste fatal caminho, cuias difficuldades sô pode vencer ou o amor de Deos ou a inçaciavel e temeraria cobiça dos homens; porque o caminho he pello recosto destas desesperadas serras que as vezes escaçamente nos dão lugar pera por o pe, tão escorregadiço que se resvalais, o Ganges vos espera e vos recebe tão furioso que sem remedio, nhum momento desapareceis nelle. Não he este rio navegavel entre as serras assy pello arrebatado cursso com que vay, como por hir tropeçando em penedos desformes dos que descarna das serras, derruba, e recolhe.

Nestas mesmas serras desta manhã por serem tão alcantiladas sobre o Ganges, vão lançando pera fazer caminho huns páos, como quem os botara unidos a alguma parede inclinados pera sobir por elles, sobre os quaes em partes vão algumas trapeiras, pelas quaes sobe o caminho sendo temeridade e risco da vida manifesto a passagem por ellas, mas so posto que o não ha melhor, he necessario bebela, ou vertella, fazendo mil vezes actos de contrição com o santo nome de JESU e Maria na boca e no coração. Crea
fol. 28. | V. R. que não he possivel nem com isso significarlhe a menor parte do perigo desta manhã porque a cada passo quando menos o cudais ou vós resvalais, ou as traves se deixão cahir no rio comvosco.

Muito pode o dezeio de ver a Deos com huma Alma, que se isso não fora, creame Padre meu que o que ca veo huma vez, que ainda que lhe puzerão diante pera voltar outras, a honra pontifical, pode ser que responderia: Eis aquy antes o pescoço pera morrer huma vida que mil. Mas como digo o amor de Deos pode tudo, tudo facilita e a obediencia verdadeira tudo vence.

Depois que passamos as trapeiras, demos com huma cafila de carneiros que vinhão do Tibet carregados de sal, aonde tinhão levado arroz, como burrinhos de Castella a Setubal que trazem trigo e levão sardinhas e sal. São estes carneiros grandes e fermosos, fortes pera a carga; elles são o serviço destas serras; alguvs tem sinco pontas, carneiro ha de sete; a carne he muito boa, sua lã preciosa; a vista delles começamos a sentir o frio das nevadas serras de Manâ.

Antes de chegar a esta 2 coices, demos num vale entre serras, mas dezabafado, sem arvore nem erva verde, todo queimado da neve de que aquellas serras nunca carecem; nelle ao pe da serra da mão esquerda se ve o afamado Pagode Badry. Bem lhe podemos por tudo chamar o val do ynferno. Ao pe delle passa o Ganges. Todo aquelle se resolve em tres cazinhas de pouco momento, terreas, nem o demonio merece mais. Nhuma dellas a melhor está sobre hum Altar o mesmo, em duas figuras huma de ouro outra de prata digo de pedra. Ao pé delle vem a romper tres grandes fontes entre duas dagoa fria huma tão quente que se não pode nella sofrer a mão metida espaço de duas palavras, de que o Padre Antonio de Andrade fas menção na sua. Derivace esta agoa em varios tanques em que se banhão os perigrinos. Bem desejei de fazer outro tanto pera remedio de certas dores que nos joelhos tenho e trouxe des rios de Cuama, mas aquelle mimo so aos gentios o fazem. Alem das grandes riquezas que de toda esta Asia se offerecem a este Demonio, os reys vizinhos lhe tem dado grande numero de Aldeas pera suas despezas como lá os Reys catholicos a Sam Tiago em Compostella porque em tudo o Demonio e Bugio. Cada dia lhe dam tres vezes de comer, ao almosso 4 ceres do milhor e mais fino e alvo arros, com certos cocos em pedaços, e boa copia de manteiga,com algum doce; ao jantar quatro mãos de arros cozido e mil outras moxinyfadas; a merenda alguma couza leve. O Bramene lho poem diante, logo se sahe e feicha a porta; passado certo espaço, abrem e tirão o comer que o Bramene reparte concigo, e com seus servidores; dizem que o seu badry não quer mais que o cheiro, que com elle se sustenta, e de ver comer os seus.

He todo o destrito destos terras do Pagode cojto e sagrado em que os chriminosos dos Reynos vizinhos vivem seguros; a pouvoação em que vivem os servidores e devotas servidoras, esta a vista, mas bem afastada; dizem que não sofre o Pagode vizinhança de homem e molher por casto. He verdade que a não tem aly o seu Bramene ordinariamente, mas algumas vezes vay saber de sua saude e cozinharlhe hum bocado.

Neste mundo Indiano se tem por bemaventurado sô aquelle que veo a seu Badry, e porque V. R. veia quão bugio he de nossas couzas, assi como nos em Roma o anno sancto cada 25 annos, tem este pagode cada doze Jubileo plenario que foi o de 630, aonde por tão desesperados caminhos concorrerão então mais de oitenta mil gentios com suas ofertas, e basta chegarem ao val do inferno donde lhe veião as portas pera tornarem sanctificados e contentes pera toda a vida. Hum veo aquelle anno tão chêo de devação pello Reyno de Mogor, e pellas serras que veo sempre de joelhos até a porta do Pagode. Vem cegos, mancos, aleijados, mas tam alejados tornão, e mais cegos do que vierão. Aly lhe vão beijar as portas os mores calaceiros desta Asia que são os jogues, que so o são pera viverem com mor liberdade. Andão por aquelle frio quasi nus, e muitos sem mais roupa que a que a natureza lhe deu pera aparecerem a primeira vez no mundo, e estes são avidos por mores sanctos. Lançãose a esta vida velhaca | Assy porque fol. 29.
ninguem lhe pede conta della, como porque tem o comer certo. E verdade que o anno passado vindo de Bengala huma tropa de 8 mil bargantes ou Birbantes destes (que são agigantados, gordos e nedios) com suas armas fora de seu costume, não pareceo bem naquella conformidade ao Rey de Siranagar, e assy lhe mandou que ou voltacem, ou pera hir ao Pagode entregacem as armas. Não estam por isso, poemse em som de guerra, toca o rey caixa, marcha, da nelles, mortos muitos e muitos, e a cabeça do magote lançado vivo no Ganges, faz voltar ao mais com menos alvoroço e mor pressa do que vierão.

E não foi este Rey so, tambem Jangir que tinha a esta sorte de vadios avorrecimento notavel matou a muitos em seu tempo, e pera Cabul vendeo a 4 mil a troco de cães de cassa, aonde lhe cortão os nervos de hum pe, com o que sem esperança de fogirem os fazem trabalhar as direitas. Com hum Vice Rey dos nossos sej eu que mandou elle tratar que lhe esquiparia as galés todos os annos com certas condições bem racionaes, mas nem com isso veo a effeito.

Aly lhe vem bejar o pe ao Demonio Badry, o qual bem cuido que se poz aquy não so pera os enganar, mas tambem pera se vingar destes dezalmados com o excecivo trabalho de tão maos caminhos. Nos seis mezes em que por ser o sitio inhabitavel por frio e neves que todo o cobrem, e que se vão os moradores pera lugares mais habitaveis, lhe tem as portas fechadas, ouvem naquelle tempo grandes tangeres e muzicas. Mas quem as viu? que naquelle tempo não pode aparecer nem viver pessoa alguma aly; assy e com estas mentiras o Pay dellos engana a estes pobretes, por seus ministros.

He Manâ huma tristissima povoação; vivem seus moradores assy de seus carneiros como de levarem arros ao Tibet, e trazerem no sal nelles. Ha nos matos desta pouvoação grande copia de bichos de almiscar que dam o mais limpo e precioso que se sabe. He o bicho como duas vezes huma lebre e da mesma cor e feitio, quasi; tem os cabelos mais grossos e compridos; da boca lhe sahem dous dentes como de porco montes, agudos e de volta pera cima; pare a femea sempre cazal inteiro. A carne dizem os cassadores que a comem que he muy cheirosa e preciosa. Come a femea hervas peçonhentas que mastigadas e mal cozidas no estamago, as vomita e da ao macho, das quaes elle so cria no embigo hum polmão pera fora em que esta o almiscar, ao qual chamamos papo, o que tudo vy com curiosidade no mesmo bicho. Cassace com cães que os vão mordendo e descendo emquanto os cassadores as pedradas os matão; vivos se tomão alguns, mas não vivem muito. Vendesse o Almiscar no papo com seus cabellos que elles lhe deixão pera pezar mais dizendo que são nelle como os bigodes no homem, a pezo de Prata, e as vezes por mais.

Daquy me party dia de S. Lourenço tão ferido ainda dos pés que se achara quem me levara, sem duvida fizera o caminho nos alheos. Fuy so por me ser necessario deixar ao Irmão em Manâ esperando os carneiros pera levarem o fatinho; ao segundo dia dej ao passar do Ganges com sua ponte mea desfeita; não hera ella mais que 2 páos de meo Palmo de grosso, unidos ambos com as pontas sobre hum penedo, hum quá outro lá, e hum delles tinha cahido na corrente, pello outro se não atrevião a passar os mesmos serranos. O vão sobre o medonho rio hera de tres braças. Cheguey, fixej de bom modo o pao que estava, encomendandome a Deos e a sua sanctissima Mãy, foy elle servido que passou o moço sem perigo, e fixa de sua parte a outra ponta, passej com o sobroço que se pode crer por tão estreito pao sobre tal rio. Daly a huma legoa dei com outro rio detraves pera o Ganges com a ponte que era semelhante toda levada. Aly me vy sem remedio e pouco pera cantar a que diz: Vay o rio de monte a monte, como passarey sem ponte. Mas como Deos acode nos mores apertos, socedeo que não era passada mea hora, quando da outra banda aparecerão 2 moços nossos que vinhão com alguns carneiros de Chaparangue demandando a ponte. Forão logo dando busca pellas ribeiras abaixo e quis nosso Senhor que nas da sua parte acharão os paos com que restaurada a ponte pudemos todos continuar o caminho.

Naquelle citio, ainda que entre serras, dezabafado, vy ao longe huns fol. 30
ramos vermelhos perto das prayas do Ganges, que me parecerão de coral, vista de grande recreação, e ao perto que de humas relvas nascyão ynfinitos ramalhetes de folhas vermelhas pequenas em huma vergontea de palmo e meo, na figura cada hum delles hum sipreste, a terceira parte da vergontea limpa. Tem consigo estes ciprestes de flores fabricados polla mão da natureza esta graça que no mesmo tempo e na mesma relva vedes que huns são de flores encarnadas outros de flores muito vermelhas e outros de flores brancas quasi, e achei que nascia tão aprazivel variedade de serem humas prymeiro que outras na nacensa na qual aparecem vermelhas, passados alguns dias se vão tornando emcarnadas, e depois mais brancas que vermelhas durando na varia vista de suas cores muitos dias. Pera qualquer jardim não forão por la de pouca estima. Devem de ser as que o nosso poeta já celebrou com aquelles versos: Escrevem varios autores que iunto da clara fonte do Ganges os moradores vivem do cheiro das flores que nacem daquella fonte.

Outra flor melhor vy tambem ao longo do Ganges, misterioza; não hera mayor que hum tostão, na qual sobre huma pequena varinha se ve de folhas verdes fabricada huma salva, e sobre as sinco folhas que a fabricão sobre outre pee assenta outra de sinco folhinhas de cor de sangue na figura como gotas, no meo da qual se ve hum bem feito coração de cor de ouro cheo de cabelinhos muito finos de cor de sangue os quaes tem as cabecinhas como de prego que ficão acompanhando em roda ao coração. O cheiro he suave e pareceome como o dos cravos que la chamão d'Arrochella. Ja V. R. ve que não deixara de ter alem de sua graça seu misterio.

Por meo destas flores me fuy achando na afamada serra do Candá, que tambem entre as floridas hervas se vê a venenoza serpente, afamada digo por cruel porque alem de que o anno todo está cuberta de neve, he sempre nela o frio deshumano, o qual apertou aly comigo, e me renovou ou encarniçou algumas chaguinhas dos pés de maneira que me foi necessario por não acabar aly, rogar e peitar a hum serrano dos que hião com carneiros que me levace tres jornadas que so restavão, o que ele fes por seu interece metendome nhum cesto, a que chamão carandy e levandome nelle as costas com não menos trabalho meu que seu.

Do meo desta serra descobry o Tanque donde nasce o rio Ganges, e tambem o Indo comforme as informações que tomey e diligencias que por minha curiosidade fiz o Ganges se fas na volta do sul, o Indo na do norte, ambos por bom espaço escondidos por baixo da terra mas com ruido notavel sentidos; pequenos quando aparecem, mas logo com o cabedal de muytas ribeiras se fazem ricos e poderosos. O Ganges, como ia disse, depois de desabafar nos campos Industanos, se fas na volta do nascente e vay pellas fozes de Bengala pagar ao oceano seu tributo; o Indo por entre serras vay pera o norte até ver a cidade de Chaparangue, a vista da qual feito na volta do ponente banhando a cidade de Lahor se vay meter no mar pela fos de Sinde. De Lahor pera la he navegavel.

Fesnos esta serra o gasalhado que costuma, chovendo aquelle dia sobre nos muita saraiva, e tanta neve que nos cubrio a todos, mas não nos enterrou pella bondade de Deos Nosso Senhor, como a muitos fas, se se lhe atrevem maxime de novembro até abril, e quando os não enterra de todo, queimalhe mãos e pes, de modo que não faltam no caminho atras muitos assynalados deste posto; a mym so crestou e esfolou o rosto, e me abrio os beiços como se forão figos. Finalmente cheguey ao Chaparangue como fruita em cesto aos 25 de Agosto tão moido e magoado dos pes que me não pude servir delles por mais de 20 dias.

Naquella cidade e Reino achey que reinava outro farao que não conhecia, mas opremia o pouvo de Deos com grande centimento meu. He este
fol. 31. Reino hum dos que se contem de- | baixo do nome do Pot, e não o menor antes hum dos mais antigos e ricos. Mil annos avia que se conservava na posse de hum Rey e seus antecessores, a que chamão Chodàpô, o dono do livro, porque o seu rey foi o que lhe trouxe de alem de Vzangue ou da China o livro de sua ley pello que era tão estimado das Reys vizinhos que todos se honrravão de se aparentarem com elle; dos mais Ricos, ou mais rico e buscado dos mercadores de varios Reinos de Vzangue que lhe trazem as sedas e chas de China, porçolanas etc., dos Casmeris, Lahoris, Industanos etc. que lhe levão as roupas o coral alambre que são as joyas que mais estimão, donde trazem grande cópia da mais fina e precioza lam que ha no mundo que aquelles estrangeiros por ser tal vão lá buscar por taes caminhos com tanto risco de suas vidas. Está esta cidade sobre huma serra toda aberta em buracos a que chamão pugus em que vivem seus moradores mais abrigados do frio alem de outras cazas que tem sofriveis. No cume della se vê a fortaleza em que o Rey morava por sitio e arte inexpugnavel.

He a gente destas regiões do Pot, que quer dizer terra de neve, nas feições e olhos achinada, nos rostos tão ajavada, ou abocetada que de maçam a maçam tem de andadura mea legoa pouco mais ou menos! Homens, molheres e meninos tão pouco airozos como malfeitos, e nelles o sujo do rosto e de corpo entra com a vida e com ella sahem, assy como nos vestidos que huma so vez metem no corpo donde não sahem senão em farrapos, podridão e mao cheiro; a indole he muito boa e branda. He gente em que ha poucos siumes, as vezes andão os fretes, e acontece que o marido o pede ao amigo sem pejo. Quando querem cazar, o terceiro que concertou e os apalavrou tem licença pera a ter a premeira noyte em sua caza e assi se pratica; a outro dia a entrega a seu marido. Enfadado qualquer dos cazados ajunta aos parentes e diante delles tomão ambos hum fio de lam pellas pontas e puxão, e quebrão levando cada hum seu pedaço, se vão quebrados, dezatados e livres cazar com quem querem; ella leva as filhas, elle os filhos.

Vestem cabaias de pano de lam grosseiras, calções do mesmo, com suas botas elles e ellas; não trazem estas couza alguma na cabeça, trazem os cabelos em trancinhas sobre as costas até abaixo bem emmanteigados; por joyas huma cambada de alambres e coraes ao pescosso sobre o peito, tão sujos huns como outros. Da testa pera o meo da cabeça hum fio de pedras verdes toscas, a que chamão turquinas; algumas são preciosas; comem carne crua ou mal assada, e farinha de sevada assada, hervas cozidas frescas em todo o anno porque no verão as secão em casa a sombra e quando as querem comer verdes e frescas, lançãonas de molho em agoa por meo dia e ficão tão frescas como as colhidas de pouco. Se lá servir, a menuta não he mâ.

Tem por costume não se vizitarem sem algum saguate, nem ainda se manda huma carta sem elle; o contrario he desprimor. O vizitado tambem vos hade dar de comer e beber toties quoties. Se tendes com o Rey negocio da Justiça, meteislhe na mão o sauguate e a petição; mas se lida esta não tendes justiça, tornavolo. O que vos sobeia do comer que em sua caza vos põem diante levailo pera vossa caza sob penna de serdes avido por descortes.

Nem são mouros, antes lhe tem aversão, nem gentios, nem christãos; a ley que tem herrada, da nossa divina teve seu principio, mas como lhe foi dada escrita de mão, e a forão por tantos seculos tresladando, forão della tirando o que lhe não pareceo a seu gosto e metendo ynfinitas patranhas. Tem que Deos he trino e uno a quem chamão Conjá sumbô, ao Pay chamão Lamâ comjô, Deos Padre; ao filho Choconjô, ao Espirito Santo Gi-undu conjô; que o pay gera ao filho à sua palavra, e que dambos nasceo a terceira pessoa. A nossa Senhora Gelobó lunzé. Tem que a segunda pessoa encarnou nella e que querendo o eterno Pay mandarlhe por embaixador
a hum Anjo, | ouvera arrufos nos homens por averem que lhe tocava, e fol. 32.
que Deos então por evitar contendas, mandara a hum elefante por embaixador. Assi o tem escrito no lyvro, mas alguns entendidos, poucos, dizem que hum Anjo lhe trouxe a embaixada, que a Virgem o concebeo e pario ficando Virgem, ma que pera o ficar o concebeo pello sobaco, que se lhe fes aly hum inchaço que creceo e durou 9 mezes e que arrebentado elle, nasceo Deos homem; com tudo alguns mais previstos dizem que concebeo como a vidraça aos Rayos do sol que passão por ella sem quebrar. Dizem que nasceo não em estrebaria que não convinha a Deos, mas em seu leyto e que morreo nelle quando quis, mas não na Crus; que foi muy tentado de molheres, mas que sempre resistia; que resurgio e que quando quis se foi pera o Ceo. Tem purgatorio pera faltas pequenas, que chamão Choquiceiro, Inferno pera grandes pecadores, confissão de que não uzão salvo algum muito devoto a hum lamâ grande vertuozo; tem que as almas são ab aeterno e que quando nasce o corpo, Deos lha aplica; tem grande reverencia aos seus lamas, que são os seus sacerdotes e tanta fee em sua vertude que quando alguma está de parto trabalhada, logo lhe vão pedir reliquias com a oferta nas mãos; elle benze huma pouca de mainteiga e a põem sobre a que esta de parto, e socede por vezes que logo lança a criança com a mesma manteiga sobre a cabeça, tanto coopera o demonio com os seus devotos, Deos sabe o porque lho permite; delles tomão reliquias que trazem ao pescoço; mas quaes cuida V. R. que serão? huns pilouros como de cabras em que vay confeitado o excremento do mesmo Lamâ que tem por grande reliquia, e aconteceo que ferindo no rosto de hum que levou a guerra tal maventura, a seta lhe quebrou nelle, sem lhe fazer mal. E pera que V. R. veja a barbaridade desta gente, o mesmo Rej de Ladac tem o seu lama mor em tanta veneração que se lava todas as menhas com a sua orina e logo bebe a que fica. Estão tão senhores destes cegos os lamas que quando morrem os pobres, se lhe não levão alguma couza, fazem que fique o corpo no

campo aos cães e ainda lhe fazem crer que a alma lhe fica fora do ceo emquanto elles lhe não passão cartas pera o enterrarem que lhe vendem a pezo douro.

Em todo o anno se não ajuntão na igreja senão quando lhe dão alguma couza pera rogarem por elles a Deos nosso Senhor; então levão o comer que lhe dão á igreja, rezão he comem nella; muitos comem em cascos de caveiras de homens, e nas igrejas tangem como com frautas, com canas de pernas e braços humanos, como lhe vy fazer; dizem que o fazem pera se lembrarem da morte e alembrarem aos outros. Estes são os costumes desta gente e os seus erros.

O Rey naturalmente he bem inclinado; emquanto Reinou foi verdadeiramente Pay dos pobres [?] e gram favorecedor da christandade; desejava muito fazerse christão e tinhao prometido aos Padres. Hia devagar porque se lhe não rebelacem. Entre as cauzas que eu acho porque nosso Senhor lhe tirou o cetro da mão, foi huma fiarse pouco de Deos neste ponto e o dilatar o sancto Baptismo tanto tempo depois que conheceo a verdade e bondade de nossa sancta ffé, tambem em castigo de viver publicamente cazado com duas irmãs alem do que o ajudou a malquistarse com seus vassalos apenados demaziadamente, donde nasceo chamarem ao seu imigo pera lhe entregarem o Reino; alem de tudo isto o malquistou fazer de muitos milhares de lamas deixados os habitos ecclesiasticos soldadesca pera as guerras, golpe que o Demonio sentio nelles tanto que pellos mesmos lhe enviou a dizer que elle adoeceria em castigo de tal crime, e que quando escapace das mãos da morte, que seu mor inimigo o de Ladac lhe tomaria o Reino sem golpe de espada e o levaria cativo com toda sua familia.

Assy foi que o pobre escapou de huma mortal doença, mas não da treição com que seus vassalos o venderão a seu imigo. Veo este, põe lhe serco,
fol. 33. recolhece o pobre rej a fortaleza, | os moradores abrem as portas da cidade, entra o Rey de Ladac, cahe logo ao nosso o coração aos pés, sendo assy que pudera conservarse na fortaleza seguro por muitos annos; sem embargo do que elle he o que comete partido de pax, fazemce as pazes que ficara no Reivo pagandolhe cada anno tributo, mas que sera com condição, que deça a lhe fazer salamâ, no que se deixava bem ver o refolho e alejvozia do Rey de Ladac; fiasse delle o mal afortunado Rey, desce, faslhe tascelima, quebralhe a fee, não esta pelo concerto, roubalhe os tezouros e levao por cativo pera Ladac com toda sua familia com o que o Demonio e seus ministros triumpharão delle e dos do sagrado evangelho com a professia comprida.

E como sobre a muita benevolencia deste pobre Rey, nosso Senhor fundou ou principiou aquella nova christandade, ja V. R. pode ver a grande quebra que ella tera, sendo tão tenra, e o novo Faraó tão fino idolatra, como imigo dos Padres; elle lhe roubou a precioso da igreja, calices, casteçaes e frontaes etc., grande numero de carneiros, cavalos e outras couzas que herão o meneo e sustentação da missão; sobre o que mandou dizer aos Padres que lhe perdoava a vida e que se quizecem ficar, ficassem e que ao diante o faria com elles como elles o servicem e lhe decem; ficarão os Padres roubados deste Pirata e oprimidos por não deixarem os novos christãos, muy confiados na divina bondade que os remediaria muito cedo melhorando o estado das couzas como dezejamos.

Entre estas montanhas Tibetenças, no meo de tamanhas ingnorancias tem nosso Senhor plantado de novo sua santissima ffeê, por meo dos excessivos trabalhos do P. Antonio de Andrade, que hora governa esta Provincia de Goa, e de seus companheiros a que deu feliçes principios com huma nova igreja que o antigo Rey lhe edificou as suas custas em bom sitio, não muito grande mas muito capas, toda pintada de oleo, e repartida em paineis da vida do Senhor Jesu. Nesta se ajuntão es novos christãos, que ficarão porque antes de tomada digo, nesta cidade real depois que foi tomada e roubada pelo novo rey; digo que ficarão porque antes de tomada, averia nella e nas povoações vizinhas quasi quatroçentos, alem de que cada dia se pedia o santo bauptismo por muitos e muitos a mor Parte dos quaes forão captivos pera Lee, cidade real do novo rey daly a duzentas legoas e pera outras de seu Reino. Os que ficarão quando aly cheguej me vierão buscar, nesta igreja me alegrei e consolei com elles. He verdade que nos não empedem os ministros reaes a converção das almas, mas com o estrondo de tamanha ruyna, e com a mudança do Rey tão amigo em rey tão pouco afeiçoado as couzas do verdadeiro Deos, quebrou algum tanto aquelle fervor primeiro assim en alguns dos novos christãos como nos gentios, que com tanto calor o pedião.

Partiose o novo Rey pera Ladac deixando em Chaparangue presidio e levando consigo o Chodapô e a muitos christãos captivos; os que ficarão continuam com sua obrigação. Neste estado achej aquella missão em 26 de Agosto. Dahy a poucos dias recebemos huma do Padre João Cabral que por morte do Padre Estevão Cacella e Manoel Dias rompeo a Vzangue com grandes trabalhos e perigos. Aquy porey o capitolo della pera que V. R. saiba o estado em que ficava em breve, a vida morte dos Padres:

„O Padre Estevão Cacella e eu passamos de Bengala pera esta missão. No caminho nos reprezou 7 mezes o rajâ Manâ Rupâ; no fim delles, avida licença delle, o Padre Cacella se partio pera Vzangue, e me mandou a Bengala buscar algumas couzas necessarias. Fuy por via de palpo; cheguej a Oguly quando chegavão as Naos da India e nellas o Padre Manoel Dias com a ordem do Padre Alberto, que passaçe a missão, se o Padre Estevão Cacella mandace chamar algum Padre; e porque não pedia gente resisty eu a ida do Padre Manoel Dias que o Padre Reytor de Bengala mandou de poder absoluto. Com estes embaraços me detiverão no Ogoly de modo que perdij a moussam de poder voltar pelo Nepal, e assi arremety pelo Cocho donde avizey ao Padre Cacella me mandace gente deste Rey pera poder passar, porque como o Reino de Cumbá junto ao de Cocho não tinha rey, não se passa sem guarda. Chegou o meu recado tão tarde que o Padre Cacella era ido a Bengalla, não podendo por cauza das neves penetrar a esse Chaparangue, aonde primeiro arremeteo, e achando por Bengala, que estava no Cocho com o Padre Manoel Dias, nos veo logo buscar tão doente que escassamente se podia ter nos pés, e em setembro de 629 se partio com o Padre Manoel Dias deixandome com algum fato no Cocho, pera em Janeiro me mandar buscar. Forão taes os trabalhos que na viagem padecerão que por força delles morreo o Padre Manoel Dias no Reino de Morongo aos 3 de novembro com hir muito sam.

O Padre Cacella chegou tal a este Vzangue que sete dias depois de che-

gar, antes de ver a el Rej, o levou nosso Senhor aos 6 de Março de 630. Sentio o Rey muito sua morte e logo me mandou chamar ao Cocho, o que não teve effeito por ser inverno. Este anno de 631 tornou a repetir com gente, com o que me resolvy a passar pelo não agravar e por não deixar o fato da igreja em suas mãos; mes e meo ha que cheguey; estou aceito ao
fol. 34. Rey. O Padre Provincial Gaspar Fernandez não mostra | gosto de continuar esta missão e desystirá sabendo da morte dos Padres. Eu lhe tenho pedido me desse por subdito de V. R. O Rey não [?]he mais afeiçoado que a sua ley, faz me honrra, a tenção Deos a sabe. Veja V. R. se sera bem fazer aquy residencia porque o rey não hade resistir etc."

Itto he o que o Padre escreve. O Rey favorece muito e he muito necesario que aly se faça acento e se aprenda de rais a lingoa, porquanto aly tem os lamas deste Imperio sua Vniversidade e letras; feitos aquelles capazes de seus erros e da verdade da nossa sancta ffe, todos os mais Reynos se sogeitarão a elle facilmente e a rezão porque o P. Antonio de Andrade dezejou tanto de meter lá o pê, o que não fes por ser a missão da Provincia de Cochym, e agora cuido que o fara por aquella lhe ter entregue a mesma missão de Vzangue por rezam das grandes dificuldades com que por via de Bengala se lhe pode acudir e da mor facilidade com que de qua pelo Chaparangue pode ter recurso.

Vendo eu o estado da missão, tratej com os Padres do remedio della e acentamos que o seria em parte ver me com o novo Rey com algum prezente soposto que hera tão cubiçozo pera o benevolear [?] na forma possivel, o que ainda que não tinha por ordem e o caminho era comprido e difficil, ouve comtudo que aquella seria a vontade de Nosso Senhor e da obediencia e que puderia com minha ida melhorarse de alguma maneira aquella missão tratando e pedindo ao Rey que nos fizesse respeitar no Chaparangue como dantes e de novo licença pera a sua sombra na sua cidade real de Lee, viveremos e pregar nossa sancta ley, porque com o bom modo dos Padres aly puderia ser que o ganhacemos e daly podiamos favorecer com isso e acudir aos Padres que estiverem por outras partes do Reino; pellos que logo me puz ao caminho porquanto o inverno dos frios que naquella partes são tão desconformes como veremos, estava ja a porta.

O capitam me empedio o caminho que seu Rey se temia de bexigas (que entam avia no Chaparangue) que não podia hir; depois o peitej e me partij, mas na terceira jornada me achej impedido so penna de morte por ordem do Rey que estava com outro em campo e se não fiava da gente de Chaparangue. Voltej bem magoado por serem ja andados muitos de setembro que he o fim do verão. Quando foi aos 28 me mandou o Rey que fosse; o capitam, sem embargo do inverno, me fes logo partir, o que foi dia de S. Francisco levando comigo pera lingoa o Padre João de Oliveira em companhia dos mercadores de Uzangue que por ordem do Rey lhe levavão seus cavalos pera lhos comprar, ou tomar. Puzemos 21 dias no caminho com as jornadas serem de sol a sol, sempre com o rosto no norte, de modo que quando la chegamos o achamos quasi sobre as cabeças, partindo de 33 graos; he o caminho quasi todo deserto por entre serras nevadas todo, não se vê quasi por toda esta terra folha verde porquanto a neve he tanta que não só não cria, mas escalda e queima a terra em forma que se não vê nella arvore alguma. Ha neste caminho muitas lebres, infinitos pombos bravos, muita cabra montes, muitas aguias, grandissimos corvos, muitos burros do mato que cassam e comem os serranos, muitas hyaças que são humas bufaras como vacas cubertás de fermoso e comprido cabello com que a natureza lhe tempera o rigor do frio de que se fazem cordas boas e fortes, cujas pelles servem de moles colchas, de cujos rabos quando são brancos se faz em muitas partes muita estima. São muito finos e compridos de braça, e braça e mea alguns; na India fazem as portuguezas delles, curados com agoa douro, fermosas cabeleiras de que se servem e nos nas festas. A carne he pera se comer muito boa.

Na primeira jornada chegamos a cidade de Sâze que he pequena toda aberta em criptas e cavernas em que morão, alem de outras cazas que fazem, com a fortaleza no cume. | Pareceome huma cidade de presepio, fol. 35.
assy são as mais, poucos moradores, ao pê lhe passa hum fermoso rio. O segundo manzel fomos fazer ao pe de outra junto de huma ribeira aonde achamos nabos verdes que não são pequeno regalo assy comidos; por datiles secos nos derão boa quantidade delles. O terceiro manzel fizemos junto de huma povoação de pastores; aquella noite nos choveo tanta neve que nos enterrou 3 palmos com grande frio qué já nos hia fazendo bem ma companhia. Os 7 dias seguintes caminhamos por grandes montanhas de neve todas desertas, sem aver nellas nem pouvoação nem pessoa ate que chegamos a Alner em que vive o Papa dos Lamás; vive este no cume de huma serra aonde se vêm 6 ou 7 cazinhas a modo de força; pelos vales ao longo della demos com 30 tendas de pastores, nas quaes vivem com suas familias, gente cingela e bonachã, fartos, ricos e contentes, tinhão por aly 18 ou 20 mil corneiros por terem ao longo dalgumas ribeiras boa relva pera pasto. Com algum leite nos acodirão a troco, não de dinheiro que o não uzão nem conhecem, mas de tres passas de uvas tamanhas como ameixas que do Industão levavamos, que elles estimarão tanto que de huma comerão com muita festa tres pastores.

Logo seguimos o caminho por tres dias de dezerto; no fim delles demos em hum largo vale, em que nasce e se ye huma grande marinha de branco e fermoso sal que a natureza aly cria por suas mãos sem ajuda alguma da arte; neste posto nos vimos mais mortos de frio que nunca, os moços com a força e dores postos em pranto e dezanimados, sem fogo porgue nem bosta se achou que he a lenha destas partes pera nos abrigar de seu rigor; aly me gretarão as mãos e se me lavarão em sangue com não pequena dor; o rosto se me crestou, os beiços abrirão em feridas, e o que mais senty foy abriremseme os pes como figos com extraordinarias dores, e isto quando eu pera caminhar e pera sobidas desesperadas tinha mor necessidade delles. O mesmo rigor e crueldade sentio o Padre meu companheiro naquelle posto sem embargo de a ter outras vezes exprimentado por aquelles clymas.

Cuidara V. R. que ja lhe dice muito deste frio. He tal que em sahindo o cuspo da boca nhum instante se converte em caramelo, em pedra; os narizes sem çocego estillam e em aparecendo o estilado ja he caramelo. He pera ver os cavalos ordinariamente com duas pontas compridas de christal nas ventas pendurados. Passavão estes pellas ribeiras feitas caramelo e tam de pedra que pera beber no caminho nos valiamos dos pedaços dele que na boca se desfazia, e pera fazer humas papas de farinha de sevada que foi em tão largo caminho a nossa sustentação, era necessario derretelo caramelo primeiro ao fogo no caldeirão, e o mesmo se fazia pera os cavalos beberem. Muitas ribeiras achavamos que por cima tinhão o caramelo de dous palmos, aonde os cavalos pera se fartarem de agoa com o focinho e mãos davão tantos golpes ate que por entre os pedaços chegavão a beber. Aqui aconteceo que com a força do frio por mais que de noite lhe fugis debaixo de godorins e mantas se as tendes, amanheceis com a boca cuberta de pedra e caramelo que he o bafo, o cuspo e as mais humidades que della vos sahem dormindo, e isto aconteceo tambem noutras partes deste Reyno.

Desta marinha continuamos o caminho tres dias por outros desertos ate que chegamos a cidade de Guiar de que he senhor hum régulo a quem o de Ladac despojou daquelle Reino de Mariul. E este regulo grande nosso amigo como bem mostrou não só no gazalhado que fes ao Padre Antonio de Andrade mas tambem a nós tratandonos como se fora hum Irmão nosso com tudo aquillo de mostras de amor que a terra sofre. Entre outros mimos que a régula sua molher nos pos diarite, foi huma duzia de maçans como as grandes de Lisboa, bicaes, excelentes. Eu como avia 37 annos que não tinha visto outras alvoroceyme e agradecy-lhas, com o que ella cuidou que lhe pedia outras que logo trouxe com muita benevolencia do que nada me pezou; e como aviamos aly de voltar, despedidos delle nos partimos.
fol. 36. Daly a dous dias chegamos a hum posto ja no Reino de Ladac | aonde estão a vista 6 cidadinhas em serras huma legoa cada qual da outra, semelhantes as passadas no mayor e mais comprido valle que vy por quá, entre serras, aonde ha muitos varzias de sevada. He esta sevada, não como a de nossa terra mas no grão como trigo anafil muito sustencial e gostosa.

Hum dia depois chegamos a cidade real de Lee edeficada em huma serrinha de cima até o pé; sera de 500 fogos, mea legoa por baixo a vista vay o rio Indo na volta de Lahor; ao pee desta cidade vay huma ribeira que das serras nasce com que moem grande numero de azenhas; aly ha algumas arvores ainda que poucas e quasi todo o anno sem folha. Confina este Reino de Ladac pela parte do sul com o de Chaparangue ou Cogê, pello nascente com o Reino dos tres mouros [por] profissão, gente branca tam bem afeiçoada como esforçada, chamace por outro nome Archande cuja cydade real he Cascai, donde em cafilas levão á China o barro de que se fazem as porçolanas. Por aly passou o Ir. Bento de Gòes da nossa Campanhia de Jesu que Deos tem, não dista deste Reino de Ladac mais que 6 jornadas; pera o ponente confina com o Reyno dos Baldijs, gente não tão branca, mas muy bem feita e de grandes corpos. Indo a vista da cidade me fizerão descavalgar e esperar, descavalgar por cortezia, esperar por costume de não entrar nella pessoa estrangeira sem ordem del rey; entramos com ella, derão nos cazas, lenha, agoa, e algumas medidas de sevada de reçam que aceitamos por ser do paço; ao dia seguinte nos chamou o Rey mais apetitozo de nos aliviar do prezente do que de nos ver. Era elle duas pessas de melique boas, 6 armas de fogo pequenas e grandes, duas rodelas de China e outros dourados, hum escritorio dedio e outras couzas curiozas; entrey, pus lho diante, mandouo recolher, fiz lhe minhas reverencias, assentamonos!

Estava com a rainha ao soalheiro; he homen alto de corpo, nas cores baço, nas feições Jao, na postura severo, com cabaya de pano vermelho grosso, e pouco limpo, com huma capa do mesmo, barrete vermelho bem safado, as gadelhas da cabeçà ate os hombros, em cada orelha huma turquina e hum grande coral, ao pescosso hum colar de ossos humanos de caveiras, e na mão outra pera memoria da morte, acentado e encruzado sobre huma colcha de velludo carmezim do tempo de Matusalem, a casa bem ornada de teas de aranha, mais suja que limpa. Junto a Sua Magestade estava a da rainha sua senhora, huma perra [?] jaoa que o governa, de ma natureza, balofa, e tão abotoada nos olhos que escassamente se deixavão ver, vestida como o marido.

Em nos sentando, nos forão logo dando o chá que ja tinháo dado aos Reys; esta he a sua primeira e mor cortezia. He o cha huma erva que vem da China pelo Reino de Vzangue muy conhecida e celebrada em Japão e China. A estas folhas cozem em agoa em huma panela de pedra com alguma manteiga e pouco leite, cujo negro caldo he o que tomão quão quente he possivel, estas são suas delicias, de modo que o que da mais numero destes negros caldos he o mais honrado e magnifico; so os ricos tem posses pera o dar. Mitiga esta herva assy bebida as dores dé cabeça, he boa pera as de pedra, concerta o estomago, faz vontade de comer; apos ella nos puzerão hum pedaço de carneiro cru, hum grande pelouro de maça de cevada que chamão zané. Comeis o que quereis e o mais levão pera sua caza os vossos moços que se sentão aly e lhe fazem o mesmo que a vos.

Passados 4 dias lhe propus ao que vinha, respondeo me que tomaria seu conselho sobre nossa assistencia na sua cidade. Passados 8, nos despachou por hum privado seu pello qual nos mandou dar formão pera podermos viver e estar como no tempo do Rey passado, não so' no Reino de Cogé mas tambem em Ridocho e na sua cidade real. Esta reposta nos não quis dar peçoalmente por se não obrigar a favores, nem a muitas despezas, se pera aly viessemos, com o que nos mandou dar hum cavalo | que se parecia fol. 37.
muyto com o de Dom Quexote, 4 panos de lam e dois rabos de hyaças e licença pera partir, e pera pregaremos nossa sancta ley como dantes.

Como era ja inverno e aly não tinhamos aparelho pera celebrar, nem eu sabia da vontade dos Superiores não me deliberey a deixar lá ao Padre meu companheiro; partimos com grandes frios, e neves pera a cidade de Guiar aonde chegamos em 3 dias; o de antes ao longo de huma ribeyra por entre estreitas serras me sacodio o cavalo da lombada de huma serra sobre a ribeira de lugar tão alcantilado que o Padre que vinha de tras e me vio cahir sobre a ribeira, me deu por acabado; mas Nosso Senhor por entercessão de sua Mãy de quem o Padre e eu nos valemos, me fes empessar no meo da rocha, aonde me achey acentado em huma tam pequena quebra della que não acabavamos de nos maravilhar de como podia eu ficar aly! O certo he que de novo nascy, e me deu o Senhor a vida de graça. A este Rey tão nosso amigo fiz algum saguate em sinal de amor ainda que não como eu dezejava. Vime ahy duvidoso do caminho que tomaria e porque erão jâ 10 de novembro, os frios cruelissimos; se voltava por Chaparangue achavaos muito mayores agora que quando vym, e daly pera lá avia de cursar 18 jornadas alem do caminho do Chaparangue pera Manâ por Syranagar que ja avia de tomar em Dezembro com manifesto risco de vida; se cometia o caminho de Lahor era caminho novo por grandes dezertos e por muitos Reinos diversos ainda que em 9 dias fugiamos por elle ao inverno. Porfim me resolvy a romper este novo caminho pera Lahor por me não arriscar a envernar no Chaparangue sem necessidade e o aver de achar muito verde com as neves e frio do inverno.

Este bom regulo me rogou muito que fizece com o Padre Provincial lhe puzece naquella sua cidade hum Padre ou dous pera sua consolação e que nella e noutras que tem insinariamos Nossa Sancta ley pera o que nos fazia cazas e daria terras pera a sustentação. O despacho desta petição pende da vontade do Padre Provincial. Despedidos deste regulo e cheos de suas charidades com hum homem que nos deu pera guia, nos partimos huma segunda feira 10 de novembro; nove dias caminhamos por hum deserto de montanhas e serranias sem nellas veremos pessoa alguma, atravessando ribeiras e rios emcaramelados, fomos dar em paragens em que as serras se dezentranhavão em fontes cuja agoa em sahindo dellas se coalhava e empedernia logo. Serra vy da qual em espaço de hum tiro de mosquete de sua chapada contamos que rompiam cento e vinte e sete fontes, algumas hum boj dagoa, sem em toda ella se ver huma erva verde. Alguns nabos e maçans doçes que levavamos, com o frio se emcaramelarão de maneira que sem fogo não prestavão pera se comer. Alguns trabalhos extraordinarios tivemos neste deserto; hum delles foj subir e decer huma impinada serra cuberta de neve, e em partes de caramelo, por espaço de hum dia atolando na neve por sima dos joelhos, caindo muitas vezes e metendo nella as mãos com a dor, ainda que breve [, ?] qual so Deos sabe, descambando e escorregando pello caramelo, em que se para com summa dificuldade. Não forão poucas as quedas e cambadelas deste dia que meu companheiro e eu demos, e foy nosso Senhor servido darnos nelle bom sol e faltar o vento, porque a ventar então aly ficavamos mortos de frio, porquanto quando em semelhantes serras cursa o vento ,vem tão cruel e frio que não ha golpe de navalha com que se possa comparar.

No cume desta grande serra entre outras faz a neve derretida hum tanque em que se podem menear 200 navios, então cheo de agoa sem gota de agoa, todo feito huma fermoza pedra de caramelo. O que nelle notey por couza maravilhoza foi huma serca em roda do mesmo caramelo de altura de hum homem, feita pellas mãos do frio e arte da natureza; aquelle muro, aquella sô pedra de fermozo christal de grossura de tres palmos coroada de huma renda de pontinhas tão bem feita que erão muito pera ver, e foy
fol. 38. que quando a agoa do tanque se foi congelando | foi abatendo aquella altura deixando a parede congelada naquella conformidade sobre que com as quebras da agoa a foi a natureza coreando com aquela artificiosa renda de pontas em que os rayos do sol fazião fermosissimos christaes. Não cuide que lhe pinto, porque não digo nada a respeito do que naquella parede tinhão os olhos que estimar.

Daly a dous dias caminhando por huma aberta de serras dyreita, nos deu o dia todo de rosto hum vento tão fero que nunca cudej nem tive a morte mais prezente que então. O lugar hera deserto e sem huma abrigada em que delle nos pudecemos esconder; eu vinha nhum cavalo, tão entangido que nem pes, nem mãos erão meus; so da sinta pera sima vivia, mas com extremas dores, e como homem de pao pera via de me menear daly; cudej que ficasse cego, porqur o olho direito com o frio se destemperou de modo que me persuady que se me acabaçe de vazar, e assi de ambos estive por tempos bem atrabalhado. Emfin o Padre me tomou nos braços, me deçeo, me confessou e consolou quando me pareceo que ahy ficava, porque ja não tinha alento pera viver muito. Emquanto me reconsylyej com elle, o nosso guia que se compadeceo de mym ferio fogo, com que Nosso Senhor me deu de novo a vida de que ja não fazia cazo, tornei a reviver nos pés, nas mãos, rosto e olhos que tudo estava imovel, com o que pudemos dar fim aquella jornada no fundo de humas serras dentro em huma lapa ao longo de huma ribeira emcaramelada, aonde com o fogo nos regelamos e refizemos aquella noyte e com algumas apas de farinha e farelo mais pretas que todo o mais preto pão que la ha, com humas papas emxabres de cevada.

Chegamos ao nono dia a hum posto em que já o frio era menos e o limite daquelle deserto nos ficavà vizinho quando la pellas 11 do dia o Padre que vinha detras gritou "boa viagem" duas vezes; parej perguntando a cauza de seu alvoroço. Então me tornou: V. R. não ve arvores? E me mostrou 4 grandes cyprestes ao longo de huma ribeira e logo se forão seguindo pelo caminho matos e matos de rozaes e fontes sem numero fresquissimos, até que pelas 4 chegamos a primeira pouvoação do Reino de Carjâ donde huma filha espiritual de hum lamâ que não estava em caza, nos recolheo nella e regalou com hum prato de trigo assado que são es confeitos desta pobre gente e com algum leyte.

Daquy nos partimos a manhã sequinte na volta do Reino de Culû a que este de Carjâ he sogeito por entre serras, mas verdes, bem assombradas e muito pouvoadas de aldeotas, a gente muy bem figurada, mais limpa que a do Tibet ainda que a lej he a mesma, de boa natureza, vestem da mesma laya, as serranas andão coroadas de pedras turquinas toscas, vivem de suas lavouras e gado, he muy lympo de ladrões, salvo os senhores que o são tão finos que se o que levaes lhe contenta, ou de graça, ou pello que querem se ficam com elle.

Nos limites deste Reino de Carjâ tres dias antes de nos meteremos pelo de Culû nos choveo tanta neve que a cada passo perdiamos o caminho porque vinhamos atolando em 2 e 3 palmos della. Trazia en então a barba de meo palmo de comprido que não era toda branca, mas a neve ma branqueou e sepultou de feição que nec campus uby Troja fuit; esta he a cauza porque os do Tibet ârrancão toda pera que se lhe não emcaramele a neve nella com o que se lhe fas huma pedra.

Assy molhados, cheos de neve e bem cortados de frio chegamos aquelle dia ao pê da serra, que mais temiamos, descalços porque a muita neve do caminho nos destrujo os sapatos que levavamos; achamos pera repouzar huma choupana de boes tão esfarrapada por cima, tam rota nas paredes que toda a noite que foj muy ventosa, o vento nos meteo por sima e por ellas grande copia de neve sem teremos com que nos pudecemos reparar e abrigar. Ve V. R. todo o trabalho deste | dia e noyte? Não foi mais que fol. 39.
vesp oras do que nos esperava naquella serra conforme aquillo: Se qua cho-

ve e neva que fara na serra? Não na acometemos ao dia seguinte, porque os serranos nos reprezentarão o perigo de a neve estar muito fresca e que facilmente nos enterraria sem remedio, que nem elles se atrevião.

Ao terceiro dia as 6 da manhã a começamos a sobir impinada quanto se pode imaginar toda cuberta de neve, sem sinal de caminho que os serranos que levavão os cavalos nos hião mostrando; levavamos huns sapatos de cordões de palha (nunqua ninguem diga deste pão não comerey) de que eu zombava nos serranos, mas a verdade he que com elles se escorrega menos pella neve, valem tres bazarucos, [?] durão dia e meo. Fomos achando a neve de 4 e de 6 palmos dalto, as bestas davão nella mil cambadellas, atoladas ordinariamente até a barriga. Eu hia remando com summo trabalho, sem folego muitas vezes, tambem dava minhas quedia e não poucas não tinha sobre que me sentar senão a neve ate os peitos, quantas vezes afocinhej, quantas mety os braços e mãos. Lá pellas onze cheguei ao meo tal que ja não fazia conta de passar avante por não poder; aquy venceram os dezeios âs forças de 52 annos; so me dava pena hir o Padre muito diante com quem me queria reconsiliar, e de quem me queria despedir; nisto chegou hum serrano que se lastimou de me ver quasi enterrado na neve e sem força, animoume que jâ faltava pouco, e meteome na mão o seu bordão, com o que fiz das tripas coração e soby outro pedaço ate que tornei a cahir; então pedy a hum moço que vinha perto que me fosse chamar o Padre e que se algum dos serranos por interesse me quizesse porventura tirar daby, que fizesse nisso o possivel.

O Padre estava ja no cume da serra (que como mais mancebo e que a tinha ja curçado muitas vezes a estranhava menos, comtudo este dia a sentio mais que nunca e passou a mesma fortuna, alem das muitas quedas, queimandocelhe as pontas dos dedos dos pés e das mãos de que nos ficou largo tempo que sentir) pera o qual me restava a terceira parte. Foi Deos servido que os serranos levados do interece decerão a me buscar por preço de alguns rupias, mas como cuidará V. R. que me salvarão? Cada hum me levava as cavaleirâs como minino quando o açoitão na escola 10 ou doze passos atolando comigo ate os peitos e botando a alma, outro me levava os pees por de tras por alyviar e ajudar o que me levava, por não hirem metidos na neve. Aquy, padre meu, me quis Nesso Senhor não acabar, que lhe não merecia eu huma morte tão honrada, mas açoitar como menino; permita sua divina bondade que a vida que aly de novo me deu seja pera melhor o servir.

Assym me puzerão no pino da serra, e quis Nosso Senhor que fazio bom sol e nenhum vento com que pudemos melhor com o rigor do frio. Logo fomos descendo da serra o que restava do dia; ainda nos ficou por acabar de decer o meo dia sequinte. No baixo della erão os cedros infinitos e fermosissimos, na altura peregrinos, na copa grandes, na grossura de 3, 4 e de 6 braças; o ar era ja outro, o lugar em que fizemos manzel muito fresco ao pé de huma fermoza fonte em huma lapa aonde a lenha sobejou, mas não se achou na nessa despença couza que comecemos; os serranos da nossa companhia nos forão bons com seus pedaços de apas.

Aquelle dia me lembrara pera sempre assy pollas mercês que Nosso Senhor nelle me fes, como porque delle me ficarão as mãos estropeadas.

Tinha as en desmentidas de muitas | quedas que dey pellas serras, e como fol. 40. os nervos dellas estavão magoados, o mesmo foj metelas na neve tantas vezes nesta bemdita serra que ficar quasi aleijado dellas; muitas vezes se me adormecem e esquecem com parte do braço de modo que as não sinto, mas aquentandoas tornão; qualquer frio nellas agora mas trata mal.

Daquella serra até a cidade de Magar Sarâ cabeça do Reino de Cullu puzemos 3 dias por aldeas muy frescas que estão nas chapadas. São terras de muyto mantimento e muito barato. Mea jornada antes de chegar a cidade real indo pelo cume de altissimas serras nos hião contando os amaes como em hum tanque grande que nhum fundo mas desabafado vale ao pee dellas fazião as agoas do inverno, estava o seu pagode em huma moita que sobre a face delle se movia, todas as vezes que lhe levavão ofertas, a moita as vinha receber a borda e se tornava logo pera o meo do tanque, senão que vindo nos zombando com elles do que cudavamos ser patranha, vimos o que dizem e que no tanque se movia polla agoa pera qualquer parte sem nelle se ver quem a movia, eu vyo o mesmo, e fiquey tão maravilhado como confuso. O tanque muito limpo e a moita era de huma braça de grandura cuberta de erva verde. Estâ aquella cidade sita na chapada de hum monte muito aprazivel assy por rezão de muitas ribeiras que das serras a vem regando, como pella multidão e fermozura dos cedros que acompanhão [?]. He muito povoada, a casaria boa. Fazem estes huma torre quadrada de pedra de cantaria e nella por todas as 4 faces varandas de fermosas taboas de cedro, algumas de largura de 14 e 15 palmos, com as quaes cobrem tambem os telhados. A gente muito bem afigurada, as crianças lindas no cabelo de ouro, algumas molheres tão alvas como as da terra de V. R. mas não todas, vestem calções e cabaias de pano como os maridos, os maridos, os cabelos soltos pera tras, hum barrete redondo na cabeça, os homens com barretes de duas pontas huma pera diante outra pera tras, mais puderão trazer seguramente. Todos assy serranos como serranas trazem nos barretes algumas rozas ou ervas cheirosas como mangerona.

Estava o Rey no campo; aly me agazalhou hum parente seu, que com palavrinhas doces me roubou do que lhe contentou, muito contra minha voutade, como foj de hum cavalo que me tomou quasi de graça e muito sujamente, o que so foy por aver licença pera me hir. Puzemos 4 dias em chegar ao Reino de Mandj. No caminho atras e neste nos deu não pequeno trabalho a falta de moeda, pera nos proveremos quis Nosso Senhor que traziamos alguns naruhçys que são certas raizes como ararâs secos ou mais pequenos, que vem da parte de Vzangue ao Chaparangue, que servem de mezinha pera febres, toce e feridas. He notavel o modo com que se acham. Cria os a natureza debaixo da terra sem delles aparecer fora della rasto algum; os que sabem o posto vão áquelle campo de noite, e delle em algumas partes vem romper hum rajo de luz, logo naquelle lugar fazem sinal, a outro dia vão e cavando aly, os tirão; são estimados e os serranos que se aproveitão delles nolos tomavão em troca de mantimento.

No Reyno de Mandy tambem de serranos nos não fizerão agravo algum. He o Rajâ tributario ao Mogol; de la de longe lhe metem hum osso de tantos mil rupias na boca a este grão cão pera que o não venha engulir ao seu Reino. Deste Reino que he como os outros nos custumes, frescura, abun-

dancia etc. nos fizemos na volta do Ponente buscando o de Lahor. Todos estes caminhos viemos a pé assi porque as serras dão pouco lugar pera cavalos, como porque em estes dando nestas terras quentes, não prestão mais
fol. 41. pera nada, donde | me nacerão nos pés algumas mataduras que me davão mao trato e me forçaram a tomar hum gemany que he huma paviola levada par 4 homens em que o Padre e eu hiamos alternadamente muito a nosso gosto. Ao terceiro dia ja nas terras do Mogol, nos deu busca hum governador gentio e nos roubou do que lhe contentou. Chamaçe esta villa Mellã que pera mym o foy em parte, em parte fel. Esta vão com o capitão gentio alguns mouros graves; acertou de aparecer na busca entre o fato huma imagem do Senhor crucificado; hum destes conhecendoa me perguntou estando eu com ella na mão, quem hera eu e quem era aquelle? Então a tornej a beijar e por sobre a cabeça, dizendo que aquelle hera Azarat Isâ, o Senhor JESU Deos verdadeiro, e que eu era Isay, christão, Jesuita, adorador e servidor daquelle Senhor; tudo monta aquella palavra. Inchouse o soberbo mouro e apanhou do alfange dizendome: Se não estiverão aquy estes gentios, com esta vos ouvera de cortar esse pescosso. Tornej a por sobre a cabeça a imagem e a dizer: eu sou Isay, vos fazei o que quizerdes. Os gentios o forão aquietando. Parte de minha desgraça foi não saber a lingoa industana pera falar o que tão boa ocazião estava pedindo, então fora pera mym mel quando fora tam bem afortunado que me cahira tão boa sorte, mas não he semelhante mel pera tamanho peccador.

Finalmente passados as serras em que andey sinco mezes sem ver outra couza mais que estas nevadas, chequey a Bayoarâ Reino pequeno do Mogol sogeito a Lahor so quatro dias longe delle, aonde não chequey por não alongar o caminho por 8 dias mais, antes o atalhey e rompy no Reyno de Synande aonde dej no caminho real pera Agrâ que elrrey Jangir de boa memoria fes; real lhe chamo porque verdadeiramente o he, o mais real do mundo e bem differente do que o emperador Vespeziano fes tralos montes de 17 legoas, grande parte delle por huma serra, por onde o caminho vay como se fora por razo campo, e bem differente digo porque não he de 17 mas de 200 legoas por campo tão lhano como a palma da mão, murado de grandes e fermozas arvores por ambas as partes, tão largo que cabem a par por elle 15 e 18 carretas; em cada coyce (3 coices fazem huma legoa) esta huma bem feita piramide pera sinal, em huma pedra de jaspe vermelho em letras parsias a memoria de elrrey Jangir que o fes. Estão as arvores por linha direita tão juntas que sempre podem os passageiros hir a sombra pera o que escolheo elrrey as melhores e muitas frutiferas, como amoreiras etc. pera os passageiros colherem dellas mais que boa sombra; conteias de coice a coice por minha curiosidade e achey quinhentas de cada parte entre padrão e padrão, com o que V. R. como bom aritmetico dará logo no numero dellas. Sam todo o alivio aos caminhantes no tempo das excecivas calmas desta terra. Ha neste caminho ordinario em cada coice hum posso de boas agoas com escadas ate o lume da agoa alem de muitas ribeiras que o atraveção.

Outra couza tem não menos real este caminho, a cada 4 coices hum recolhimento a que chamão saray, feito pera repouse e segurança dos caminhantes, em quadro como huma boa fortaleza de muro forte e bem feito de tijolos, de 4 braças de alto, em cada canto hum fermoso baluarte, logo de canto a canto na mesma parede de muro se vão sequindo por cada lado 36 ou 40 cazas de abobada com seus alpendres da mesma, muito bem feitas, cada qual agazalha duas e tres pessoas em seus catres.

Estando no saray vos vem logo rogar a meteranym, a hospedeira (que ha muitas, pera muitos) com a caza varrida e agoada, catres nella pera dormir, agoa quente pera os pés, fria pera biber, | lenha, fogo, panellas, fol. 42. saĩ e ella pera vos cozinhar, pelo que tudo lhe dais quando vos ides 10 ou 12 reis, com o que vos ficais agazalhado, e ella contente. Pello meo do saray vay huma rua de boticas em que tendes a carne, o peixe, o pão, o arros, a verdura e tudo quanto vos he necessario em preço acomodado; repouzais nelle a noite sem sobroço, porque no principio della se fechão as portas e não se abrem ao romper da manhã sem primeiro se lançar hum pregão, se alguem acha menos alguma couza sua pera se buscar o ladram dentro. Alguns destes saraes fes el Rey Jangir, outros a raynha Nurmal, outros outros Navabos com grande magnificencia e despezas por fazerem grande seu nome; e he muy necessario avellos porque sam os ladrõis muitos. Este caminho fes Elrrey assy porque por elle hia muitas vezes a Lahor, como por aliviar com as commodidades delle ao infinito numero de passageiros que o frequentão perpetuamente.

Depois que party de Sinande cheguey em 8 dias ao Reino do Delŷ aonde o Mogol se coroa e donde se entitula porque nelle reinou muitos annos antes gue decesse mais ao Industam e Decam. He a cidade real grande, os edeficios ordinarios rõis; a fortaleza, passos reaes nella, muitos saraes que tem magnificos, é muito pera se ver, como tambem grandiozas sepulturas. Daquy nos partimos pera a corte de Agrã passando pela cidade de Maturâ que he a penultima jornada aonde hum rajâ gentio vassalo delrrey edificou ao seu Pagode hum templo custosissimo, soberbissimo, e tão grandioso que se pode por entre as maravilhas do mundo e com muita rezam vir ver por tal. Creame V. R. que não pode a pena nem as palavras chegar ao que os olhos vêem nella de architetura, lavores, laçarias, relevos, grandiosidade em geral. Sera no comprimento como o do Bom JESUS de Goa, ou São Roque. Tem sinco muy altas cupulas ou abobadas que fazem o vão de dentro emfiadas e emcadeadas maravilhozamente, lavradas e cozidas em laçarias soberanamente; todo de jaspe vermelho. A primeira cabe na entrada do templo, e he mais baixa, duas mais altas fazem o corpo delle, a quarta o cruzeiro, na ultima, da primeira a quinta, a capella mayor, e mais alta que todas. Dizer agora a perfeição das figuras, a arte dos debuxos, a galantaria dos lavores, a graça dos ramos, a formozura das laçarias, porque não ha palmo de pedra nelle que não esteja lavrada as mil maravilhas tudo de pedra mindissima por dentro e por fora sem aver em tamanha machina hum palmo de madeira, não he possivel não escrevelo a pena nem pintalo a lingoa. Sobre es sinco simborios se levantão pera o ceo sinco piramidas com au mesma perfeição obradas. Em toda esta machina dizem que se despenderão 9 milhões de ouro pera que? Pera o Diabo na figura de hum cafre ser nelle adorado desta cega gentilidade; dizem elles que este he o filho de Deos que veo ao mundo 4 vezes e que ainda hade tornar, a ultima deve de vir na burra manca dos judeos, e que elle

he o que matou os gigantes do mundo na terra e no ynferno, donde quando ja sobia vitoriozo lhe çahio das cavernas infernais huma cobra venenoza pera o tragar, e que matandoa elle, o bafo das cobra peçonhenta o defumara, donde lhe ficarão as cores negras como elle ahy tem, por nome Caná, assentado em hum altar ornamentado de brocado com es pés emcruzados tangendo huma frauta de ouro, assy como o fazem muites cafrinhos. Ahy me disserão que aquella frauta era o instrumento com que elle obrou grandes maravilhas no mundo assy como temos de fee que as fazia e fes o Se-
fol. 43. nhor Jesu nosso verdadeiro Deos so | com sua divina palavra que elles quetem significar com a gaita na boca deste negro cafurrão, tão vizitado aquy como festejado e adorado deste mundo oryental. Ninguem aly entra senão descalço, naquelle cruzeiro se estyrão beijando mil vezes aquelle chão com muitas lagrimas de devação.

Mea legoa antes de entrar na cidade di Agrâ, no caminho demos com [a] afamada sepultura de elrrey Acabar em Scandarâ, grande machina e de grandissimas despezas, setuada em hum jardim em quadro que tera de largura sinco carreiras de cavalo com huma porta em cada lado, de real archytectura por dentro cozidas em relevos de ouro sobre varias cores, por fora de pedraria emtertalhada nas mesmas pedras, como se uza por Italia, obra de grande preço porque as pedras são finas, de varias cores, e muy escolhidas. Fica o corpo de elrrey mouro hum pouco levantado do andar do chão dentro de hum soberbo tumulo de prata lavrada com relevos e rica pedraria, suspensso em cadeas da mesma prata. Tem esta machina tres andares de varandas, ou crastas de pedra jaspe vermelha grandemente obradas, em que as colunas e charolas respondentes são em grande numero, e toda se vay apiramidando proporcionadamente em grande altura mas sempre em quadro. No cume della no vão de dentro que responde ao lugar em que ficão os ossos por baixo, se vê maravilhosamente emcaixada huma pedra de finissimo porfido de varias cores da grandura do tumuio que custou mais de 14 mil rupias. Emfim a machina he soberana e de muitos milhões. Aquy o adorão como se fora grande sancto prostrados por terra beijando o pavimento emquanto no ynferno o triste e dezaventurado rej paga com eternas penas gostos temporaes e terrenas honras.

Por fim cheguey a cidade de Agrâ aos 3 de Janeiro de 632 depois de onze mezes menos 12 dias que gastej nesta perigrinação e trabalhos da qual so tocc nesta a V. R. muito por alto porque nem a modestia religiosa permita outra couza, nem a memoria pode chegar aonde elles; porque relatar a V. R. os rijscos da vida a sobir e decer por impinadas e desesperadas serras, o passar de furiosos rios, hora a vao com a agoa frigidissima pellos peitos, hora por pontes de cordas perigosissimas, as topadas, as quedas por estreitissimos caminhos de hum sô palmo as vezes de largo, pelo recosto das serras, o sobir de gatinhas edecer escorregando de costas, o dormir por vezes não digo so no chão todc anno, mas despido algumas por ter o fatinho ensopado em agoa da chuva, sem ter farrapo com que me abrigace, nem herva, ou palha que com sua brandura me fosse boa; as calmas de 3 verões, os frios de 3 invernos que tomey em diversos climas e regiões, as fomes não tendo pera matalas humas vezes mais que humas papas de se-

vada mal cozidas, e sem sal por não aver pera as cozinhar mais lenha que o esterco de cavalos, que muitas vezes faltava, outras hum pedaço de apa preta mais de farelo que de farinha, e outras em que até este mimo nos faltou; a sede de jornada inteira sem mais remedio que algum pilouro de chumbo na boca, ou pedaço de caramelo; cheo de infinitos piolhos de extraordinaria grandeza, os quaes com os mataremos ao meo dia, quando a quentura do sol nos dava lugar, ja a noite tinhamos tal novidade, que muitas as não dormiamos inteiras com a crueldade desta praga; os sobresaltos de ladrões em tão novos e perigosos caminhos, o andar em trajos de mouro com toucas e cabaias quasi todo este anno, com o alfange de huma parte na cinta e da outra o coldre com o arco no hombro e pistolete ou espingarda, o que tudo hera necessario alem de outras muitas rezões por amor daquelles; as perrarias dos alcavalistas; | a semrazão dos servidores e fol. 44.
amaes que no mato nos deixavão muitas vezes, sem guia desemparados, a deshumanidade de nos não quererem algumas vezes dar agoa pera beber por lhe não contaminaremos seus vazos, nem emprestar huma panella pera cozer o nosso arros, por nos terem por casta baixa, sendoo elles de baixissimas, por averem e dizerem que só nos o heramos por comer vaca; emfin e tantos outros trabalhos e molestias que referilos a V. R. fora grandemente canssalo. Permita nosso Senhor que os tomace eu com algum proveito spiritual de minha alma, e algum delles lhe foce agradavel.

Isto he, Padre meu amantissimo, o que se offereceo escrever a V. R. desta minha perigrinação, não porque com os descontos della entenda que lhe meto pavor, antes o faço porque sej o animo de V. R., seu fervor e Religião e que ouvidos lhe servião de lenha com que se acenda mais o fogo de sua charidade em seu coração, e o dezejo que tem da salvação das Almas etc.

O PADRE FRANCISCO DE AZEVEDO

APPENDIX II

RELAÇÃO QUE MANDOU O Pe ESTEVÃO CACELLA DA COMP.ª DE JESU AO P.e ALBERTO LAERCIO PROVINCIAL DA PROVINCIA DO MALAVAR DA INDIA ORIENTAL, DA SUA VIAGEM PERA O CATAYO, ATÉ CHEGAR AO REINO DO POTENTE.

fol. 1. Nas cartas do anno passado escrevi a V. R. todos os sucessos da nossa jornada até chegarmos a Biar cidade principal do Reino do Cocho; mas por não saber atégora se aquellas chegarão a V. R. referirey nesta toda nossa peregrinação até este Reino de Cambirasi, que por esta parte he o primeiro deste Potente, abreviando o que toca até Biar por não me pôr a risco de causar a V. R. com repeti-lo, dando mais copiosa relação do restante do caminho.

Saimos do Golim aos 2 de Agosto de 1626; chegamos a Dacà aos 12 do mesmo mez; daqui partimos em 5 de Setembro, e aos 26 do mesmo passamos par Azó e chegamos a Pandó onde estivemos com o Raja Satargit alguns dias, e vindo a Azó nos partimos aos 8 de Outubro p.ª Biar onde entramos aos 21 do mesmo; aqui foi necessario esperar quatro mezes p.ª poder passar as serras, e aos 2 de Fevereiro de 1627 nos fomos p.ª Runate, ultima terra do Cocho, e aos 21 do mesmo mez entramos pollos Reinos do Potente, e começando a sobir as serras aos 23, depois de desoito jornadas, que por ellas fizemos, aos 10 de Abril chegamos a ver nos com Droma Raja Rei e Lambà maior deste Reino, e tido pollo maior letrado, e mais authorisado de todos os mais Lambás maiores, que são seis em todos estes Reinos do Potente.

Partimos do Golim o P.e João Cabral, o Irmão Fonteboa, e eu já vestidos de soldados portugueses por ser assim necessario ao segredo com que nos convinha sair de Dacà p.ª não ser impedidos dos mouros que a governavão em auzencia do Nababo, que então estava em Rajamol; e por rezão de conhecimento que o P.e Simão de Figueiredo já tinha com elles, e da benevolencia e respeito com que sempre tratarão ao P.e veyo comnosco, porto que bem doente p.ª ajudarnos na saida daquelle cidade; na qual logo que chegamos nos prenderão a embarcação e dous mossos que nella estavão com todos os marinheiros; a causa foi, porque no mesmo tempo chegou outro barco de Portuguezes em que vinhão alguns soldados que o anno dantes acompanharão o Mogol no saco de Dacà; foi hum em desembarcando conhecido, e preso, e com elle as embarcaçois que tinhão chegado com a

gente que nelles estava, avendo que era gente do Mogor mandada a espiar a terra; passados doze dias soltarão os mossos e a embarcação, a qual mandei logo a Siripur p.ª trazer o P.e João Cabral que la ficara com o Irmão Bertolameu Fonteboa, vindo eu so com o P.e Simão de Figueiredo p.ª nossa chegada ser menos sentida. Ao Irmão escrevi as difficuldades, que tomadas as informaçois da Viagem nos representavão, dizendo não ser possivel irẽmos todos, e assim com grande magua minha pollo deixar, lhe ordenei tornasse p.ª o Golim e que na primeira occasião que ouvesse, sendo possivel lhe mandaria ordem, e modo com que viesse; o que parece ordenou Deos nosso Senhor p.ª do Collegio do Golim, e não nas incommodidades do caminho levar o Irmão a gozar na gloria o premio dos bons dezejos que tinha de fazer esta viagem, avendo se por bem servido delles. O P.e João Cabral não pôde vir logo de Siripur, por lhe impedir a vinda o mouro capitão mor da armada do Mogor, e prendendo-lhe a embarcação; e em oito dias mais que la o detiverão socedeo em Dacà o sucesso de Jorge de Souza, que logo direi, com que os Portuguezes ficarão tão amedrontados que os que alli estivãro de fora se forão com toda a pressa p.ª o Golim, e os moradores da terra se derão por perdidos, procurando os que se forão persuadir ao P.e fizesse o mesmo, e os que ficavão se consolávão muito com sua companhia, edificando-se huns, e outros grandemente do spirito com que o padre [*fol.* 2] por não arriscar sua missão não tratou sair-se do perigo, fol. 2.
quando o fazião tantos, que tinhão por temeridade ficar nelle; pôde comtudo o P.e com ajuda e companhia dalguns portuguezes sair de Siripur sem o saber o Mouro, — e chegou a Dacà quando já a tempestade era passada, mas muĩ prezente ainda o medo que causara nos christãos que nella vivem. Socedeo a cousa nesta forma.

Hum Portuguez bem velho, que envelhecera em Dacà pretendeo matar outro soldado, e não o fazendo seus mossos com espingardadas que lhe tirarão, veyo elle com outros m.tos a buscalo sem o poder deter ninguem fazendo alguns muito por isso; levavão a morte que poucos mezes antes dera a outro christão, e o castigo de seus peccados. Concorrerão da parte contraria tambem m.tos e em chegando a vista huns dos outros, o velho que foi o primeiro que apareceo, foi o primeiro que logo cahio morto com a primeira espingardada que se tirou sem poder confessar-se, como tambem o não pode fazer o que ella dantes matara, p.ª confirmação do que em Bengala se tem observado, que quem sem confissão mata, sem confissão o matão, do que trazem muitos exemplos. De huma e outra parte tudo erão soldados christãos e como capitão de todas acodio Jorge de Souza desarmado a apartalos; com esta voz de sua vinda fugirão os christãos de huma e outra parte e apareceo huma companhia grande de Resputos soldados gentios, feros e barbaros, cuyo capitão era hum parente muy chegado do seu Raja; derão todos sobre Jorge de Souza, em cuja defensa com huma espingardada derrubarão do cavalo o capitão dos Resputos; caido este, se detiverão os mais, e deixando a Jorge de Souza sem ferida se forão todos a queimarlhe e roubarlhe as casas, como em effeito fizerão; que por serem casas grandes e estendidas ardendo com outras muitas que lhe ficavão junto com seu incendio, furia, grita, forças, roubos dos Resputos naõ acudindo a nada por muito tempo justiça algua, se fez o dia muy medonho: vendose ser tudo traça, e ordem que cadahum a seu modo imaginava; foraõ muitos os feridos, de doze mortos se soube; e muitas mais serião se depois de alguas horas não accudira o Catual, que é a justiça da cidade, que posto que não trazia poder de gente p.ª castigar e prender tanta multidão de soldados; com tudo a enfreou com sua prezença.

Pera todos foi de grande espanto ver como em hum tão evidente perigo saira Jorge de Souza, não só com vida, mas sem ferida algua attribuindo a particular providência de Deos nosso Senhor, que parece lhe quis mostrar ser lhe acerto algum serviço que naquelle dia lhe fizera, como na verdade lhe tinha feito, avendo do governador de Dacà o formão comque aviamos de fazer nossa viagem p.ª o Cocho, o qual me mandou huma hora antes da briga, querendo Deos nosso Senhor, que só me mandasse este, e guardasse outro que p.ª nos juntamente tirara, do qual em effeito naõ tivemos necessidade e se perdeo no incendio das casas; p.ª que tivessemos por partar merce sua a providencia com que lhe tirou das maõs o que nos era precisamente necessario, nem se podera na mesma forma tirar outro, se este se perdera, porque o estado em que ficou Jorge de Souza não era para pedir formão de mandar cortar madeira e fazer muitas embarcaçóis no Cocho que era o teor do formão passado, e demandava gasto de muitas mil tangas, ficando elle depois deste suceso, sem huma. Alem desta merce do Senhor experimentamos aqui outras muy especiaes de sua divina mão. No meio da mor furia dos Resputos, que não perdoavão a christão algum que encontrassem, que não ferissem ou matassem, pondo fogo a todas as casas de soldados que estavão naquelle bairro, morando nos e estando actualmente em huas da quelle paragem, onde dantes morava hum soldado, que por nosso respeito se saira dellas alli nos deffendeo o Senhor sem nos chegar o fogo, nem saberem de nos os soldados gentios, estando nos ouvindo sua grita e as lastimas e prantos da gente nos incendios, e roubos que padecião. E p.ª o Senhor nos mostrar mais esta merce sua quis, que grando aqui chegamos, tendo nos primeiro aparelhado outras casas em que morassemos sem nos avermos nem sabermos dellas nos aparelharão aquellas em que estivemos, não querendo morassemos nas outras, as quaes forão as primeiras em que os Resputos derão e pegarão fogo; onde com muita diffi-
fol. 3. culdade escapou hum mercador portuguez vestindo [*fol.* 3] se de cabaya, e touca e pagando muy bem a hum mouro vesinho que o livrou. As causas e principios deste suceso são assaz sabidos, o que toca a culpa dos males que aqui se executarão, deixo por excusar até os que tão publicamente são culpados.

Com aquella traça de mandar cortar madeira e fazer embarcaçóis ao Cocho viemos acompanhados da gente que Jorge de Souza tambem p.ª esse effeito mandou; e nos servio muito p.ª poder passar os Choquis, que saõ como alfandegas onde se vê o fato, e se paga delle hum tanto, e são secenta, e tantos nestes rios até Azò, indo sempre por gangas mui frescas e aprasieis de muito boa agua, e com as muitas povoaçais que lhe ficão junto abundantes de tudo. He Azó a cidade principal e cabeça dos Reinos de Cocho, terras grande, muy populosa e rica; onde residia Liquinarane Rei do Cocho que hora he morto; e onde esta o Nababo de Mogor a quem estas terras pagão tributo. Passamos a vista desta cidade e chegamos a Pandó, onde tem seu assento Satargit Raja de Busna gentio, capitão geral do Mogor contra os Assanes; he Pando terra não muito grande mas muy frequentada; e de não se alargar muito polla terra dentro, mas estar estendida na praya deste fermoso Rio do Cocho, he a causa a guerra que tem de continuo com os Assanes que confinão com Pando terra ultima do Reino par aquella parte. Recebeo nos o Rei Satargit com grande benevolencia fazendo nos muitas honras entre grande multidão de gente sua muy grave, e capitaĩs mogores que o acompanhão, e lhe saõ necessarios p.ª trecentas coças que tem de guerra. Intendendo de nos e das cartas que lhe trouxemos, que a causa de nossa vinda era passar ao Catayo, tomadas as informaçois se naõ achou alli quem tivesse noticia daquelle reino mais que hum mouro pessoa grave que nos disse ficar alem de huma cidade que se chama Coscar por onde se vai a elle, e que do Cocho não sabia caminho para lá, mas que passadas as serras do Potente o achariamos. E tratando o por onde entrariamos no Potente quis o Rei Satargit que p.ª isto fossemos ver-nos com Liquinarane Rei do Cocho a Azo que como Rei da terra sabia mais della, e tinha muito conhecimento daquella gentẽ, que por varias portas dece a seus Reinos. Naõ quis o Raja que fossemos sós, elle em pessoa se abalou e foi sò a aprezentarnos a Liquinarane, e dally nos aviar p.ª nossa viagem; aparelharão se algũas coças muy fermosas em que viemos a Azó; e ao dia seguinte fomos com elle visitar o Rei. Naõ he de estimar pouco a benevolencia desta Rei de Busna, as honras com que nos tratou, e o cuidado que pos no nosso negocio, porque não se ha de imaginar o estado destes Reis, fausto e aparato conforme o que se vê em alguns da India; he isto muy differente, tratão se estes Reis muy bem e tem estado Real, que não consiste em multidão de gente nua, mas muy bem trajada e grave, assi de pé como de cavalo: em particular este Rei Satargit por seu saber, e condicão he em todo este Reino, com ser nelle estranho, muy estimado como vimos em Azo onde pollas ruas o aclamão como se fora Rei proprio, ao que ajuda muito a liberalidade com que de suas rendas reparte com muytos, que posto não passem de duzentas mil tangas cada anno com tudo lhe luzem muito.

Pera fallarmos ao Rei Liquinarane passamos tres grandes pateos, que em roda tinhão largas varandas cheas de gente, que em toda a parte pareceria muy luzida; de huns p.ª outros se passava por grandes portas, e muy fortes, que sempre estão fechadas com porteiros e muita gente de guarda; nos dous ultimos era grande a multidaõ de soldadesca que servia de guarda do Rei, e sempre alli assiste com muita ordem divididos em estancias conforme as armas de cada hum, sempre tão a ponto e tam bem providos como se estiverão em campo de guerra. Sequia se logo hum grande e fermoso jardim, no meio delle estava huma casa de prazer bem ornada onde nos esperava o Rei. Recebeo nos com muita benevolencia, e depois de varias praticas acerca do Reino de Portugal, e de outras partes, tratando de nosso negocio lhe pareceo fossemos a Biar onde governava seu filho Gaburrasa, e que dalli por Runate ultima terras sua passariamos ao Potente; offerecendo nos cartas suas para seu filho em tudo nos ajudar; despedimo nos delle e mandando nos as cartas nos mandou com liberalidade [*fol. 4*] prover fol. 4.
de dinheiro p.ª o caminho; o que fez ainda mais liberalmente o Rei Satargit alem de nove peças de ceda que nos mandou com grandes desculpas do

estado em que estava incapar de poder mostrar doutro modo o amor que nos tinha, e mandando hum parente seu muy chegado que nos acompanhasse a quem p.ª isso deu huma coça, dando nos a nos outra, e mandando outro bramenene de sua casa com carta sua p.ª o Principe Gaburrasa, se foi p.ª Pando e nos nos partimos p.ª Biar.

Esta a cidade de Biar situada junto a ganga fazendo por espaço de alguas leguas huma aprazivel vista, e pollos campos em que está assentada se estende do modo que assi ao largo como ao comprido tem distancia de leguas; e a não ser nos edificios humilde como as dos mais Reinos de Bengala, fora muito para ver; tem muita gente, e he de tudo muy provida, assi do que tem o Reino, como do que lhe vem de Patana, Rajamol e Gouru de cujos mercadores he frequentada: os bazares saõ muitos onde se acha tudo o que estas terras de si dão, en particular he Biar sinalada nas fruitas de espinho que tem com notavel ventagem as que tenho visto na India; e principalmente nas laranjas de toda a sorte. Não estava ao prezente o Principe em Biar, porque poucos mezes antes desgostando das inundaçoĩs que o Rio na cidade fazia, fez seu assento mais polla terra dentro junto a hum esteiro muy fresco do mesmo Rio; lugar que dantes se chamava Colambarim: e derão se os mercadores de Biar tanta pressa em dar gosto ao Principe e fundar a nova cidade, que ja quando alli chegamos estava muy fermosa na ordem e grandeza das ruas com ventagem a Biar. Em Colambarim fomos bem recebidos e agasalhados por mandado do Principe, e tratando com elle de nossa vinda cujo intento soube pollas cartas dos Reis, seu pai e Satargit, se offereceo a nos favorecer emtudo; e logo com gente sua parti p.ª Runate onde achei sete ou oito pessoas destes Reinos, com cuja vista o gosto que recebi correspondia bem ao dezejo que tinha de ve los tão largo e dilitado. E tomando delles as informaçoĩs que puderão dar me, dizendo me não ser possivel passarmos naquelle tempo as serras, a respeito das muitas neves, ventos e chuvas de que dizião cousas notaveis, por mais que fiz, e instei por todas as vias p.ª intentar logo a passagem me não foi possivel, e assi fomos obrigados a esperar naquelle Reino do Cocho mais quatro mezes.

Com este occasião, e necessidade de detença tratei logo de escrever ao Irmão Bertolameu Fonteboa, p.ª que viesse buscarnos e continuarmos todos nossa missão, pois a gente do Potente nos facilitava o restante do caminho: a este fim, e tambem p.ª dar relação a V. R. de como estavamos já naquelle Reino mandamos ao Golim o lingua que traziamos, por ser homem experimentado em caminhos, e que traria muito bem o Irmão, mas posto que as cartas o acharão vivo, foi o Senhor servido de dahi a poucos mezes lhe premiar o fervor com que intentou esta missão, quando já a idade, e compreição parece o podião retrahir della: tinha o Irmão Fonteboa zelo e spirito fervoroso de se aproveitar a si nas virtudes, e a outros com seu trabalho; mas quando elle tratava de causar e trabalhar pollo Senhor, quis elle dar lhe o eterno descanso. Nos como aviamos de esperar quatro mezes naquelle reino, ordenou o mesmo Senhor com paternal providencia os passassemos em tal exercicio, que nos ajudasse a tomar forças espirituaes p.ª o que nos restava de viagem: e assim adoeci eu logo, e dahi a tres dias o P.ᵉ João Cabral ambos de cozois e juntamente hum moço a

quem a doença em começando deu muy gravemente, ficando nos so outro que não sabia a lingua, e era p.ª pouco, e que dahi a poucos dias tambem cahio doente mortalmente; de mim não fiou o Senhor doença larga, em breve sarei e convaleci, ao P.e João Cabral foi a doença sopeando tanto por mais que elle se animava, que o chegou a estrema fraquesa, e o teve por muitos dias em grande perigo da vida; no mesmo tempo estavão os dous mossos que so tinhamos tambem a morte, ja sem faila e sem juizo esperando lhe sua hora; deste modo estavamos sos todos quatro em huma casinha em os mezes de Novembro e Dezembro que a força das doenças durou, recebendo de continuo muy particulares merces de nosso Senhor, que bem mostravão ter nos elle alli por sua conta [*fol. 5*] e que elle era o que nos go- fol. 5.
vernava e regia; pois no meio daquelle estado em que aos olhos humanos pareceria faltar tudo, nada nos faltou; sem medicos; sem mezinhas, sem serviço necessario, sem muitas commodidades, que as doenças precisamente requerem, como se todas ouvesse, e nada faltasse, deu o Senhor saude a todos.

Chegando se já o tempo em que aviamos de continuar o caminho ficando o P.e ainda doente me fui despedir do Principe Gaburrasa, e aver delle suas chapas p.ª o capitão de Runate, e gente do Potente as quaes logo mandou passar e dar nos com elles em sinal de benevolencia hum cavalo, mostrando compadecerse de nos entregar aos de Potente, pollo grande medo que os cochos tem daquella gente, vendo a liberdade com que se hão em Runate sem temer a ninguem; mas facilitando lhe tudo com o gosto que tinhamos na empresa me despedi delle. Esperamos todo Janeiro em Biar para alli nos achar o Irmão de cuja morte não sabiamos, e o lingua que fora buscalo do qual tinhamos precisa necessidade, porque os dous mossos inda andavão doentes, e hum delles avia de ir p.ª o Golim: porem vendo que nao vinha aos 2 de Fevereiro, dia da Purificação de nossa Senhora nos partimos p.ª Runate, p.ª alli esperarmos mais alguns dias e tratar do necessario p.ª o caminho, e resoluto em o começar aos 20 de Fevereiro; aos 19 do mesmo a tarde nos entrou pella porta o lingua que vinha da Golim e nos pareceo hum Anjo vindo do ceo, que parece quis o Senhor trazelo naquelle dia ultimo de nossa estada no Cocho p.ª que mais claramente experimentassemos ter elle de nossa jornada muy particular cuidado, ordenando o mesmo Senhor que este homem se adiantasse e deixasse na companhia em que vinha alguas cousas que nos trazia, porque se assi não fora já nos não acharia em Runate, nem era possivel seguirnos; com esta occasião foi necessario esperar mais o dia sequinte e assi partimos e entramos nas terras destes Reinos aos 21 de Fevereiro, que foi o primo domingo da coresma, recebendo particular consolação com a jornada que a igreja naquelle dia reprezenta do Senhor para o deserto, com cuja companhia não duvidamos aver de vencer os encontros do enemigo que em semelhantes viagens são certos.

Aos 26 de Fevereiro depois de quatro jornadas destas serras chegamos a prima aldea destes Reinos e querendo passar adiante o não pudemos fazer logo, porque o homem com quem nos tinhamos concertado p.ª vir com nosco, que he pessoa principal entre esta gente se ficou em Runate p.ª seus negocios e nos deu gente sua com que viemos, dando lhe ordem que

nos detivessem nesta aldea até elle vir que seria dahi a seis mezes, nem nos dessem aviamento p.ª poder passar avante. Assi o fizerão de modo que por mais dilligencias que fizemos não avia romper os impedimentos, que nos puserão; até que passados ja doze dias nesta aldea me resolvi a acometer o caminho, eu com hum mosso christão, e dous gentios do Cocho, que sabião alguma cousa desta lingua, deixando aqui o P.e João Cabral p.ª chegando a outra aldea lhe mandar gente com que podesse continuar o caminho; não se pode dizer facilmente a força que a gente de toda esta aldea nos fez, pª. que não partisse della, reprezentando nos se o fizesse, como então o fazia sem guarda, roubos, cativeiros, mortes, e outras cousas com tanta efficacia que era espanto: porem parecendo nos ser tudo traça do enemigo p.ª nos empedir o caminho, não dando por nada me pus a elle, no qual encontrei algumas pessoas que vinhão p.ª Runate, estas me puserão as mesmas difficuldades, acrecentando que tornasse p.ª a aldea, e elles deixando de ir adiante nos levarião ao Rei; mas como já tinha visto que na aldea donde sahira nada se fazia mais que o que queria a gente que nos detinha, por aquelle homem, por cuja ordem vinhamos, ser capitão della, não voltei então, mas escrevi ao P.e João Cabral fizesse tudo o possivel por vir com elles. Econtinuando o caminho me vierão demandar dous soldados destes Reinos dizendo me que hião p.ª a mesma terra p.ª onde eu caminhava, com os quaes monstrando fiar me delles me. concertei para me acompanharem, e guiarem; porem ao segunda dia se concertarão com os dous gen-
fol. 6. tios pª. roubar nos, e derão logo tantos sinaes deste conselho [*fol. 6*] que não pode encobrirse, e o menos era o roubo mas delle provavelmente se sequirião outros impedimentos p.ª a viagem, e como ao passar de huma ribeira deixando me ja um pouco atras tornassem aos mossos essa pobreza nossa que levavão repartindo lhe de suas armas comtinuarão todas quatro o caminho com tanta pressa que mostravão dar se lhes pouco de ja os entender. Eu vendo me sem os mossos que me servião de lingua no meio de serras frequentadas de ladroĩs sem ter quem me guiasse avante, julguei por necessario voltar p.ª a aldea, e buscar outro remedio de poder continuar o caminho, e porque nesta volta avia os mesmos riscos, a fizemos aquella noite seguinte o mosso christão e eu caminhando toda ella acompanhando nos muy bem o frio, e vento passado pela neve, que neste mez de Março aqui não falta e assi polla escuridade da noite, como pollos caminhos destas subidas, e decidas serem muy estreitos, e de serras muy alcantiladas era necessario andar boa parte da noite com pes e mãos juntamente p.ª o que me ajudava muito terem me deixado os companheiros desembarçado so com o meu breviario e bordão. Assi cheguei a aldea ao dia seguinte, onde achei o P.e João Cabral concertando se com os que primeiro encontrei, e foi o Senhor servido mover a gente que nos detinha p.ª que nos não impedisse, antes nos ajudasse a negociar nos p.ª ir adiante, e assi continuamos o caminho todos aos 16 de Março.

Partidos desta aldea a cabo de seis jornadas sempre por serras, chegamos a outra maior que se chama Rintam, onde achamos a prima casa deste Rei com gente sua, que nos agasalhou, no mesmo dia chegou alli hum homem parente do que nos negociou a vinda em Runate, e nos disse como vinha p.ª nos levar avante até Pargão cidade principal deste Reino, e dalli tam-

bem passariamos com elle até o Rei; nos que grandemente dezejavamos escusar detenças o recebemos e ouvimos com muito gosto e ao outro dia nos partimos com elle, e chegamos a Pargão depois de quatro jornadas. Começa esta cidade em hum campo muy fermoso, largo, e aprasivel entre serras que de huma e outra parte o vão acompanhando, ellas em si alegres a vista, e muy accommodadas as searas de trigo, e arroz de que então estavão cubertas; reparte se o campo com duas grandes ribeiras que o fazem muito p.ª ver, principalmente com a frescura que tem de grandes sinceiros, e muitas levadas de aguas que das ribeiras sahem; com o campo começão os edificios das casas muy grandes, e altas, que comummente saõ de tres, quatro, cinco sobrados, de paredes muy grossas, com janelhas e varandas que as fermoseão; naõ estão estes edificios em forma que fação ruas, ficão divididas hums dos outros em todo o campo, e pollos pes das serras em forma que fazem huma cidade, mas tão comprida que so o que andarmos e vimos della serão tres leguas, ficando nos inda o mais por ver; porque o campo vai continuando na forma que tenho referido até dar em huma serra que o parte pollo meio com qual vem as duas ribeiras de huma e outra parte que regão o campo, e nesta serra faz a cidade dous grandes braços que pollos lados della vão pollas ribeiras acima grande espaço. A gente parece innumeravel, e lançada a conta a menos que alli vivera hão de ser mais de quinhentas mil almas; ao que ajuda muito o modo que commummente tem de morar naquellas casas, porque em cada hua dellas ha muitos moradores divididos pollos sobrados e repartimentos que p.ª isso fazem; aos 25 de Março entramos neste cidade, dia em que o Eterno Verbo vestido de nossa humanidade entrou neste mundo, e de sua infinita bondade esperamos que a entrada em tal dia naquella terra seja p.ª todo aquelle povo o reconhecer por seu Salvador. Não pudemos logo chegar a casa do companheiro que nos guiava, e quando ao dia seguinte entramos nella achamos ter nos aquella manhãa roubado tudo quanto traziamos p.ª nosso sustentação; meteo nos em huma casa sua tão escura, que ao meio dia nos não viamos, e mais parecia carcere que outra cousa. Logo lhe pedimos nos quisesse buscar o que nos faltava, pois p.ª nos trazer com segurança vinha por nosso guarda; mas elle muy seguro, e sobre si nos respondia, que descansaria, e depois faria a dilligencia mostrando em tudo o pouco que se lhe dava de nos ser tão infiel depois de nos fiarmos delle, e assi se enfadava notavelmente de lhe fallarmos na [*fol.* 7] materia dizendo que aquelle negocio não era de hum dia, fol. 7.
mas que avia de durar mezes, e que vindo de Runate o homem que la nos negociara, elle faria o que lhe parecesse. Vista a danada resolução deste homem, e outros sinaes que dava de coração inficionado com ruins traças, de que o Senhor nos livrou, e depois soubemos, nos resolvemos a sahir de sua casa, p.ª o que avia grandes difficuldades, mas passados dous dias vendo que elle faltava muito tempo em casa, nos saimos della, ao que acudindo logo os parentes nos detiverão e lhe levarão recado do que passava; era notavel a paixão com que este homem veyo a nos impedir, e querer outra vez a força meter em casa; valendo se das armas e de tudo o que pode contra nos; mas foi Deos nosso Senhor servido que com a paciencia o vencemos resistindo so com esta, a paixão e colera de que vinha arrebatado. E como neste tempo acodio muita gente que vio a sem rezão que aquelle ho-

mem nos fazia, e se compadecia de nos procurando aquietalo e recolhelo em casa, nos desembaraçamos delle; e recolhendonos aquella noite em casa de hum bom velho que por amor de Deos nosso Senhor nos fez gasalhado, ao outro dia hum Lamba authorisado quem o P.^{e} João Cabral primo tinha fallado, nos mandou cavalos e gente sua que nos levasse a sua casa, que ficava muito longe desta paragem; mas chegando nos a elle o achamos mudado a respeito de temer brigar com o homem que nos roubara, se em casa nos recolhesse: porem foi nosso Senhor servido que se animasse a não reparar naquelle inconveniente, posto que depois de estarmos em sua casa por respeito do mesmo homem nos impedia ir avante em tal forma que querendo outro Lamba levar nos, a gente deste com armas lhe defendeo o não fizesse. Vendo nos assi, e com outras muitas circumstancias de difficuldades e impedimentos, que deixo de apontar em terra onde não ha quem acuda a nada sendo cada hum destes homens em sua casa senhor absoluto sem aver fora della quem lhe peça rezão do que fizerem, encontramos o Lamba principal que aqui tem o Rei, o qual sabendo dos impedimentos que tinhamos p.^{a} chegar ao Rei, nos disse que por sua via iriamos por ser elle o que alli estava p.^{a} negocios do Rei, e que logo nos passassemos p.^{a} sua casa; assi o fizemos com beneplacito do Lamba com quem estavamos agasalhados, antes elle mesmo nos levou, e acompanhou até o Rei; mas nem aqui deixou o inimigo suas custumadas dilligencias p.^{a} impedirnos, de modo que tratando com o Lamba principal de querermos passar avante, nos quis persuadir não fossemos mas esperassemos alli o Rei, que dizia viria dalli a hum mez (o que era tão falso que são hoje passados seis sem ir la). Vendo nos esta mudança nacida tambem do homem que nos roubara; nos despedimos do Lamba, e começamos a caminhar sos determinados levar avante o caminho confiando em nosso Senhor nos guiaria e guardaria, pois tendo feito as dilligencias possiveis não viamos outro meio p.^{a} passarmos adiante. O Lamba vendo nossa resoluãço foi obrigado a nos pedir esperassemos mais alguas horas p.^{a} nos aviar e fazer suas chapas e iremos por sua via ao Rei, que se la nos visse sem irmos como convinha, ou se no caminho nos sucedesse algua cousa o castigaria gravemente. Com isto esperamos aquelle dia, elle nos deu gente e cavalos p.^{a} o restante do caminho, e em companhia do primeiro Lamba partimos de Pargão na 2ª oitava de Paschoa a cinco de Abril.

A cabo de tres jornadas achamos em huma aldea hum Lamba parente do Rei, que de sua parte nos vinha buscar com gente e cavalos, e nos acompanhou: este escreveo logo ao Rei como hiamos chegando, o qual mandou outros Lambas que em outra paragem nos esperassem com dous cavalos p.^{a} nos muy bem ornados; e caminhando assy com toda esta companhia hum bom espaço antes de chegarmos mando outra gente sua convidando nos com o seu cha, de que elle e os seus usão muito, e continuando depois o caminho que era per serras bem altas indo ja perto do lugar onde estava mandou outros Lambas mancebos em seus cavalos que nos festijassem com muitas carreiras que derão em huma paragem onde a serra lho soffria, e logo descobrimos por entre as arvores grande multidão de gente, que nos esperava e soarão as charamellas e trombetas, que com isto tem algua
fol. 8. [*fol. 8*] semelhança os instrumentos de que usao em suas festas. Aqui

estavão cem Lambas todos de pouca idade de doze té vinte annos, que postos em ordem em duas fileiras nos vinhaõ receber, no meyo tres Lambas pequenos com cheiro que levavão em seus toribulos, que he honra unica do Rei. Assi nos levarão ao lugar que nos tinhão aparelhado, que era huma tenda muy bem feita forrada de ceda da China com seu dacel e lugar onde descansassemos; e mandando nos dahi a pouco o Rei recado que podiamos ir o achamos em outra tenda bem ornada de ceda, elle assentado em hum lugar alto vestido de ceda vermelha broslada de ouro; a mão dereita, e muy junto a elle estava em outro lugar correspondente huma imagem de seu pai com huma alampada aceza, que alli sempre ardia; aqui ficavão dous lugares altos p.ª nos, não tendo alli nenhum Lamba, por grave que fosse, lugar senão nos esteirois que pollo chão estavão. Recebeo nos com demonstração de muita benevolencia significandoa na alegria que mostrava de nos ver, e saber de nos donde vinhamos, donde eramos, de que Reino e nação com as mais perguntas ordinarias nas primeiras vistas: puderamos dizer lhe que eramos portuguezes, porque a estas serras, como nunca vem gente estranha, nem se lembrão de terem visto, ou ouvido ter por aqui passado semelhante gente, assi não chegou a elles o nome de Franguis que em todo o Oriente tem os portuguezes.

Naõ foi para nos pequena desconsolação acharmo nos aqui quasi sem lingua, porque trazendo nos quem sabio muito bem o indostan, parseo e cocho, comtudo so achamos aqui hum Lamba de Chaparangue muy querido do Rei, que entendia algua cousa, mas muy pouco, do indostan; por este fallavamos como podiamos com assaz trabalho e pena nossa e do Rei que dezejava muito nos pudessemos declarar bem p.ª as largas praticas que cada dia com nosco tinha; mas sabendo de nos como vinhamos aqui mandados p.ª lhe pregar a fé de Christo nosso Senhor por teremos sabido que antigamente a tiverão e depois com a mudança dos tempos, e falta de mestres foi esquecendo, tendo ainda della alguas cousas, mostrou estimar nossa vinda, e disse que aprendessemos bem a lingua p.ª nos lhe podermos fallar, e que não poderia deixar de aceitar o que lhe ensinassemos, pois deirão ser causas muito boas, pollas quaes vinhamos de tão longe a buscalo e assi mandou logo aquelle Lamba de Chaparangue continuasse cada dia, em ensinar nos e elle p.ª isso o desocupou muito.

He este Rei, que se chama Droma Raja, de idade de 33 annos, el Rei e juntamente Lamba-maior deste Reino de Cambirasi primeiro dos do Potente por esta parte, que le muy grande e povoado; preza se muito da mansidao que tem, polla qual he muy estimado, mas menos temido, e actualmente tem em sua casa hum Lamba parente seu, que lhe fez hum notavel agravo, trata o bem e disse nos que o soltaria logo, e que naõ tinha coração p.ª lhe dar outre castigo, posto que soubesse que em saindo da prizão se avia de alevantar contra elle, como custumava. He tambem mui celebrado polla abstinençia que faz nao comendo nunca arroz, nem carne, nem peixe, sostentando se de leite e fruitas, e tambem pollo recolhimento que guardou os tres annos passados antes de aqui chegarmos, metendo se em huma casinha que fez muy pequena no meio de huma serra sobre grande penedia, naõ vendo nem se deixando ver de pessoa alguma e o comer lhe punhão em duas cordas que da sua casinha decião a outras que lhe ficavão

abaixo, e elle o recolhia sem fallar em todo esto tempo com ninguem; occupava se como elle nos disse em orar e no tempo que lhe ficava fez algumas pessas que tem e nos mostrou huma dellas por melhor que era, huma imagem de vulto de Deos em sandalo branco, pequena, mas excelentemente feita, e he esta arte a de que elle muito se preza, como tambem de pintor, que le bom, e nos mostrou algumas pinturas suas muito, e vendo hum Anjo S. Raphael que traziamos em hum painel, quis fazer outro por elle e logo o começou, e foi continuando muito bem, posto que por muitas occupaçãis o
fol. 9. não tem inde acabado. Tem tambem este Rei [*fol.* 9] grande nome de letrado e como a tal o reverencião todos os outros Lambas maiores e os Reis lhe mandão presentes e he buscado de todas estas partes, tendo consigo Lambas de Reinos bem distantes. A causa de o acharmos alojado em tendas nesta serra; he porque custuma a gente das povoaçõis chama lo cada huma p.ª a sua, e assi se vai pôr em alguma paragem donde possa ir a mutas, dando lhe então largos prezentes de cavalos, gado, arroz, panos e outras cousas, que a sua principal renda e os que por ficarem longe o não convidão, o vem buscar tambem com suas offertas. Por este respeito estava neste serra com a escola dos seus Lambas que sempre tras consigno, e tem mais de cento com notavel exercicio de aprender, e fazer suas ceremonias: chamão se este Guelõis, e são os principaes Lambas, porque não casão, e não comem mais que huma vez antes do meio dia, depois do qual não podem comer arroz, nem carne, nem peixe, nem bebem vinho nunca, e nisto se distinguem de outros Lambas, que não são tão apertados; estaõ todo a dia recolhidos na escola, na qual comem, e dormem, saindo todos juntos duas vezes no dia, huma polla manhãa, outra á tarde, e recolhendo se logo todos em ordem huns apos outros com muita composição e modestia, tam bem ensinados e acustumados, e faz magna grande vê los por outra parte tão occupados nos erros que lhe ensinão, que grande parte do dia gastão em suas rezas, e de noite se levantão todos a hum sinal que lhe daõ, e rezão como por espaço de mea hora e outra vez de madrugada, cantando a modo dos clerigos em choro.

Nestes serras e noutras o acompanhamos dous mezes até chegar a sua caoa que esta naquella serra onde teve seu recolhimento sem ter consigo mais que os seus Lambas, nem o sitio he capaz de se povoar, porque para se fazer huma casa he necessario quebrar muita penedia e aplainar com muito trabalho algum espaço da serra, que e muy alcantilada; e he sitio que elle escolheo p.ª se defender de hum Rei que le fica daqui a oito dias do caminho e he o maior do Potente que se chama Demba Cemba, e lhe fez guerra os annos passados por lhe não querer dar, como elle nos disse, hum osso de seu pai defuncto que o Rei lhe pedia, deixando a este respeito de habitar em huma cidade sua, grande e boa que se chama Ralum e fica daqui a cinco dias de caminho; nestas suas casas nos acommodou muito bem em huma parte dellas, onde pudemos fazer, e ornar bem huma capella p.ª a qual o convidamos dia de nosso Santo P. Ignacio e foi o Senhor servido, que depois de dous roubos nos achassemos inda com todo o aparelho que trouxemos p.ª o altar, e com todas as imagens, que posto que no primeiro me levassem huma lamina da Virgem Senhora nossa, com tudo hum Lamba que a achou na mão dos que nos roubarão no la trouxe aqui com mais huma biblia que tambem la tinhão; veio o Rei ver a capella com o seu mestre que he hum Lamba muito velho a quem elle tem grande respeito, e com os mais Lambas, que ficarão todos muy satisfeitos do que vião, gastando algumas horas em ver, e perguntar por tudo.

Em estes mezes procuramos com toda a dilligencia aprender a lingua, e posto que andavamos por tendas e caminhos e casas estranhas que tudo nos tirava o tempo, com tudo nos fez Deos nosso Senhor neste materia como em todas as mais muitas merces; o maior trabalho de todas ero a falta do mestre, porque com o que tinhamos nos entendiamos muy difficultosamente; e por não ser deste Reino, mas de Chaparangue não sabia a lingua desta parte de que ao prezente tinhamos mais necessidade porque posto que estes Reinos todos tenhão a mesma lingua, ha muita variedade na pronunciação e nas terminaçõis, e a corrupção della em alguas partes a faz quasi outra particularmente neste Reino que por ficar neste canto sem trato, nem muito comercio dos outros Reinos esta muito mudada: porem os Lambas todos e comummente a gente entende tambem a lingua dos mais e assi com a que sabemos ficamos aptos para todas estas partes e tambem fazemos muita dilligencia p.ª nos formar bem no desta mesmo Reino, em que o Senhor he servido façamos a'prima estançia e assi ao prezente graças a Deos nosso Senhor nos [fol. *10*] entendemos muito bastan- fol. 10.
temente e praticamos as cousas de nossa Sancta Fe, e compomos as oraçõis e instrucçõis necessarias nesta lingua, e as fazemos escrever nos seus caraрteres pª. que mais facilemte aprendão ajuda nos tambem muito sabermos ja ler seus livros posto que naõ os entendamos ainda bem por estarem compostos no milhor e mais polido da lingua; erão em todo esto tempo muy frequentes as praticas que com o Rei tinhamos acerca das cousas de nosso Senhor, que elle muito folgava de ouvir; mas entendendo tambem que entre nos e elle avia grande differença acerca do que criamos em nossa Sancta Fe, vimos claramente nelle desgosto e frieza p.ª nossas cousas; e assi lhe dissemos depois de lhe agradecer muito o amor que nos tinha mostrado, que o ouvesse por bem dar nos licença e companhia p.ª passar adiante até os partes de Chaparangue, pois neste reino não tinhamos que fazer: ficou o Rei muy alcansado com esta pitição e differindo nos a resposta p.ª alguns dias fez nestes por via doutros Lambas dilligencias comnosco pª. que disistissemos de ir avante; mas presistindo nos no que lhe tinhamos pedido nos deu elle mesmo reposta, dizendo que era descridito seu deixarmo lo e ir avante; que todos estes Reinos sabião como estavamos com elle e que o ter nos aqui era grande honra sua pello [que] pª. diante não aviamos de passar; particularmente tendo lhe nos dito que estariamos aqui sempre, nem o deixariamos. A isto lhe respondemos que o avermos de estar aqui era tendo elle muito gosto de se pregar em seu Reino a verdadeira Lei de Christo nosso Senhor, e mais particularmente aceitando a elle e fazendo se christão, e como viarmos nelle pouco gosto desta materia, que he o que so mente aqui buscavamos, não avia p.ª que fica aqui. A isto nos disse que era verdade mas que elle avia medo, que se agora tomasse nossa Lei, de morrer logo, que seus antepassados tiverão a lei que elle tinha e que nunca forão christãos, mas que fossemos lendo o seus livros e praticariamos mais de raiz sobre a materia da lei, que por hora começassemos a fazer

christãos e pregar nossa Santa Fe, que era muito boa, e elle assi o entendia e que logo teriamos muitos christãos que era o que dezejavamos e que p.[a] começarmos nos dava, como logo deu, em sua prezença, a hum mancebo Lamba de vinte annos muito familiar seu e primo comirmão de outro Lamba que he todo o governo do Rei, e que logo nos daria mais dous e que a estes seguirião muitos e nos faria casa e igreja em Pargão. Vendo a resolução do Rei lhe dissemos que lhe queriamos dar gosto, pois elle o tinha em ficarmos neste Reino com as esperanças que nos dava de nelle se aver de estender a Fe do Senhor e lhe agradecemos muito os Lambas que nos dava e se querião fazer christãos, e a igreja que em Pargão queria fazer; que no que tocava a aver de morror logo tornando a Fe do Senhor, elle veria o contrario nos que se fizessem christãos, porque sendo Christo nosso Senhor verdadeira vida das almas não matava os corpos antes com elle teria todos os bens do corpo e alma.

Do que neste Reino ha acerca da Religião direi a V. R. o que colhemos das praticas com este Rei e com o velho mestre seu: dizem primeiramente, que nunca forão Christãos nem achão em seus livros que seus antepassados em todo este Potente conhec[ess]em a Christo nosso Senhor e tivessem sua Lei, dizem que não são gentios, antes si ri[e]m, e zombão das cousas da gentilidade, como de adorar animaes e abominão o matar gado a pagodes, e outras ceremonias dos gentios; dos mouros dizem muito mal, e he nome que chamão a quem querem chamar homem muy mao. Dizem que adorão a hum So Deos e delle tem imagens bem feitas, huma nos mostrou o Rei muy composta, modesta e authorisada, de metal dourado, que tinha entre as mãos huma vasilha pequena de agua, e disse nos que aquella agua era significação de como Deos lavava as almas dos peccados. Tambem nos mostrou outra pintura de Deos em pano toda de hum azul escuro, e estranhando lhe nos a cor nos disse que pintavão assi a Deos não porque nelle
fol. 11. ouvesse cor, mas porque sua morada ero o ceo por isso [*fol. 11*] o pintavão com aquelle cor de ceo: mostrando nos tambem outro painel em que estavão pintados os ceos, e no meio delles huma casa quadrada em que dizia morava Deos, posto que conforme seu ordinario fallar conheção a Deos por immenso e que como tal esta em toda a parte; dizem que em Deos ha tres, que são hum Deos, e que dous delles não tem corpo, e hum tem corpo, ao que tem corpo chamão Togu, que quer dizer Filho, e no modo com que fallão de seu nascimento dão a entender quererem dizer que nasceo ficando a mãi virgem, e nos mostrarão a imagem de huma molher que dizem ser a mãi de Deos. Tem noticia da bemaventurança aonde vão os bons e do inferno onde são castigados os máos, no qual dizem aver grandes tormentos de fogo e frio. Bem se vê nestas cousas ter aqui chegando dalgum modo a luz do Sancto Evangelho e outras ceremonias e bençãos de que usão mostrão muita semelhança com as cousas da christandade; mas tem tambem outras muitas desbaratadas; dizem que ha seiscentos annos não avia neste Potente gente nenhuma, que tudo era agua, mas secando se esta ficou a terra com arvores e so com dous bugios, dos quaes dezem decende toda a gente do Potente, e que estes bugios forão depois p.[a] o ceo; e que logo no principio destes Reinos ouve hum Rei que tinha doze cabeças. E rindo nos nos a isto e dizendo lhe que tudo era falsidade e zombaria, nos respondeo muy

firme no que tinha dito, que assi o dizião seus livros. Tambem fingem huns tres paraisos donde os bons passão de hum p^{a}. outro até ficarem spiritualisados de todo, e os que vão ao ceo dizem que entraõ no mesmo Deos e ficando Deoses; e assi adorão os seus mestres e Reis que tem por Sanctos como o Deos depois que morrem; donde vem que este Rei toda a sua arte e curiosidade emprega em fazer imagens de seu pai e orna las muito bem, e fazer lhe festas e esta tem em huma casa, que aqui fez de sua oração na qual so está imagem de vulto em hum sepulchro bom e fermoso de prata. Em ouvindo nos dizer que so na Lei de Christo Senhor nosso ha salvação, nos affirmarão que muitos antepassados deste Rei sobiraõ ao ceo em corpore e alma a vista de muita gente e que não era isto cousa muito antigua, mas de poucos annos a esta parte e que o pai de Droma Raja era tão sancto que onde punha o pe em pedra se imprimio algumas vezes a pegada, contando juntamente outras cousas de seus antepassados com que o demonio os tras cegos, e enganados. Acerca do Filho de Deos que dizem nasceo affirmão ser o seu Chescamoni, que he hum pagode muy famoso n[illegible]tas partes, e fica daqui a doze dias de caminho, e dizem que nasceo ha dous mil annos e que andou doze mezes no ventre do mãi: isto nos disse aquella Lamba principal, que he o que governa a casa do Rei, tendo nos o Rei dito primo que Chescamoni não era Deos e que os Lambas letrados não o adoravão, mas so a gente commua e que não sabia; e o Rei ouvindo agora isto ao Lamba o não contradisse, antes estavão ambos como embaraçados e confusos, não sabendo quem era este Deos filho que parece conhecião e não sabrão nada delle, de que nos lhe davamos muy differentes novas; nem ategora temos alcançado terem noticia alguma dos outros misterios da vida do Senhor, nem da Sancta Cruz achamos aqui mais sinaes, que alguma semelhança no nome; porque o que nos chamamos cruz elle chamão cruca, mas não conhecem este sancto sinal por causa sagrada. A este Rei e Lamba maior estimão todos muito, e dão do que tem p.^{a} quando morrerem, elle os mandar ao ceo; e a ceremonia he que quando estão vesinhos a morte ja arrancando he chamado o Rei e assiste a morte com suas rezas e em espirando lhe puxa o Rei pollos cabellos da cabeça, e então lhe faz aquella que elles chamão grande obra de misericordia de mandar lhe a alma p^{a}. o ceo. E perguntando eu a hum destes Lambas em huma morte doutro que aqui morreo, se lhe puxava pollos cabellos antes de morrer se depois; se espantou muito da pergunta dizendo que puxar-lhe antes de morrer seria gravissimo peccado. Depois de morto o homem repartem o que lhe achão polla mais gente, porque va bem a alma na outra vida, e os que estão ausentes em a morte dos parentes trazem ao Rei as principaes cousas do defuncto, e o levão a fazer sobre elle suas deprecaçóis. Deste modo pouco mais ou menos he o culto do Deos que adorão todos estes Reinos do Potente como entendemos do mesmo Rei e dos Lambas [*fol. 12*] que aqui estão de todos estes Reinos. fol. 12.
Fizemos todas as dilligencias de perguntas acerca do Reino do Catayo, e não temos delle noticia alguma por este nome, que he aqui totalmente não sabido; he porem aqui mui celebre hum Reino que dizem ser muy grande, e se chama Xembala, e fica junto a outro que chamão Sopo, daquelle Reino de Xembala naõ sabe este Rei que lei tenhão e no lo tem perguntado por muitas vezes. Deste Reino cuidamos poder ser o Catayo, porque o de Sopo

he o dos Tartaros como entendemos polla guerra, que este Rei nos diz tem aquelle Reino de continuo com a China, acrescentando que o Rei da China tem mais gente: porem que a do Sopo he mais esforçada, e assi comummente esta vence os Chinas, o que tudo diz com o que he tão sabido da guerra dos Tartaros com as Chinas, e como o Reino do Catayo seja muy grande e o unico que fica por esta banda junto aos Tartaros conforme as descripçõis das Mapas, parece podemos com alguma probabilidade cuidar ser o que aqui chamão Xembala. Nem faz contra isto não aver aqui noticia do outro nome, pois nem a China nem a Tartarea, nem o Tibet são conhecidos por estes nomes, dos quaes não tem noticia; e a China chamão Guena, a Tartarea Sopo e ao Tibet Potente;do caminho para o Reino de Xembala dizem muitas difficuldades; confio porem em o Senhor, que pois até qui nos trouxe com os olhos naquelle Reino, nos leve onde o vejamos demais perto, de modo que o anno que vem possa mandar a V. R. novas delle; não podera ser irmos ambos o P.[e] João Cabral e eu, vista a resolução deste homem com que não que passemos avante; e assi sendo Deos nosso Senhor servido ficara aqui o P.[e] Joaõ Cabral nesta casa e igreja que o Rei nos faz, pregando o Sancto Evangelho a esta gente com ajuda destes tres que o Rei nos deu, e vendo juntamente o fruito que neste Reino se podera fazer em as almas, p.[a] conforme a isto tratarmos do assento desta missão, e eu com ajuda do Senhor procurarei passar ao Reino de Xembala, que pode ser ou nelle, ou em algum dos que neste meio ficão nos tenha Deos nosso Senhor aparelhado ocasiõis de maiores serviços seus avisando o anno que vem a V. R. de tudo o de que pudermos ter noticia.

Deu nos este Rei os dous Lambas mais, que nos prometeo, hum delles he de doze annos menino ingenuo, e de habilitade, e outro de desanove, que tem particular aplicação em aprender o que se lhe ensina: a todos tres himos cathequisando e instruindo nas cousas de nossa Sancta Fe. Tambem outro Lamba de 27 annos muy principal e de muitos parentes, que todos estes meses esteve aqui com o Rei ajundando o nas obras de sua curiosidade de pintura, scultura e macenaria [sic] em que sempre esta occupado p.[a] ornato da imagem de seu pai, me tem prometido de se fazer christaõ por muitas vezes, como acabar estas obras do Rei, que sera daqui a mez e meio, deste me ajudo para me escrever e por em boa linguagem as oraçõis e doutrina christãa; e escrevendo hum dia destes o capitulo da cartilha sobre a Sancta Cruz ser signal do Christão, e outras cousas acerca do nascimento de Christo nosso Senhor, e da pureza da immaculada Virgem Senhora nossa, ficou muito satisfeito e me disse depois que o tinha no coração e lhe contentava muito. Tambem outro homem, que de outra aldea veyo aqui, vendo a capella que tinharmos e ouvindo algumas cousas de nosso Senhor, nos disse que queria ficar comnosco, e que indo para nossa casa estaria comnosco p.[a] nosso Senhor lhe perdoar hum peccato que o trazia muy desconsolado, e era que por desastre com huma frecha matara hum homem; este tornou outra vez e presiste nos mesmos propositos. Tambem outros affeiçoados a nossas cousas nos tem prometido de nos trazer seus filhos p.[a] os ensinarmos, e hum destes esta mais em particular agradecido polla merce que diz nosso Senhor lhe fez de dar saude a hum filho, que nos trouxe doente estando nos com o Rei nas tendas, ao qual pedinho alguma cousa santa

p.ª remedio, deu o P.ᵉ João Cabral huma reliquia, a qual o homen attribue a saude do filho e outros pedem muitas vezes a agua benta com que dizem se achão bem de seus achaques. E os Lambas e a mais gente que vem aqui a ver nos tambem com suas offertas de leite e fruitas, vendo as imagens e ornata da capellinha ficão [*fol. 13*] pasmados e se prostraõ muitas vezes fol. 13.
diante da imagem da Virgem Senhora nossa, e de Christo nosso Senhor beijando com muita devaçao o pe do altar. Tindo isto he dentro desta casa do Rei, junto a esta casa do seu pagode, que temos vesinha onde he continua a guerra que o demonio faz as almas com o cantar e rezar dos Lambas da escola do Rei e o som de varios instrumentos com que semper estão occupados em seu culto, e com a prezença do mesmo Rei que sabe de tudo quanto aqui passa, e a gente tudo o nosso compara com o seu, e lho antepoem do que bem se vê no Rei o pouco que gosta; e assi de aqui aver estes principios podemos conjeiturar progressos milhorados no bem das almas, confiando em Deos nosso Senhor, que saindo deste forte que aqui tem o demonio nos dê muitas victorias delle, desapossando das almas que aqui tem sugeito: porque fora deste não ha outros pagodes, senão rarissimos e andando por estas serras as primeiras desaseis jornadas não encontramos nenhum, mais que no alto de huma serra hum alpendre de pedras humas sobre outras bem mal feito com algumas pinturas do demonio e alguns idolos; e em Pargão com ser a cidade que disse não vimos mais que huma casinha pequenina de hum Lamba particular, que lhe servia de pagode, e assi fazendo se igrejas a que a gente venha e concorra se pode esperar com o favor do Senhor fructo em o bem das almas, nas quaes se vê bem a sede que lhe causa a propenção que tem ao conhecimento de seu criador na vontade, e gosto que mostrão de ouvir as cousas do Senhor que lhe praticamos, e na piedade e reverencia que mostrão a qualquer imagem que lhe dizemos ser de Deos e as cousas de seu divino serviço e ajudara muito a este bem a liberdade que neste Reino ha, que he assaz grande, e estendido e muy povoado, tendo a este Rei huma sugeição muy voluntaria sem obrigação de lhe averem de differir nem sequir sua doutrina, nem elle ter poder de gente p.ª constranguer ninguem a nada; antes como sua principal renda esta no que lhe dão voluntariamente, a ninguem quer ter descontente, e cada hum he muy livre p.ª fazer o que quiser, como o mesmo Rei por muitas vezes nos disse fallando nos inda acerca dos seus Lambas que são os mais sugeitos.

Este he o estado das cousas em que as prezente estamos, p.ª cujo progresso pedimos a V. R. as faça nessa provincia encomendar a nosso Senhor muy de continuo, pois aos sacrificios e araçõis de toda ella attribuimos todo o bem, que o Senhor he servido obrar e as muitas merces que de sua divina mão recebemos, assi em cousas exteriores, como na consolação interior de nossas almas, pois p.ª estes caminhos parece tem o Senhor guardado muy differente provimento do com que nos sustenta nos collegios e casas suas: e como se se esquecera de que tudo quanto por seu amor fazemos, he divida em que lhe estamos e merce que delle recebemos, parece que vão comprando a mor preço de consolaçõis de espirito qualquer passo que por seu amor se da, e custumando o Senhor com paternal affecto esconder se algumas vezes aos seus p.ª que mais o agradem soffrendo a pena

de o não sentirem tão presente; aqui parece naõ trata mais que de ser huma piadosa mãi, occupada toda em recrear e se recrear com os filhos pondo tanta belleza nos objectos em que a vista da por estas serranias, tanta facilidade nos caminhos destes rochedos, tanto gasalhado e amparo nos frios, chuivas e neves das noites que se dorme pollas lapas das penedias, tanta abundancia, e fartura na falta do neccessario, tanto alivio nos contrastes, e difficuldades, tanta suavidade na companhia e trato de animos e vontades danadas que da ao spirito huma satisfação tão plena, que bem se experimenta ser a medida por onde o Senhor mede estas merces, como elle disse, cheia, e bem cheia: e posto que nesses collegios se sinta muito destes bens cujo sabor o Senhor da a provar p.ª com elle atrahir a esta conquista sua as almas de seus servos, comtudo la se cuida, e aqui se vê, e experimenta, e nesta materia tem muy particular lugar o que se dis que huma cousa he cuida lo e outra ve lo: como tambem milita nesta o contrario do
fol. 14. que nos cousas [*fol. 14*] humanas, nas quaes o que antes da experiencia se cuida, com ella se acha falso: porem quem la sentir muito da consolação do spirito, na consideração da pregação do Sancto Evangelho, metido na obra experimenta a com muita ventagem: falando sem confusão aos Reis acerca da lei do Senhor, confudindo os letrados das seitas infernais, mostrando lhe a falsidade dos erros em que vivem, ajudando a muitos a sair da boca do inferno, em que ja estão, acudindo polla honra do verdadeiro Deos, persuadinho as almas o conheção e adorem fazendo guerra ao inferno com lhe tirar vassallos dando ao ceo alegres vistas nos actos do entendimento, e vontade com que os infieis vão entrando em si, e finalmente cooperando com o sangue preciosissimo de Jesu Christo Redentor, Senhor, e todo o bem nosso, que p.ª prova do amor que as almas dos seus lhe tem se quer servir delles no testemunho, que devem dar aos infieis de como elle he seu Salvador: tudo isto faz hum thesouro riquissimo de gostos dalma taes, que fica sendo nada o preço de grandes trabalhos quando os aja, e a abnegação de tudo o mais com que deve comprar se. Pera mim peço eu a V. R. muito em particular o favor de suas oraçõis, p.ª não por impedimentos a estes bens, mas possa tambem com os servos fieis entrar no gozo do Senhor grangeando lhe com o seu dinheiro ganhos e usuras de muitas almas, pois elle por na sua infinita bondade neste emprego quis ter seu ganho.

Tenho faltado atégora em dar a V. R. nesta algumas novas particulares da terra em si e do clima della; he elle muy sadio, e depois que entramos nestes serras sempre tivemos muito boa saude, e eu a não tive nunca na India tão boa; e he isto geral em todos, porque rarissimamente encontramos aqui algum doente, e são muitos os que sendo muy velhos tem saude e vigor; alguns mossos que trouxemos vindo assaz imdespostos, e sendo dantes doentes, aqui tem cobrado perfeita saude: ja temos destas serras passante de sete mezes, em todos elles foi sempre o tempo muy temperado sem frio, nem calma de momento; nestes quatro mezes que se seguem de Novembro até Fevereiro ha mais frio, ma ha p.ª elles muy bons panos de lãa de que todos andão vestidos. He a terra muy abundante de trigo, arroz, carnes, que tudo val muy barato, de fruitas que são muitas e boas, peras de muitas castas, algumas bem grandes, todas boas, pecegos muito bons, maçãs,

nozes, marmelos tudo em muita abundancia, e não faltão tambem os zambolõis da India, ha tambem ervilhas e nabos muito bons, afóra outras cousas, e fruitas mais proprias da terra. Peixe não tem aqui mas vem lhe muito bom seco do Lago Salgado, donde tambem lhe vem o sal, qui fica daqui perto, ou de Reino do Cocho, donde o trazem tambem; e algumas cousas que nesta terra não ha, se achão em outros lugares que não distão muito daqui, como uvas que aqui não ha, e se dão em huma cidade chamada Compo, que fica daqui a vinte dias do caminho, e delle se faz la vinho. He esta terra provida das cousas da China, como de ceda, ouro porçolanas, que tudo vem aquella cidade de Compo, e dalli dece para estas partes, e tambem de Caximir por via de Chaparangue ha comercio com as terras que ficão vesinhas a este Reino, e vem muitos estrangeiros a Guiance, que he a Corte de Demba Cemba, Rei mais poderoso deste Potente, e fica daqui a oito dias de caminho e a Laça, que he a cidade onde esta o pagode Chescamoni muy frequentada de jogues e de mercadores de outras partes; porem a estas serras em que estamos não vem pessoa estrangeira e so se lembrão de algum jogue ter por aqui passado, mas muy raramente, nem do Cocho aqui vem ninguem mais que os cativos que de lá trazem os que deste Reino decem áquelle; e hum tio do Reĩ deCocho, que há poucos annos por curiosidade e dezeio de ver terras, entrou por estas serras e poucas jornadas o cativarão e puserão ao arado, do que tendo noticia o Rei do Cocho mandou prender toda a gente destes Reinos que estava no seu e tratando de fazer justiça delles, se lhe não entregassem o tio, se obrigarão a lho trazer, como trouxerão. Fica esta terra pouco mais de hum mez de caminho do Reino [*fol. 15*] de Chaparangue e assi depois que aqui estamos fol. 15.
tivemos algumas vezes novas dos Padres que lá estão, não por sua via, que parece não sabem inda de nossa chegada a estas serras, mas por via de Lambas, que de lá vierão, e por outros que para lá forão escrevemos já aos Padres tres vezes e juntamente lhe mandei cartas p.ª por via de Goa as mandarem a V. R. He a gente destes Reinos branca, inde que a pouca limpesa com que se tratão faz que o não pareção tanto; todos trazem o cabello da cabeça crecido em forma que lhe cobre as orelhas e parte da testa, no rosto de ordinario não concente cabello algum, e trazem ao peito humas tanazes muy bem feitãs que só servem de arrancar todo o que aponta; os braças trazem despidos, e do pescosso até os giolhos se cobrem com hum pano destes de lãa, trazendo mais outro pano grande por capa; cingem se com cintos de couro, com chapas de muy bom lavor, como tambem são muy bem feitos, e lavrados os braceletes, que comummente trazem nos braços e os relicarios com que andão lançados a tiracollo; de ordinario andão descalsos, mas tambem usão de botas de couro, ou meyas destes seus panos particularmente por caminhos; suas armas são arco e frecha terçados e adagas de ferro excelente, aos quaes ornão con muita curiosidade e obra muy bem feita. Os Lambas não trazem armas, cortão o cabello da cabeça; alguns, mas poucos, deixão crecer a barba; o Rei a tem grande, e alguns cabellos della lhe chegão a cintura, os quaes comummente tras envolto em alguma ceda, e por festa os tira e aparecem, como fez no nosso recebimento; os da cabeça tem tão compridos, que tem quasi dous covados; delles parece se preza muito, e os tem por insignia de grandeza: porem disse nos que

tinha propositos de os cortar como tivesse filho, que lhe sucedesse no Reino e que então se avia de recolher e deixar o mundo porque não queria que a morte o tomasse com elles, como morreo outro Rei seu antepassado e foi materia de escandalo não cortar até aquelle tempo os cabellos. Vestem se todos os Lambas de humas meyas cabayas que lhe cobrem bem o peito, deixando os braços descubertos, e o mais corpo até os pes trazem bem cuberto com outro pano grande, servindo lhe outro de capa; a qual nunca largão, nem andão em corpo. Queira Deos nosso Senhor pôr em todos os olhos de sua divina misericordia, e traze los a seu divino conhecimento, fazendo que se aproveitem da mercê que lhe faz em lhe bater as portas com as novas de Sancto Evangelho, para o que peço a V. R. outra vez a continuação das oraçõis e sacrificios de toda essa Provincia; e na benção de V. R. muito me encomendo.

Deste Reino de Cambirasi, e casa deste Rei em 4 de Outubro de 1627.

Filho em Christo de V. R.

Estevão Cacella

APPENDIX III

RELAÇÃO DA MISSÃO DO REINO DE UÇANGUE CABEÇA DOS DO POTENTE, ESCRITA PELLO P.e JOÃO CABRAL DA COMP.a DE JESU

Nas cartas de Outubro passado escrevemos a V. R. o successo da nossa fol. 1.
Missão até a chegada e estada com o Droma Raja ou Lama Rupa, que he o seu proprio nome; nesta darei conta da mudança que fizemos para oReino de Uçangue chamado Deba Camba, do qual ja nas outras faziamos menção; relaterei tudo em breve summa, porque vai por hum patamar. Resolvemo nos a fazer esta mudança, porque achamos, que todos os favores de Lama Rupa, erão traças p.a nos impedir nosso intento movido do zelo de sua falsa seita; effeituou se por via de outro Lamba seu inimigo p.a quem o Padre [1]) se passou em huma occasião que teve da ir ver hum sitio p.a as casas e igreja que nos prometia fazer. Era este Lamba de quem o Pe. se valeo, alçado com o Rei de Uçangue, e por esta causa sabendo de seu intento sem reparar em nada o ajudou, ou por melhor dizer o aviou dando lhe gente de guarda, mantimentos, cavalo e todo o mais necessario para poder chegar a Gigaci, corte do Rei; chegou o P.e em 20 jornadas e foi muito bem recebido do Rei e da toda sua gente. E logo despedio hum homem seu com cartas de agradecimento ao Lama que ajudou o P.e e outras p.a o Lama Rupa em qua lhe mandava me posesse a mim; e a todo o fato em casa do Lama seu inimigo p.a dalli me aviarem tambem a custa do mesmo Rei; assi se executou sem nenhuma replica, ficou porem o Lama Rupa sobre maneira enfadado e se declarou por inimigo nosso, e por mais que com rezõis o procurei abrandar, tudo foi baldado. Parti a 18 de Dezembro e cheguei a 20 de Janeiro fazendo algumas detenças no caminho em quanto não cheguei as terras do Rei. Aos 21 pola manhãa sabendo o Rei da minha chegada nos mandou chamar mostrando de novo muita alegria da nossa vinha a seus Reinos. Ao dia sequinte lhe propusemos em forma a causa, que nos movia a emprender esta jornada; ouvio com muita atenção e gosto, e respondeo que fossemos com muita dilligencia formando nos bem na lingua, porque gostaria fallar muitas vezes naquellas materias, e isto foi confirmando sempre nas mais praticas, e o seu Lama grande passou hum formão, em que dis que a nossa sancta Lei he a melhor de todas, e que he bem que todos a aprendão p.a salvação de suas almas, do qual formão soube o Rei e o confirmou.

[1]) **Father Stephan Cacella.**

Mandou nos logo dar humas casas muito boas e em muito bom sitio e provernos de alfayas e mossos p.ª o serviço, tudo com muita liberalidade; p.ª a sustentação manda dar huma reção quotidiana que se da a toda a gente da fortaleza na despença do Rei e a fora esta outra de cada mez, que he so dos capitãis; o que he nao so bastante p.ª o nosso comer ordinario, mas ainda p.ª fazer muitas esmolas, e porque o Rei não sabia do nosso custume, e do que nos era necessario, deputou hum pagem p.ª avisar do que nos faltasse. Sobre tudo nos fazia muitas honras mandando nos chamar quasi todas as dias e tomando nos as mezes trabalho de nos ensinar a lingua. Era esta nossa entrada tão franca muito fallada entre os seus, por que este Rei não ada tão facilmente, nem ainda a gente principal. Nesta conjunçao se acharão na Corte dous Lamas, criados de Lama Rupa, e ao que parece, mandados por elle afim de nos impedirem o assento naquelle Corte, procurarão fallor pessoalmente ao Rei, e nao sendo admitidos, o fizerão por via dos officiaes; e o que mais insistirão, foi em excitar todos os Lamas desta cidade, que são sem numero, contra nos, dizendo, que eramos padres mandados so a destruir os seus pagodes, gente ma, destruidora e blasfemadora de sua Lei; foi nosso Senhor servido que nesta conjunção naõ se achasse na Corte algum dos Lambas grandes que fallão com o Rei, posto que bastou o vir lhe as orelhas p.ª se mostrar menos alvoroçado da nossa vinda, não no tratamento que sempre foi o mesmo mas na graça e afabilidade em que parece (se não foi nossa imaginação) diminuio alguma cousa; e he para dar graças o nosso Senhor não causar isto mor mudança, suposto o Rei nos não conhecer ainda e se temer muito das feiticerias do Lambas. Nestes dias em que isto andava revolto lhe davamos nossas rezõis, as quaes lhe quadravão muito, e respondia sempre com a boca chea de riso, segundado nos de tudo, queira o Senhor por sua infinita misericordia conservalo ainda que naõ sera mais que neste favor, que delle neste principio temos, por que so este basta p.ª podermos esperar grande fruito.

fol. 2. [*fol.* 2] Parti no mez de Janeiro da cidade de Uçangue e cheguei aeste Golim em Abril por causa de algumas detenças do caminho. A causa da minha vinda foi principalmente vir descobrir este novo caminho do Reino de Nepal p.ª se poder por elle continuar a Missão, supposto o do Cocho ser tão perigoso e arriscado. Vim tambem p.ª negocear algumas cousas p.ª esta Missão, que entendo pode ser huma das mais gloriosas da Companhia; e he porta p.ª toda a Tartarea, China e outros muitos Reinos de gentios.

He este Rei mancebo de 22 annos muito bem entendido, branco, bem affeiçoado, e sobre tudo muito pio e liberal p.ª com os pobres. A cidade real he esta de Gigaci; esta situada ao pe de hum monte, no cume doqual fica a fortaleza onde mora o Rei com todos seus officiaes, e guarda de soldados; o edificio della e traça he como as de Portugal, e não lhe falta mais que a artelharia, as casas por dentro todas são douradas, e pintadas e o quarto dos aposentos do Rei he muito p.ª ver, principalmente algumas casas de brincos que tem de toda a sorte, porque como o Rei he rico de toda a parte lhe vem o melhor; usa muito de armaçõis em todos seus aposentos, as somenos são de damasco da China, outras tem que podem competir com todas as boas de Portugal; a gente que o serve se traja muito limpa, e pode aparecer em toda a parte, a gente popular he pouco mais ou menos doque temos escrito da gent lo primeiro Reino, que agora soubemos se chamava o Reino de Mon.

O Reino que se ch a Uçangue he muy estendido e por qualquer parte que se tome, dizem q io menos tem mez e meio de travessa, e taõ povoado que em 20 dias q aminhei da Corte até os confins do Reino de Nepal (que he o novo cami por onde vim) sempre vim vendo e passando por entre aldeas; o clima frio; em Janeiro e Fevereiro passei muitas ribeiras por cima do caramelk a cavalo, mas as neves não saõ demasiadas; tem grandes campinas de igo, e não vi terra mais parecida com Alemtejo em Portugal. Pollo nort onfina com os Tartaros com os quaes este Rei as vezes briga, e aqui ve muitos os quaes dizem que a sua Lei he a mesma. Pera o Oriente fica C chinchina da qual vem muitas mescadorias, como tambem da China, qu demora ao Noderste [*sic*], e não semete este Reino, e ella mais, que o Rei de Cam, que he o donde vem o almiscar; Xembala que a meu ver não he Catayo, mas aquella que nos Mapas chamão gram Tartarea fica mais des iada para o Norte.

Neste Reino de Uça gue estão as cabeças do todas as castas de Lambas, e porisso lhe chamão escola de sua ley; os mosteiros (aque chamão Combas) não são ao nosso modo, mas cada Lamba grande tem sua cidade, na qual não morão mais, que os seus Lambas com elle. A Comba dos Lambas de Chaparangue esta a huma ilharga desta fortaleza, dous tiros de falcão, e por esta causa temos cada dia novas dos Padres dos quaes ficamas distantes como hum mez de caminho, mas o Rei não fas nenhum caso destes Lambas, porque dis que he ma casta. Tratão se estes Lambas grandes com aparato de Rei, e entre elles o Lamba Rupa de quem tantas cousas se tem escrito, he o quinto na dignidade; por onde V. R. pode julgar oque serão os outros, mas tem hum grande bem, que nemhum destes assiste de ordinario com o Rei.

A ley e seita destes Reinos, agora acabo decrer que são gentios, porque alem de elles se terem e confessarem por taes, achei que tem os mesmos pagodes do Reino de Nepal e algums de Bengala e so na superstição de castas e comeres que não tem, são diversos. Do Catayo quanto mais imos sabendo da terra, menos sabemos delle, so nos disse o Lamba do Rei que passou o formão que avia huma terra chamada Cata cuja Lei naõ sabia de certo, mas que ouvira dizer era huma lei antiga diversa desta destes Reinos e o caminho p.ª este Reino dis, que he por Coscar cidade muito nomeada e concorda isto com a informaçao do Padre Hieronimo Xavier, onde falla nesta mesma cidade.

Isto he o que por hora posso dizer a V. R. desta Missão, doqual bem se deixa ver de quanto effeito pode ser dando nos nosso Senhor pe neste Reino de Uçangue, perque não so em si he o que digo, mas ainda porta para todos os mais Reinos que se seguem. O que resta he mandar nos V. R. encomendar muito a nosso Senhor p.ª que as oraçõis de tantos servos seus suprão nossos defeitos e lancar lhe hua benção p.ª que [*fol. 3*] arreigue e fol. 3.
ereça. O caminho para estes Reinos naõ he pollo Cocho, mas pollo Nepal, oqual confina com as terras do Mogor: Em Patana e Rajamol he caminho segurissimo frequentado de muitos mercadores. Comigo mandou o Rei hum capitão até o Nepal com carta e prezente p.ª o Rei, pedindo lhe que

me ajudasse em tudo o que lhe pedisse, porque era pessoa aquem elle estimava muito; assi o fez o Rei do Nepal e me aviou muito bem até Patana, onde achei Portugueses com osquaes passei aeste Golim, donde faço esta a V. R. Do Reino de Nepal escreverei a V. R. mais largamente porque ahi hei de achar novas do P.e Cacella e do que tem socedido. Nos santos sacrificios de V. R. muito me encomendo. 17 de Junho de 1628.

APPENDIX IV

LETTER OF FATHER JOHN GRUEBER TO FATHER ATHANASIUS KIRCHER AT ROME

Rev. in Chro. Pater,

Pax Christi et felicissimus novus annus.

Quid agit meus amantissimus Pater Athanasius, numquid aut in Mundo Subterraneo ita sepultus, aut in itinere exstatico ita ad Superna abreptus est ut in casu causaque propria ad tot ad se a me datas [epistolas] nec unico verbulo respondere dignetur; estne „ein so seltsämer Män", sicut me saepius Romae vocabat, ut promissum litterarum commercium et plane per R. P. Provincialem nostrum a me extortum adeo cito interrumpat? Certo hoc numquam supposuissem, nec cum patientia, sed sciat me tam diu nec litteras, nec descriptionem itinerarii amplius submissurum donec sciam initium illius aliasque meas epistolas ad manus pervenisse; non enim deest mihi occasio (si ea uti volo) nec sculptores, nec maecenates notata mea Viennae imprimendi; verum cum V.ae R.ae gloriam totam hoc in opere transscribam, rogo sit diligentior in respondendo ad meas, ne animum plane abiiciam.

De itinere alio per Sinas meridionales usque in Regnum Tenassari quod adiacet regno Bengalae, aperto etiam mihi constat, practicare tamen difficile est, maxime iis qui linguam ignorant, nam transitus per provinciam Sinicam Quantunus in Quicheu, ex hac in Funam, ac inde per fluvium in Regnum aut Tunkinus [sic] aut Camboia, aut etiam sed difficulter in Champa, quod Regnum adiacet Regno Siang, inde facile in Tenassari ex quo per Pegu in Bengala usque ad Gangem ac deinde nostro itinere trito in Agram metropolim Mogorensem; verum hoc iter vix non impracticabile est ob varietates gentium linguarumque ac morum per quas transire necesse est, alterum a me factum sub una nempe Indica aut Persica lingua facillimum, quod omni modo manu teneri et promoveri a Societate nostra deberet.

Haec breviter, in posterum plura, si bonus P. Athanasius diligentior fuerit in respondendo, in cuius maiorem diligentiam affectum, sancta Sacrificia precesque me humillime commendo.

Tyrnaviae, 13 Januari 1670. R.ae V.ae

Servus in Chro.

IOANNES GRUEBER

APPENDIX V

EULOGY ON FATHER JOHN GRUEBER

(Austriae Necrologia 1615—1685. p. 937—938).

30 September 1680. Patakini.

P. Joannes Grueber, Austriacus, Lincensis, absolutis in Societate cum laude altioribus studiis cum quarto Theologiae anno mathesim repeteret seque pro Missione Dacica pararet, a P. Marco Tieste[1]) pro missione Chinensi interpellatus et impetratus cum eo Romam inde in Chinas profectus, Macaum pervenit, ubi quator vota professus. Inde ad Regiam Pekinensem P.[1] Adamo Schall socius triennio adhaesit: quo exacto cum P. Alberto Droville [sic] diplomate Monarchae Chinensis instructus, itinere vasto in Indiam rediit multum terris et alto iactatus. Ex India Romam regressus breviorem per Moschoviam inituros viam, Româ ad fines Moschoviae penetravit, irrito quidem conatu, sed non sine fructu, redux in Provinciam per Constantinopolim ad suos Chinenses penetraturus cum Legato Caesareo abiit. Sed infirmitate gravi praepeditus, Chinas sibi in Hungaria invenit finem laborum. Tot spatia confecit itinerum indefessus, ut testimonio viri gravissimi[2]) abusque Româ datis intimetur: „non ego arbitror in universa Societate hominem vixisse, qui maiora itinera fecissit." Et rursus: „Nullus hucusque e Societate maiora terra marique itinera quod R[a]. V[a]. confecit".

Natus ad labores Apostolicos vilibus delectabatur, incommoda ultro quaesivit, in aegritudinis molestiis patientiae exemplar, siquidem putrescentibus iamiam carnosioribus corporis partibus in summo dolore nil aliud quam patientia: „Fiat voluntas Dei" ingeminabat. Obiit resignatus omnino in Dei voluntatem Sacramentis omnibus munitus.

[1]) Father Bernard Diestel.
[2]) Father Athanasius Kircher?

INDEX

A

Abdullah Isaï, Persian name of Goes, — 13.

Aconterzec, halting-place in Tarim basin, — 32.

Agra, — death of d'Orville at, 197.

Aingaràm, halting-place, — 18.

Akbar, Great Mogul, — invites Jesuits to his court, 10; contributes to Goes' expedition, 12.

Aksu, oasis in Tarim basin, — 31, 33, 42.

Alaknanda, river, — described by Andrade, 48; principal source of the Ganges, 59, 60.

Alceger, halting-place in Tarim basin, — 31.

Alner, monastery in Ladakh, — 103, 303. *vide* Hanle.

Amaral, Michael de, S. J., — desires to re-establish the Tsaparang-mission, 206, 207; biographical note, 207.

Amulets, disgusting, — 101, 191, 299.

Andrade, Antonio, S. J., — *main entry*, 43—82; chronological summary, 90—91; his letters, 92—93; suggests the establishment of a station in Utsang, 120; — 8, 130, 148, 153, 196, 288, 292, 295, 301, 302.

Anjos, Alado dos, S. J., — describes the mission at Tsaparang, 75; sent to Srinagar, 86; biographical note, 72; — 71, 90, 92.

Aramuth, halting-place in Tarim basin, — 36.

Attock, on Indus river, — 14.

Azevedo, Francis de, S. J., — on Tsaparang king, 78, 80; appointed Visitor to the mission, 81; *main entry*, 94—118; chronological summary, 119; — 73, 77, 90, 158, 159, 214.

Azo, in Assam, — described by Cacella, 123; — 122, 125, 126, 314, 316, 317. *vide* Hajo.

B

Badakshan, district of, — 13, 20, 22.

Badasciàn, Tenghi, — 20, 22.

Badrinath, village and temple, — visited by Andrade, 50, 51; described by Raper, 51, 52; by Azevedo, 97; — 294, 295, 296.

Baltistan, — 109, 212.

Bara-lacha, pass, — crossed by Azevedo, 112, 113.

Barantola, — 188, 190. *vide* Lhasa.

Barbaro, Josaphat, — 5, 12.

Barreiros, S. J., — biographical note, 83.

Beauchère, Alain de la, S. J., *vide* Anjos.

Bhotias, — described by Andrade, 52; 53.

Bhutan, — first visited by Cacella and Cabral, 133; the Bhutan Duars, 134, 135; introduction of Buddhism, 140; first Dharma Rajah, 140—141; language, 144; religion, 145, 146, 156; temples, 148; origin of the country, 146; climate, products, trade, etc. 149—151; appearance, dress, arms of the people, 151—152; intercourse between Bhutan and Ladakh 151. *vide* Pargão, Potente.

Biar, town, (Cooch Behar), — described by Cacella, 127, 128; — 122, 130, 131, 317, 318, 319.

Bosmans, H., S. J., — his opinion on Grueber's return-journey, 175, 176.

Breebung, monastery, — 225, 241, 242, 243, 267.

Bree-me-giong, (Sikkim) — 143, 226.

Bucarate, — 19.

Buddhism, — introduced into Tibet, 99; into Bhutan, 140.

Burrard, Sir S. G., — his remarks on lake Deb Tal, 61.

C

Cabral, John, S. J., — *main entry*, 121—161; chronological summary, 162, 160, note 2; — 101, 163, 301, 333.

Cacella, Stephen, S. J., — *main entry*, 121—161; chronological summary, 162; his letters, 163; — 73, 301, 314.

Calcia, mountain-tribes, — 18, 19.

Caldeira, Balthasar, S. J., — biographical note, 83.

Cambaluc, capital of Cathay, — 4, 5, 6, 11, 13, 36, 172, 178.

Cambasci, halting-place in Tarim basin, — 32.

Cambirasi, Kingdom, — same as Mon, 142, 143; — 120, 138, 323.

Camul, *vide* Chami.

Can Sanguicascio, mountain, — 28, 29.

Capece, Dominic, S. J., — biographical note, 80.

Capetalcol, halting-place in Tarim basin, — 31, 32.

Capuchins at Lhasa, — 208, 209, 210, 222, 223, 267.

Cara Cathai, — 33, 185.

Caravans, as pseudo-embassies, — 25, 26.

Carja, kingdom, — 113, 114, 307.

Carpini, John of Plano, — 4, 5, 33.

Cartoâ, (Gartok), — 216, 226, 258.

Carvalho, John, S. J., — 206, 207.

Casciani, halting-place in Tarim basin, — 34.

Castro, Joseph de, S. J., — biographical note, 81; his letters, 93; — 77, 82, 86, 87, 159, 283.
Cathay, — empire, 3, 4, 5, 7; Christians in C, 11, 12; proved to be China, 36, 39; Andrade's opinion on C., 71; Coresma's, 84; inquiries made by Cacella, 125, 147; Cabral's opinion, 155, 156; — 317, 327, 328, 335.
Çeri, place of pilgrimage, — 251, 252.
Chami, oasis, — 31, 36, 37, 42.
Chang, a kind of beer, — 213, 259.
Chaparangue, *vide* Tsaparang.
Charikar, iron at, — 17, 20.
Chaudhuri, H. R., — note on change of capital in Cooch Behar State, 129, 130; on Runatc, 135.
Chescan, settlement, — 19.
Chia-yu-kuan, — 37, 38.
Chiang-ze, — described by Desideri, 233, 235.
Chichiklik, pass, — 23.
Chieê-rong, Tibetan province, — 226, 231, 232, 233.
Chodakpo, supposed name of Tsaparang king, — 79.
Christians, — in Cathay, 11, 12; in Tibet, 46, 47, 264; in Bhutan, 145, 146.
Chumbi, Tibetan territory, — 143, 158.
Ciacor, halting-place in Tarim basin, — 32.
Cialis, oasis, — 30, 34, 37.
Ciang Thang, — described by Desideri, 215.
Ciaracàr, *vide* Charikar.
Ciarciunar, in Badakshan, — 20, 22.
Ciecialith, *vide* Chichiklik.
Cilàn, halting-place in Tarim basin, — 32.
Clavyo, Gonzales de, — 5.
Climate, — of Bhutan, 149; of Tibet, 226, 227.
Cocho, kingdom, — 122, 123, 126, 130, 149, 150, 158, 330. *vide* Cooch Behar and Koch.
Colambarim, capital of Cooch Behar, — 128, 129, 130, 318.
Compo, town, — 150, 331.
Congbo, Tibetan province, — 150, 251, 253—255.
Cong-me, Tibetan province, — 226, 253, 254.
Cong-tó, Tibetan province, — 226, 253, 254.
Contel, or Zo-ji, — 211.
Conti, Nicholas, — 5.
Cooch Behar, state and town, — described by Ralp Fitch, 127; different capitals, 129, 130; *vide* Biar and Cocho.
Cordeiro, Antonio, S. J., — silent on Goes, 8, 9, 10.
Coresma, Nuño, S. J., — his verdict on the Tsaparang mission, 84, 85; on the mission in Utsang, 160; his letters, 92—93; biographical note, 82.
Correa, Ambrosio, S. J., — 83, 91, 92; biographical note, 83.
Corvino, John e Monte, — archbishop of Cambaluc, 5.
Cotan, *vide* Khotan.
Cruce, Ignatius a, S. J., — biographical note, 86.
Cucià, *vide* Kutsha.
Cullu, — 307, 308. *vide* Kulu.

D

Dacca, — 122, 123, 314, 315.
Dalai Lama, — 156, 190, 266—269.
Dam, Tibetan territory, — 244, 267, 268.
Darcha, hamlet in Lahul, — 113.
Death-ceremony, — in Bhutan and Tibet, 146, 147.
Deb Tal, lake on Mana-pass, — 60, 61, 98.
Delhi, — 311.
Dellai, halting-place in Tarim basin, — 34.
Demetrius, Goes' travelling companion, — 14, 16.
Denis, F., — his appreciation of Goes' journey, 1; of Andrade's, 45.
Desideri, Hippolyte, S. J., — why he went to Lhasa, 208, 209, 210; *main entry*, 210—272; chronological summary, 273; his letters and manuscripts, 274—281; — 74, 83, 94, 135, 143, 144, 150, 151, 159, 191.
Dharma Rajah, — receives Cacella and Cabral, 137—139; first in Bhutan, 140—142; 147, 153, 155.
Diaz, Manuel, S. J., — 158, 159, 161, 301; biographical note, 159.
Diestel, Bernard, S. J., — 173, 174, 338.
Dras, in Baltistan, — 212, 214.
Droma Rajah, — 138, 139, 142, 314, 323, 333. *vide* Dharma Rajah.
Duars of Bhutan, — 134.
Dukpa-sect, — prominent in Bhutan, 140—42; headquarters at Ralung, 142. *vide* Red-caps.

E

Egriàr, halting-place in Tarim basin, — 31, 32.

F

Fernandes, sent by Ricci to Goes at Su-cheu, — 38, 39, 40.
Ferreira, M. E., — his inquiries about Goes' name, 9.
Figueiredo, Simon de, S. J., — 123, 315; his appeal in favour of the Utsang-mission, 160—161.
Fitch, Ralph, — describes Cooch Behar, 127; Bhutan, 134.
Fonseca, Anthony da, S. J., — biographical note, 77.
Fontebona, Bartholomew, S. J., — 122, 123, 131, 315, 318; biographical note 123.
Franciscan Friars in Cathay, — 4, 5, 6.
Francke, Rev. A. H., — on the name and the conduct of the Tsaparang king, 79, 80.
Freyre, Manuel, S. J., travelling companion of Desideri, — 209, 210, 214, 222; biographical note, 222.
Freytas, Pietro de, S. J., — biographical note, 83.
Funeral, — of Garhwal Rajah, 95, 292; different kinds of funerals in Tibet, 263.

G

Gaburrasa, king of Biar, — 126, 131, 135, 317, 318, 319.
Ga-den, monastery, *vide* Kaa-n-den.
Gama, Aloys de, S. J., — biographical note, 86.
Ganges, source of the, — 56, 57, 58, 60, 61, 98, 219.
Garhwal, *vide* Srinagar.
Gartok, — 216, 226, 258, 268.
Gaso, halting-place in Tarim basin, — 34.

Gelugpa-sect, *vide* Yellow-caps.
Gerbillon, J. F., S. J., — on Chinese Wall, 180.
Ghideli, halting-place, — 14.
Gialalabath, halting-place, — 19.
Giegazze, town, — 221, 234, 235, 236, *vide* Shigatse.
Gigaci, town, — 142, 153, 154, 334, 335. *vide* Shigatse.
Gill, Peter, S. J., — 206.
Ginghes Khang, king of Lhasa, — 241, 265—268.
Gnee-lam, — 232, 233. *vide* Kutti.
Godinho, Francis, S. J., — 72, 77, 90; biographical note, 72.
Goes, Bento de, S. J., — *main entry*, 1—41; chronological summary, 42; — 71, 109, 156, 161, 176, 304.
Gold-digging, in Tibet, — 228.
Golim, town, — 120, 122, 314, 315, 334. *vide* Hugli.
Gonçalves, Luiz, — Goes' real name?, 8—10.
Grassi, Hildebrand, S. J., — 201.
Grimanus, Leo, travelling companion of Goes, — 14, 16.
Grueber, John, S. J., — 73; the materials for the present account, 165—172, 204, 337; *main entry*, 172—202; chronological summary, 203; euolgy, 338.
Guebedal, halting-place in Tarim basin, — 32.
Guge, kingdom of Tsaparang, — war with Ladakh, 75—76; 70, 156, 159, 213.
Guiar, town, — 104, 304, 305. *vide* Gya.
Gya, in Ladakh, — 73, 104, 106, 107, 110, 111.
Gyantse, — 142, 221, 227, 235, 269. *vide* Chiang-ze.

H

Haack, Dr. H., — his remarks on lake Deb Tal, 60.
Habagateth, halting-place in Tarim basin, — 31.
Hajo, in Assam, — 124, 126. *vide* Azo.
Hancialix, halting-place in Tarim basin, — 31, 32.
Hanle, monastery, — 103, 104.
Hedin, Sven, — his tribute to Desideri's work, 272.
Hedonda, town, — latitude determined by Grueber, 195, 196.
Hiarcan, — 24. *vide* Yarkand.
Hircanda, — letter of Goes from —, 21.
Hoang-ho, — 179, 182, 183, 184.
Holdich, Sir Th., — his verdict on Andrade; 44; on Desideri, 209, 233.
Hor, — 245, 246.
Horling, inscription at, — 79, 80.
Horma, halting-place in Tarim basin, — 31, 32.
Hsi-ning, — 179; Great Wall at —, 180, 181, 182; 226, 267, 268.
Hugli, town. — 122, 123, 131, 152, 157, 158, 160. *vide* Golim.

I

Indus, source of the, — 99, 219.
Influenza, in Nepal, — described by Desideri, 270.
Inscription, — at Si-ngang-fu, 5; at Horling and Tabo, 79; on d'Orville's tomb at Agra, 197.
Isaac, Goes' travelling companion, — 2, 4, 16, 23, 29, 31, 39, 40, 41.

J

Jacorich, halting-place in Tarim basin, — 24.
Jade, — 25; mines near Khotan, 27, 28, 29.
Jenkinson, Anthony, — 12, 13.
Jogis, — mentioned by Monserrate, 47; by Andrade, 48; by Azevedo, 97, 295.
Jolci, halting-place in Tarim basin, — 31, 32.
Josimath, village, — 50, 51; visited by Azevedo, 95, 96.
Jus primae noctis, — mentioned by Azevedo, 100.
Jussy, — 95, 293, 294. *vide* Josimath.

K

Kaa-n-den, monastery, — 245, 267.
Kabul, — 16, 20, 42.
Kafiristan, — 15, 16.
Kailas, Mts, — 217, 218, 222.
Kan-sang-i-Kash, — 28.
Kargil, in Ladakh, — 214.
Kashgar, — 13, 14, 25, 32, 108, 125, 156.
Kashmir, — 24, 47, 48, 65, 150, 205, 209, 212, 232.
Katmandu, — latitude determined by Grueber, 194; — 157, 226, 232, 270.
Kherum Shahr, *vide* Chieê-rong.
Kham, — 155, 228, 255, 256.
Khitaï, — 4. *vide* Cathay.
Khotan, oasis, — visited by Goes, 26; jade-mines near —, 27, 28, 29.
Khri-bkra-shis-grangs-palde, king of Tsaparang, — 79, 80.
Kircher, Athanasius, S. J., — erroneous statements on Andrade, 58, 59; 196; account of Grueber's expedition, 166—172.
Kiron, *vide* Chieê-rong.
Koch, Francis, S. J., — 207.
Koch Bihar State, — 124.
Koch Hajo Sate, — 124.
Koko-nor, — mentioned by Grueber, 183, 184.
Korea, — 183, 184.
Korla, oasis in Tarim basin, — 34, 35, 36.
Kulu, — visited by Azevedo, 113—117; 213. *vide* Culu.
Kutsha, oasis in Tarim basin, — 31, 34.
Kutti, — 192, 231, 233, 269, 270.

L

Ladakh, — kingdom, 70; the king invites Andrade, 73; war against Tsaparang, 75—77; Azevedo's description of land and people, 99—102; Desideri's, 213; intercourse between Ladakh and Bhutan, 151, 304, 305.
Laertius, Albert, S. J., — 122, 158, 160, 162, 301.
Lahore, — 10, 11, 13, 17, 42, 117, 118, 211, 310, 311.
Lahul, district, — 111; visited by Azevedo, 114—116.
Lamas, — mentioned by Andrade, 74; by Cacella, 144. *vide* Red-caps, Yellow-caps.
Langur, Himalaya Mts., — 192, 222, 269.
Leh, capital of Ladakh, — 77; visited by Azevedo, 108—110; described by Desideri, 213, 214, 221; 304.

Lha-brang, temple, — 238, 239, 240.
Lhasa, — mentioned by Cacella, 150; visited by Grueber and d'Orville, 188—189; latitude determined by Grueber, 190; by Desideri, 226; description of Lhasa by Desideri, 238—244; — 205, 209, 267, 269.
Lho-bàs, tribes, — 226, 230, 253, 254, 261.
Lho-rò, — 226, 253, 254.
Liquinarane, king of Cocho, 123, 125—127, 316, 317.

M

Macao, — 174, 175, 178.
Macassar, — 178.
Machado, Anthony, S. J., — 14.
Magar Sarā, capital of Kulu, — 116, 309. *vide* Nagar.
Magro, Anthony, S. J., — 7.
Malpichi, Stanislaus, S. J., — 86, 87, 91; biographical note, 88.
Mana, village, — 54, 98, 296.
Mana, pass, — pool on Mana pass mentioned by Andrade, 56—62; by Azevedo, 98; — 55, 67, 297.
Mandi, kingdom, — 117, 309.
Mansarowar lake, — 44, 47, 56, 57, 58, 62, 218, 219, 220. *vide* Retôa.
Mariul, kingdom, — 70, 73, 75, 107, 304.
Markham, Sir Cl., — his statement on Andrade, 43, 57; on Grueber, 202.
Marques, Manuel, S. J., travelling companion of Andrade, — 47, 62, 70, 87, 88, 90, 91, 95, 98; biographical note, 88.
Martinetti, Joseph, S. J., — 207.
Martini, Martin, S. J., — biographical note, 177.
Mellah, town, — 117, 310.
Meselelec, halting-place in Tarim basin, — 31, 32.
Minapor, town, — 195, 196.
Mingieda, halting-place in Tarim basin, — 31.
Mohammedans, — in Cathay, 11; at Yarkand, 24; at Lhasa, 256.
Mon, territory, — 142, 143, 226, 248, 249, 335.
Monserrate, Anthony, S. J., — 46, 100, 116.
Morando, Francis, S. J., — 80, 81, 283; biographical note, 80.
Moranga, kingdom, — 159, 195, 196.
Morro, Guiseppe da, — 225, 269, 270.
Mountain-sickness, — described by Goes, 21, 22; by Andrade, 54; bij Desideri, 269.
Mutgari, town, — 195, 196.

N

Nagar, capital of Kulu district, — 116, 117.
Nang, Tibetan province, — 253, 254.
Nepal, — visited by Cabral, 154, 157; by Grueber, 192—195; by Desideri, 270; — 260, 261, 268, 269, 334, 335, 336.
Nephrite, *vide* Jade.
Nesti, town, — 193, 226, 233, 270.
Ngari Giongar, — 217, 218, 219, 258.
Ngavang Lobsang, Dalai Lama, — 78, 155, 156, 190, 191.
Nilam Dzong, — 192, 233. *vide* Kutti.
Nyi-ma-nam-gyal, king of Ladakh, — visited by Desideri, 215.

O

Oitograc, halting-place in Tarim basin, — 34.
Oliveira, John de, S. J., — 71, 77, 81, 90, 92, 101, 302; biographical note, 71.
Om mani padme hum, Tibetan prayer-formula, — noticed by Andrade, 74; by Grueber, 191; Desideri's interpretation, 264—265.
Ortelius, — 6, 13.
Orville, Albert d', S. J., — *main entry*, 172—198; chronological summary, 203; — 73, 223.

P

Padmasambhava, *vide* Urghien.
Pamech, desert, — 21.
Pamir, — 20, 21, 22.
Pando, district and town, — 122, 123, 124, 125, 314, 316, 317, 318.
Pargão, town, — described by Cacella, 133; — 132, 136, 148, 320, 321, 322, 326, 329. *vide* Paro.
Pari, district, — 226, 248, 249.
Paro, town, — 136, 137, 148, 149, 151, 152, 153.
Parwan, pass, — 17, 20.
Pashkyum, in Ladakh, — 214.
Patna, — latitude determined by Grueber, 196.
Pekin, observatory at, — 174, 178.
Pelliot, Paul, — his remarks on Goes' route in Tarim basin, 32, 34.
Pereira, Anthony, S. J., — 72, 77, 80, 86, 90, 92; biographical note, 72.
Peshawar, — 14.
Pimenta, Nicholas, S. J., — 11, 12; biographical note, 11.
Pinheiro, Emmanuel, S. J., — biographical note, 10.
Polo, Marco, — 4, 6, 20, 21, 27, 172, 182.
Polyandry in Tibet, — mentioned by Desideri, 262.
Pordenone, Odorico de, — 4, 63, 188—189.
Potala, — described by Desideri, 243; — 156, 190, 221, 244, 267, 269.
Potente, — Tibet, 66, 70, 99, 298; Bhutan, 122, 125, 126, 131, 133, 142, 314, 333.
Pseudo-embassies to China, — 25, 26.
Puccian, halting-place in Tarim basin, — 36.

Q

Queyros, Fernão de, S. J., — refers to a lost document of Cabral's, 121; 159.

R

Rakas Tal, — 57, 58, 220.
Ralum, town, — 139, 142, 324.
Ralung, monastery, — 140, 142, 220.
Ramo-cce, monastery, — 224, 240, 241.
Rangamati, town, — 135.
Raper, *vide* Webb.
Rawlinson, H., — his remarks on Goes' route, 20.
Rebat, — 12.
Red-caps, Dugpa-sect, — 74, 142, 151, 156.
Régis, J. B., S. J., — on Goes' halting-places, 31; his remarks on Tangut, 188; — 57, 58, 196.
Retink, monastery, — 187, 188.
Retôa, lake, — 213, 218, 219, 220. *vide* Mansarowar.

Revolution, — in Tsaparang, 76—78; in Tibet, 265—269.
Ricci, Matthew, S. J., — his account of Goes' expedition, 2, 40; holds Cathay to be China, 6, 38; on pseudo-embassies, 25; biographical note, 3.
Rintam, village, — 132, 136, 320.
Ritter, C., — his estimate of Goes, 1; of Andrade, 45; of Grueber, 164.
Roebroek, William, — 4, 33.
Rongmati, town, — 135, 230, 253.
Rotang pass, — crossed by Azevedo, 115.
Roth, Henry, S. J., Grueber's travelling companion, — 59, 194, 199, 203, 204; biographical note, 199.
Rudok, district, — 43, 59, 71, 77, 81, 196, 213.
Rudok, town, — mission-station begun by Andrade, 72, 73; destroyed, 77.
Runate, town, — the same as Rangamati, 135; — 122, 130, 131, 132, 317, 319, 320, 321.
Rupshu, district, — 111.

S

Sacrithmà, — 23.
Saka Dzong, *vide* Serkia.
Sa-kya, town, — 269; *vide* Secchia.
Sa-m-yeê, town, — 245, 246, 247.
Sandberg, Gr., — his verdict on Andrade, 44; on Desideri, 209.
Sanze, village, — 103, 303.
Saraswati, river, — 54, 57, 60, 61, 62.
Sarcòl, district, — 23.
Sare, halting-place in Tarim basin, — 32.
Saregabedal, halting-place in Tarim basin, — 32, 34.
Sarikol, district, — 19, 23.
Satargit, (Satrjit), — 123, 124, 125, 126, 317.
Schall, Adam, S. J., — 174, 178; biographical note, 174.
Schiltberger, John, — 5.
Schlagintweit, A. von, — on Andrade, 54.
Secchia, town, — 221, 234, 235, 236, 251.
Semedo, Alvaro, S. J., — on pseudo-embassies, 26.
Senge-nam Gyal, king of Ladakh, — his war against Tsaparang, 75, 76, 78; visited by Azevedo, 109, 110, 304.
Sera, monastery, — 224, 244; 245, 267.
Serkia, town, — 221, 231, 233.
Serpanil, — 23.
Shangtze, village, — 88, 103.
Shigatse, — intercourse between Shigatse and Tsaparang, 155—156; — 153, 154, 158, 159, 192, 236, 267, 269.
Si-ngang-fu, inscription at — 5.
Sikkim, *vide* Bree-me-giong.
Siripur, town, — 123, 315.
Small-pox, — at Tsaparang, 101; at Lhasa, 261.
Socceo, *vide* Su-cheu.
Sopo, kingdom, — 71, 147, 327.
Sousa, Gonzales de, S. J., — 70, 77, 90; biographical note, 70.
Springs, thermal, in Tibet, — 229, 230.
Srinagar, (Garhwal), — 47, 48, 49, 50, 52, 67, 70, 83, 86, 88, 95, 199, 291.
Srinagar, (Khasmir), — described by Desideri, 211.
Stein, Sir A., — regard for Goes, 39.
Su-cheu, town, — 2, 37, 38, 39, 42.
Surate, — latitude determined by Grueber, 173, 174; — 83, 208, 210.

T

Tabo, inscription at, — 79, 80.
Takpó-Cigni, Tibetan province, — 250.
Takpó-Khier, Tibetan province, — 224, 228, 250, 251, 268.
Takpó-rŭ, Tibetan province, — 250.
Takpó-tŏ, Tibetan province, — 250.
Takpó-trù-lung, Tibetan province, — 250, 253.
Talhan, halting-place, — 19, 20.
Tallec, halting-place in Tarim basin, 31, 32.
Tanghetàr, — 23.
Tangut, — 43, 59, 187, 188.
Tashigong, *vide* Treêscy-Khang.
Tashi-Lhumpo, monastery, — 155, 156, 190, 236.
Taze, Tibetan province, — 245, 246, 268.
Tenghi Badascián, — 20.
Teshkàn, town, — 19.
Thévenot, M., — his account of Grueber's expedition, 170—171.
Thoghi lake, in Ladakh, — visited by Azevedo, 104, 105.
Tibet, — boundaries, climate, rivers, products, etc. described by Desideri, 225—231; administration of justice, 257—258; medical profession, 260—261; polyandry, 262; funerals, 263; language: Cacella's remarks, 144—145; Desideri's, 260; revolution and Chinese occupation, 265—269. *vide* Potente.
Tieffentaller, Joseph, S. J., — 58.
Time-notices, — in Goes' journey, 17, 24, 36, 38; in Grueber's journey, 189, 195, 198, 200.
Toantac, halting-place in Tarim basin, — 31, 32.
Toktokai, river, — 183, 185, 186, 187.
Torres, Peter, S. J., — 207.
Totling, town, — 61, 62, 73, 79.
Transhimalaya Mts., — crossed by Grueber and d'Orville, 188; why not mentioned by Desideri, 222.
Treêscy-Khang, — 215, 216.
Trigault, Nicholas, S. J., — biographical note, 2.
Trong-g-nêe, — Desideri's residence, 225, 251, 268, 269.
Tsangpo, river, — mentioned by Desideri, 230.
Tsaparang, town, — described by Young, 64; by Andrade, 76; by Coresma, 83; by Azevedo, 99; first Christian Church at, 71; the king favours the mission, 75—76; but was never a Christian, 78; his name unknown, 79; revolution, occupation by Ladakh king, sufferings of the mission, 76—78; destruction of the mission, 85, attempt at re-establishment, 206—207; intercourse between Tsaparang and Shigatse, 155—156; — 101, 110, 138, 148, 151, 158, 159, 160, 206.
Tsaparang, district, — described by Andrade, 64; by Coresma, 84. *vide* Guge.

Tsari, — 252. *vide* Çeri.
Tsetang, town, — 230, 248. *vide* Zze-thang.
Tsongkapa, — 80, 245.
Turfan, oasis, — 31, 36, 42.

U

Uçangue, — 79, 81, 99, 153, 155, 158, 159, 160, 302, 333, 334, 335. *vide* Utsang.
Ugan, halting-place in Tarim basin, — 34.
Urghien, — founder of Lamaism, 217, 218; temple at Sa-m-yeê, 247.
Utsang, — kingdom, 71; the king invites Andrade, 73; Andrade advises the establishment of a mission-station, 120; first visited and described by Cacella and Cabral, 153—157; Figueiredo's appeal in favour of the mission, 161.

V

Verbiest, Ferdinand, S. J., — moves the question of a Siberian route, 175.
Vishnu-Ganga, river, — 50, 51, 54, 60, 62.

W

Wall, Chinese, — near Hsining, 179—182; — 172, 180.
Webb and Raper, — their expedition to the sources of the Ganges, 34; their mistake, 53.
Wood, John, — his expedition to the river Oxus, 17, 18.

X

Xavier, Jerome, S. J., — 10, 11, 13, 156, 335; biographical note, 10.
Xembala, kingdom, — 147, 148, 155, 327, 328.

Y

Yakka-arik, halting-place, — 24.
Yarkand, oasis, — 18, 21, 24, 25, 30, 32, 42, 11.
Yarlung, Tibetan province, — 247, 248.
Yee, Tibetan province, — 247, 248, 250.
Yellow-caps, Gelugpa sect — 74, 156, 240, 245.
Young, G. M., — describes Tsaparang, 64; makes enquiry for relics of the mission, 88.

Z

Zeodary, a plant, — 228, 231, 233.
Zoji-la, *vide* Contel.
Zzang-to, Tibetan province, —221, 226, 231.
Zze-ri, Tibetan province, — 226.
Zze-ring Ton-drup, commander-in-chief at Lhasa —223; 267, 268, 269.
Zzé-thang, town, — 230, 247, 248.